SPIRITUAL HEALTH

An Exploration of the Gospel of Jesus Christ as
Guide to Wholesome Living Here and Now

SPIRITUAL HEALTH

BY ROY A. CHEVILLE

"I am come that they might have life, and that they might
have it more abundantly."
The Great Physician

Copyright © 1966
HERALD PUBLISHING HOUSE
INDEPENDENCE, MISSOURI

Library of Congress
Catalog Card No. 66-25062

Printed in the U.S.A.

CONTENTS

Part IV

Part V

FOREWORD

"The future is to the fit!" says a contemporary slogan. Right! Two questions need to be asked: What kind of future? What kind of fitness? We are needing to inquire about the kind of world society we are wanting and the kind of healthiness we have in mind. Some ideas of health will not do. Recent decades have disclosed some programs advocated and pushed that would make persons physically strong but shriveled in soul. So we ask, When is a person inclusively healthy?

Furthermore we are needing to go to work on realizing this fitness here and now. This is no time for postponement. Certainly it cannot be a matter of waiting for some after-death transportation to a land of health. Good health takes time to achieve, but we shall start now.

This exploration rises out of a deep, well-seasoned conviction that the gospel of Jesus Christ, rightly understood and rightly expressed, produces healthy persons. It does not result in collapse or surrender or escapism. This view needs to be examined and affirmed, for much that passes under the name of religion is not health-producing. Some of it actually undermines health. Sometimes pictures of the spiritual person suggest weakness and retreat and neurotic trends. The gospel of good health is referred to in such passages of scripture as II Timothy 1:7. Here it is the antidote to fear, self-pity, worry, superstition, and the like. This gospel enables men to stand strong in daily living. It is more than a message of "health in heaven"; it looks to soundness on earth.

This exploration rises, too, out of a sense of pressing urgency. This is prompted by the awareness that ever so many persons are spiritually unhealthy. Many are spiritually undernourished. They are needing the hope of the gospel of good health and the ministry of the church of good health. And the church has something to contribute that is indispensable.

The title "Spiritual Health" was slow in coming. For several years "spiritual hygiene" was guiding and stimulating my studies. The word "health" won out because it was nearer to the idea of "wholeness" that Jesus of Nazareth used to teach. In his healing ministry he would speak of a man's becoming whole. He was forthright in saying that he came to earth to enable all persons to experience an abundance of health.

Such a work is long overdue. Our people are needing it. Others need to hear this gospel, free from fads and fallacies. There has been little printed about "spiritual health." It will be noted that no bibliography is given for reference reading. I have gone through many publications but little material pertains to spiritual development as this term is used. We are on a pioneering exploration.

This is a consideration of spiritual health. Those who explore will need to identify quite soundly, quite clearly what constitutes good spiritual health. We shall need to avoid tangents, fads, and quacks. We shall need to look to the total health of the total person. Physical, mental, and social health will be considered, but spiritual health must go beyond these others. Any program of health that leaves out the spiritual is incomplete. A program that looks upon the spiritual health as a compartment of its own, separate from the total person, will be partial and disconnected. We shall see the total man as a son of God in God's total universe.

The course involves thirty-four explorations—a chapter for each. A group may find it expedient to devote several sessions to one exploration.

We can work in this with a sense of commission. The directive will run something like this, "Go and share the gospel of spiritual health! Go to everybody, beginning in your home, on your street, in your congregation!" And the counsel continues, "Live out this gospel of spiritual wholeness in yourself!" The Restoration Church is called to such a mission.

ROY A. CHEVILLE

PART I

THE MEANING
OF HEALTH
IN GOD'S UNIVERSE

This opening section lays the foundation for the entire exploration in spiritual health. This part may not be hurried through. It requires much more than reading through. It has to be thought through, explored through, prayed through. It has to be understood as laying the foundation for working out a spiritual fitness program.

This section sets forth four basic affirmatives which put spiritual health in the process of God's total universe, in the program of God for the physical and spiritual fitness of every person in the world. Here is a crusade of the highest order and of the widest scope. It makes the whole world a laboratory, a gymnasium in spiritual exercising. The topics of the four lessons set forth the four affirmatives concisely, clearly.

This section sets forth the viewpoint of the entire course. God is healthy. He designs persons to be totally healthy and happy. The life and person of Jesus Christ reveals this healthiness. The Spirit of God functions in developing and maintaining dynamic spiritual health. God intends for us to learn how to use the health-affording resources in his universe and to learn how to live together healthfully. The Restoration movement reaffirms this gospel of spiritual health lived and enunciated by Jesus of Nazareth.

Take plenty of time on this first section. Practice the art of exploring together rather than of defending some single tenet. Do laboratory work in healthy spiritual living. Think of the family and the congregation as units for carry-on and checkup and lookout.

Look to the interrelatedness involved in all this. If any person is going to be totally healthy he has to see to it that others are healthy too. There is a contagious quality in health, good or bad. Any spiritually healthy person is concerned with the spiritual welfare of others. When he loses this interest his own health is deteriorating. The healthy Saint is a sharer of the gospel of spiritual health.

The natural way in God's universe is the healthy way.

CHAPTER 1

HEALTH MEANS
WHOLENESS

One day in Jerusalem Jesus of Nazareth noticed a halting, withered man by the pool of Bethesda. It was believed that when the waters from the spring were agitated, healing power would come to the first one who stepped in. This man, an invalid for thirty-eight years, had never been able to get in ahead of other patients. Jesus noticed his predicament. This Physician of Nazareth asked him forthrightly if he really wanted to be restored to health. Then Jesus told him to get to his feet, to pick up his pallet, to start walking. It may be that Jesus was not going to do anything until the man showed he was willing to make some effort. Something had to happen within this cripple. Jesus always made this requirement.

Read all the story from the beginning of the fifth chapter of John. It climaxes in Jesus' charge to the recovered man to go out and live worthy of his blessing. He was to "sin no more." The incident discloses how the physical healing and the spiritual renewal were combined. The entire personhood, the entire life of the man was involved. Here were physical, mental, social, and spiritual aspects of one healing experience.

Health and Wholeness

The Authorized Version puts Jesus' question this way, "Wilt thou be made whole?" The Revised Standard Version reads, "Do you want to be healed?" The two mean the same. The words for *health* and for *whole* come from the same rootage. In this conception the well person has wholeness. This provides the viewpoint for this study of spiritual health. In other words, the healthy man functions in one harmonious, integrated personhood.

He who is healthy is a living whole,
Well-joined, well-cheered, a fresh, creative soul.

Our explorations into healthy living will take us into consideration (1) of the total person, (2) of the total universe in which this person lives, (3) of the ends for which he lives, and (4) of the total way he goes about living. Health is a great inclusive field. Can anything be left out when we vision becoming "whole"? We shall be looking at life in its broadest aspect. Faddism will have no part, for it deals with extremes and tangents. "Quickies" will have no place, for they do not get at the sources of good or of ill. Local spiritual ointments will have little consideration, for they apply to only one segment. In this we shall seek "to see life steadily and to see it whole."

An Honest Wanting

Jesus' first salutation was, "Do you really want to be healthy?" If the man had made an evasive or indifferent reply, Jesus probably would have left him hobbling on the steps to the pool. A first question for us, starting out on this exploration, is, "Do you want to find out about spiritual health?" We shall presume that those setting out want to discover about this phase of health something they do not yet see. We shall suppose that all of us are wanting a quality of wholesome spirituality beyond what we now have. God can do little for and with the self-satisfied man. Said Frederick Amiel, "There is no curing a sick man who believes himself in health." There is little if any help for the sick man who gives up and will not try and hope and dare. The cripple at Bethesda pool had to want to recover and to try to get up. We have to come with honest, questing spirit if we are going to understand the wide, deep field of spiritual health.

A Common Salutation

In many cultures persons greet each other with phrases that say something about the health of the other person. A common greeting in the Western world is "How are you?" or "How do you do?" This expresses how one of the first concerns of a person for his friend is his health and his fortune. It is a token salutation. We would be surprised after we say, "How do you do?" if the person addressed were to tell us in detail the condition of his health and his wealth. Usually the person responds by saying in return, "How do you do?" Neither person is informed about the condition of the other. Yet this long-expressed greeting reminds us that friends are concerned about the health of each other. We can be well pleased that associates care enough to inquire, if only symbolically. As long as person meets person with friendly concern we shall be saying something like, "How are you?"

This health greeting reaches back into the centuries. When the maneuvering Joab wanted to get rid of Amasa, his rival in King David's military generalship, he took hold of Amasa's beard and inquired, "Art thou in health, my brother?" (II Samuel 20:9). The exegesis of this verse presumes that Joab had a second sword concealed under his military cloak while he let fall the visible sword, thus banishing from the mind of Amasa any suspicion of foul play. Thus his left hand could be on the hilt of the sword under his coat. This incident has become a classic example of perfidy. Such an inquiry about health is pretense. Friends inquire with genuine concern.

An Identification of Health

A century ago we were thinking of health as referring only to the physical body. Today, this concern with the physical aspect of health continues but we are including more. Now we are thinking of physical health, of mental health, of social health. In this study we are pushing out farther and farther. Here we shall be considering *spiritual health*. The physical, the mental, the social aspects of health remain basic. We are saying, however, that the *spiritual* aspect must be included. Without the spiritual factor any consideration of health falls short and is incomplete. Our identification of health must include all phases.

In *Psychology, Religion and Health* Leslie Weatherhead has set forth a usable and meaningful identification of health. It has merit in its expandability. It is sound in its inclusiveness. This is his statement:

"Health is the complete and successful functioning of every part of the human being, in harmonious relationship with every other part, and with the relevant environment."—Page 311.

When we use this identification we shall have to indicate what we mean by the following: (1) complete functioning, (2) successful functioning, (3) the human being or person, (4) harmony within the person, and (5) the relevant environment. These get at big questions about (1) the nature of the person, (2) the goals of personal living, and (3) the universe in which man lives and is sustained. In the inclusive sense this involves "the spiritual."

Health Is Relative

Many of us tend to drop a line and divide persons into two groups, the "sick" and the "well." Some think of the sick as those whose bodies are in bed horizontal with the surface of the earth and the well as those whose bodies are perpendicular to the earth's surface. This black-white sort of classification has about the same lack of soundness as dividing all persons at judgment time into those assigned to heaven and those consigned to hell. Our company of humans does not divide this way in matters of health.

Traditionally, we have come to think of those confined to bed and those who ought to be there as "sick." Many times, however, those who are "up and about" include many who are "not well." Health is much more than merely not being "sick in bed." Normal functioning of all parts of the body means more than the ability to do a full day's work without more than a healthful fatigue. It means efficiency and zest, courage and enthusiasm for life. We need to build into our conception of health the picture of complete personal fitness.

There is no sharp dividing line between the mentally healthy and the unhealthy. There are many different degrees of health. This refers to the physical, the mental, the social, and, of course, the spiritual health. Well can we say that in healthful living there are many degrees of glory. We are wiser if we think of a scale that ranges from excellent health to collapse of health and then chart our health on intermediate points between these extremes. Our places on the scale will vary from day to day, from circumstance to circumstance. We need to inquire concerning the degree of our health.

A Complex of Many Factors

The body is an organism in which any one part affects all parts. It is intended to be fitly framed together into a whole. This means that we are not free to isolate some single factor and have it stand alone as the index of our health condition. The quack tends to select one thing and make it speak for the whole person. Thus an herb doctor had a mixture of "nature's remedies" that would insure the top-rate functioning of the kidneys. In his teaching, if the kidneys were functioning well the entire body would be in a state of good repair. We recognize the essential role of the kidneys but we also recognize the necessary place of many other organs. Another diagnostician centered everything on the weight. Obesity was the cardinal sin. The way to health was to take off pounds. The wiser man sees how our food consumption and our weight have tremendous significance in our health condition but sees good health involving more than nutrition and weight. Certainly the way to good physical health takes in more than any one pill or tonic or article of food.

In this complex of factors and functions, then, we cannot name the presence or absence of any single factor as evidence of good health. Nor will the carrying out of any one single habit insure this desired health. Nor is the absence of any one characteristic evidence of poor health. This applies to mental health as well as to physical. Nobody has all the traits of good mental health all the time. One person may be strong in one aspect of good mental health and be weak in another.

This applies in the same way to spiritual health. It is not an either-or situation but a more-or-less condition. No one of us can pose as one hundred percent perfect in all aspects of physical, mental, social, and spiritual health. It is the trend of our health that matters.

The Inclusive View

Someone has said that we can determine health only as we study "the total person at work over a period of time." More and more we are seeing the soundness of this viewpoint. Health involves the total person and his total pattern of living. It brings in what he lives for. This inclusive view sees how all the factors are to function together in one harmonious whole. When all factors and traits are in tune and in cooperation, good health results. When one or more of these are out of tune, discords occur in the life harmony. Today we are looking at the total person in his total world. Any study that leaves out the spiritual potentials and needs in man is incomplete. Any study that omits spiritual resources available to man leaves us lacking in achieving full health.

The Emphasis on Environment

Some texts on health such as Van Buskirk and Kline's *Principles of Healthful Living* open their studies with consideration of "our environment." This presumes that a healthy environment is required for healthful living. Man cannot live in a vacuum. He has to have an environment with which he reacts, as a physical organism, as a person. Man needs health-producing air to breathe and health-producing food to eat. He needs a complex of factors from supply of oxygen to climate to water in quality and quantity. Sometimes conditions in the environment operate to his detriment. Exceptionally small disease-producing organisms can endanger his life.

One thing stands out to man's advantage. He is the only form that is able to remake his environment to any marked degree. He can create new conditions. From the health standpoint these can be to his advantage or to his disadvantage. Man can pollute the air with foul chemicals destructive to living, or he can purify and humidify and control the temperature of the air in his immediate living quarters. This holds true of his social environment. He can charge it with smut and superstition and suspicion or he can make it healthy with wisdom and fraternity and cleanness. The atmosphere for healthy living includes the intangible factors. Here we are thinking, too, of the environment of the spiritual factors and the requirement that they be health-producing. We do well to recognize that some factors that are called "spiritual" may not be conducive to good spiritual healthfulness.

Health and Natural Law

Health is the natural product of living in complete accord with life-producing forces. Vic Terry has commented, "Health is nature's reward for getting into harmony with her laws." We aim, then, to discover how our bodies, our minds, our persons, our souls function, how they draw from resources about them. These descriptive statements about the way nature operates, we call *natural laws.* When we state a natural law we are simply saying of some phenomenon, "This is the way nature works." We go ahead on the assurance that given the same conditions nature will always behave this way, with these results. It is a description of cause-and-effect.

Good health is not a matter of magic or of gambling. We do not throw dice and cast lots and expect returns to come out favorably to us if we chance to speak the health-giving word. We do not wear some amulet that will charm away the evil and induce the good. We have to live for good health. We have to accord with laws of health. This applies to all phases of healthful living, bodily and spiritual.

We are honest enough and humble enough to say we know few of the natural laws that bring to pass healthful living. We are always living beyond our understanding of the workings of things about us. We go on breathing when we know so little about oxygen and the respiratory system. We go on turning on electricity when we are comparatively unschooled about electrical energy. We live through the complex operation of a heart about which we are comparatively unschooled. Yet we know these functionings are orderly and explainable. We keep trying to discover more and more in every one of these fields. Then we can manage our living more wisely so we can have improved health.

So often we discover one factor in healthful living, one operation in the health process. Sometimes we act as if taking care of this phase will insure good health, even if we disregard a score of other factors and processes. So a person brushed his teeth punctiliously and meticulously and presumed he would have "perfect dentition." He left untouched the matter of diet and general health. Living is complex and calls for the keeping of many natural laws. No amount of attention to one phase will take care of lack of attention to a score of other things. There is no one-track salvation in health.

This way of accord with natural law applies to spiritual health.

More than Physical

Until recently texts on health had to do with physical well-being. One treatise said, "Good health is a state of complete physical efficiency." In these approaches good health, basically a physical expression, was interpreted as being a social asset. Physical efficiency would enhance attractiveness, charm, appeal, and this would have profitable returns in occupational achievements and social advance. Such sentences as this appeared: "The quality of this [first] impression may be largely determined by one's attention to personal health." Such factors as these were considered: hair, eyes, mouth, teeth, skin, hands, feet, posture, hearing, vision, voice. Attention to these physical factors would pay off well.

None of these factors in the physical body are to be disregarded. They are part of the picture, but they are not all. More and more we have come to see mental health inseparably associated with physical health. The field of mental hygiene has come to be concerned with (1) attaining an integrated personality, (2) releasing the potentials of a person for creative expression, (3) achieving purposive self-management. The goal of all this as stated by Dr. S. H. Kraines is "to cultivate positive mental health."

The expanding outlook is to look upon good bodily health as the means for realizing personal and spiritual values. These ends can be achieved more effectively through a healthy body. This is said with the realization that much of the creative work and sacrificial contributions through the centuries have been made by men and women who often lived in discomfort. We are seeing more and more how the emotions and the mental states affect the body. Today objectives in healthful living are expressed in such terms as these: (1) enjoyment and zest in work and play; (2) general attitude of cheerfulness and confidence in relation to life; (3) freedom from persistent worry and anxiety. H. F. Hilander in *Health for Modern Living* gives this picture, "A normal person shows emotional maturity, accepts reality, gets along with others, and has a philosophy of life that holds him up when the complications of daily life become burdensome" (page 31). Such a person, he continues, "is happy, has peace of mind, has a sense of humor, and enjoys his work."

Such a portrait of the healthy person rises above physical health alone, above mental health, above social health.

Spiritual Health Too

The foregoing identification of health as the functioning of the total person in harmonious relationship with his total "relevant environment" carries some very significant implications. It calls for an inclusive conception of man as a person. It calls for an inclusive conception of the environment in which man comes to be a person, in which man can expand his personalism. This pushes us to explore the spiritual potentials and needs in man as person. It pushes us to reach out to discover and to tap the spiritual resources available for achieving good spiritual well-being. It leads us to study *spiritual health*.

Almost thirty years ago Alexis Carrel wrote his monumental book, *Man, the Unknown*. He was a physiologist and might have been expected to write only of man as a biological organism. He went beyond the data of his field. He said we would never know man by compartmentalizing him, by analyzing segments by themselves. Rather, we must see man as a whole. We are needing, he said, "a synthesis that can be utilized" (page 54). Man does not know himself as a whole. Often he has become imprisoned in the cosmos picture that he himself has created (page 320). Now he needs to be liberated from faith in an exclusive material reality. His life and his health go beyond this world of inanimate matter. His image of himself must go beyond these fences. Men must "learn the necessary relations of the cosmic universe, of their fellow men, and of their inner selves, and also those of their tissues and their mind" (page xiv). Dr. Carrel, the physiologist, was saying that man must come to see himself in his wholeness, functioning effectively in his total universe. He says, "We do not apprehend man as a whole. We know him as composed of different parts" (page 4). So he speaks of "man, the unknown."

This study is an exploration into spiritual health. We move forward with the conviction that there are resources in this universe, if utilized, for developing us as persons and for achieving in us an inclusive health—physical, mental, social, and *spiritual*.

Questions for Discussion

1. What is your reaction to the comment that if people are "told too much" concerning health, they will come to worry unnecessarily about themselves?
2. How is healthful living more concerned with the quality of living than with quantity of living?
3. Under what conditions is it desirable to prolong the length of man's life-span?
4. The life expectancy in New England in 1940 was 68 years, in India 27 years. Would it be desirable by some tonic or pill to increase the life-span in India to that of New England?

5. What do you see involved in healthful living besides living to "a ripe old age"?
6. How do you account for the fact that the first studies in health were concerned with physical factors?
7. What did Alexis Carrel have in mind when he said we do not know man as a whole but that we know only segments of him? How is health concerned with "the whole man"?
8. Contrast physical health as an end in itself and as a means to achieving spiritual well-being. What kind of program would we develop if physical health became a goal in itself?
9. Interpret, "The total health of a person involves his spiritual possibilities." Contrast seeing this as a part of an inclusive health program with considering this as a field to itself.
10. Do you consider it possible and desirable to study spiritual health? Some consider spiritual well-being a gift of God with which we have nothing to do.
11. What difference does it make whether we take environment into consideration when we build a program of health?
12. What is the implication of saying that a person has to take the resources of his spiritual environment into account if he is going to have an inclusive program of health?
13. What is your response to the inquiry as to whether persons want to make an intelligent approach to health? Or do you see persons preferring to follow fads, notions, "quickies," prejudices? Does this hold true for spiritual health?
14. Name some traits of the spiritually healthy person.

CHAPTER 2

RIGHT RELATIONSHIP
BRINGS SPIRITUAL HEALTH

Good health is a consequence of good relationship. It does not come by chance, or through some charm, or through maneuvering with some health-dispenser. Many of us happen to have good health because we happen more or less to comply with health-providing factors. We are like the boy who said he liked to "breathe down." He was complying with requirements in sound respiratory health, but he did not know why. He had discovered he felt better when he breathed deeply and he concluded, "I feel good when I breathe way down." Today we are advised to breathe deeply if we want to feel well and be in good spirit. The next step up for this boy will be to understand his own body and his own breathing processes so he can comprehend more of the *why* and the *how* of what is going on in his own living. Then, too, he will come to include the *what*, which will involve the kind of air that makes for good health. He will see to it that he lives in an atmosphere of good air for breathing. Such a boy has risen above ideas of "good luck" and "great charm": he is seeing causes and consequences and relationships.

We want to be able to see this way in spiritual health. We have the confidence that we can.

An Inclusive Process

Good health includes all of a person, every bit of him. A teacher told some children that health includes everything from their toenails to their hair-tips. Right, if we truly include everything. And this includes the range from faith in digestion to faith in Deity, from a liking for candy to love for Christ, from what takes place in the swimming pool to what takes place in the baptismal font, from the feasting at a family dinner to the communing at the table of the Lord's Supper. No segment of our living, no factor that touches our living can be left out. So we can say our health includes every portion of our body and our personhood and every force that we are related to in the business of living.

A Matter of Relationships

Everything in the universe exists in and operates in relationship with what is about it. Nothing exists in a vacuum. Even the atom does not exist to itself. It is dizzying to think that billions of atoms make up the ink in the period that closes this sentence as I write with pen and ink. It is amazing to think that eighty million oxygen molecules, placed in a row like marbles, would stretch a distance of only an inch. Atoms join in molecule formations. They are constantly in motion. They jolt each other. Scientists seek to map what is on the inside of atoms and how they unite to make up "the stuff" of all we see about us. This stands out clearly in the world of atoms: (1) all things exist in relationship; (2) all things are predictable and explainable; (3) the universe is one great system of operation.

Our Own Selves in Relationships

Everything in us exists in and operates in relationship. To understand any one part of us, we have to understand the whole in which it functions. Before we get far, we are reaching out to the universe itself. For instance, the eye does not live to itself. It is conditioned by the circulation of the blood of the total body. The position of its lenses and the sensitivity of its nervous network are factors. The alertness of the brain affects the interpretation of sensations received. The health of the eye depends upon establishing harmonious relationship with light, which is highly relevant in its environment. We are reminded that our diet has bearing on our vision. Lopsided diagnosticians prescribe this or that as insuring clear vision. We see that if any of these inward functions or these outward relationships are interrupted, the health of the eye is impaired and we speak of the eye as being in a state of dis-ease. Literally no organ lives to itself.

What is said of the eye can be said of a multitude of situations. The mind of a person can get at war within itself, so that no longer is there harmonious relationship within its parts. It can get out of harmony with many factors in its environment, as with the world of healthy persons, with the world of true ideas. All this holds true for spiritual health. When we include the spiritual in the totality of functioning, in the wholeness of environment, we can well refer to health as "the harmonious relationship of the person at all points with the total relevant environment."

Spiritual Life Too

In like manner we shall get along better in spiritual health as we let the divine process function, as we further conditions favorable to good functioning. If we become nervously concerned about some aspect of our spiritual health, we can actually get in the way and disqualify ourselves for good spiritual living. We could become as ineffective as the person who keeps wondering if his heart is contracting as it should, if his salivary glands are secreting properly, if his breath is smelling sweet, if his kidneys are taking care of impurities. Such a person can become a nervous wreck and a social nuisance. A few years ago a young man became concerned about the odor of his breath, feeling that this was an index to his social acceptance or rejection. Every few minutes he would put his finger to his tongue and endeavor to smell the deposit, as unnoticeably as possible, to ascertain the state of his breath. He not only induced stomach difficulty; he broke down in nervous health. His preoccupation got in the way.

This can happen, and does happen in spiritual health. A young man got so concerned with "thinking pure thoughts" that he wrecked his own "spiritual thinking." He used good energy in wondering whether this thought or that thought was pleasing to God. When his mind happened to turn to anything connected with sex he mustered his powers to turn to something "high and holy." Instead of concentrating on something with pull upward, something spiritually creative, he used up his energy in keeping "away from" the "carnal" and "the corrupt." He isolated one field of thinking from his total thinking and pulled it out of natural relationship. He became unhealthy by trying so hard to be healthy. In time, he broke down.

We Need to See Basic Relationship

We are healthier today because men of medicine are coming to understand the nature of the blood, its circulation, and its function in the body. Misconceptions used to get in the way. We live more understandingly because explorers, notably William Harvey in the middle of the seventeenth century, set forth how the blood circulates. Before this time some thought the veins carried the blood and the arteries conveyed air. Many considered the liver to be the major organ for blood operation. Many thought persons became ill as the blood got in bad condition. In this conception the thing to do was to "let" the blood, that is, to drain off the impure blood. This was practiced even in cases of anemia. Dr. Harvey set forth the picture of circulation of the blood with the heart as the motor power of the movement of the blood. He saw this circulation in relation to the total body. Dr. Harvey helped us to see how to help the body in achieving and maintaining healthy blood. And the studies are still going on. Problems, such as those of leukemia, are with us. These basics stand out: (1) we do well to understand what is going on, (2) we do well to let the bodily processes go on without our fretting about them and concentrating on them.

We need to see these basic relationships in ever so many aspects of our bodily functioning. In time, we learned how the cells of our body divide and how growth continues. We shaped such words as "mitosis" to indicate the processes. Yet at this instant we get along better if we do not stop to wonder if our cells are dividing in the right way, if metabolism is proceeding normally. We could become quite nervously indisposed if we were to start concentrating on every cell of our body. Rather do we endeavor to get the picture of the whole body "fitly framed together." We see each part in relationship to the whole.

Seeing the Whole in Spiritual Life

A wise man said recently, "I know a little about the circulation of the blood; I would like to know something about the circulation of the Spirit." He was seeing that what he knew about the blood helped him to understand his own body and to further his spiritual health. The man went on to say that he believed if he could understand more clearly what he called "the circulation of the Spirit" he would have improved spiritual healthiness. He was thinking that if he knew more about the nature and the functioning of the Holy Spirit, if he realized more about the qualities essential in a person for experiencing the Holy Spirit, if he knew more about the "circulating" of the Spirit in his own body and person, if he knew more about the healthy circulation of the Spirit in the group life of the Saints, he could be healthier spiritually. He believed that good spiritual health is more than chance and supplication; it is achievement through utilizing what God graciously makes available to us.

For God Only?

Once men felt it wrong to explore the human body. This was in God's domain. The attitude was something like the Greeks' attitude toward the gods on Mount Olympus: mortal man was to stay away. To probe into matters of the physical body was sacrilegious and unwarranted. Man might pray but not probe. Man might expect but not explore. Whatever came in physical health was given of God and man was to accept. This is represented in the viewpoint of the woman who limped with fallen arches. She commented, "God gave me bad feet. He must have intended that

23

I suffer in this way. It is not for me to alter his desires." She laid the responsibility for her discomfort on God and considered it wrong to try to remedy the situation. She had no idea of the why and the how of her misery. She was sure of this: her suffering was sent by God.

There have been those who considered the physical body one of the "mysteries" of God. Only he should and could understand. Those who tried to get inside the mystery or change the divine decree were out of their assigned place. Add to this viewpoint the outlook that the physical body was carnal and that man should center his attention on spiritual matters and the case was pretty well closed. When disaster came to an explorer, the case against tampering with and speculating with the body was strengthened. For instance Miguel Servetus (1511-1553) studied both in medicine and theology. He is credited with the first modern understanding of the pulmonary circulation of the blood. He spoke out against doctrines of the Trinity. He came to Geneva. There John Calvin prompted his condemnation as a heretic and Servetus was burned at the stake by order of the city of Geneva, October 27, 1553. It was presumed that his heresy in theology about the Trinity and his heresy in medicine about the blood would be burned together.

Quite often this same viewpoint has been applied to mysteries about spiritual phenomena. This is in God's realm. To these the Spirit of God "falls" on those whom God chooses to endow. Here the phrase in Ephesians 5:32, "This is a great mystery," is often quoted. More specifically, the working of the Spirit is looked upon as beyond man's power to comprehend. Paul's statement in I Corinthians 14:2 can be torn from its total setting and turned to support this view, "in the spirit he speaketh mysteries." In this classic discourse on the Spirit Paul was endeavoring to get the Corinthian saints to understand the Spirit to their edification rather than putting it in the realm of the not-to-be-examined. He was wanting these Corinthians, fairly recently converted to the Christian faith, to rise above misconceptions and misapplications of the Holy Spirit to purposeful and uplifting expression. Paul wanted them to follow his guiding direction, "Let all things be done unto edifying." He was concerned that they have more than a temporary exhilaration in a meeting; he wanted the Spirit to effect transforming influence in their lives.

Paul wanted them to get a comprehensive view of the Holy Spirit. He wrote frankly, "Now concerning spiritual things, brethren, I would not have you ignorant" (I Corinthians 12:1). He called them to see the wholeness of the working of the Spirit. He spoke

24

of "diversities of gifts" in the functioning of "the same spirit." He outlined various "manifestations." Then he moved on to affirm how "the body is one," how the body has many members. Then he moved on to the "more excellent" expression of the Holy Spirit, the fruitage of love. Here is a remarkable call for the inclusive ministry of the Holy Spirit in the total person, in the fellowship of the one body. Paul was instructing these inexperienced members in a comprehensive overview that would further their spiritual health. He was advising how love was understanding, was involving their entire living, was of God.

Religion Is Relationship

For our study of spiritual health we shall identify religion as the personal relationship between man and God. In man's wholesome religion, he is endeavoring to experience right relations with God; he is seeking to live with God soundly and helpfully. At first thought we can see that relationship between person and person can be narrowing or expanding, stimulating or deadening, creative or perfunctory. Personal association can lift and leaven a man's life or drag him down. Religion with an unsound conception of God, of man, and of the relationship between God and man can work defeat and deterioration. When these basics (1) God, (2) man, and (3) religion are soundly conceived, understanding of this relationship leads to the cultivation of enduring spiritual health.

We are not free to indicate all that passes under the term religion as conducive to this good health. Some ways of living that pass under the name religion are actually health-undermining. It is our business to develop expandable, explorable conceptions of God, of man, and of their relationship (religion). Only as we do so can our spiritual health be wholesome and enduring.

A Comprehensive Relationship

A simple-speaking man prayed this way, "Lord, we want to get together, so that all of me gets next to all of you." Then he added, "There's not so much of me, but there's a powerful lot to you. Every bit of me needs you so much! And I need to see more of you." An honest, heartwarming prayer! He was voicing a basic principle in spiritual health, that of the involvement of one's total self in an inclusive relationship with God. This involves all of God's universe. It involves all of God's children. It brings in all of God and all that is God's in the wide-flung meaning of religion. There is no compartment of our living that we can leave out by crossing our fingers. There is no area we can disregard by saying that it is not spiritual. The word of September 1830 rings out to us, "All things unto me are spiritual" (Doctrine and Covenants 28:9 a). All of a man's personhood is concerned in spiritual health.

All of God's personhood is involved. This includes God as Person and the works of God as creative manifestations of his Personhood. We cannot disregard anything in God's universe. We always have to keep differentiating between things as God intends them to be and things twisted and out of line with God's intentions. Many things are malformed and malfunctioning at present as forces not God-minded have gotten hold of them. Yet we may not disregard them even if they are not as they ought to be. It is so easy for us to focus on one facet of God's total nature and consider this the total character of God. Thus some have centered on "the wrath of God." Others have stressed an indulgent love with little consideration of cause-and-effect. The truly healthy person endeavors to keep himself sensitive to the fullness of God.

Law and Relationship

Natural laws describe relationships and operations. They are the descriptive affirmations of the way God operates in all his phenomena. They speak of order and predictability. They operate in every phenomenon in God's universe. They range through the structure of the soil, the movements of the planets, the reproduction of animals, the interaction of persons, and the spiritual insight of saints. The more we understand these natural laws, the more we shall be able to accord with God's health-giving forces. This is universe-wide in application. Everything in God's universe is designed to function in orderly and causative procedure. What takes place in every field or "kingdom" can be described in terms of natural law (Doctrine and Covenants 85:8 ff.). In this predictability, in this relationship lies the assurance of the continuance of the universe. In it, too, lies the promise of good health.

And Persons Too

The wholeness of God's universe includes all other persons. We are related, closely or distantly, with all people. Their total health, good or ill, affects us. Their cleanliness or lack of it, their interests or lack of them, their manner of speaking, their values in living, their faith in God or lack of it, have bearing on us. The man with biological ulcers affects us. So does the man with spiritual ulcers. The neighbor with wholesome faith contributes to our well-being.

The Hebrew prophets kept reminding their people that right relations with God involved right relations with others. First they referred to fellow Hebrews. Then they pushed out to include Gentiles. Jesus kept reminding his disciples of this inescapable relationship. He was saying that no part of the world could be healthy until all the world was healthy. He had in mind spiritual leprosy as well as physical leprosy. This conviction is reexpressed in our Latter Day Saint program of Zion building. This concentrates on health in Zion that shall reach out in influence into all the world. The gospel of Jesus Christ says that what happens between a man and all other men conditions his spiritual health.

And This Is Atonement

The word "atonement" occurs again and again in the scriptures. Literally it means at-one-ment. The prophets were concerned in getting men into right relationship with God, at one with God. Priests and prophets were concerned with ways of achieving this. Priests tended to emphasize things to do—"works." Prophets tended to focus on what was to take place in the lives and character of persons that would qualify them for oneness with God. They recognized "things to do" to the degree that they functioned in making "men to be." Once Booker T. Washington told his students in Tuskegee Institute that they should endeavor "to share the character of God," to become one with God. He told them, and tells us all, that as we would do this, "we shall then become strong where we have been weak, wise where we have been foolish." He urged these Negro youth "to incorporate God's laws" into all their living. This would bring them health which he called "a requisite for effective living."

Questions for Discussion

1. How may we think of good health as coming about "by chance" or "through charm"?
2. Illustrate how a faddist or a quack in physical health or in mental health or in spiritual health tends to stress some single phase of healthful living rather than the total life of a person.
3. How does it affect our picture of the universe to say that everything in the universe exists in relationships?
4. How can we interfere with a natural functioning of the body,

27

such as breathing and digesting, by focusing too much attention on the process?

5. How may we interfere with processes of spiritual health by focusing too much attention on them and fretting about them?

6. Evaluate the statement, "A truly spiritual man does not concentrate on and worry about the condition of his spirituality."

7. Contrast understanding the basic process of health with anxiety about the working of the process in one's self. Apply to spiritual health.

8. Why is it advisable to understand "the nature of the Spirit" and "the circulation of the Spirit" if we are going to achieve good spiritual health?

9. What guidelines did Paul give us concerning the Holy Spirit and spiritual health?

10. How might some react against exploring the process of spiritual health? How might they consider it contrary to God's intent?

11. What do you consider a sound outlook for investigating spiritual experience and its influence on spiritual health?

12. How is wholesome religion concerned with the inclusive relationship of man with God? What is included in this relationship (religion)?

13. How is religion basically a process of atonement?

CHAPTER 3

HEALTH RESOURCES
ARE AVAILABLE
IN THE UNIVERSE

"There is enough and to spare" is an assuring phrase. We feel at home when a host invites us to dinner. We feel we are wanted. There is going to be nothing skimpy in either hospitality or table supply. There is going to be material food and there is going to be social food. Then with good sense and sensitivity we try to fit in with our host's service and resources and we endeavor to contribute to the joy and fellowship of the meal. At the close we can say, "I feel good. This has been a good meal."

Such is the nature of God's counsel and his invitation to us. God reminds us that he has ample resources for healthy living. If there is shortcoming it is in us. In many fields we have not yet discovered these resources. Or we have not learned how to tap them and develop them. Or we have not learned how to use them together for the good of all of us. Or we may do what some juniors did: they invited too many persons to one picnic in one place when their refreshments were planned for half the number invited. Or we may carry on and have a situation comparable to that of the social gathering that was ready for food at ten o'clock but did not have it arriving until two o'clock in the morning. Many times we have to say with Cassius in *Julius Caesar*, "The fault, dear Brutis, is not in our stars, but in us."

An Affirmation of Amplitude

The person who starts out on an adventure is presumed to examine what he has to work with as he launches forth. This includes the tangible things he will be able to mobilize and the not-so-tangible resources. Certainly a survey of what Christopher Columbus took with him from Palos, Spain, enumerates ships, food supplies, sailors, and so on. It must also include the indomitable spirit and the faith in his venture that were in the navigator himself. So when we look about to make inventory of the resources that God provides we shall include both the material and the spiritual. We shall conclude that there is an amplitude of both.

In April 1831 when the idea of Zion was taking shape some significant advice was given about available provisions. The pioneers were told that there was enough in God's resources for them as they moved into this endeavor. What would be needed would not be coming in ready-to-wear or ready-to-cook packages. The colonists were to work and produce. There were to be no lazy spongers among them. Doctrine and Covenants 68:4 is the reminder that there was no place for "idlers among them." The resources were not to be used in a helter-skelter and live-to-oneself way. Here are the major affirmations as set forth in Section 101:2 of the Doctrine and Covenants:

"I, the Lord, stretched out the heavens, and builded the earth as a very handy work. . . . It is my purpose to provide for my saints, for all things are mine; but it must needs be done in mine own way; . . . the earth is full, and there is enough and to spare.

"It is expedient that I, the Lord, shall make every man accountable, as stewards over earthly blessings, which I have made and prepared for my creatures."

This message is clear and inclusive. It is affirmative and assuring. It is a statement about the divine abundance. There is no suggestion of skimpiness. The supply is well planned and well supervised. These are the basics:

1. There is abundance of resources in God's universe for the good of his people.
2. Use of these resources requires accord with God's purposes and plan; they are available only for healthy living. They may not be misappropriated by those who pull out of accord with God.
3. These resources are inclusive; they are available for all phases of balanced healthy living.

The Processes Go On

In God's universe the processes of operation keep going on in their own right. We do not set them going or stop them. We would have a pretty unstable world if we had to press a button or push a lever to set some process going. Some of us would forget; some of us would press the wrong button; some of us would pay attention only to some little corner that we thought affected us for good; some of us might be inclined to interfere with the life arena of others, for good or for not-so-good. Such processes as air movement and light radiation and oxidation keep going on. We can change conditions under which they operate but we cannot vote them out or in.

These processes are available to all. This used to bother the ancient Hebrews. Sometimes they seemed to feel that God should turn on his beneficial resources for the righteous, notably themselves, and shut off these resources from the wicked. One day Jesus told them how God made these natural resources available to all: "He maketh his sun to rise on the evil and on the good, and sendeth rain on the just and on the unjust" (Matthew 5:47). Well he realized that if good things were provided only for "the good," there would be an inclination to hold out a false motivation for complying with God's righteous way. Life could become a bargaining counter for getting identifiable benefits. The air we breathe is available to persons of all kinds as they live to appropriate the good air.

The Use Makes a Difference

God leaves it to us to discover these processes of operation. For centuries men lived in the midst of what was going on around them but never discovered what was going on. They saw no relation between air pressures and wind movements. They did not make connection between soil content and quality of crops. More and more we have been discovering the nature and the operation of the resources in God's universe. We are still in kindergarten in understanding them and using them.

We can discover these processes and use them for good or ill. We have learned something about atomic energy. We used it to bring destruction on Hiroshima and Nagasaki. We can also use it to help undeveloped regions of the world. We suspect that misused atomic energy can bring about radiation that can wreck humans and transmit deformities. We are also seeing that this energy through radiophosphorus can function in locating diseased cells. God puts this atomic energy in the universe. We can employ it for healthful living or diseased and deformed living. This holds true for ever so many resources—water, air, soil, chemicals.

Let the Processes Go On

We do well to remember that in many health matters we get along better when we let processes operate without our consciously trying to supervise them. This applies to many fields. We learn that heated air rises but we do not sit down at the moment and get fidgety, wondering if the warm air is rising in our vicinity. We assume that it is. Of course we do well to look to the heating system or the cooling system and their effective functioning. But we expect the air itself to go on behaving as air does with temperature changes.

It is so with our bodies. We learn that we need oxygen in the lungs and that this oxygen-changed air needs to get circulated through the body. Of course we shall need to consider ventilation and related fields to see that good air is available, but we do not stop every few minutes to wonder if we are breathing or if the oxygen is getting circulated. Such concern would get in the way of natural breathing. Our dispositions would become neurotic and our respiration spasmodic. We expect life-giving respiration to go on. This applies to ever so many life processes. Preoccupation with these bodily procedures would make us like the centipede that got along very well in his locomotion until someone asked which leg went first. Then in confusion and concern the troubled centipede became unable to move at all.

Spiritual Resources Too

One of the great essentials for us in this modern world is the recognition of "spiritual reality." Through recent centuries men have tended to discount what they could not explain and manipulate. Things had to be describable in terms of formulas, equations, specific data, and so on. What could not be explained in the science laboratory was put aside as imagined. The "spiritual," whatever this was, was looked upon as something to be disregarded in consideration of what was "real." Today we are seeing that there is much of reality that we do not know about. We are less inclined to doubt or deny what we cannot explain or handle. We expect that as years go by we shall come to explain many things that are mysterious to us now.

At present we are looking upon the universe as involving much more than that which we can pinch with our fingers, weigh in scales, and describe as to motion. We are more inclined to listen to a man like Physicist Jeans who says that the universe is more like a great idea than an assemblage of inert stuff. There is place for *mind* in the universe as well as *matter*. This view indicates that omission of spiritual reality leaves the picture of the universe incomplete. Once Lynn Hough said, "A secular world is only half a world."

A program of healthful living has to consider the fullness of reality. This includes spiritual reality. We shall be honest enough to say that we are not very well schooled about it. We shall admit we are going to try to find out more about it. But we are going to say that this spiritual reality enters into our building of a way of inclusive good health. Leave this out and we have man as animal; include it rightly and we have man as person. We shall not discount what we shall call the physical, for this enters into the process of living. We shall, however, go beyond the physical reality; we shall include spiritual reality in the total picture and process. Herein is a distinctive affirmation and contribution of the Church of Jesus Christ.

It is a mission of the church today to identify spiritual reality and to guide persons in uilizing this in healthy living. The church will keep reminding us that any health program that leaves this out will be partial and temporary. The person needs the spiritual light from the Son as well as the physical light from the sun. And we are seeing that the two are not opposed to each other. We are coming to think that they are aspects of one reality, one phase of which we call spiritual and the other physical. We have made the separation in our thinking; God has not made the division.

Recent Approaches to Spiritual Resources

The field of health and healing is being enlarged by recent developments in physical sciences. What we are calling "the new physics" is helping to break down the barrier, the artificial barrier that used to be set up between the material and the spiritual. Sir James Jeans in his *Physics and Philosophy* speaks of "ingredients" which are not describable in the techniques and language of the physical sciences. He advises,

> "These are just as real as the material ingredients, but do not happen to make any appeal to our senses. Thus the material world as defined above constitutes the whole world of appearances, but not the whole world of reality: we may think of it as forming only a cross-section of the world of reality."— Page 113.

He goes on to say that we cannot ever "understand the world of appearance without probing into the deeper substratum of reality."

How this spiritual reality functions we have yet to discover. We are yet amateurs. We do not understand these resources. We do not know how to tap them. We cannot even identify them. Our framework of thinking is too limited to interpret this little known reality. Yet in clearer moments we can sense the possibility of bringing ourselves, our bodies and our minds, into right relationship with those invisible resources. Without this right relationship our condition can become partial, disturbed, distorted. And we are in danger of getting off on some sidetracks and half-truths. There can be quacks in matters of spiritual health as well as in physical health. We have so much to learn. Just now it is important that we do not deny the existence of the higher reality.

We are often tempted to ascribe the functioning of spiritual reality to some inexplainable realm and call it supernatural. It is truer to fact and more helpful to consider that everything in God's universe can be explained even if we are unable to make explanations at present. It would be inconsistent with God's nature to have one aspect of his universe describable in terms of natural law and another aspect left to unpredictability. Yet we shall have to be very careful that we do not jump to conclusions and explanations about the operation of spiritual reality. We need genuine humility.

In *A Doctor Heals by Faith* Dr. Christopher Woodward sets forth the view that just as there are "waves" in what we call physical reality, so it is likely that there are waves in beyond-the-physical reality which can function as wireless waves do, which are yet "undiscovered by scientists." He sees this reality, whether explainable by waves or otherwise, as constituting great resources for augmenting healthful living. He makes this conclusion.

"I believe the next great step forward in Man's progress toward uncovering all that God has given us is the realization of the existence of healing powers on the spiritual level, which as yet have not been understood, though they were seen clearly when Christ was on earth."—Page 117.

In *Psychology, Religion, and Healing* the Reverend Dr. Leslie Weatherhead sets forth his faith in the availability of help and healing through rapport with these spiritual realities. He writes, "Let us never forget that there is a spiritual power to heal which has not been withheld. It has not been appropriated" (page 495). We see that if this spiritual reality is available for healing the sick, it is also available for achieving and maintaining good health. It is available for preventive as well as remedial services.

Physical Resources for Spiritual Health

What we do with our bodies conditions the kind of spiritual health we are going to have. Effective care of our physical bodies provides for and contributes to spiritual health and effectiveness. It

34

is true that many men and women of great spiritual capacity and creativity have not had good health. On the whole these persons rose above their handicaps by will power, by strong faith and good discipline; they were not spiritual giants because they were sick. Paul never explained his spiritual conversion or his spiritual advance as due to his "thorn in the flesh" (II Corinthians 12:7), whatever that was. We can infer, however, that this weakness or affliction may have helped to keep him humble and more reliant on God. He advised the young Timothy to take good care of his health, of his stomach in particular. He told the Corinthian saints to regard the body as "the temple of the Holy Ghost" (II Corinthians 6:19).

The junior boy was quite right when in the days of long periods of kneeling for prayer he said that after so long he did not feel prayerful anymore. After his legs got cramped and in time went to sleep he was more concerned about getting up than he was with praying. More and more we have come to see that we want to take such good care of the physical health and posture that we do not need to think about the body; then we can turn without interruption to the spiritual expression of our selves. We want to utilize available resources that we call physical to achieve healthy living.

To Be Discovered and Developed

God provides us with an amplitude of physical resources for healthy living. Generally, they are in the raw, undeveloped state. There are no placards around to say what they are and what they are good for. We have to find out. Sometimes we get confused about them. For instance, a little more than a century ago the tomato was considered poisonous and injurious to health. At the same time fresh air in the wintertime was looked upon as very undesirable. And milk could not be taken safely with an orange since the milk would curdle in the stomach. We keep getting unfounded ideas which we think agree with the way of things in God's universe. God expects us to explore and discover the great supply of health-producing materials.

We have to develop these resources. Generally, God does not set up a free lunch food corner with all supplies ready-packaged, clearly labeled, and medically prescribed. Except in rare emergencies God is not going to provide us with "manna from heaven" for which we do not work, for which neither cooking nor recipe is required. He does not provide us with ready-made dynamos for furnishing electricity. Nor does he hang ready-to-wear, health-built clothing on the trees about us. If he did he would end up with a race of lazy, incompetent nincompoops without creative power or initiative.

And the Means of Supply Too

God leaves it to man to take care of the means of production. He expects us to take care of the soil, of plant culture, of animal husbandry, of storage of what we produce, of distributing what we raise and manufacture. The kind of soil makes a difference. The way we take care of this soil and maintain its richness affects the quantity and the quality of foodstuffs and clothing stuffs. The kind of seeds we provide and use, the kind of stock we breed affects our health. So does the supply and the control of water. It is not enough that we have something to eat. What we eat and how we eat is of great consequence. We are stewards over supplying and consuming and sharing what we have in food and clothing and fuel and more. It is and ought to be disconcerting to all of us to realize that more than half of the world's population goes to bed hungry every night. We admit there can be enough food produced to meet these needs, but we have not learned how to make an adequate distribution of products produced.

The List Is Long

The stewardship applies to so many things: to pure water to drink, clean water for bathing and washing, good air to breathe; to plant and mineral products for soaps and other cleansing materials, disposal of refuse; to plant products, furs and hides, synthetic materials for clothing; to petroleum and related materials for fuel, for transportation, and for medicines; to stone and wood and mineral products usable for constructing of our living quarters. We are jolted when we realize that more people on the earth live in houses made of mud and straw or paper than in houses of more substantial materials. The list might go on and on. All these things affect our health. And we are stewards over all these.

For Renewal and Recuperation

God does not have in mind a run-down earth for a run-down race. When this deterioration occurs, it is because we have been doing a poor job of utilizing what God has for us and of lining up with him so that we live his way. Such words as "restore" and "renew" and "refresh" are in God's vocabulary in health matters. Even death can be looked upon as a transition in eternal living rather than as an end to everything.

In this universe of God's are astonishing powers of resiliency and recuperation. This earth on which we live can stand some mighty severe shocks. Volcano and earthquake strains have ripped at the earth as if they would tear things apart. In the longer view we come to see them as steps in building up our planet. What at the time seemed setbacks have turned out to be setups. When our planet gets tired and old and worn its resources will probably continue in some shaping of other planets.

The universe is full of health-building resources. The powers of the sun are considered the outstanding purifying force in the world, better than sprays and powders. The decomposition of dead matter gets rid of the putrid and the decadent and also contributes producing powers to the soil. Left to itself, the air gets rid of what is foreign to good breathing.

Our human bodies are miracles in resiliency. The corpuscles of our blood function in defense and in creation. A single drop of blood contains about three hundred million red corpuscles. Every one of these makes a complete circuit of the body in a few seconds, each time with a load of oxygen. Each corpuscle makes about a half million journeys in its lifetime of three months. It is a miracle in life-giving power. When some part of the body is wounded white corpuscles literally throw themselves by the thousands to counteract the danger and restore health. How these corpuscles are able to identify what is foreign to the well-being of the body and come out as the police force to protect the total organism is miraculous. In ever so many ways this miracle of recuperation appears.

The body exhibits remarkable comeback expression. The forces of restoration are inherent in God's universe. He intends for us to be willing, to be worthy to draw on them.

Lining Up for These Resources

God's universe requires us to *line up* in the universe way if we are to draw on resources available. The man who wants to transmit electricity knows that he cannot carry it through dry wood. The man who plans to fatten cattle knows that he cannot do this on nutritionless grass. The man with sloping fields knows that he cannot permit erosion to carry away his topsoil. The man with iron exposed to the weather knows that oxidation will go on unless he provides protection. There is no wishful thinking, no hocus-pocus charms. There is no substitute for wise compliance with the way natural things operate. In every field we have to learn how things function and then work accordingly.

It has to be this way in God's universe. If every person could wish things around to suit his private fancies, the whole universe would go to pieces. The order and the predictability of things as described in natural laws provide us with possibilities of drawing on natural powers and working with them. They do not make slaves of us; we can use them to our service. What confusion there would be if electricity traveled well on a copper wire one day and on a wooden stick the next day, if water boiled at 212 degrees Fahrenheit one day and 63 degrees the next day, if heated air rose one week and cold air the next week. In predictability and order lie our assurance for getting help.

This is true of spiritual reality. These spiritual resources are available to us only as we line up with God. We have to go along with God if we are going to draw on his powers. The universe would go to pieces if every man were able to set up his own program through which he could acquire these spiritual resources. Many plans would go directly against what God is working to accomplish. Suppose the schemer could draw on divine wisdom to help him devise more complicated schemes of wickedness. Suppose the robber could draw on sources of divine strength to enable him to become a second-to-none pugilist. Suppose the singer could draw on divine artistry to glamorize his sensuous actions. What a mess of confusion and conflict we would have! No, in the long run, those who draw on divine resources have to line up with God.

This holds for spiritual resources, too, in every way. Mere asking in praying is not enough. Conniving so we seem to be working to further God's purpose when we are really looking to our own schemes will not carry through. A farmer may presume he is asking God for a good crop so he can contribute generously to the church, when his major motivation is to add to his own treasury. A preacher may pray for support that he may speak convincingly for the sake of the people when he is really thinking of his own standing. In all this it is good for us to remember the comment of a twelve-year-old boy, "God is quick to catch on to why we do things."

Spiritual resources are available to those who (1) see how God's forces operate, (2) understand what God has in mind to do, and (3) line up their living with these plans and these processes of God. This lining up with God is the way to good health.

Questions for Discussion

1. What are some factors that enter into the shaping of your life that would be called nonmaterial, which cannot be weighed and measured by systems for describing physical reality?
2. Henry Drummond once wrote of "natural law in the spiritual world." What does this mean to you? Do you consider that spiritual reality can be described in terms of "natural law" as can physical reality?
3. What difference does it make in "living healthfully" if we separate reality into two parts, the material and the physical, and think of them as separate from each other or opposed to each other?
4. What difference does it make for healthful living if we deny the existence of material reality and consider it only as the product of our imagination?
5. What would happen if persons would draw on God's spiritual resources and use them without regard to His purpose and plan? For instance, what would happen if "power to heal" were granted to an irresponsible person?
6. How does physical fitness affect our spiritual fitness?
7. How are physical resources for healthy living provided as potentials to be discovered and developed rather than as ready-made, packaged products handed out by God? How does this make a difference in man's longtime development?
8. How may both material and spiritual resources be present in the universe and yet be unknown to us? Give examples of the discovery of resources.
9. How are we equipped in body and in spirit for recovery and restoration? What resources are there for our spiritual restoration?
10. What constitutes quackery in spiritual health? How may quackeries misinterpret resources for spiritual health?
11. How shall we go about discovering spiritual resources and utilizing them for healthful living?
12. How are we normally obligated to use spiritual resources wisely and usefully, even though we say there is an abundance in these resources?

CHAPTER 4

HEALTHINESS IS
GOD'S NATURE

"God is the altogether healthy!" So speaks one designator of what God is like. "If he were not, he would have broken down long ago." Fittingly we can say that to be eternal is to be "everlastingly healthy." Considering health as wholeness, we are able to look upon God as the perfect expression of inner harmony. No one part of him is fighting any other part. No one phase of him is undermining any other phase. He is completely one and operates in a great creative expression that is one, his *universe*. Right fittingly have the Jews, for more than two thousand years, chanted their Shema, "The Lord our God is one . . . !" This says not only that there is only one God; it says there is oneness in this God (Deuteronomy 6:4).

The words "health" and "whole" and "holy" all come from the same root. To be healthy is to be whole and to be whole is to be holy. God is all of these.

Another View of God

Some critics do not see this oneness, this wholeness in God. One critic draws a conclusion like this from the pictures of God that he has seen: "It appears to me that God is all tied up in knots. He is a complete neurotic, if there ever was one." He sees God as an expression of nervous conflicts and emotional outbursts. Such a comment calls for frank inquiry about the way God has been pictured. The youth who imaged God this way pictured him as lashing out in jealousy and anger to whomever displeased him. Like the ancient Thor the God of the Bible would send plagues and hurl thunderbolts and cut down enemies. To this observer such conduct looked like a case of juvenile tantrums.

To another critic God appeared to be like a small child who has special favorites. With this nature he might neglect or work against the not-so-favored peoples. This portrait of God makes him look like the child who is able to play with only a few playmates and who becomes peevish if his close friends play with more. Sometimes God is portrayed as somewhat sadistic about those he does not like. In this portrayal he finds happy satisfaction in chucking into hell those who oppose him and then watches them wriggle in pain. Such carrying on bears characteristics of an unhealthy personality. If God had such a disposition as this he would be the picture of "dis-health." We do well to be honest and admit that such portrayals of God have existed and do exist. We shall also do well to concede that a God of such ill health could hardly produce good health in us. Our studies in health need to stem from a God who is healthy and health-giving.

A Healthier God in the Bible

Early books of the Old Testament do give us the impression that the ancients did not give God a very healthy personality. Writers often pictured him with strong traits of jealousy and wrath and vengeance. He was thought of as "visiting his wrath" to the third and fourth generations (Exodus 20:5). Writers often pictured God as letting loose on those who crossed his path. Thus David incurred hot displeasure when he took a census of the Hebrews. The chronicler saw this as invading God's territory and as calling down the wrath of God in either seven years of famine, three years of pursuit by enemies, or three days of pestilence (II Samuel 24). Such an ill-tempered God would be a plague in himself.

It is a long way from this God pictured as striking down thousands when he became angry and the God of Jesus who is portrayed as the Father who loves all with understanding concern. It is a long way from the vengeful God who prompted the frightened Hebrews to fall prostrate on the ground before the awful Jehovah and the God described by Paul in his second letter to Timothy. Paul wrote in this uplifting vein, "God hath not given us the spirit of fear, but of power and of love, and of a sound mind" (II Timothy 1:7). A great development had been taking place in picturing God. It was a development that carried through many centuries. This later picture portrayed a healthy God who would make persons whole.

We Can Grow in Picturing God

Today many are demanding a more worthy and more adequate conception of God. Achieving a worthier idea of God has always been a major problem of religion. Only a dead religion can escape this. Only a blind religion will not see the need of it. Every living religion keeps seeking more adequate conceptions of God's nature and function. This is especially true of a religion that believes in and practices continuing revelation. We need the humility and the faith that prompts us to sense the need of expanding understanding of God. Each move forward should increase the health-stimulating powers of the conception.

This growth in conceiving God pertains, too, to the scope of the universe and to God's functioning in it. A few centuries ago through the thinking of Copernicus, Galileo, and Kepler the universe was pushed out into incredibly vast proportions. Multitudes thought that they would have to give up God since now there was no place for him to be. Yet God was not lost. Those who would grow saw their conceptions of God expand and deepen. Still he "was not far from every one of us." Now in the space age we are going through more growing pains. Light-year proportions, galaxies, atoms, and protons are stretching the images we have of the way God works. We keep needing a larger idea of God. We have to keep remembering that we tend to mistake San Francisco Bay for the Pacific Ocean. We have to remember that we shall be able to live more soundly when we sense that the great ocean is here, too. And we can be healthier.

The Character of God, Too

We tend to think of God in terms of our own selves. Perhaps this is the only thing we can do. We make a grave error, however, when we limit God to our circumscribed pictures of ourselves. Thus we often ascribe to him our petty qualities as well as our nobler ones. We tend to see God speaking our language and reacting as we said. Thus a young girl on first hearing that Jesus was a Jew said, "Jesus may have been a Jew, but God is a Baptist." John Fiske of Harvard University said that in his boyhood he thought of God as living a long, long time, so he pictured him as a venerable bookkeeper with flowing white beard, standing behind a high desk writing down everybody's bad deeds. And he wore spectacles.

The God of many persons does not show a very good picture of healthiness. He sits on a throne in regal splendor. He wants his own imperial way. He has no time for anyone who differs from him. He pronounces stiff sentences on offenders. He holds ingrained jealousies. He sends plagues and pestilences as punishments. He picks some to be saved to heavenly glory and some to be sent to hell. All this is at his own whim. Such a portrait depicts a strangely unhealthy God. Such a picture could only breed unhealthiness in those who believed in such a God.

Jesus Revealed Good Health

Jesus of Nazareth gives us the true picture of healthy living. We can look at him and say, "This is life at its best." His life did not come to an end because he collapsed internally. He kept his inner harmony. He disclosed confidence in eventual victory, even when he was facing the cross. He could say to his disciples on that last Thursday evening, "Let not your heart be troubled; I have overcome the world." In the Garden of Gethsemane he faced his captors and tormentors with courageous poise. He died from external causes.

When Jesus faced exacting situations, he carried on with certainty and strength. When his disciples requested him to eat, he calmly replied, "I have meat to eat that ye know not of" (John 4:34). He was drawing on sources of spiritual supply that the disciples did not know existed. The wise man is aware of resources for healthy living. Jesus knew how to tap these resources.

The Evergreen Life

The evergreen tree has long been a symbol of eternal life. Scientists who study the age of forests by examining tree rings conclude that the oldest living things on our planet are pine trees growing in the upper timberline of mountains in eastern California. Bristlecone pines in the White Mountains northeast of Bishop, California, are believed to be something like 4,100 years of age. This pine is sturdy enough to have survived flood and drought and climatic changes of forty centuries. The California pine trees were living when Abraham set out from Ur of the Chaldees. The first Psalm tells us that the good man, the wise man, is like a tree that has an evergreen life:

> "He is like a tree planted
> by streams of water,
> that yields its fruit in its season,
> and its leaf does not wither."
> — Psalm 1:1, R.S.V.

The Dead Sea Scrolls put this imagery this way: "a plant evergreen for all time to come."

God and Consistent Living

There are no quackeries in God's healthfulness. There are no shortcuts, no magic cults. Healthful conditions come out of

43

living consistently in God's universe, which universe has resources for producing health in persons. The term "quack" came from the likeness of the medical braggart to a duck when this supposed expert was going around making noisy boasts. The quacksters go about boasting of wonderful cure-all remedies. So there have been devices for making short persons tall, garlic tablets for blood pressure, electric blankets for cancer, salves for baldness, tonics for infertility, and more. All these guarantee a quick cure for sundry maladies. They have no sound relationship to healing factors.

It is estimated that every year Americans hand over one billion dollars for quackery health products. Of this amount some 350 million dollars go to some form of vitamin buildup, 148 million for laxatives and elimination aids, 250 million for useless "cures" for arthritis and rheumatism. Salves, tonics, pills and the like seek quick action and easy application.

God provides for us to live soundly in an inclusive program that is health-producing. He calls us to "see life steadily and see it whole." No one compartment will do. Any one phase pulled out of proportion becomes a fad or even a fanaticism. God does not specialize in liver pills or skin ointments or stomach tonics. He looks to the whole person. The cynic sees all parts of the person but he has a blind spot when it comes to seeing the meaning of the whole. The quack plans to distort the picture by concentrating with nearsighted vision on some part for which he has a nostrum. God's way is the program of concern with the total body and the total personhood in relationship to God's total world. To keep all this body and spirit healthy calls for continuing, consistent living with God's life-giving and person-producing factors.

The Healthy Image of God

There is considerable loose talking these days about imageries of God. He is the "Man Upstairs," the "Heavenly Porter," and even for one actress, a "Livin' Doll." Much of this is cheap and juvenile, contrary to what really exists. Nowadays it is not enough to believe in God: the kind of God we believe in is of utmost consequence. What we think of the nature of ultimate reality in God is going to determine what kind of persons we are going to be, what kind of lives we are going to live, what kind of health we are going to have. Some images of God cannot be conducive to spiritual health or physical health.

This does not mean that we can go out on the market and select some image of God that suits our fancy. Our image has to square with the way God behaves in the universe. We cannot select an image of a God who lets us follow our whims and go our own undisciplined way, and then gives a shot of spiritual vitamins or serves us some celestial tonic so that at an instant we are charged with spiritual energy.

The God of popular song and sentiment and of all-of-a-sudden preaching does not make serious demands on his children as to what they do with their lives. Not infrequently persons who indulge in sensuous or self-centered activities tell how God aids and abets them in what they do. One worldly agnostic would say when he was dealt a good bridge hand, "There is a God" and when dealt a poor hand would say, "There is no God." Often God is credited with making a contest come out a certain way so the one who won could win the prize. One baseball pitcher commented, "I wouldn't have been able to work this kind of pitching without the help of the Man Upstairs." All these are self-concerned, self-constructed images of God that do not glimpse the functioning of divine purpose and divine process in God's universe. A sound program of health cannot be built on such flimsy, fanciful thinking. Well might a high school student say, "I cannot believe in a God like this, incompetent and inconsistent."

Socrates is credited with saying that the unexamined life is not worth living. It may be wise for us to add that an unexamined faith is not worth having. We might go further and say that the unexamined image of God may actually undermine our spiritual health. This examination involves all of our personhood. The Bible charges us, "Thou shalt love the Lord thy God with *all* thy heart, and with *all* thy soul, and with *all* thy strength, and with *all thy mind.*" We explore and we experience and we evaluate with every bit of ourselves.

The Healing God Revealed in Jesus Christ

Jesus Christ enables us to see what God is like. He lived out on earth in human terms the eternal qualities of God. Jesus once said, "He that hath seen me hath seen the Father" (John 14:9). We speak of the revelation of God's love, of God's wisdom, of God's forgiveness. Let us also add that Jesus Christ reveals God's health, that he reveals how God is concerned with the health of all his children.

When Jesus went home to Nazareth and spoke in his own synagogue he set forth his mission as expressed in the Book of Isaiah. In his text was this phrase, "He hath sent me to heal . . ."

45

(Luke 4:18). Jesus went about healing the sick. He gave sight to the blind. He made the lame to walk. He restored muscular action to the man with a withered hand (Matthew 12:10). He stopped the hemorrhaging in an afflicted woman (Mark 5:21-26). He lowered the body temperature of "Simon's wife's mother" who "was taken with a great fever" (Luke 4:38). He brought health to an epileptic (Mark 9:15-24). All this he did out of humanitarian motivation. Never did he parade his healings. Never did he use his healings to attract followers. Rather he requested those healed to refrain from publicizing what had happened. He ministered in healing to restore good health to persons.

And this good health was inclusive. He was concerned with the total person. Often he said, "Be ye whole!" While he looked to easing physical suffering and to bringing to pass physical competency, he would say, "Thy sins be forgiven!" He always wanted spiritual health to go along with physical health. He seemed always to think of the two as functioning together. Essentially, they are not separable.

Jesus was a minister of healing. In this he reveals the healing intent and the healing outreach of God. A hymn of a few decades ago sang of Jesus as a healing doctor.

> The great physician now is near,
> The sympathizing Jesus,
> He speaks the drooping heart to cheer,
> Oh, hear the voice of Jesus!

Here was a simple affirmation of the healing power and purpose of the Father expressed in his Son's ministry on earth.

In the Mosaic Code

The book of Exodus tells how a servile people were led out of Egypt toward the land of Canaan and then entered it. Attention was given to health regulations. The first annual report of New York City's health department referred to the Mosaic Code as "the greatest collection of health laws ever published." It is important to note how this code envisioned a close relation between religion and health. The book of Leviticus sets forth regulations regarding the conduct of the priests as they were charged with preserving the health of the community. At a distance, some of the regulations seem harsh, even cruel. These people, however, had to function on the level of their capability. The regulations had to be specific and the penalties specific. In this Mosaic code we find provisions for detecting leprosy, for quarantine, for disposal of excretion, and so on. These regulations had to do with physical health. The Hebrews were reminded sternly that a chosen people had to be a healthy people.

These chapters in the Pentateuch are considered some of the least appealing in the Bible. Seen in their day they stand out as highly significant because they speak so far beyond the standards of three thousand years ago. The Mosaic code says that religion can never be regarded as a compartment separate to itself. It says that physical well-being is an essential part of community living. It says, too, that taking care of one's physical health is a stewardship related to the total group life.

It was several centuries before the prophets and Jesus of Nazareth could go on to teach about mental health and spiritual health. But the Mosaic code gave something in its field that was much more advanced than anything in the ancient world.

Jesus' Directive

When Jesus sent out the twelve apostles, he commissioned them "to cure diseases, . . . to preach the kingdom, . . . to heal the sick" (Luke 9:1, 2). He sent them out with concern for a better *mind,* a better *spirit,* a better *body* for those *afflicted.* Jesus sent them out to be *medical* missionaries, *teaching* missionaries, *preaching* missionaries. He meant for these appointees to go out to restore the sick—some of them sick of body, some of them sick of soul, some of them sick of mind, and some of them sick in all phases of their living. These men were to go with appreciation of the healing power that had come into their own lives from God. "Freely ye have received, freely give" (Matthew 10:7). Good health was to beget good health.

Our Need for Image of the Healthy God

In *Green Pastures* the lone Jew, Hezdra, fighting before Jerusalem, discloses how he had rejected the longtime God of wrath and vengeance of the ancient Hebrews for the God of love of Hosea. If he could have met Jesus of Nazareth, his image would have moved on still further. He would have come to know the God Jesus pictured in the parable of the good Samaritan, the God of the Great Commission; his image could have leaped far ahead as he came to vision God in terms of the best he experienced in Jesus.

Today we are needing to see these basics: (1) God himself as everlastingly healthy, (2) God's provision for resources for man's good health, available for producing healthy living, (3) Jesus Christ as the revelation of the healthy nature and healing outreach of God, (4) the Saint as the well-disciplined follower of God's way of living, (5) the wholeness, the completeness of inclusive health, (6) the church as a laboratory fellowship for bringing about healthy living, (7) the Holy Spirit as life-giving and person-producing dynamic in healthy living, (8) the gospel as the good news about spiritual health.

Our God is help and hope for living that does not run down or run out. Our God intends for his people to be happy and productive in their healthfulness. This is set forth definitely in the counsel about looking well to our health in the "Word of Wisdom" (Doctrine and Covenants 86). Here Saints who are wise are to "receive health" and "find wisdom" and "walk and not faint." Our God promotes our total well-being and furthers our self-managing development—all this in the framework of God's own healthy and health-radiating Personhood. Confidently we can affirm with Paul, "We know that in everything God works for good with those who love him, who are called according to his purpose" (Romans 8:28, R.S.V.).

Questions for Discussions

1. How can some conceptions of God make us neurotically unhealthy?
2. What is the conception of God involved in this comment, "God must have sent me this headache for a purpose"? How would you help this person to rethink his concept of the nature of God?
3. How must God be "everlastingly healthy"?
4. What is the significance of health regulations in the Mosaic code? How would this be inadequate for a code of health in a contemporary Zionic community?
5. What do you see as Jesus' motive and plan of ministering when he healed persons? What was he wanting to achieve?
6. How may we read our partial conception of what constitutes good health into God as to his purpose for us?
7. In terms of God's purpose and plan when do we have the moral right to "enjoy good health" in what we do?
8. How are the motivation and the method of quackeries not consistent with God's purpose and procedure?
9. How was "wholeness" an essential concern of Jesus Christ in his ministry of healing? How does this reflect God the Father?

10. What qualities do you see inherent in a healthy and a health-producing God?
11. How are the healthy and the holy one and the same in God?
12. Why is it not enough just to believe in God? How does the kind of God we believe in make so much difference?

PART II

Very early in the life of the Restoration church the founders were advised, "All things shall be done by common consent in the church, by much prayer and faith." Such counsel places a high estimate and a heavy responsibility upon members. All are to be participants in developing and using this "common mind." Such a "consensus" cannot be superimposed, handed down, or left to chance. It comes to be through the enlightened and effective thinking and feeling of the members as they interact freely, as the Spirit of God guides in this sharing. There is no place for the way of common ignorance and superstition. There is no place for uninformed acceptance of edicts of authoritarian leadership. Members are to see, so that a "common mind," sound and functional, shall emerge.

This section looks to the developing of "common consent" about spiritual fitness: what it is, how it comes to be, how it is to be used. It calls for a questing, examining attitude that avoids presumptions. Sometimes it may appear negative. It is not intended to be so. When it speaks against quackery in spirituality, it is endeavoring to clear the deck of misconception and mispractice. When it says that it is not enough to be "religious," it is wanting to push aside malpractice and malbelief in order to get at soundness. Let it be clear that much that passes under the name of religion is unhealthy, that much that is considered "faith in God" is contrary to God's nature and is conducive to spiritual ill health.

Let the chapter that affirms that the Restoration movement has a gospel of health ring clear. The next section will be devoted to expanding this affirmation. The chapter about a healthy theology used healthfully is highly important. Some portraits of God, some pictures of man, can only end in unhealthiness. Let it be evident that religion can further spiritual ill health. Our own church is not foolproof.

51

The consideration of the requirement that our leaders be spiritually healthy applies to every one of us. In the inclusive sense each one of us is both leader and follower. Each parent is a leader. Each youth leads somebody. It is never the privilege of leaders to push off their unhealthy phobias, fears, prejudices, fallacies, half-truths, and anxieties on others. We are saying, let our physicians of the soul be spiritually healthy! The main thing is that we all shall want to function in a searching, expressing way. There is no place to point fingers to other leaders and refer to them as "they."

Throughout this section we shall be asking what the mind of the church is about healthy spirituality, about the spirituality we want to see develop in the church. One of the main objectives of this course is to build a common consent about spiritual healthiness.

CHAPTER 5

THE KIND OF RELIGION
MAKES A DIFFERENCE

This truism stands out boldly: Religions differ and the effect of these differing religions upon the spiritual health of a person and of a group varies widely. We do not lump "food" into one category and suppose that all has identical influence on the body. Some foods provide chewing without nourishment. Some things taken into the body do little good, and some are injurious. Nor do we put all persons together as if they exerted the same influence upon us. Some persons have a kind of neutral air; some undermine us; some build us up. There are qualitative differences with respect to the ways they affect us. And this is true of religions.

Here are some of the fundamentals that stand out: (1) A person needs sound religion if he is going to have continuing, inclusive spiritual health. (2) There are great diversities among existing religions as to their effect on the health of persons. (3) Some religious systems in beliefs and practices are conducive to spiritual healthiness; some are not. (4) Within a religious movement there can be considerable difference with respect to influence on spiritual health. This stems from the diversity of thinking and practicing within it. (5) It is imperative that a religious group develop sound consensus about its functioning in producing spiritual healthiness. (6) Each person needs to evaluate the religion of his espousal and his practice with respect to its effect upon his spiritual health and upon the health of others. (7) This cultivation of spiritual healthiness is a lifelong stewardship. Each one of us needs to guard against the unthinking presumption that the religion of our own affiliation and participation is one hundred percent pure while the weaknesses and errors are in the religions of other persons and groups. And we shall do well to avoid thinking that the shortcomings are in the faiths of others while our own is simon-pure.

Differences within a Group

We are discovering that we are not warranted in making widespread generalizations about the healthiness or health-affording

...ues of groups as a whole. We cannot say that the Roman Catholics are more or less spiritually healthy than are Methodists or Nazarenes. We can point out that there are differences in resources in the several groups and that it makes a great difference how a given group utilizes its resources. Thus the confessional of Roman Catholicism can be highly significant in affording counsel and in providing inner release, or it can be a perfunctory participation in a rite that means little more than supplying escape. The belief in "salvation and sanctification" in a rather "pentecostal" group can bring a conviction of cleansing and security or only an emotional surge that never touches the ethics of living. It is sound for members of the Reorganized Church of Jesus Christ of Latter Day Saints to take this examining look at our own faith. We may not elevate it as totally good or denounce it as totally bad. We shall see what happens in the life of a person or of a group and ascertain whether it works to the good or otherwise. We shall see how our gospel and our church interpreted and slanted in certain ways can push toward not-so-healthy expression, how with misdirection it can move toward neurotic self-censure, superstition, and social withdrawal. We shall also see how with sound, inclusive, and balanced understanding and practice this gospel and this church can produce persons of wholesome spirituality.

Dr. Wayne Oates has reported studies of the mentally ill in different groups with respect to the functioning of religion in their several cases. His opening chapter in *Religious Factors in Mental Illness* carries the significant title, "The Hindering and Helping Power of Religion." In his study he is asking this question, "What can we learn from mental illness as to specific ways whereby Christian teachings may enable the religious person, with all his believing, to be mentally healthy?" If he includes living out these teachings as a part of the program of teaching we would accord with his objective. The living out will include his communing and his serving which is something more than finding out some printed teachings. He is searching for what is "sound," with "sound" meaning "health-giving" rather than "conformity." He came out with these conclusions:

1. "Religious affiliation with this or that group has little or no correlation with mental illness." By this he meant affiliation with a "particular denomination." To say a person belonged to the Roman Catholic faith, to the Presbyterian Church, to the Assembly of God, or to something else does not give clue to his difficulty. Apparently there is wide range among the members of any specific group.

54

2. "The way in which religious teachings are presented to the person," however, has much to do with what happens inside him. He may accept the teaching and the practices, he may reject them, or he may fall into "interminable conflict" over what he has been taught and how this is to be carried out. It would appear that such a tenet as *repentance* could be interpreted and preached and included in the program so that a person could find release and renewal or continuing inner strain and conflict.

3. The role of persons in parental functions is of great consequence. This includes the mother and the father of the person, or persons who fill the role of parents in the event of the death or defection of the parents. The kind of teaching and the kind of practicing of parents, particularly with reference to their concept of God, is of marked significance. The God-concept and the family relationship were interwoven with the illness of the patients.

Such studies bring us face-to-face with the realization that mere membership in the Latter Day Saint movement is not going to insure spiritual health. We have to ask further questions. (1) What kind of Latter Day Saint believing and practicing furthers spiritual health? (2) What kind of Latter Day Saint family living provides a developing ground for spiritual healthiness? (3) What kind of Latter Day Saint do we vision as being spiritually healthy? (4) What kind of conception of God and what kind of communion with God fosters spiritual healthiness? (5) What kind of approach shall we develop for achieving spiritual healthiness through the latter-day gospel and the Latter Day Saint Church? Certainly the brand of Latter Day Saint faith we vision as good and encourage as essential is going to condition the spiritual health of our people.

Facing Reality or Repudiating Reality

Sound religion faces reality. Rudyard Kipling once wrote of "the God of things as they are." This is right if we include in "things as they are" the potentiality to develop what is now into what yet can be. In reality there is always potential for things "as they may become." The spiritually blind are aware only of what is before their eyes in present form. The spiritually alert see hidden possibilities. The healthy person carries this more inclusive conception of reality. He faces all of what is and visions what good or bad can come out of it. He lines up with God in making the desirable to come to pass. The workman of the early sixteenth century saw only a rough chunk of stone while Michaelangelo visioned a statue of Moses in it. The spiritually healthy religion is aware of the total reality.

The healthy religion does not encourage the person to run away or to repudiate reality. The weaker expression would be to get away from it all. Some religions are expressed by the fervent preacher who wanted his eyes "closed to this world of sin." He prayed "for the wings of a dove" that he might fly away to God and get away from all troubles and trials. Dr. Karl Menninger once wrote in *The Human Mind* that from the standpoint of the psychiatrist, "a religion which merely ministers to the unconscious repudiation of reality . . . cannot be regarded as anything other than a neurotic or psychotic system" (page 466).

Jesus taught his disciples to see reality and to stand up to life. He spoke out against escaping and self-deceiving. He said that in the universe there is nothing that "shall not be revealed," nothing that "shall not be known" (Matthew 10:23). There is no place for covering up and excusing and pretending in the gospel of Jesus Christ. This applies to motivations, rationalizations, and validations. Dr. Menninger speaks bluntly on this matter.

> "The manner in which a man utilizes his religion— whether it be to enrich and ennoble his life or to excuse his selfishness and cruelty, or to rationalize his delusions and hallucinations, or to clothe himself in the comforting illusion of omnipotence—is a commentary on his mental health."—*Op. cit.,* page 467.

We need religion that serves a positive and creative function in maintaining a vital, purposeful relationship with reality. We need a religion that is aware of total reality, including spiritual reality. We need religion that sees God as he is, so that the person is able to grow in healthy relationship with God, with others, with God's universe. We need religion that sees the person in his real self and this includes the person he may become. We need religion that beholds reality as something to be used enjoyably and creatively with God for carrying on God's purpose. We need religion that recognizes and uses man's capacity for reality. This is the kind of religion we want and the kind God intends the Latter Day Saint gospel to be.

Living Together with God

What does a man's religion do to his relationship with others? Three general courses are possible. (1) He can withdraw from others and consider them evil or undesirable. He may retire to a cell where he literally lives to himself or he may withdraw into a shell of his own making that isolates him like a hermit in a woodland. This apartness may come from different factors. (a) This may arise out of elevation of himself and the discounting of others. (b) It may be prompted by his low estimate of himself, which low estimate he transfers to others. (c) He may feel constrained to deny himself the association he enjoys so much. (d) He may believe that God needs his worship more than others need his association. In cases of spiritual illness the person may lose imagery of himself and of others so that he can no longer communicate in the world of reality.

Sound religion enables the person to communicate with others and to commune with God as one integrated process. The two go together. Those who come to know God and work with God come to live together and with him in maturing love, in growing understanding, in effective mutuality. Dr. Oates, in *Religious Factors in Mental Illness,* summarizes the matter this way:

> "In essence, then, healthy religion binds people together in such a way that their individuality is enabled both to be realized and to be consecrated to the total community of relationships to which they belong. This is a religion of mature and responsible relatedness."—Page 113.

We need religion that sees every man as worthful in the sight of God. We need religion that enables a person to see others as they now are and as they may become as they respond to God. We need religion that stimulates and assists persons to live together with brotherly mutuality. And God wants his church to develop this kind of religion.

Religion for a Unitary Life-span

A social welfare program of Britain was once described as being concerned with the life of a person from the womb to the tomb. Certainly the religious program as conducted by the church is to have no shorter concern. It is to be concerned with the total life-span. What is more, every segment of this span is to be an integral part of an integrated, continuing program of living. Every unit is to be considered as essential and important. No bit can be separated or left out. Sometimes adults talk as if childhood is merely a preliminary and youth is merely a preparation. Such a view is foreign to God's purpose and proceeding and is unfair to these non-adult years. If productivity becomes the criterion for worthful living, productivity as measured by the industrial world, then the senior years become a burden and a liability without appeal and without fruitage. This is not to be the case.

Sound religion sees every span of life as important and worthful in its own right. Every stage is preliminary to and preparatory for the next stage. This applies to adult living. The closing months of life are viewed as preface to the post-death existence. This reverence for every age of the life-span was emphasized by Jesus Christ. His recognition of children and his blessing of them was almost revolutionary. Small wonder that his disciples were surprised that he would do so. He reached out to the crippled, the ill, and the old and found a place for everyone. He had no cult for youth, no closed circle for the zenith-of-life adults, no high seats for the bewhiskered. There was no age-group to be tolerated or endured. Each one was essential for the total fellowship of the saintly community and every age group was elevated in its own right, in its own resources.

Sound religion sees the church as a company of persons rather than as an aggregation of identicals. God is not in the business of mass production of robots or yes-men. The God who does not create identical leaves on an oak tree is not planning to manufacture saints out of one mold. Even identical twins are not exactly alike. Sound religion recognizes that we cannot make all-inclusive generalizations and snug classifications in dealing with this infinite variety of more than two billion persons on the earth. Apply the following to children, youth, and adults: (1) Persons differ widely in resources and backgrounds. (2) Persons differ in their worlds of varied interests. (3) Persons differ in the problems they are facing. Often everyone could say with Dwight L. Moody, "I have more trouble with myself than with any other man I know." (4) Persons differ in their conception of God and in their communion with God. (5) Persons differ in their ability to express themselves to others and to themselves. Sound religion is aware of this infinite variation in man, God's highest creation, and functions accordingly.

In Outreaching Self-Expression

Religion that keeps persons spiritually healthy stimulates them and guides them in creative expression. They are active, meaningfully and consistently. There is no place for surrender to inactivity. There are no time clocks by which we "call it quits." This does not mean that the healthy person is in a buzz, in a dither, on a racetrack. A person can be very busy thinking and planning without making any demonstration of being busy. Nor does he picture Zion as "sitting under a vine and fig tree" and heaven as relaxing in a celestial rocking chair. He thinks of keeping on in creative work with God. And his God is no past tense *He Was*.

This creative expression gets him outside himself. This person gets outside his own little kingdom into God's great universe. This does not mean that he discounts himself; it means that he believes that as he works with God he will find his own self-fulfillment. Some religions hem persons in and turn their sights inward and leave them there to manufacture their own anxieties, concerns about themselves, and hope for rewards to them.

A few years ago Julius Schreiber wrote an article, "Mental Health Flowers in Democratic Soil." This is quoted in *Mental Health Planning for Social Action*, by George S. Stevenson. He sees good health or ill health reflected in what persons do in relation to the world about them. This is his picture of the behavior of a mentally healthy person:

> "Our lucky friend knows how to love on a mature basis where giving to others and doing for others is more meaningful and gratifying than receiving for oneself. . . . Further, our emotionally mature (or mentally healthy) individual has learned the trick of being quite honest with himself. From time to time he examines his values—all of them—to see if they can stand up under the careful scrutiny of newer experiences and newer information. . . .
>
> "Healthy living—or mental health—means that an individual . . . is able to pursue reasonable, purposeful goals; may use his capacities and talents fruitfully; experiences a sense of security, of belonging, of being respected . . . : has a sense of self-respect, of self-reliance, and achievement; and, in addition, has learned to respect others, to accept others, to love others, to live fairly and in peace with others."—Pages 4, 5.

Place all this in a universal context with God as the chief and central character and we have a picture of good spiritual health. Here we are in harmony with those persons who are in harmony with God. This lifts religious living above hobnobbing with all sorts of persons and trying to agree with all of them. Such attempts only lead us into shallow schizophrenia, spiritually speak-

ing. This harmonizing with God puts us into the world of outreach to all of God's children and youth and adults everywhere.
And this is a very real world.

Involvement of the Whole Person

Every aspect of life affects spiritual health and spiritual healthiness affects every field of our living. Over and over it has been
pointed out that health means wholeness. Dr. George Stevenson
makes this summary statement:

> *"The Wholeness of the Person.* This principle is basic to
> healthy human functioning. It means that, when a person be-
> haves, he behaves with every part of him or wholeheartedly.
> Academic and professional disciplines may seem to compart-
> mentalize human functions rather neatly. But in real life peo-
> ple do not function separately at home, at work, at play, and
> at church. Man resists fragmentation."—*Op. cit.,* pages 5, 6.

Religions are most effective when they help man to function as a
whole. Sometimes spiritual ill health is identified as failure to
function as a whole. This applies to more than dual personality
of the Jekyll-Hyde type or the shattering of personality into fragments in cases of schizophrenia. It applies also to persons who
through confusion in loyalties, chronic indecision, mixtures of love
and hate, judgments on partial data, and conflicts between doubts
and certainties live in disturbance and distress.

Health-producing religion summons the whole person to live,
integrated in himself in right relationship with his total environment. And this total environment is the universe, with God the
Source of oneness, order, and predictability. The call of Christ
still rings clear, "Be ye whole!" And we add "—in a whole society,
in the whole universe." Part of a man in a part of his living in a
part of God's universe will not work well.

Expandable Meaning and Enduring Value

Some religions do not encourage adherents to ask questions
except the questions that are officially stated. They do not expect
believers to inquire about meanings; these are prepared by those
in charge and the followers are to memorize what is supplied. They
do not investigate value, for it is stated categorically that God is
Value and that is enough. The lines of Tennyson's "Light Bri-
gade" are fitting.

Theirs not to make reply,
Theirs not to reason why,
Theirs but to do and die . . .

But such directives stand in the way of spiritual health. Sooner or later such as this will happen: (1) The person will split into two parts, one for thinking in religion, one for thinking in other matters. The two will keep apart for peace's sake. Such a person remains unintegrated. (2) The person will experience conflicts within himself as he endeavors to be honest in his thinking about religion. (3) The person will shut off exploratory thinking and will maintain what authoritarian leaders have dispensed to him. (4) His meanings and values will remain suspended without expression in daily living. They remain abstractions.

Persons require adequate meanings and enduring value. Without these life gets to wobbling about. Searchers for meaning ask, "What's the sense of it all?" And searchers for value ask, "What's the good of it all?" And we need the companionship of those who are searching with us and discovering with us and validating with us. Paul M. Johnson in *Personality and Religion* sets forth this need of ours:

> "A study was conducted by Braden at Northwestern University, in which more than two thousand people were asked why they were religious (if they were). Of all the answers given, the one most frequently offered was that 'religion gives meaning to life.' . . . The need to find meaning and enduring value in the face of separation and loss is one of the most persistent searchings of the human spirit. To discover an order of spiritual values that will not fail when other goods decline is the basic difference between confidence and despair. Some larger meaning such as the faith of religious affirmation is urgent if we are to hold life together in the depletions and destructions around us."—Page 138.

Yet everything that passes under the terms "meaning" and "value" will not suffice. Here are things that cannot be superimposed by authoritarians or by scriptures without understanding on the part of the searcher. The person has to see what they mean, what they imply, how they hold up. He wants values that are rooted in the nature of the universe, in the nature of the God of the universe. He needs to discover values, not to concoct some with brand-new price tags. Memorizing generalities and listening to platitudes will not satisfy.

The religionist who believes in revelation expects to increase in insight about value. He will hold to the values by which he lives while he examines their validity and seeks for expanding understanding of what they mean and how they apply. He will test his meanings and his values in the laboratory of living. He will distinguish between the eternal quality of God and his own partial conceptions of God. He will blend humility and honesty and hunger.

So Quality Matters

The kind of religion we choose and adhere to matters ever so much. Whether it has spiritual vitality, intellectual honesty, inner integration, relevance to daily living, breadth and inclusiveness, reverence for personhood, enduring value, foundation in the way of the universe, universal love, and the like will determine whether it can further spiritual health in persons and in groups. Certainly quantitative factors alone will not be enough. Yet the notion persists that possessions and population and prestige attest spiritual soundness and efficiency.

In Lewis Carroll's *Through the Looking Glass,* Alice meets the White Knight. He is cumbered with contraptions: a beehive to capture vagrant bees, a mousetrap for rodents that might turn up, and a dish for plum pudding if anyone should give him some. He was laden with gadgets. He represents the many persons who expect to gain health and happiness by accumulating things. They do not see that spirituality has to come from within, even if outside factors may help in gaining it. This view is found in those who think that if they had more money they would be spiritually well-to-do. Health does not come this way.

We need religion that helps us to gain wholeness, religion with integration, meaning for living, values worth living for, honesty toward reality, fellowship with those who line up and live with God and who love him and his people in all this. We need to be rooted in spiritual reality. Then temporary rebuffs and frustrations will not tear us apart. Some religions get in the way of becoming whole. The gospel of Jesus Christ, rightly interpreted and validated in everyday living, enables us to become complete, and completely healthy.

Questions for Discussion

1. Some radical sects practice handling poisonous snakes during their meetings and consider this a great demonstration of

faith. In the light of its motivation and its effects and in consideration of the way God works in his universe, how do you evaluate this practice? How do you evaluate this as faith?

2. What would be the effect on a person of praying Beerholm Tree's agnostic prayer, "O God, give me the faith to believe in those things which the common sense Thou has given me tells me are not true."

3. Einstein once devised a motto, "God is a scientist, not a magician." Does this have bearing on your working with God? One admirer of Einstein has said, "This is good if we make God a scientist, not a book on science." What difference does this make?

4. What would you name as "hindering" factors in religions that get in the way of man's achieving spiritual health?

5. How may "faith" be a hindering or a helping factor in achieving healthiness in our personhoods? How is our conception of what faith is very important?

6. What would be the effect on you of your holding to the view of Lord Londonderry who wrote in his diary, "Here I learned that Almighty God, for reasons best known to himself, has been pleased to burn down my house in the county of Durham"?

7. What are some quantitative criteria by which men often adjudge the merit of a religion? To what degree are they sound? How are they inadequate for furthering spiritual health? Yet how can these observable things serve in expressing and developing spirituality?

8. How does a sound religion include images of ourselves as well as images of God? What are some images of man that get in the way of experiencing spiritual health?

9. What did Alfred North Whitehead mean when he said, "That religion will conquer which can render clear to popular understanding some eternal greatness incarnate in the passage of temporal fact"?

10. Illustrate how a given institutional religion may include both hindering and helping factors in its beliefs and its practices. Indicate how both can be in one system.

11. By what criteria would you determine whether a given religion is "sound," that is, "health-giving"?

12. What implications for our church are there in the observation of Wayne Oates that we cannot say whether a given denomination is health-producing but that the difference is in the way the beliefs and practices of the denomination are taught and carried out?

CHAPTER 6

THE RESTORATION MOVEMENT
HAS A GOSPEL OF HEALTH

Now comes the exacting question, What does the Restoration movement have in its way of life that can and does foster and further good spiritual health? What does it hold up as desirable spirituality? What does it teach as a health-producing gospel? What kind of God is held forth and worshiped and worked with? Is the God of the Latter Day Saints a wholesome Person, as they see him? What kind of saints does the movement set out to develop? What kind of fellowship does it encourage and attain? Does this fellowship further spiritual healthiness? How does Jesus Christ, who is heralded as centering the movement, affect the living of the Saints? How does the much emphasized Holy Spirit affect the living of believers as far as spiritual health is concerned? What does the emphasis on priesthood authority do to the tone of the life of ministers and members? Is the heaven of Latter Day Saints healthy in motivation for spiritual, fruitful living here and now? (A people's image of heaven is a good index of the maturity of their spirituality.) What is visioned as the health condition of the Zion which Latter Day Saints wait and work for?

These considerations are inescapable. In our answers lie the soundness and the service of the Restoration gospel. We have to face up to the question, What kind of saints is the Restoration movement producing? What kind is it capable of producing? So we are asking ourselves, What potential resources and what operative resources for healthy spiritual living were available in the Restoration movement at its inception, 1820-1830? And we ask further, What resources are available in the movement of 1966-1976?

God Provides Resources to Be Discovered and Developed

The Restoration movement is not going to provide bargain counters to which persons may come for free supplies of health-producing pills to be taken with ease. There will not be gospel hawkers crying out spiritual tonics that transform persons from skinny spirituality to marvels of heavenly health. There will be no exhibitions of paragons of spiritual power. God's resources have to be worked for and worked with.

Natural resources are not supplied by God in packaged, labeled products. Few can be titled "ready to use." Rather does God provide ample provisions for creative endeavor, for making things come true. Only in emergencies does God provide on-the-counter supplies ready for the table. The story of the flight from Egypt tells of God-supplied manna and quails on the trek through the desert. If he had continued to do this through the centuries, his people would have become a spoon-fed, dependent people without ability to make decisions, to act creatively, or to stand on their own feet. When they came into Canaan he left them to learn how to till the soil and make a living. He kept reminding them that they were to do this with him as a stewardship. He kept telling them that they would get along well insofar as they lined up with him and worked to realize what he had in mind for them in his world. It was up to them to discover the resources in their new land to utilize them. God may be identified as the Source of resources for righteous living. And this is happy and healthy living.

The Church, a Resource Company

The Church of Jesus Christ is a company of believers who come together and work together because they can do things in mutual support that the disciple cannot do alone. God initiates and endows the church because the kind of person he plans for and provides for needs the church. The church exists for man's sake. It has organization and administrative procedures, not as ends in themselves but as means to getting the job done in human living that God has in mind. There are rites and sacraments and scriptures in the church, not for their own sakes but for what they can contribute in developing God's type of man. The church is a community of those who respond to God's love and who want to live together in this kind of divine love. The church exists because it has something to do; it exists in doing this. The church is a fellowship of children and youth and adults who constitute a laboratory in living.

The church is an exploratory corporation. This company is busy exploring (1) the resources within a person that can be developed and devoted in living of saintly caliber, (2) the resources in the church fellowship that can be increased and utilized in community living of Zionic quality, (3) the resources out of foregoing life and learning that can throw light on the business of abundant living, and (4) the resources in God and in God's universe that can be drawn on and utilized for this God-way of living. The

65

church might be entitled "Research in God's Resources." We may think of a fivefold purpose: (1) to discover resources, (2) to develop resources, (3) to direct resources, (4) to "dynamize" resources (there is no adequate word to express putting dynamic into them), and (5) to "divinitize" resources. This last means to link them with God so that they express the nature of God.

It is the church's job to function as resource for getting God's job done. And this job is to assemble, assess, and associate these many resources in a great, ongoing program of building persons who will be "everlastingly happy" and "thoroughly healthy."

The Restoration Was for Persons

The Restoration movement was brought into being for ministry to men. The original happening was a very simple reaching out to God by a youth and the responding by God to this youth. In 1820 a boy who would be in our junior high division today sought direction. God, ever ready and always waiting, gave such elemental direction as the youth could receive and understand and follow. In the next years God stimulated and instructed this young man so that his resources would be increased through linking with the resources of God. When in July and August 1828 the young man mismanaged what he had been given to do, God stayed with him and helped him to straighten out his life. The divine counsel was clear: "See that you are faithful and continue on. . . . Be diligent. . . . Remember him who is the life and light of the world." This last phrase pointed up what God was interested in doing. He was planning to bring into this youth expanding *life* and increasing *light*. And this young prophet would experience this through reaching out to bring life and light to others, to all others. He was to grow in spiritual stature as the resources for this life and light came into him from God. The concern in one person, in all persons is the genius of the Restoration movement.

The ten years between 1820 and 1830 constituted a period of laying foundation for the movement. The pioneers had to see clearly what was the purpose back of this restoring that was going on. They were reminded again and again that the bringing forth of the Book of Mormon and the reconstituting of the church and all else was for ministry to persons. In May 1829 they were told that the Holy Spirit was to minister to persons for enlivening and enlightening them (D. and C. 10). To an inquirer, Joseph Knight, came counsel that God's chief concern was in the spiritual quality of persons and that only those qualified in spiritual virtues might participate and make the ideal come true (D. and C. 11). Then in June 1829 the trio most influential in ministry in those early years were told that their first assignment was to invite men to God and to help them appreciate his gospel. Therein they would find joy, enduring and unspeakable. When instruction came about how to proceed in organizing the church, everything was pointed toward ministering to persons. The ordaining of men to the priesthood was for ministering to others. Those ordained were to preach, teach, exhort, visit, pray, and baptize for the good of those receiving. No exaltation of priesthood here. The prayer for the Lord's Supper centered in what was to take place in the lives of those who participated.

The Restoration movement came forth for the redeeming and the revitalizing of men and the recommitting of men to God. All the while the message kept saying that men could be freed from bondage to sinful living and be freed to live continually the kind of life that would deliver them from spiritual disease and deterioration. In the freshness and immediacy of life-giving powers from God they could be happy and healthy. The Church of Jesus Christ was restored that men might be renewed and remade through life with Jesus Christ.

Resources in the God of Restoration

In theology we portray as best we can who God is and what he does. The image a man carries of God—that is, the image he uses—affects his daily living. Some conceptions get in the way of achieving spiritual health, some exert little influence, and some contribute well. The experience of Joseph Smith in 1820 is foundational. This experience reveals a contemporary God, a responsive-to-man God, a revealing God, a light-emanating God. Here is a God who works with man to help him solve his problems in ways that will develop him gradually, from step through step. Here is a God who is interpreted and disclosed to man through Jesus Christ. Here is a God who starts with men where they are and then continues with them to advancing levels. Here is a God who outlines the assignment of a man with longtime perspective. Here is a God whose program is eternity long and universe wide. What happened in ancient America expresses the eternal program and the universal Christ. Here is a God who is available, even to a farm boy of western New York. Here is an adventurous God who is not held to conventions and institutionalism: he will do the extraordinary and utilize the not-on-the-beaten-path procedures. Certainly the happenings of 1820 to 1830 could not be thought of as the grooved procedures of a senile deity. Here is a God who wants a person to live with him until he senses with some clarity what God is setting out to do. This God of the Restoration movement is a stimulating, creating, revealing, responding God with a big purpose and plan, with a big heart and mind, with a big confidence and high expectancy of man. One youth put it this way, "When I get hold of what was said and done during that decade, I discover an on-the-job and out-of-the-groove God."

Such is the God of 1820-1830 when he is seen at his best. The directives addressed to the pioneers of the movement are to be heralded today. These stand foremost: "A great and marvelous work is about to come forth," "The works, and the designs, and the purposes of God, can not be frustrated," "Seek to bring forth and establish the cause of Zion," "Fear not, little flock," and "This is my work and my glory, to bring to pass the immortality, and eternal life of man." Here was a calling to a great enterprise. No place here for any waiting for God to do the job or for watching while God did it. These pioneers were to risk with God, and to realize with God. Such work was to make sturdy saints. This pioneering is to operate now as then. The God of the Restoration movement invites his people to move out adventurously and expectantly with him.

God's Universe Is Loaded with Resources

The way a man thinks of the universe and of the way God does or does not function in it conditions strongly what his spiritual health is going to be. One man put the matter this way, "A man has to have something to stand on and to count on." Sometimes our pictures of the universe make it so uncertain, with God so capricious in his moods, so affected by praying that suits him, or so indifferent to man that man is left pretty much to himself. Then man has few foundations for reliable living. Sometimes God is pictured as so abstract, so far away that he could have little effect on what is going on on our planet, our galaxy, or our universe. One youth said that the God pictured to him in his boyhood was "so clean and so holy that he would never think of getting his hands soiled in real work."

In Restoration theology God is not an absentee landlord or a monarch on an ivory throne. Rather, he is in the business of running his universe. He provides and makes available resources by which man will be able to live the good life. H. L. Mencken in the twenties wrote, "The cosmos is a gigantic flywheel making 10,000 revolutions a minute" and "man is a sick fly taking a dizzy ride on it." And Joseph Wood Krutch in *The Modern Temper* concluded, "There is no place for us in the natural universe." There is no hope for support or supply in such outlooks. Some theologians offer little more: they make God so removed and so impersonal that little can be expected from him except a groundwork for their rationale. In contrast is the voice of the Restoration prophet in 1834.

> "I, the Lord, stretched out the heavens, and builded the earth as a very handy work; and all things therein are mine; and it is my purpose to provide for my saints, for all things are mine; but it must needs be done in mine own way."—Doctrine and Covenants 101:2 d.

This statement sets forth how God is involved in and expressed in his universe, how its resources are for man's good life, and how man has to use these resources in God's way. If it were not so, the universe would fall apart as each man pulled off to operate in his own scheme of living.

The Restoration movement affirms that God is not separable from his creative expression and his eternal purpose in persons. There is nothing of W. H. Auden's view of an indifferent world and an unresponsive God as he wrote,

> Looking up at the stars, I know quite well,
> That for all they care, I can go to hell.

Restoration theology recognizes the universe with God creating and sustaining it, thus providing something stable and appealing on which and by which man will be able to live healthfully. Man needs a universe he can explore, understand, and utilize for living of eternal quality. Pessimists and cynics find nothing reliable or responsive in the cosmos. The Restoration conception of God's universe sees resources, spiritual and material, that God provides for man to discover and use. Here is a stable groundwork and a usable framework. Such a universe requires man to be on his toes.

And This Universe Is Reliable and Reasonable

Man needs a universe that combines the known and the unknown. On the one hand he needs certainty and stability. On the other hand he needs the risk of the not-yet-traversed and the thrill of exploring the not-yet-understood. The universe, as visioned in Restoration prophecy, affords both.

1. Restoration cosmology affirms, "The elements are eternal" (D. and C. 90:5). It has no place for notions of creation out of nothing. There are no grounds for fears that it will ever lapse into nothingness. Creation means the reorganizing of this fundamental stuff, with purpose. God will never discontinue creating. Man can count on this eternally.

2. Restoration theology affirms the oneness of God's universe. There is no cosmic war going on between the material and the spiritual. With God all things are of spiritual quality (D. and C. 28:9), so man can plan for integrated living in an integrated universe. Man need have no battles in himself on this score.

3. Restoration scriptures depict how natural law is operative through all reality, spiritual and material. There is no magic, no happenstance, no whim of God. There is predictability. There is order (D. and C. 85:8, 9). Man, then, is able to probe, to prove, to predict.

4. Restoration prophecy says that the creative process of God is continuous. It is eternal (D. and C. 22:23). One earth may decline and even disappear as such, but other earths can come into being. The working of God does not harden into some fixed mold. Things are not going to shape up into monotonous fixedness, nor are things going to come to an end next year or next century.

5. In Restoration theology the Holy Spirit is the dynamic agency in this creative process. This Spirit affords insight into purpose and process and power for creative work. This brief sentence is basic, "The power of my Spirit quickeneth all things" (D. and C. 32:3). As man is endowed by this Spirit, he acquires the understanding and the dynamic to enable him to be a co-creator with God. He is not stranded in a hostile, dizzy world but is a participant in an ongoing creative endeavor.

Man Is Endowed for Living Nobly

What God thinks about man and what man thinks about himself stand high in the resources for spiritual health. If man thinks God is against him or has a low estimate of him, he will live accordingly. He may ignore what a neighbor or an alien thinks of him but he cannot ignore what he thinks God thinks of him. He is not inclined to buck the divine opinion. One man put it this way, "If God thinks I am no good, how can I think I am worth anything?" Another man phrased his view, "If I am as low-down as some picture I am, then God created me a mess and he has no moral right to expect me to be anything else." On the whole, Latter

Day Saint theology places a high estate on man, as a potential son of God. This theology does not make man a law to himself. It affirms that man has to find his being and his meaning in God and in God's universe: he cannot live atomistically to himself.

Here are foundational conceptions of man in Restoration theology. They set forth resources and relationships that are to contribute to a high quality of healthfulness and happiness.

1. In the program of God every person possesses infinite worth and is to live for eternal quality (D. and C. 90:4, 16:3). No man starts his life as a reject or a no-account.

2. At birth man is a candidate to become a person. He is not yet developed for decision-making. He is not held responsible for sins that occurred before his time. Children are born free from guilt, but they are affected by the sins of the social order, especially of the family into which they are born (D. and C. 28:13).

3. Man is born to be self-managing. He has potentials of agency within him. He is not born with freedom to choose, but he has native resources out of which he is to develop capacity to choose. He is accountable for the exercising of this endowment to choose (D. and C. 101:2). God wants a man to be self-managing; he wants a man to choose to line up with God's want and way.

4. The major purpose of God and the zenith of God's creative expression is the eternal development of man as person (D. and C. 22:23). The material resources of the universe are designed to contribute to man's spiritual welfare. This is stated succinctly in counsel given about developing the Jackson County community in 1831 (D. and C. 59:4): "All things which come of the earth . . . are made for the benefit and the use of man, both to please the eye, and to gladden the heart . . . to strengthen the body, and to enliven the soul."

5. The physical and the spiritual aspects of man are intended to be complementary, for maximum effectiveness and good health. There is to be no conflict between the two phases of man's total being.

Social Resources Are Available and Essential

Man is conditioned by his social relationships. He has the responsibility of developing the kind of social relationships that will nurture and further his spiritual health. Man's total nature and all his needs as a person are involved in the community that is designed to make possible this health-producing social order. These three affirmations about man require a basic assumption: God is the center of this living together and is the great resource for social health. All this is part of Restoration theory and practice.

Mere living with others is not enough. Mere gregariousness can get in the way of healthy living. It may consume time and energy without productive returns. It may bog the person down under social pressures until he loses his initiative and creative powers. So the Restoration gospel emphasizes strongly that the kind of interpersonal relations matters ever so much. The Zionic community is called to balance responsibility to others with responsibility to one's self, both with a sense of responsibility to God. It calls for recognition of both freedom to think and responsibility for developing community life in which there is freedom to think. It aims to blend the right to "the pursuit of happiness" with the responsibility for building a social order in which persons can be happy with enduring happiness. And such a combining of these two aspects could go on and on with application to many fields of living.

Here are some of the resources and responsibilities in the social living visioned in the Restoration movement. It is clear that the kind of living together matters ever so much. It is also clear that it is up to man to work with God and with his fellows in bringing such a community into existence and maintaining it and advancing it.

1. Persons are to function with a sense of stewardship for their contribution to group life (D. and C. 70). This implies specialization of function. It pictures a community of stewards who carry a sense of brotherly responsibility to one another.

2. In all social relatedness there are to be attitudes and techniques for reconciliation and resolution of tensions (D. and C. 42:23). Strains are to be recognized and resolved before they fester into antipathies.

3. Members develop in the arts of communication that function in the achieving of consensus (D. and C. 27:4). This is the way of *common consent*. This views the art of Zionic deliberation as the art of thinking independently together with the ministry of the Holy Spirit pervading, affording enlightenment and harmony.

4. Mutual instruction, counsel, and support is foundational for planning, for processing, for fraternizing (D. and C. 83:3).

5. This Zionic community functions as a social nucleus in the world mission of the church, as center of spiritual dynamic, as evangelizing agency, as laboratory school in saintly living. This outreach to and sense of responsibility to the total world order delivers the community from provincialism and inbred blight.

What Do We Have to Work With?

Every movement that stands up to assert itself needs to be asking these questions: (1) What do we think we are going to do? (2) What resources can we mobilize and use to get this done? (3) What kinds of persons will be drawn into the project? (4) How are we going to find out whether we are getting the job done? In this mission of developing good spiritual health we shall need to be asking all of these questions. The concern in this chapter is with the resources that can be mobilized, developed, and utilized.

Every leader of a far-visioned movement knows he has to look to the producing of manpower. General William Booth of the Salvation Army once spoke of the army he was going to shape up. He mentioned how there would be needed corporals, lieutenants, generals, and more. "Where are you going to get them?" he was asked. His company did not look very promising. They looked like the riffraff of lower London. Confidently he replied, "We're going to raise them." And this is the way the Church of Jesus Christ must ever proceed. It takes ordinary or less-than-ordinary persons and quickens them and directs them so they become workers and witnesses of merit. It takes groups of unpretending members and blends them and blesses them as they evolve into a community of saints. These persons and groups become spiritually healthy as they draw on divine resources for health-producing resources, as they support each other and spread contagiously healthful influence, as they constitute, each one in his own personhood, sound disciples of the way of healthiness.

Here are basic resources inherent in the Restoration movement. The are to be recognized, mobilized, utilized. (1) The heritage of a people who believe in restorative, resilient, and re-creative spiritual empowerment from God. (2) A God of eternal healthfulness who supplies resources for healthful living. (3) A gospel that centers in the ever living Jesus Christ who lived healthfully and continues in wholesome outreach to all persons who will respond. (4) The Holy Spirit with dynamic, enlightening ministry and spiritual fruitage in good health. (5) Scriptures containing guidance, past and contemporary, about man's living together with God in beneficial relationships. (6) The project of building Zionic communities out of whose building emerges spiritual well-being. (7) The portrait of saints as happy and healthy in their creative association with God, in an inclusive program of living. (8) The practice and theory of contemporary inspiration that functions in problem-solving, in group consenting, in spiritual confidence. (9) The institutions and ministries of the church that educate, evaluate, encourage, and enliven. (10) A world mission that enlists all members in service that expands and enlivens their personal resources. These resources are in the making. They are beneficial in the using. When operative we are able to speak of the *Restoration movement*.

Questions for Discussion

1. A man said to his friend as they were discussing their faiths, "Your God is not on active duty. He is on reserve." What did he mean?

2. Illustrate in the field of physical health how we have the responsibility of keeping God's resources for healthy living in good condition. Apply to water supply, to condition of air, to soil fertility. How may we misuse these resources so they contribute little or nothing to our health or undermine our health?

3. Illustrate how we may misunderstand or misuse spiritual resources so that the end result is spiritual unhealthiness. How may they be utilized for spiritual healthiness?

4. How may a Latter Day Saint believe in "divine healing," "faith healing," "healing through administration by elders" in such a way that his kind of belief works against his spiritual well-being? How may he believe in this so that the belief "heartens and healthens" him?

5. Dr. Oates in *Religious Factors in Mental Illness* observes, "The religious experience of persons may reach a point of sterility and nonproductiveness. Yet all the while the other processes of the individual's life go on because of external necessity." Illustrate how this can happen. How does religion affect the person when this situation occurs? How would you go about making religion become an asset in such a person?

6. Two Latter Day Saints believe in the Holy Spirit. In one the belief leads to narrowness and superstition and hostility to learning; in the other the belief prompts him to explore fields of study, to improve patterns of thinking, to tackle problems. How do you explain this difference growing out of belief in the Holy Spirit?

7. What is the effect upon individual living and on community living of thinking through and working through the counsel given in Doctrine and Covenants 59:4 concerning the purpose and the appropriation of natural resources? What effects in the life of persons are indicated here?

8. How may the living together of members in branch association

be asset or liability as resource for spiritual health? How is healthy living together an essential in an inclusive program of saintly living?

9. How may desire for Zion work to the healthiness or to the unhealthiness of Latter Day Saints? This includes what we are wanting, how we are expecting to get it, and what we are looking toward doing in a Zionic community. What conceptions of Zion do you consider unhealthy and which ones healthy?

10. A nonmember attended a prayer-testimony meeting and went away saying it was "weepy," morbid, and self-centered. Another nonmember attended another prayer-testimony meeting and went away saying it gave him "a lift" and a hope. What might be the difference in the two meetings? In the two congregations? In the two visitors? When are such meetings resources for happy, healthy spirituality?

11. Two men attended the World Conference in 1964. One commented, "There wasn't much to it and I didn't get much of anything out of it." The other said, "Here we faced basic problems of the church and laid foundations for the work before us. The delegates and ministers faced conditions honestly and came through well." How would it happen that the Conference was great resource to one and not to the other?

12. How is evangelizing a bringing to persons the resources of the Restoration faith and fellowship?

13. What do you list as the major resources the Restoration movement has in its history and in its present life that can contribute to achieving spiritual health for those who will see well and use well these potentials in the movement?

CHAPTER 7

GOD'S OBJECTIVE
IS PERSONS
OF ETERNAL QUALITY

Most of us take better care of things that are worth good care. We do not waste energy on tidbits and trivia. Silly, inconsequential ideas do not merit our protection and devotion. A person of good judgment wants to be sure that what he gives his life to deserves his support. He wants to understand what makes this thing, this idea, this person worthy of undivided allegiance. This applies to health. A farmer has a horse that is deteriorating and moving in the direction of what some call "the bone heap." Is it worth veterinary care and expense? That depends upon what the horse has done. Sometimes emotional attachment and sentimental association may rate the sick horse above considerations in practical work value. Or the farmer may judge that with health restored the horse would pay for its medical cost and keep. Every day what we do with and for something or someone is conditioned by our sense of their worth.

Worth and Spiritual Hygiene

If Saints are not worth very much, we are not going to spend much time and energy and money and thought and love on them trying to keep them in good state of repair. If they are sick of body, of mind, and of spirit they can slip out of the way; if they constitute a drag on others they can be neglected. A society and a church have to indicate rather clearly what they consider the worth of persons to be if they are going to carry on programs of developing and maintaining healthy living in persons.

Sometimes through the centuries maimed babies and unwanted babies, the worn-out and nonproductive old people, and the indigent and useless adults have been put out of the way. Crippled children might be abandoned to exposure. The very old might be left behind when the tribe marched on. Conditions other than physical would also be considered. Once in Sparta, for instance, if a person were found to be without a friend, he would be put to death for being a liability to the group. In ancient Israel those considered to possess powers of witchery might be put out of the way. Quite often persons and groups looked upon as inferior would be deprived of religious privileges. Thus the Jews would not desecrate their faith by permitting Samaritans to join them. Their God was looked upon as quite particular with respect to admittance to the circle of the approved.

A program of physical health and of spiritual health always involves the question of the worth of persons. These are basic questions: (1) what constitutes the worth of a person, (2) which persons possess this worth, (3) how does God estimate the worth of persons, (4) what constitutes a program of healthful living, and (5) how are persons related in the business of healthy physical and spiritual living? We have to begin by asking what God thinks of man (1) as he is, (2) as he can become. Does God consider man worth spending time and resources on in order to make him spiritually healthy?

Jesus Concerned for Every Person

Jesus of Nazareth shocked his contemporaries by being genuinely interested in all persons, in all classes of society. There was neither caste nor privilege of birth in his program. He valued all persons as potential sons and daughters of God. The leper, the prosperous publican, the small child, the wayward woman, the rugged fisherman, the dying thief, the rich young man, the begging cripple, and more were all in his concern. The Samaritan was there, too. Jesus set up criteria for evaluating persons that was revolutionary to Jews and to Romans. There was no priority in the society he had in mind that would come from political or priestly privilege. He who served most would have high place. He put it this way: "Whosoever will be chief among you, let him be your servant" (Matthew 20:27). Sometimes the people chided him because he took time to associate with those they frowned upon. Sometimes his own disciples made this same criticism. When Jesus chose a person as one who would express what a member of his kingdom should be like, he "set a child in their midst," a child with potentials for developing, with a natural curiosity, with freedom from imprinted phobias and animosities, with zest for living.

Jesus did not talk of man as depraved and hopeless, as sons of perdition, as doomed to hell. He began with men wherever they were, whether up a sycamore tree, in a pigpen, or a fishing boat. He wanted them to respond to him so that he might help them to become sons of God (John 1:12). He looked to unpromising persons as having promise in them. He associated with persons who were getting nowhere and left them changed, transformed. A new, an enduring purpose grew within them and they in turn became interested in the welfare of others. In contrast we tend to look persons over, take their measures, and size them up according to prevailing notions. Often if they do not meet our requirements, we leave them. Jesus left no one, saw no one as beneath his interest, as inharmonious with his dignity. Jesus became the supreme life-changer of all time. Whenever he met anyone he started thinking about what could be done with this life, how it could be "made whole"; that is, how it could become healthy. Jesus let his disciples see that whenever one of them sized up another, he was taking his own measure. Jesus always said to a man who would listen to him, "You need not stay the way you are; you can be spiritually healthy."

The Christian Doctrine of Personal Worth

In general, the ancient world did not have a high estimate of man. In warfare the conquered were to be killed or enslaved. A man could be looked upon as a target for an arrow or an animal for labor. In the heyday of Roman prosperity, if a slave gave out another could be purchased. The Roman sense of humor and excitement called for combats between persons or between persons and animals in which life itself was at stake. There were no qualms about killing persons by sword or by lions to appease the taste for death struggles. The wincing and the suffering made up the thrill of the entertainment. Jesus came to a world that placed a low value on human life. He himself was a victim of this outlook.

The Christian gospel preached the fatherhood of God, in which he cared for all. It affirmed the equality before God of all men and of both sexes. It said that every individual was sacred in the eyes of the Father. Thus an entirely new conception of the individual was proclaimed to the world. The Jews had taught this, but it became entangled in their provincial limitations. The prophets had sought to release it from these limitations. Paul led the crusade to keep early Christianity free from Jewish boundary lines and to make the gospel truly universal. What is more, Christianity promulgated an entirely new ethical code. God was pictured as righteous, so that those who would live with him would need to reconstruct their lives and achieve this righteousness. Men would live together in mutually helpful righteousness. It was the duty of every person to become healthy in righteousness. It was his privilege to become so. This doctrine of a righteous, loving Father who was interested in every person brought to ancient society a new hopefulness and a new energy.

It was a world-shaking teaching when Jesus opened the way for all men, of all conditions, of all cultures to say together, "Our Father." There were no rejects by God. Man only could bring on separation and rejection by alienating himself from God.

Then Man Discounted God's Estimate of Him

Christianity had a hard time holding up this hopeful outlook. Pessimistic patterns of thinking in the ancient world bore down upon it. Man's physical nature was denounced. Man himself was discounted. Doctrines of man's fall left him sunk in the hopelessness of depravity. He came to be thought of as born in guilt. He was helpless in his sinfulness. God came to be thought of as a sovereign rather than as a father. He was thought of as arbitrarily consigning some to hell and some to salvation. It looked as if God's major concern was with himself. He was thought of as saving some so there would be enough to praise him. Man was thought of as a worm.

This discounting was heightened as the Roman Empire declined and barbarians swept in. Chaos prevailed. It looked as if men were indeed a bad lot. After A.D. 200 the empire was on the defensive and on the decline. The virtues of citizens of the early days of the republic had given way to vices and corruptions which sapped the life of the ruling classes and, in time, of others. The resisting power of the empire went down. Then the barbarian deluge from the east and the north poured over Europe. To many it seemed as if the end of the world were approaching. Force reigned. Work declined or ceased because there was no security for the results of labor. Learning declined. The church itself became paganized before the barbarians were Christianized. Small wonder that man lost faith in man's nature and in his potential. It was God who would have to work the miracle of salvation. This would be done through the sacramental services of the church administered through priests. To most persons, salvation was something brought in from outside to a helpless, originally depraved creature. Appropriately could men come to say of themselves, "There is no health left in us."

An Early Reaffirmation

It took God several centuries to build up a background, a climate that could recover what Jesus had taught and practiced about man. A new continent had to be opened where there would be liberation from some of these restricting ideas about God's estimate of man.

The Restoration movement of the early nineteenth century is a re-affirmation of this original gospel about man.

In the spring of 1820 a farm boy in western New York not quite fifteen years of age was facing a question of great consequence to him. He was confused by the diversity of churches and the conflicts between them in the revivalistic activities in his neighborhood. He did not know how to make a decision about joining one of them. He read the promise in James 1:5 that God would respond to anyone who was honestly seeking. He took the quotation at its face value. So he went to the grove on his father's farm and bared his soul to God. He testified that God responded to him. The height of the counsel was this salutation of the Father, "This is my beloved Son: hear ye him!" In this elemental experience the boy was directed to Jesus Christ. He would be pointed toward the life and message of the Son.

The experience itself enacted the message. Here God was responding to a farm boy of simple, unpretending background and means. Here was no eminent ecclesiastic or theologian or official. Here was a young boy who reached to God in honest faith, in a quest for direction. Here was ground to testify that God cares for the very ordinary, very needy person. And he does so in the living now.

A Basic Directive about Persons

The pioneers of the Restoration movement went through a training-school period before they organized the church. They had to see what the church had to be for and how it was going to function. Joseph Smith and Oliver Cowdery were concerned about their ordination to the priesthood. Here, too, they needed to discover what priesthood was for. In June 1829, ten months before the organization of the church was effected, they received instruction that is numbered Section 16 in the Doctrine and Covenants. They were directed to look to "the foundations of my church, my gospel, and my Rock." It is significant that in the first revelation that dealt specifically with the organization of the church, the emphasis was on what the church would be doing for persons. It was to be an agency, a fellowship for ministering to specific persons, not for humanity in general. The counsel given constitutes a classic in Restoration scriptures.

"Remember the worth of souls is great in the sight of God . . .
And how great is his joy in the soul that repenteth.
Wherefore you are called to cry repentance unto this people.

And if it so be that you should labor all your days,
in crying repentance unto this people,
and bring save it be one soul unto me,
how great shall be your joy with him in the kingdom
of my Father!"

Foundations for the organizing of the church were involved here:
(1) the worth of all souls in the sight of God; (2) the divine joy
when a soul turns repentantly to God; (3) the evangelistic concern
of persons who know God that others come to know God, too; and
(4) the satisfying fellowship of the witnessee. The satisfaction would
be in this companionship, not in getting stars in a crown or tangible
awards. Here God's concern for persons and the concern of his
people for other persons become one. They are concerned that all
persons become spiritually healthy.

The Stated Objective of God

A year after the foregoing counsel was given a message of rare
importance was brought to the young church. It is presented as a
vision of Moses. This brave prophet had a tremendous responsibility
to carry through. He was to lead the Israelites out of Egypt across
desert regions to their promised land, Canaan. These people were
unschooled in spiritual discipline. Their major concern seemed to be
in getting away from slavery in Egypt without any clear idea of
what they were being liberated for. Sometimes their chief interests
seemed to be in their comfort, their security, and an adequate food
supply. Sometimes they showed accomplishments in complaining
and whining. They found fault with Moses and with God. A
prophet needed a fairly clear idea about what God had in mind.
He had to see what he was doing in the light of God's total program.
This is a requisite for any of us who are going to carry responsibility
effectively and consistently.

So Moses was taken to "an exceeding high mountain" where God
showed him the great panorama of the centuries. First Moses was
told that God's works "are without end." This means that his
creating never ceases, that it has always been going on. Then
attention was focused on man. At first this was bewildering. For
a time Moses collapsed under the strain. Then Moses made this
observation, "I know that man is nothing." This has to be taken
in its total context or we shall jump to the conclusion that God has
a zero estimate of man. Not so. Moses was realizing that man in
his own strength, apart from the sustaining power of God, is helpless

and incompetent. Right. Everything in the universe exists in relationships; everything continues through right relationship with God and his universe. This does not mean that God counts man as worthless. In the first place Moses sensed convincingly the call of God to lead his people out of their bondage. In current terms, they were a worthless, servile people. On first thought God should have selected for his own people some nation more powerful in military might, in riches, in prestige. These Hebrews would be less than others in the rating of the day. Here Moses could sense the humanitarian compassion of God for the downtrodden. Here was evidence of God's love for all peoples. One might say that if he could love these Hebrew slaves, he could love anybody.

Moses pressed for more understanding. What about the earth? What about man? What was the purpose of this ongoing creation? What was the place of man in this great program of creating? Then came the majestic statement of God's intent:

> "There is no end to my works, neither to my words;
> for this is my work and my glory,
> to bring to pass the immortality, and eternal life of man."
> —Doctrine and Covenants 22:23.

Here is a remarkable combination of work and glory. The two ought always to go together. Work without glory is drudgery; glory without work is parasitism. God finds in the unending process of developing persons of eternal quality his greatest satisfaction. Here is the joy in constructive creating and the rewarding thrill of seeing his purpose come to pass. This statement is saying that God experiences an indescribable satisfaction in seeing the emergence of personhood that is worthy to continue. Here he could say, as is told in Genesis, "Behold he is good!"

Of High Calling and Expectancy

Today we can see considerable despairing about man and a discounting of what man is. There is much talk of man's hostilities within himself, of hostility between man and man, of man's hostility to God. No honest observer will deny these things. Looking only at these strains, deep and active, we may be inclined to say with some, "Mankind is a mess." But the wide-eyed observer will see something more: he will see things in man that are to the good. He will note motivations to altruism and satisfactions in man when he is kindly disposed to others. He will note that in man there is hunger for community which is as much a part of man's original equipment as his drives for preservation of himself, which drives may lead to crushing others. He will note that a man can change the course of his living and can lift his values. What is more, he sees that men do. About us we see man's despair in man, which despair cripples effort to rehabilitate man. About us also we see those who stake their lives on the conviction that man can change and respond to the good.

Is this bias against man in God's thinking? Hardly. Is God inclined to surrender man to dog-eat-dog animalistic urges? Not at all. The gospel of Jesus Christ places a high evaluation upon man. It recognizes man's trends toward self-centered sinfulness, but it also affirms that in God are resources for enabling men to become God's sons. The gospel has faith that man's egoistic and altruistic motives and actions can become compatible with a unifying allegiance to God. Man can come to see that when he acts for the good of others he is also acting for his own good.

The honest analyst of human life today will see the wretched state in which a large part of the world's population lives. He will see men who deliberately warp the lives of others. He will see men as sinners living in their own self-contained little kingdoms. This is an honest admission of *some* things about him. The honest analyst will also see men of integrity who give themselves to help others. He will find men, though not enough of them, who adhere to enduring principles. Such an observer finds evidences of devilish expression. He also finds in man evidences of spiritual viability. He can see the misuse of potentials God has given us and he will see the disuse of resources for saintly living, resources with which God has endowed us.

The larger view does not surrender to pessimism. It joins with the comment in Genesis that after God had created man and then surveyed the whole process of creation God said it was "very good." Man was included in this evaluation.

God Has Hope

The Old Testament sometimes pictures God as looking at disobedient man and wondering if he should wipe mankind off the earth and get along without men or populate the earth with a more promising breed. God never followed any such course of action. Rather he would renew his efforts in a fresh start. He would give men who would hear some signs of promise that he would keep carrying on. The rainbow was to be such a "sign of promise" to Noah. God would send prophets to invite men to a better way of life. Eventually he sent his own Son. This Son lived among men and he loved them. He arranged for his church to be a witnessing community that was to reach out to all the world, to every man. In time the Restoration movement came as a revitalizing ministry to give man another help forward. In the early days of the Restoration movement God was saying to the pioneers, "The works, and the designs, and the purposes of God, can not be frustrated" (Doctrine and Covenants 2:1). This does not sound like a surrendering God, like a God who is about to give up on man.

Winfred E. Garrison reaffirmed his confidence in man in an affirmation, "God saw that it was good." He admitted shortcomings and dangers in the human situation but saw also goodness in the original stuff of man. He testified, "I lean strongly to the opinion that God is not wholly discouraged about us, and that his purpose in creation . . . has not been frustrated and will not be." (*Criterion*, Winter 1964, pages 24-25). If God is a God of hope, such must be our outlook. Such is our voice. The Restoration movement is not preaching a God who is giving up in his ageless objective of developing persons of eternal quality.

Implications for Our Carrying On

When we catch hold of God's objective of developing persons of eternal quality, we come to sense some very important implications. They concern each one of us; they involve us all as a church.

1. God takes a risk in setting out to develop persons. To be a person means to be self-managing. Persons who choose for themselves may not choose with God.

2. God will work patiently and consistently to help men to choose understandingly and willingly to line up with him rather than compel men in such a way as would deprive them of self-choosing.

3. The ability and the disposition to choose with God is one expression of spiritual health.

4. God wants men to join with him in this objective of developing persons of eternal quality. Personhood develops in interaction with others, with God as Person. Joining effectively in this social enterprise is a phase of healthful living.

5. God places a high evaluation on persons. It is an incalculably high estimate. He wants men to live together with high estimates of all persons with respect to their worth and their potential.

6. God's evaluation of man entails developing man to the fullness of his possibilities, to the fullness of healthful living.

7. God expects us to use the plenitude of resources in the universe for achieving this fullness of health in all men.

8. Men of eternal quality are thoroughly healthy in physical and spiritual wholeness. They are healthy persons in a healthy community with a healthy God.

9. Men are called to explore their own nature and potentials and also God's intent and his resources in an inclusive program of achieving total healthiness in men.

10. Men are to achieve healthy community living that will be conducive to the achievement of spiritual health. God is the Integrator and Source of health in such a community.

11. The Restoration movement affirms the worth of man, the potentials of man, the concern of God in man's healthy condition.

12. The gospel of Jesus Christ, re-expressed in the Restoration movement, is a message, a program of inclusive healthful living.

Questions for Discussion

1. How is our conception of the worth of man or the lack of worth of man connected with what we shall do or shall not do to further man's health?

2. How does our conception of what makes a man worthful affect what we shall do and on whom we shall concentrate in a health program?

3. What are some bases of evaluating man that do not accord with God's estimate of man? How might these bases of evaluation warp a program of health?

4. What did Jesus teach and do that expressed his concern for every person with a sense of the high worth of persons?

5. How was man estimated too low in Jesus' day to permit a program of total healthfulness in which all persons would have been involved?

6. What happens in man if he has a low estimate of himself, or if he considers that God has a low estimate of him? What happens if he has a low estimate of some part of him?

7. How healthy is it to think of God as chiefly concerned in having men praise and adore him?

8. What experiences and counsels in the early years of the Restoration movement pointed up God's high estimate and expectancy of man? How did denial of original guilt and of infant baptism enter in? How do these early counsels have bearing on what we shall be doing in furthering man's total health?

9. What is your reaction to the comment, "Man is a mess and God is thoroughly disgusted with him"? How does such a view affect what we shall do in a program for increasing physical and spiritual health?

10. How can we consider man spiritually unhealthy and believe that he can become spiritually healthy? How is this at the heart of the church's message and mission?

CHAPTER 8

OUR THEOLOGY
IS TO BE EMPLOYED
HEALTHFULLY

"Tell me what you believe and I will tell you what you are going to become." This is sage counsel. A belief is an affirmation out of life. It points the way; it colors life; it centers faiths and values. It cannot be separated from the total personhood, from the full picture of a man's living. A man's belief is not a compartment separate to itself. If his belief becomes something apart, it is not functioning well. What a man believes and how he believes it conditions his whole character and conduct. Belief and behavior are inseparably related. The man who affirms belief in honesty and then shortchanges in handling the truth does not truly believe in honesty. It is the beliefs that function in daily living that matter.

Beliefs Can Be Unsound and Unhealthy

A belief can be sound or unsound, limiting or expanding, healthy or unhealthy. Sometimes persons will hold to theories about what they are to eat and how they are to eat and undermine their health by these notions. They can be very sincere and can believe that God has told them to follow this way of living. A conscientious woman was holding to a diet that contained scarcely any protein. She felt that this was the way God wanted her to live. She weakened and died. She lived out her belief but to ill effect. A man believed that if he rounded out his prayer with "in Jesus' name" he would get anything of God that he asked for. He did not consider whether what he wanted accorded with God's plan and program. He did not set himself to help make things come to pass. His belief about praying brought unwholesome consequences to him and to those he taught. On the other hand are sound beliefs that are conducive to sound behavior.

Belief in God Is Basic

At the heart of our stock of beliefs is what we are thinking about God, about God's universe, about man with God and with all other men in God's great world. We call this our *theology*. A man's theology indicates how he is going to go about living with God, what he is going to live for. A twisted theology will produce a twisted person. A dwarfed theology will bring to pass a dwarfed person. A full-of-worry and full-of-fear and full-of-superstition and full-of-enclosures theology will bring about this kind of person. And the reverse is true. A theology with a God of creative, charitable, consistent nature will impel persons in this direction. When God is rightly understood we see him busy developing saints with healthy spirituality. This wholesome functioning takes place in persons, in families, in congregations, in camps and reunions, in the church at large. It transforms persons and groups.

How We Believe

Listing topics of what we believe and what we do not believe is not going to be enough. How we believe and how we use these beliefs is of great moment. Three men believe in "divine healing"; that is, each man believes in some way that the healing power of God is available in case of illness. And then the divergence is evident. Number One believes that he is to rely only on administration by elders without interference by medical skill. He believes that God has decrees that determine what is going to happen. And healing is to come at a recognizable instant. Number Two believes that God's healing ministry operates through many avenues and agencies. When illness comes the afflicted utilizes ministries of administration by elders, services of doctors and nurses, helps of his own managing of diet, ventilation, rest, and so on. Number Three takes a look at the total person in his total living situation. He considers physical, mental, social, spiritual health in one operation. He is concerned with what we call preventive medicine as well as remedial medicine. He sees God's resources for health and healing used to keep us in good health. He believes that when emergencies arise he will go for administration, for medical service. He believes, too, that the elder and the doctor are to function in keeping him healthy. All three believe in "divine healing," yet so differently.

We Survey Our Basic Fields of Belief

The following fourteen topics are essentials in formulating a comprehensive, balanced theology. Here they are mentioned separately for clarity and convenience. Every one can be believed in such a way as to further spiritual health or in such a way as to make for narrowness, superstition, escape, worry, infantilism. For instance, persons may hold a portrait of God of such nature and behavior that this God robs the person of initiative, of creative expression, of concern for others, of intellectual exploration, and more. It is not enough to affirm "faith in God." The kind of faith in the kind of God makes so much difference. And this holds for every other tenet of theology. The following fourteen basics, taken together, foundation and further spiritual healthiness of the highest order.

1. *God in Restoration Theology*

God is righteous. In him is a righteousness of eternal goodness and eternal expression. This righteousness cannot be codified in final legal enactments. This goodness is creative in spirit and in function. God is concerned with persons, with all persons, for their optimum and eternal personal living. What God does is always health-producing and happiness-providing. God plans for man to be righteously creative with him. God is consistent and reliable. He does not respond whimsically. He expects this consistency and reliability in man as a person. God is creating. His creative process continues. He experiences joy and satisfaction in his creative endeavor. God expects man to utilize materials and to tap spiritual resources in working cooperatively in the divine program. God sees the emergence of persons of eternal quality as the highest expression in his universe. God is harmony within himself. All phases of his nature and expression are "fitly framed together." So God looks to the wholeness and inner harmony of every person. God's glory is intelligence and his genius is love. He looks for this glory and this genius in man. And God is ever contemporary. He focuses on the living now as it moves out of the past and into the future. God is ever the great I Am. Such a God, soundly believed in, makes for good health in believers.

2. *The Universe in Restoration Theology*

This affirmation stands forth, "The elements are eternal." The "stuff" of the universe is eternally existent. God utilizes this in his creative expression. The process of God is eternal. Earths come and go as the Creator keeps creating. The functioning of the universe is orderly and predictable. Whatever happens emerges out of casual "precedings," out of happenings of what has gone on before. Inherent in the universe are spiritual realities so that any inclusive conception of the universe will include spiritual resources. It is this reality, this Spirit that "quickeneth all things." Fundamentally, all things have spiritual basis. Everything hangs together in one God. All these resources are designed for utilization in bringing to pass persons of eternal quality. This is God's major creative expression in his universe. The universe reveals the intent, the artistry, the orderliness, the creative nature, the righteousness, the purposive love of the God of this universe. Such a universe provides foundation for healthy spiritual living.

3. Man in Restoration Theology

Man is often the great enigma in theology. He is rated from depravity to perfection. On the whole, Restoration theology places a high evaluation upon man, seeing him as highest in God's design. Man is intended to be self-managing. Therein lies the hazard and the high probability. God intends man to line up with God's will and way. If God had determined man, however, so that he would have to go one way, God's way, man could never be a choosing person. Man is responsible for his own choosing, not for the decisions that have preceded him. He is responsible for his influence on others, so far as this is in his control. Man is not born "ready-made"; he has to develop his powers and use them to wise purpose. God provides man with "power to become." He has capacity to become a "son of God." Man is a unity with material and spiritual aspects to be harmonized into oneness. Everything in man is to be directed to harmony in righteous living. And God endows man with needs, with hungers, with potentials for helpful, healthy interaction with his fellows. Men are to learn how to live together in mutual support, here and now. Corporate living together with God in the social process is called Zion. Evil is man's diversion from this divine intention for him. Restoration theology believes that it is man's stewardship to realize what God created him to become. The saintly life God intends for man is worthful and healthful. Such a conception of God's intent for man expects thoroughly healthy saints.

4. Jesus Christ in Restoration Theology

Jesus Christ is the Son of God. The Book of Mormon refers to him as "the universal God," one with the Father. He is the revelation of God in terms man can understand. He volunteered to come to earth to live as a man, among men, that he might draw persons to God in loving relationship. He disclosed what sacrificial love is like. He aims to reconcile wayward men with God. His mission is to all persons in all lands in all ages. He draws man by the quality of his life. This Jesus Christ enlists men to associate with him in creative goodness. Latter Day Saints believe that this vital, direct association of the first century was choked out by institutionalism and traditionalism. Vital contact with this Christ was restored in the experience of Joseph Smith in the opening of the nineteenth century. The Christ of 1820 is the restoring, redeeming Christ. He provides for the church to be an agency, to be a fellowship to assist persons in developing spiritual qualities through living with him and with those who hold allegiance to him.

5. *The Holy Spirit in Restoration Theology*

The Holy Spirit expresses the outreach of God to man, the indwelling of God in man. Here is the spiritual dynamic indicated by Jesus Christ that would guide to truth, sustain in living by this truth, and harmonize in oneness of truth. The Restoration movement reaffirmed that the ministry of the Holy Spirit is enlivening, enlightening, ennobling. It continues the criterion written by Paul: the Holy Spirit *edifies*. Man is uplifted and developed through the Holy Spirit as man, with God's help, endeavors to qualify to be a recipient. Man needs the cleanness, the capacity, the wisdom for utilization that he may receive. Just as light and warmth of the sun provide life and fruitage to a plant, so does the Spirit of God produce spiritual fruitage in persons. And foremost are love and wisdom. The Spirit of God furthers physical, mental, spiritual health. The fruitage includes joy, constancy, faith, and more. Such a Holy Spirit is indispensable for healthy spiritual development.

6. *The Church in Restoration Theology*

The church is a fellowship centered in Jesus Christ to enable persons to live together in brotherly helpfulness. God plans it and provides it because men are so constituted as to need it. It is a laboratory school for developing in saintly living. It is a witnessing company for enabling others to learn of the good life centered in Jesus Christ. This association in the church is designed to promote brotherly fellowship, to afford means of creative expression, to provide outreach of world proportion, to minister in clinical counsel, to enable spiritual renewal, and more. The members are to constitute a "strong and happy people." Rightly understood, and rightly functioning, the church respects each person in his own right with consideration of each as a unique person with a distinctive role in God's work. Such a company keeps alert for prophetic communion with God and develops for carrying out its commissioned ministry. Such a church is a health-producing association.

7. *Soteriology in Restoration Theology*

Soteriology is concerned with "the way of salvation." Man is saved not only *from* something undesirable; he is saved *to* something, *for* something. He is saved from all forces that would alienate him from God and would lead to his decline and deterioration. He is saved *to* and *for living* of eternal quality. This involves every part of him in a unified program. There is no instant magic through a word or a rite. The person has to "work out his soul's salvation." This continues throughout life. Salvation calls for repentance and regeneration, making of a man "a new creation." Since man's nature requires interaction with others, the saving experience includes the saving of the society in which he lives. Hence, there must be Zion. The sacraments and the ministries and the operations and fellowship of the church are to function in saving the person. In salvation all man's powers are developed, refined, alerted, and used to God's purpose. Salvation comes as a by-product. At death life continues in a condition of living suited to the level of his spiritual capacity and level of appreciation. The "saved" person is a healthy person, functioning productively with God. Such a soteriology saves man from poor health to good health.

8. *Faith in Restoration Theology*

Faith is a spiritual functioning of a person in which the person places the total adventure of his life with God. It assumes that God creates man with capacity and desire to risk, to dare. Faith is adventurous living with God. It is active, compelling commitment to God, Father and Son. Since God is ever working, the believer in God is going to be working with God. It takes a long time to mature in this consistent, reliable faith. It involves building the quality of person that can line up with God. Faith is not a content to be memorized or a code to be imposed; it is a commitment to be lived out and lived on. This kind of faith makes for vigorous, farseeing, far-trusting persons. Sound faith affects the health of persons in every field. It affects every bit of a person. Such a faith makes for vigor and confidence, with God.

9. Epistemology in Restoration Theology

This is concerned with how we know. This directive stands forth: "Ye shall know the the truth and the truth shall make you free." This involves truth in every field. There are no "mysteries" with a fence built around them with a sign saying, "Keep Out." The Restoration movement counsels believers to "study" and to "teach one another." Early in the movement a youth was told to study a thing out in his own mind as an integral part of insight through inspiration (Doctrine and Covenants 9). Man is a unity in which he learns through every part of his personhood. This includes heart, mind, and hand. Knowing involves validation in the laboratory of living. Something is not known until it is experimented, until it is interpreted. The enlightening Spirit of God is seen as functioning through the learning process. Man's powers are not turned off when he is inspired; they are quickened and his perception becomes clearer. Inspiration, when heightened so that it is termed revelation, does not turn off; it quickens and expands. We can say we know a thing when we have explored a belief, have seen its message and meaning through inspiration, have examined it in the light of available resources, and have validated it in the laboratory of living. This makes for humility in us about what we say we "know." Such an epistemology prompts men to seek deeply, to seek together, to seek with God. The process of seeking to know is lifelong, is eternal. Such an epistemology makes for healthy learning and knowing.

10. History in Restoration Theology

Some of what happens which we call history accords with what God intends and some does not. Often the evil, the trivial, the ugly, the temporary get in control. At times happenings get so out of touch with God that we call such a time an era of apostasy. But God does not go out of business. He keeps working to bring to pass his purpose. Restoration theology counsels man to stand on a high mountain and see the centuries in a great panorama. The prophetic man has to see in great sweeps of time, in extended relationships. He sees God working through century after century in a continuing cause. In the end the evil and the ineffective go down. So history is a great interrelated drama of cause and effect. God has many forces at work behind the scenes. The spiritual factors come out in triumph. Such a theology of history enables us to look with God in long, confident, healthy perspective.

11. *Eschatology in Restoration Theology*

The phrase "latter day" prompts many to inquire about views of "Latter Day Saints" on "last things." This is the field known as "eschatology." Generally it has to do with such matters as "the end," "the second advent," "the resurrection," "the judgment," and the like. Eschatological beliefs can produce differing effects through different doctrines. For instance, belief in the imminent coming of Christ can prompt believers to sit down, do nothing, and wait, or to work zealously in order to round out work that is to be done. The Restoration movement has no fixed time schedules or assigned dates for advent or for judgment. The doctrine of God's ongoing creative expression leaves place for punctuating happenings but not for cessation of his creative expression. There can be an end of an age but not the end of everything.

The "second coming" of Christ brings in his ministry; it does not put an end to it. There is no surrendering, no escaping, no sit-down ease. God's work will go on, and competent, consecrated Saints will keep on working with him. Every man will be granted whatever condition of existence he is qualified to receive. Judgment is with us, always. So Restoration eschatology is an affirmation of God's justice and of man's need to "ready" himself to live with God, to work with God. The resurrection affirms the essential unity of man as to the material and the spiritual. It emphasizes, as did the resurrection of Jesus, the making of life worthy to continue. The doctrine of judgment, rightly interpreted, stresses the reliability and the equity of God, not his vindictiveness. Saints do not ask, "How much is God going to give me as reward?" but "How shall I be fit for communing with God, for working with God?" The great satisfaction is in associating with fellow-laborers and with fellow-beneficiaries. The desire to increase in wisdom and saintly stature continues. Such an eschatology makes for healthy, hopeful persons in present-time living.

12. *Scriptures in Restoration Theology*

Scriptures are the record of the gospel, not the gospel itself. Scriptures set forth the religious living and thinking of former years. They function for guidance, for inspiration. Those who believe in revelation look for continuing counsel from God and for continuing extension and expansion in the canon of scriptures. Those who see God as ever disclosing himself wherever and whenever men will be responsive believe he will keep on prompting the writing of scriptures. So there is a multiple canon of scriptures, combining the Book of Mormon and the Doctrine and Covenants with the Bible. Restoration theology enjoins men to qualify to interpret and use the scriptures, to qualify to receive and evaluate further scriptural counsel. It offers the richness of diversity and of contemporary reception. Such use of scriptures is health-producing.

13. *Sociology in Restoration Theology*

The saintly social order is to be developed on this earth. There is no postponement to the hereafter. There is no surrender to any prevailing social system. The Saints are to be leaven in transforming the order so that it will be conducive to saintly living. The Jews were "chosen" in the sense that they had a mission to perform; they were not to function as God's favorites. This applies to the contemporary church. And it applies to the central nucleus of Saints, called Zion. This body has assigned functions as a spiritual core in ministering to the world evangelistically. Restoration sociology looks to the integration of all phases of well-balanced living into a health-producing society with spiritual values in ascendancy, with God at the core. Members in this society develop enlightened common consent. Each member functions as a steward, responsible for the competent and consecrated management of his field, for the common good. Society releases the person to achieve to his possibilities, in responsibility without submergence. Such a social program stimulates initiative, cooperation, and satisfaction in the spiritually motivated enterprise. Zion is an incarnation of spiritual health.

14. *The Restoration Itself*

The preface to, the initiation of, and the continuation of the Restoration movement expresses the way God works with man. In it stands forth the man-concerned, longtime-purposing, present-tense functioning, self-revealing God. He discloses his confident, creative, charitable nature. These are basics in the initial happenings of 1820-1830: (1) the centrality of the ever living Christ, (2) the responding and revealing nature of God, (3) the worldwide program of God to men of all times and places, (4) the essential role of the church in furthering a vital God-with-man relationship, (5) the multiple and contemporary content of scriptures, (6) a present tense, on-earth social program and social salvation, (7) the enlightening ministry of the Holy Spirit in contemporary expression, (8) the

95

worth, the nobility, the transformability, and the stewardship potential in every person, (9) the functioning of God-called men in diverse ministries for the uplift of persons, (10) the evangelistic mission of the church through ministers and members. No wonder the movement was called "a marvelous work and a wonder." No wonder pioneers were advised that there would be no place for idlers. Here was a call to men who would venture with God. Such a restoration restores men and society and church to a condition of good spiritual health.

Basics for a Healthy Theology

A theology has to be kept alive. It has to be kept healthy. It cannot be printed in a creed, preserved in archives, quoted authoritatively, and affirmed periodically. If this is all that happens, it will have about as much vitality as a mummified body of a once-alive person. A theology is a living interpretation and living affirmation of the faith men are living by and living out. Whenever a theology is divorced from contemporary spiritual experience it becomes stagnant and past-dated. The Restoration movement flourishes on present-tense communion with and direction from God.

This means that the theology is to be examined and interpreted continually. The spiritual reality continues. Our contacts are limited and our insights partial. As we develop, as our inspired experience expands, we are to increase our insights and our competency for explaining and expressing these insights. A healthy theology is always in process, using what it sees that it may see more. So we are more interested in creative than in codifying action. Living with healthy theology is more like moving ahead on a pioneer trail than in fencing in a tract. The Restoration movement was an adventure of trailblazers.

Healthy theology examines its phrasing to keep its language meaningful. In a developing, dynamic culture new words are formed to designate new experiences, new concepts. Phrases of former days may lose relationship with current thinking and doing. Religion is tempted to use outgrown words and concepts. A vital religion may have to coin new words and redefine old ones if it is going to keep abreast of the times. Thus the development of ideas of "process" and "natural law" and "person" and "space" and "genetics" called for religion to keep up and to speak the language of the times. So we continually seek more adequate words with richer content to identify enduring spiritual reality. The Restoration movement is designed to do this.

At its best the Restoration theology sets forth (1) a healthy God, (2) a man capable of being totally healthy, (3) a health-expressing Christ, (4) a health-stimulating Holy Spirit, (5) a health-furthering, a health-concerned church, (6) a health-affording contact between God and man, (7) sacraments for enabling healthiness, (8) divinely called and divinely endowed ministers for health service to all, (9) family living that looks to the health of members, (10) a world mission with the gospel of wholeness.

A Conversion to Healthiness

Don Parrish was just past twenty-five years of age. He was a devotee to the church. His allegiance to the church had priority over his loyalty to Jesus Christ. He knew the "epitome of faith" by heart. He could summon passages of scripture to support the several tenets. He organized his study of church history and of the church's scriptures to support his views. He knew which tracts would uphold which doctrines. He could turn charts and point to slides. He was a priest and expected to be ordained an elder. He had a quantum of selected "spiritual experiences" to enumerate. His theology went dead with memorization, argumentation, delineation.

Then one day he met a needing man, Joe Daniels. Don ran through his usual line of talking. The man observed, "I don't want your quotations about God, your clichés about God. I need *him*. I would like to meet the God you say is so vital, so understanding. You have given me words about him, chiefly out of books of centuries ago. Can your God speak my language?" Don was helpless. His constructed framework would not make contact. He began to see that he had been giving only phrases, historical events, credal statements, scriptural quotations. Don was honest and sincere.

Then Don went to his own grove as Joseph Smith had done. He caught something of God's concern. He saw Joe Daniels as needing "to become," as worthy "to be." And Don began to love Joe, too. He relived the experience of Joseph Smith in the Palmyra wood. He saw Christ not as a name or a symbol or a historical character—He became a person who was reaching out to Joe Daniels through him. He felt the pulling power of the Holy Spirit impelling him to return to Joe. And Don returned. The gospel of redeeming love came to life in him. He thought out the best means at his command to interpret this, to witness of all this. In Don Parrish the gospel became flesh. The staleness in him gave way to healthy spirituality. And inherited phrases were replaced by a vital theology.

Such is the genius of the Restoration movement. "All things become new"—even theology.

Questions for Discussion

1. How does healthy experience of God involve a sound interpretation of God? What can happen when we try to believe in God without examining our beliefs? What can happen when we keep examining and interpreting and lose out in vital experience with God?

2. How is belief in God inseparably related to how we behave with God? What happens when we go about divorcing believing from behaving?

3. How can we develop a lopsided or narrow concept of God so that this makes our spiritual living fragmentary, partial?

4. How shall the church go about developing an adequate conception of God, one that will be conducive to healthy spiritual living? How shall we develop this kind of common consent?

5. To what extent will it be advisable for an appointed committee to outline "what we believe" and then have the World Conference sanction this as the authorized theology of the church?

6. How shall we encourage juniors and youth to develop the questing spirit in theology while we provide something sound for them to stand on while they search?

7. What basics in Restoration theology do you see were identified, lived out, and shared between 1820 and 1830? How will you phrase these distinctives of our theology in today's life?

8. How may belief in the "glories" in the "hereafter" produce healthy or unhealthy beliefs and practices in Latter Day Saints?

9. How may belief in "spiritual fruits" and in "spiritual gifts" be interpreted and recommended to persons of ill spirituality? To persons of healthful spirituality?

10. An Oriental youth says he would like to know what we mean by the Holy Spirit, that he would like to have this explained in non-scriptural language that would be meaningful today. How would you go about it?

11. What do you see as constituting a healthy Restoration theology for a child of eight years, stated in terms a child can understand? What would be the fundamentals in this theology?

12. In your opinion what qualities characterize Restoration theology in our day for our worldwide mission?

13. Which beliefs in the Restoration movement function most healthfully in your life? How do these beliefs affect your behavior?

CHAPTER 9

"They've no right to do it. There ought to be regulations against it." So spoke a parent of two children, one of kindergarten age, the other of primary age. The usually undemonstrative father was warm and definite in his viewpoint. "Against what?" his friend asked. "Against exposing small children to persons such as these." He sounded as if his children had been exposed to measles or whooping cough or something worse. When this was suggested to him, he went on to say, "A diseased personality is more damaging to a child than a few microbes." The perturbed listener asked, "What kind of maladies are these teachers afflicted with?" Said the father, "I have no high-sounding terms, but these are what I would say: neurotic natures, whining worries, and twisted notions about God and man."

This parent was considering a situation that wise, conscientious church administrators are concerned about more and more. Their wonderings are reaching into many fields. They are thinking of teachers in church schools in every age group, of leaders in boys' and girls' activities, of directors in worship, of visitors in homes, of workers with women, and more. The concern reaches to parents and to the church's responsibility for developing fathers and mothers with wholesome spirituality. At the fore for consideration are ordained men with respect to the impact their personalities make on others. So we are asking about the moral right to lead others as we become more aware of the influence one person has upon another, as we become more conscious of the effect that a person of healthy spirituality exerts in contrast to the effect of the person of not-so-healthy spirituality. We are thinking about the qualities of spiritual good health in a man or woman or youth as these people move out to lead others in the name of the Church of Jesus Christ.

Some Cases of Unhealthy Spiritual Influence

It will be wise for us to identify some cases of the kind of poor health that was of concern to this father. We must note these if we are going to be honest, competent diagnosticians. We shall be able to help such people only as we identify their conditions. This, however, shall not be our major emphasis. We want to stress being healthy and how to be healthy. All are aware of the hundreds and hundreds of spiritually healthy men and women and youth who are on the working staffs of our many congregations and districts. These few cases of ill health are presented to prompt us (1) to avoid putting persons of unhealthy spirituality on our staffs of leaders, (2) to minister to those ill in spirit that they may recover and associate healthfully with others, (3) to become constructive in setting up criteria in selecting personnel with reference to their influence on others, and (4) to develop more functionally an expanding picture of what constitutes spiritual healthiness.

Case I. Alice Symonds has an abnormal interest in death and funerals. She says she "just loves to look at corpses." One of her favorite hymns, (not in our hymnal) is "We Are Going Down the Valley One by One." She has been teaching a class of five-year-olds and six-year-olds. She talks with the children about recent deaths and funerals. She emphasizes pain and suffering and the agony of dying. This is due, in her interpretation, to "human sinfulness." The most emphasized part of the life of Jesus of Nazareth is his suffering on the cross. The great hope that she expresses to the children is that Jesus will come so the good will not have to die or that he will heal the good so they will not face death.

Case II. Bill Hanthorne is on the staff of the youth division. He is in his early thirties. He is married and has three children. He is looked upon as a "friendly, warmhearted fellow," whom the youth "like so much." He poses as a confidant. Particularly does he like to have teen-agers confess their problems, their weaknesses and their shortcomings. He considers himself "very competent" in counseling on "sex and family matters." He speaks of "conversation," of "conferences," of "confessions." He poses as the experienced man who is able to guide the inexperienced. The warm glow of a tête-à-tête on sex matters is interpreted as "the presence of the good spirit."

Case III. John Hilton is an elder. He prefers to take a priest with him on his "priesthood visits" who does little more than go along. Elder Hilton has the dominant role. The major theme during his "official visits" is "the terrible things coming upon the earth." He interprets what he is doing as getting the Saints ready for "the perilous times" that are imminent. He has skill in graphic portrayal of disasters that are to come. Generally he leads to an intense prayer for the family that all members may be faithful during the trying days ahead when "sin shall abound" and when "the love of many shall wax cold." Often he prays that as the destroying angel shall pass by, some sign will be given that will indicate that here is a family worthy of protection. One mother told how after such a visit her children were so frightened that they did not want to sleep apart by themselves.

These things do happen.

We shall do well to go along with the elder who was talking with a young woman who was charged with fears and who said she was afraid of God and dreaded the fears that God had sent her. He said frankly and directly, "You may have fears of God and you may have fears about what God is going to do, but God never sent you these fears." He reminded her of the counsel of Paul to Timothy, "God hath not given us the spirit of fear; but of power and of love, and of a sound mind" (II Timothy 1:7).

Much of the damage done by these persons of unsound spirituality comes from their attributing to God happenings that are contrary to his nature and to his way of directing his universe and of dealing with man. So often their distorted or limited conceptions of themselves become the basis for their image of God. This image, centered in themselves and their anxieties about themselves, may be narrow or narcissistic or neurotic. Thus a college youth could say of the teachings he had received about God: they were too small, too "snoopy," and too superstitious. It is likely he was not quite fair in his evaluation, but he prompts us to look at what we are doing. And it can take years of understanding, companionable ministry to eradicate the effects of persons of unwholesome spirituality.

Some Cases of Healthy Spirituality

Then there are those saintly persons whose sound saintliness touches other lives with wholesome influence. They untie knots now present and keep others from getting tied up in knots that bind and bother. They live and lead others to live in creative, constructive relationship with God. This is well expressed by a teen-age boy who was inclined to blunder around and get off the right track— with the wrong persons. He paid tribute to a man who was taking a consistent interest in him: "He always pulls me up and pushes me on." The man was getting the fourteen-year-old boy to do something for some other person. This middle-aged man with a helping hand and a hoping heart saw his God wanting him to reach out to others, whatever their social condition might be. The boy added, "I don't feel like doing dirt when I'm with him." There are hundreds and hundreds of Saints of expanding thinking and maturing believing and wise serving who are working every day with God. These cases exemplify this healthiness in spirituality.

Case I. The Howells lived in a home not recently constructed. They were not well-to-do, so when five-year-old John was given a bar of chocolate candy it was a more-than-usual event. He and his mother decided he would eat half of the candy that evening and save the rest for the next day. As the boy said his prayer he asked God to take good care of the candy and keep the mice from eating it. The mother caught the tone of his concern and said something like this, "John, let us help God to take care of the candy. I shall get a small tin box and you put it in there so the mice will not be able to get to it. You help God protect it." The boy jumped at the chance to put his candy in the box and to help God. His unexamining faith was turned to a wiser faith that was looking toward a well-protected candy bar.

Case II. Paul Holmes was teaching a class of ninth graders. Astronauts were going far out into space and were circling the earth. The youth of this class were following these happenings on TV programs, in public school discussions, in newspapers. This morning some of them were talking about the millions and millions of years the earth had been existing. They were going out beyond our galaxy and were wondering about the vast distances out there. They were looking at the interior of the earth. One youth said the old location of hell was gone and that we would have to go without hell or get a new location for it. Some of them had encountered adults who considered these astronautical explorations and scientific calculations contrary to God's designs for men. Some members were insisting that the earth was created all at once in 4000 B.C., "as the Bible said." Some of their senior adults were saying that the universe could not be as large as newspapers were saying because such views jeopardized the location of heaven. This Sunday morning several of the youth were inclined to be negative or belligerent and were looking upon the church as holding to backward views. "In the first place," said one youth, "is there any God out there where these old fogies are putting him?"

Paul Holmes did not argue. He did not try to "set them right." He did not insist that they accept any stated position. He told them of the view of a man many centuries ago as God stimulated him to "look big." He took them to Section 22 of the Doctrine and Covenants, with its picture of a continuously creating God. He moved on to the Restoration conception of revelation that keeps "calling us from one level of insight to a higher level of insight." He spoke of the timeless quality in God's creative program. He pointed out how God expects us to search for truth in all fields, in diverse ways, and how we are to piece all this together into a meaningful whole. He referred to the Holy Spirit as intended to enlighten us in all areas of constructive endeavor. Then he said, "Let's go exploring with the Great Creator, the Great Adventurer!" He spoke of God's call to us to join in a "great and marvelous work." Then a boy more certain of Glenn, the astronaut, than of God, the adventurer, spoke out, "I didn't suppose a Latter Day Saint could be a scientist and a spaceman."

Case III. Dorothy Belrose was spastic. Her speech was impaired: she struggled to express herself. She moved about in a wheelchair. Manipulation of her fingers was limited. Now she was finishing high school. What was ahead for her? It would be so easy, so tempting, to surrender and stay at home, to be cared for by others. Her parents were facing the situation realistically. They did not know what could be done, but they were going to find out.

The parents had tried to blend the honest and the hopeful outlooks. They had endeavored to keep her from the influence of a grandmother who was inclined to say, "Poor Dorothy, I am so sorry for you." They had sought to strengthen her against the comments of those who would say, "Why did this have to happen to you?" They endeavored to help her see how God's healing help could be expressed in longtime exercising, as Dorothy kept working with God. They wanted her to rise above the view that several church members had expressed about administration for her impaired condition. These had suggested that they join in fasting and praying and that if it was God's will for her to be healed, some instantaneous healing would take place. The parents tried to develop a self-reliance in her. So Dorothy went to college and to the university. She received a master's degree in speech therapy and went to teach in a school for retarded children. To friends who knew the case she became a speaking miracle. It should be added that understanding members prayed and that elders did administer through childhood and through youth.

Leaders as Associates

Every leader has to develop a clear idea of what his role is. His image of himself can get in his way or get him on his way. It can make him conceited or concerned, legalistic or loving. The leader faces the all-important question, What am I setting out to help come to pass in the lives of these persons? Not just any persons, not humanity in general, but these specific persons now before the leader, waiting to be lived with, to be loved. And the leader continues, How is my personality going to affect them? How am I going to bring them to God or enable them to know God more than they now do? How shall I know my own self rightly so that I shall be able to influence them for good?

Socrates, always listed among the great of teachers, did not call the young learners about him "students" or "pupils"; he insisted on calling them "associates." He did not try to do the thinking for them: he sought to stimulate minds and to guide them in the art of thinking. He wanted them to discover the joy of exploring new areas of thinking and to bring all this together into a conception of what the "good life" was to be.

Jesus of Nazareth was the master for all time in the art of associational teaching. It was said of him that he selected twelve apostles "that they might be with him." He went with them in laboratory ministry. He conversed with them about their problems and their inquiries. What he himself was spoke out to them. His own personality and ministry constituted the revelation to them of what his Father was. They had to sense this gradually and expandingly. These men came out of this association with Jesus changed men. Judas changed until he surrendered to his lower self and then he realized he had betrayed his Master. The others changed into confident and capable apostolic witnesses. He touched their hearts and their minds. He opened their eyes to see what they had not been seeing. So the two disciples on the Emmaus road were able to say of him, "Did not our hearts burn within us, while he talked with us by the way, and while he opened to us the scriptures?" (Luke 24:31). Jesus set himself to motivate these men to discover what was "inside themselves" and to direct it toward the good of those "outside themselves." So in his closing evening circle he could say, "Henceforth I call you . . . friends" (John 15:15). And John could write, "And of his fulness have all we received" (John 1:16).

Healing Begins at Home

One day in Nazareth Jesus returned to his hometown synagogue for a service. He read the passage from Isaiah that depicted the nature of his ministry (Luke 4). Then he called upon a familiar proverb that he discerned they would be saying, "Physician, heal thyself." Jesus did not speak against the saying, but he spoke against their use of it. Jesus practiced a healing ministry with the men he chose that they might be qualified to extend healing ministry to others. He kept helping them to face their own lives, to know their own, inner selves. This would be necessary if they were to know others. Jesus kept reminding them that they needed to know God if they were going to know themselves and that they needed to know themselves if they were going to know God, for they were of God's designing. So now as then we may well pray the prayer of Augustine, "O God who art ever the same, let me know myself, let me know thee." The injunction, "Physician, heal thyself!" still stands before us.

Jesus spoke of his own fitness for ministering to others. He kept himself in good condition through living with and working with his Father. This is what he intended his disciples to do. They were not to withdraw from others, but were to live among them, radiating spiritual influence as Jesus had done among them. They were to have an inward quality of life that would equip them to live among others. So Jesus prayed,

> "I pray not that thou shouldest take them out of the world. . . .
>
> "Sanctify them through thy truth. . . .
>
> "As thou hast sent me into the world, even so have I also sent them into the world.
>
> "And for their sakes I sanctify myself, that they also might be sanctified through the truth."
>
> —John 17:15, 17-19

This Jesus Christ was able to call on inexhaustible sources of supply and minister with such vitality that his personhood afforded lifting power and spiritual vigor to others. Because he was "whole," he was able to help others to experience wholeness. And this is required of all leaders.

Some Misconceptions of Evidences of Spirituality

What are marks of spirituality in a leader? It is necessary that we get below the surface, beneath external manifestations, and get hold of the genuine power and potential inside the person. These qualities are not evidenced by reviewing a man as he marches by nor by seeing him only when he is in action on a platform. We have to live with a man or woman to catch their seasoning, maturing spirituality. Here are some criteria not infrequently identified as marks of spiritual quality. They are rather easily detected and catalogued.

1. The preaching of the gospel and the testifying about it with orotund voice and halo-word phraseology.
2. The quoting of scriptural passages with authoritarian tone and specific identification.
3. The portrayal of signs and wonders as describable and recognizable in overt ways.
4. The narration of personal experiences with emotional intensity, which experiences indicate divine direction and approval for the narrator.
5. The briefing of arguments to prove a case with emotional flavor that does not prompt to analytical thinking.
6. The declaration of ministerial office and the testimonies of endowments and prerogatives incident to the office.
7. The feelingful expression of friendliness and good feeling in person-with-person contacts and congregational gatherings.

Qualities in Spiritual Healthiness

We have no battery of tests that we can administer by which we would be able to indicate the rating of persons as to spirituality. There is no Spirit-meter for gauging how we stand. If there were such a test, if there were such a meter, the use of these might bring about disastrous results. We are quite sure that some commonly employed bases for rating are not valid. A man or woman may be able to quote scriptural passages, to reel off events and dates in encyclopedic fashion, to shake hands like a professional greeter, to tell of healings and visions, to move persons with dramatic stories, and yet have little spiritual depth or dynamic in character. A leader may be a cheerleader, a platform entertainer, and a social mixer and yet have shallow or superficial spirituality. A leader may tell of communing with God and yet lack content and soundness in his communication and commendable motivation in telling it.

Here are ten qualities that taken together constitute indications of the kind of spirituality we are wanting and needing in our leaders. These are qualities that made Jesus of Nazareth a man of spiritual power, a Messiah of divine endowment. They mark spiritual health.

1. Genuine concern for persons, for their spiritual well-being, with a sense of the worth of every person, each in his own right. This concern involves understanding love and brotherly outreach.
2. Joy in righteous living and satisfaction in living the righteous

106

way. True spirituality involves more than doing what duty and reason tell one to do: it involves joy in doing this. Personal integrity is basic.

3. Longtime perspective that looks ahead with God in purpose, process, program, seeing the implication of this longer view in immediate behavior.

4. Facing of reality as it is, spiritual and material, with intent to utilize this reality creatively to achieve God's purpose in man and in his universe.

5. Adventurous faith that moves out courageously and confidently, in accordance with God's faith and objective.

6. Integration of one's own self into a harmonious whole with all facets of one's personhood centered around and in the ever living Christ.

7. Fellowship with persons in furthering God's work, which fellowship entails art in communication and satisfaction in communion together with God. Such fellowship is productive of good and expanding in mutual fruitage.

8. Communion with God in many channels of communication with consequent revelation of God in multiple fields and ways, with all moving together into one ensemble of communion.

9. Sense of mission in God's program and sense of commission and stewardship as an individual and as a member of God's company of disciples.

10. Spiritual radiance that affects others with the light and love inherent in the personhood whose source of life and light is God.

Here in modern language is what Paul called "the fruits of the Spirit." He said this ministry of the Spirit affords "liberty." He told how this ministry of the Spirit transcends legalistic regulations (Galatians 5). These are the manifestations that eventuate in love and edification (I Corinthians 13, 14). These characterize the saints.

The Right to Influence

Every person needs to ask himself what right he has to influence others, to lead them. This study is affirming that foremost in consideration is to be the healthiness of the spirituality of the person who is leading. The leader will master whatever techniques he can; he will explore theories; he will make social contacts that will contribute. These are to add to his competency. Foremost, however, is the person himself with a theology concerning God that is sound, with a communion with God that is vital, with a caring for other persons that is compelling. The Christian leader does not parade his abilities in stampeding others or suppressing others. He does not boast of his skill in getting what he wants. He does not emphasize matters of protocol or prerogative. Such parading is sheer idolatry, with himself on the altar of adoration.

Thornton Wilder in *The Ides of March* has Julius Caesar make an entry in his diary concerning Clodia Pulcher that expresses pointedly the influence of the unorganized and the disorganized person upon others. He wrote, "This woman has lost intelligible meaning to herself and lives only to impress the chaos of her soul on all that surrounds her." Soul chaos like this can operate as a chain reaction. It is our responsibility (1) to prevent such as Clodia Pulcher leaving the impressions of their confused and self-centered personalities on those who cannot protect themselves and (2) to provide rehabilitating ministry for such as she.

There can be no place for leaders who fail to grow up. There is no place for adults who look upon God as a fond, indulgent modern father extended to cosmic proportions. There is no place for the man or woman or youth who expects to be pampered by the Eternal. Healthy religion is a continuously growing experience, continuing through life. There is no place for the worrier who keeps "medicining" himself. God's medicine comes as the person loses himself in God's work. There is no place for the leader who is concerned with tying others to him: the leader of healthy spirituality looks to God working through him, to tying persons to God.

A Prayer of Healthy Saints

O Lord, we bring to thee this urgent prayer,
   Keep us in love with life.

Keep us growing, in wisdom, in insight,
   In overview, in courage.

Touch us alive at many points, O God,
   with thy varied gifts and voices.

Lead us with faith into the unexpected,
   the unplanned, and the unknown.

Guide us in building inner strength and zest,
   that we may minister from the overflow
   of what is in us, from thee.

Help us to extend the radius of our fellowship
that eventually we may include in love
thy children over all the earth.

Save us from servitude to things and thoughts
lest we become incompetent to serve
those who seek larger light.

Deliver us from the stagnation of absorption
in the routines and regulations
of the operations of thy church.

Endow us with the Holy Spirit increasingly,
that our souls may be enlightened
and harmonized in thee.

God, keep us in love with life.
Enable us to follow and labor with Him
who lived and taught the Abundant Life.   Amen.

Questions for Discussion

1. L. J. Gable's *Encyclopedia for Church Group Leaders* observes, "One of the leader's greatest assets is his relationship with the group." What do you think he meant? What does this imply about his spiritual maturity and spiritual health?

2. David Jenkins says in the foregoing text that groups need "help in keeping the group in a healthy working condition" (p. 138). What constitutes a "healthy working condition"? How does the leader himself constitute part of this condition?

3. Apply to the role of the leader in social relationships, "People will trust what we say when they have learned to trust the quality of our lives." What qualities make a significant difference?

4. How are the attitudes, "Everything's all right" and "Everything's all wrong" both fallacious? How do both of them have an undesirable effect upon disciples?

5. What are some prejudices and fears that children may absorb from adults which will impair their spiritual health?

6. How is it unsound to rate the spirituality of a person on one lone factor? What might be such a factor? How does such evaluation require inclusion of many factors taken together as a whole?

7. How is the criterion "All the young people like him" an in-

adequate one for evaluating the competency of a leader to lead young people? What else is needed?

8. What do you set forth as basic spiritual qualifications for ordained men and for visitors in the women's program who are to be visiting members? What qualifies them to do evangelistic visiting? What qualities do you consider would disqualify them for visiting? How was the visit of Jesus with the disciples on the road to Emmaus and in the home in Emmaus a noteworthy visit that provides us with a picture of effective visiting?

9. In Section 119 of Doctrine and Covenants what are some qualities set forth as essential in ordained men? How is this an epistle on spiritual health?

10. How may unwise emphasis upon a few identifiable qualities of spiritual ill health create a problematical situation in families and in congregations? How might it lead to what we often call "witchhunting"? What would constitute a sound consideration of spiritual ill health and good health?

11. What are some beliefs and practices in the Latter Day Saint movement that could be misemphasized and misinterpreted so that they would get in the way of sound spiritual leadership?

12. How is the prayer, "Keep us in love with life!" suited to furthering good spiritual health among our leaders?

13. How may Socrates' use of the word "associates" promote healthy leader-disciples relationship? How did Jesus employ this notion?

PART III

BASICS FOR HEALTHFUL LIVING
IN THE CHRISTIAN GOSPEL

"Gospel" means *good news*. It is "glad tidings" about God's provisions for man's wholesome living. Jesus lived on earth as the expression, the revelation of what life is when it is lived in complete accord with God. He taught this way of living. He lived this way. He told his disciples that this fullness of living constituted the reason for his coming to live on earth as a human with humans. John recorded his saying this way, "I am come that they might have life, and that they might have it more abundantly" (John 10:10).

After Jesus left, his message got somewhat twisted and worked over. Some parts were misemphasized; some parts were misinterpreted; some parts were omitted. Through several centuries the picture of the healthy spiritual man became distorted. Often exponents of their particular ideas of what the spiritual person should be drew up ideals quite different from those Jesus had portrayed. Sometimes they discounted things which God had placed in his creation for man. Sometimes they sought spiritual well-being not by process of gradual growth in God's way but by all-at-once methods, especially through the hands of priestly practitioners. Many times man was pictured as being at war within himself or with forces that God had supplied. The physical body of man was denounced and the thinking of man was distrusted.

In the third decade of the nineteenth century the movement arose which we have come to call the Restoration. It considers itself a reexpression of the gospel that Jesus of Nazareth had taught and lived. It reaffirmed the gospel of abundant life for here and now. It called men to seek this inclusive abundance which God has ever had in mind for man.

This section of our study examines the basics in this "restored gospel" for providing the foundations for spiritual health.

111

CHAPTER 10

COOPERATION OF THE SPIRITUAL
AND THE PHYSICAL

The Christian faith affirms the *uni*verse. God intends that there is to be a oneness in all that he creates and operates. The gospel, soundly interpreted, has no place for the splitting of God's creation into two parts with one part inherently opposed to another part. On the face of everything such an arrangement would be wasteful and would end in the falling apart of everything. It is true that the early writings of the movement speak of the temporal and the spiritual, but these are to be viewed as designating two aspects of one unified creation that is intended to hang together, to function harmoniously. This conception of oneness has much to do with our thinking about good health in God's universe.

What Dualism Signifies

Often in centuries past man looked at the world in which he lived and insisted that he had found two parts in everything about him. He thought he discerned two independent substances in his world. What is more, these two parts were inherently opposed to each other. Their natures made them so. The conflict was quite perceptible. Originally they were different and contrary to each other. The creation was made this way.

This is different from recognizing opposition which came to be and which might be resolved. There is considerable difference in saying that God created evil and intended it to be forever in the order of things and in saying that God created man with potentials which could go wrong and become evil. Evil in this second conception could be changed for good and come into right relationship with God and his universe. In dualism evil is not potential gone wrong; it was started as evil and continues as such.

Quite often, the material, the physical substance was looked upon as evil. Man faced the responsibility of extricating himself from it if he was to rise to spiritual salvation. Sometimes matter was considered so vile that it would be impossible for a holy God to have been connected in any way with its origin or management. Certainly his holy hands could not have been soiled or contaminated by involvement in the creation of this foul physical stuff.

Usually this dualism produced a battling ground in man. The physical body was thought of as involving carnal qualities and devilish drives. Whenever these attained ascendancy man was slipping to damnation. These animalistic urges and propensities had to be suppressed. There could be no compromise between evil matter and spiritual substance.

The Early Christians Faced the Problem

Quite early in the Christian movement dualistic tendencies showed signs of creeping into the life and thinking of the disciples. Paul met and faced it in Asia Minor. His epistle to the Colossians tackles this dualism. Some were insisting that the material world was evil and that man's body partook of this nature. Man was in a body which was tainted and hostile to the divine. Such a body could not come directly into the presence of God. These dualists thought there would have to be intermediaries between man and God. Certainly God could not have been involved in creating this evil material. Joseph Sittler ("Called to Unity," *Pulpit Digest,* July-August 1962) summarizes it this way, "The Colossian error was to assume . . . that the real world was a dualism, one part of which was not subject to the Lordship of the Creator in his Christ."

Paul wrote boldly. He affirmed that there was no need for intermediaries. The Son of God is sufficient. What is more, "all things were created by him, and for him" (Colossians 1:16). If the Son of God effected the creation of "all things," the material world could not be evil. So man does not need to seek release from the physical order. Rather does this material order need to be redeemed from the effects of man's misuse of it. In the Christ are all things held together.

In this sentence Paul wrote with unmistakable meaning that the Son of God had been instrumental in creating the world and that he has ever been the sustainer, the unifier of this creation. No place here for dualism and for discount of the physical.

> "In him all things were created,
> in heaven and on earth, visible and invisible . . .
> He is before all things,
> and in him all things hold together."
> —Colossians 1:16, 17, R.S.V.

114

And Two Parts in Man Too

The view that man is a dichotomy has had a long history. It persists to this day. Theologians through the centuries built on the presumed gap between the physical and the spiritual. So in man there were two parts, the carnal and the spiritual. There was more than a breach: there was an opposition. Here as in the whole world the physical was opposed to the spiritual. He who would be truly spiritual must denounce and suppress the physical. This view has been called *asceticism,* the view that there are two parts in man and that these are diametrically opposed to each other.

Carried to the extreme, asceticism denounces any program that seeks to make the physical body comfortable and vigorous. Enjoying delectable food, relaxing on a comfortable bed, appreciating clothing of fine texture and the like is compromising with evil tendencies. This explains why monks of the Middle Ages wore clothing of camel hair, slept on hard beds, ate coarse food and sat in uncomfortable posture. This was crucifying the body. This is what prompted the conscientious Scotsman to refuse to eat ice cream with the comment, "Nothing could taste that good and be right."

Refutation in the Word of Wisdom

In February 1833 a message was directed to the church that came to be called the "Word of Wisdom." This section of the Doctrine and Covenants is a noteworthy message about the oneness of the so-called physical and spiritual. It is unfortunate that its major message is often overlooked by those who choose to argue about its secondary points and who want to use it to support particular theories about diet. Fundamentally, it forever puts aside doctrines of asceticism and theories about discounting the physical body. It enjoins man to take care of his body as a stewardship. It calls on man to use wisdom in taking care of his body, that thereby man may experience "wisdom and treasures of knowledge." This document is basic in any Latter Day Saint theology about health. Adequate care of the body is more than an option: it is a duty. This Word of Wisdom leaves no place for hostility between body and spiritual development.

Oneness in Restoration Theology

The Restoration does not advocate splitting the universe into two parts. Joseph Smith set forth some simple, sound postulates about the nature of reality. These have profound bearing upon our everyday living, upon our approach to matters of health.

1. "The elements are eternal" (Doctrine and Covenants 90:5).

This breaks with the conception that the creation proceeded and proceeds out of nothing as expressed in the doctrine *creatio ex nihilo*. The elemental stuff of the universe is without beginning or end. Creation means purposive rearrangement of this primeval substance. Nor is there an expectation that some day material stuff will be no more and man shall be completely released from its evil and inhibiting effects. The elements are of God. It is their misuse that gets in the way.

2. "Spirit and element, inseparably connected, receiveth a fullness of joy" (90:5).

This affirms more than tolerance of one by the other: it places them in an essential relationship. What we call "element" and "spirit" are intended to function together. They are not to be in opposition; they are to be complementary.

3. "The power of my Spirit quickeneth all things" (32:3).

The Spirit of God is identified as the force that makes all things operate in motion, in vitality, in affinity. This Spirit is described as pervasive in all the universe, with dynamic functioning. There is no trace of "the Spirit" shunning the material as evil, no leaving of matter to itself. The Spirit is the creative, impelling, unifying factor in the universe. Elsewhere (Doctrine and Covenants 10) the Spirit is identified as life-giving, as light-giving. This quickening of "all things" by the Spirit applies to our bodies, to the environment in which our bodies live, to the food that we take into our bodies. There are no rejects of any substances because they are evil in their own nature.

4. "He hath given a law unto all things" (85:11).

Here every phase of creation is described as operating in identifiable, describable, predictable ways. No field is exempt. No field is ostracized. Both "the physical" and "the spiritual" are set forth as operating by "law." Such a statement leaves place for man to misuse things and processes that operate by law but it does not leave the operation of law out of anything that goes on, out of any area of our universe. This has tremendous significance when we go about building up a program of healthful living.

The foregoing affirmations indicate that there can be only one unified program for healthful living. There can be no isolated program for physical bodies and another separate program for spiritual welfare. We are dealing with oneness in the universe and with oneness in the person. What is more, we shall not have part of the program concerned with "natural law"—what is sometimes called the "natural" or the physical—while another part, called the "supernatural," is conceived as above any kind of law. Both operate by "natural law." In both fields there are many processes we do not yet understand, and this is especially true of the "spiritual," but this does not warrant our saying that what we do not yet understand is outside the law. All this lays the foundation for the statement in Section 85 of the Doctrine and Covenants, "The spirit and the body is the soul of man." They belong together.

And This Oneness Applies to Zion

This oneness applies to the community in which man lives, the community that conditions his healthfulness. This applies to the Zion we are setting out to build. Such a community needs a living body that is visible and it needs an inner spirit that is not visible as a material thing. The material matters are to be assembled and organized in a structure and operation that makes possible healthy living. These material things alone, however, will not bring about the Zionic community. There have to be the spiritual factors of understanding love, of discerning insight, of personal cleanness, and more. Then Zion becomes a living soul. And the two forces, the spiritual and the temporal, may not be separated.

This Calls for Spiritual Resources Too

This conception of the universe recognizes and emphasizes the spiritual resources therein. It affirms that God's universe is rich in spiritual resources. Through recent centuries we have been inclined to discount what could not be explained and measured and manipulated. Once such things as radio broadcasting, unknown three centuries ago, would have been attributed to the supernatural. Many functions in biochemistry in our bodies would have been denied or ascribed to God or classed with hocus-pocus.

Men were not inclined to include as reality what could not be touched with the hand, weighed on the scales, or measured with some meter or yardstick. Now we are seeing that we include as real many things not seen or not accepted a few decades ago. Moderns are still inclined to rule out things that they cannot yet get hold of. We still need to pray the prayer of William Penn, "O God, help us not to despise or oppose what we do not understand."

We are amateurs in matters of spiritual reality. We lack fund of experience. We lack vocabulary for considering it. We lack methods of exploration and validation. Yet it is rather immature to deny the existence in the universe of that which we are not able to interpret and measure. On this basis most of us would have to rule out atoms and light waves. It is high time that we appreciate that there are richer spiritual realities available to us as we come up to the level on which we can tap them, try them, use them. In this tapping is the requirement that we tap them in God's way and use them to his purpose. We need to become willing to see that there is much in our universe that we cannot see with our eyes and touch with our hands.

Our program of healthful living must recognize the essential place of these spiritual resources. We shall go through life half supplied, half equipped if we do not get hold of the abundance of spiritual resources available to us, essential to our healthfulness. Those who leave this spiritual reality out of their living are getting only part of the universe. They are losing the not-so-visible means of support. John Buchanan has identified an atheist as a man "who has no invisible means of support."

Trends toward Conception of Oneness

During recent years considerable thinking has been moving in the direction of oneness with respect to the wholeness of things. There is less inclination to think of a *duo-verse* in which two kinds of reality oppose each other. Rather is there vision of a uni-verse in which things hang together in a unity. Even the physical sciences have been moving in the direction of a single reality. Once in this field matter and energy were thought of as being different. More recently we are seeing these as two aspects of a single reality. Our explorations in atomic studies have demonstrated how the two are one and the same.

This trend toward oneness comes nearer to us in biological and psychological studies. Once man was thought of as split into two parts, the physical and the spiritual. Sometimes these were thought of as independent, sometimes as opposed. Now moderns are thinking of electrobiological processes, of brain waves describable in biochemical terms. Now physical treatment, as in the use of electricity, is being used to correct malfunctioning in feeling and thinking. All this leaves us a little confused. Now there seems to be a tendency to crowd out anything that might be called "spiritual." There is need that we indicate clearly and soundly how spiritual reality is an essential part of God's universe, not as a separated segment but as a functioning part of God's total process. Even when we are careful to include this, we need to have some sound conception of its functioning.

The gospel affirms the oneness of the spiritual and the physical. Our modern age calls for a concept of this oneness that leaves adequate place for the functioning of both. We are needing to see how "the spirit that quickeneth all things" can function and does function through the biochemical, the electrochemical, and many other processes of our living. If this is not done, man can be thought of as a walking mechanism of biological, physical operations. This leaves out something basic in the universe, something essential to complete living. When we leave out spiritual reality, we tell only part of the story and we have only part of a world. Wholeness of health calls for use of the whole field of resources available for healthful living.

The Oneness of God

Central and foremost in the Jewish faith is the Shema. This is the declaration of Deuteronomy 6:4, "Hear, O Israel; the Lord our God is one Lord!" For centuries the Jews have chanted this creed of the oneness of God. It declares that there is one God; it also says that he is one within himself. We would say that he does not have a split personality. He does not have one hand with which he handles physical stuff and another hand with which he handles spiritual matters. The Shema expresses the idea of God's unity, of his own inner harmony. This oneness applies to what he creates. The Hebrew faith has no place for a two-compartment universe.

The next verse (verse 5) is a natural concomitant of the Shema. The word "and" connects the two. It calls the believer in this God of oneness to love him with fullness of heart and mind and strength. Every bit of the person is to be involved. Here there is the implication that the person who truly senses the oneness of

God and commits himself totally and lovingly to God will be one in his own self. In this person will be found single-minded loyalty expressed in wholehearted service. This is sound counsel for achieving inner harmony. Can a person who sees the universe divided and God unintegrated find oneness within himself? Hardly. He can see a struggle going on between man-generated and devil-concocted evil against the righteously purposed forces about him, and still repeat the Shema. God can be one and his purpose can be single, while cumulative forces brought about by man are operating against Him and his program. Yet he is one. Consistently and unifiedly he goes ahead. So can it be with the person who lines up with him. He too will function consistently and unifiedly.

Is Man Unitary or Divided?

At first glance man appears to be a creature of contrasts and contradictions. At second glance he is likely to appear even more so. It has been said that man is in a "paradoxical position," "half animal and half angel." Few fields, if any, show the diversity of attitudes and appreciations that man's views about man appear to show. The rating runs from his being "a little lower than the angels" to "a little higher than the apes." Blaise Pascal once put it this way: "What a novelty, what a monster, what a chaos, what a contradiction, what a prodigy. Judge of all things, imbecile worm of the earth; depository of truth, a sink of uncertainty and error; the pride and the refuse of the universe." Lewis White Beck once asked, "Is he the center of things, or is his birth on a middle-sized planet of an insignificant star just a queer accident in a planless universe?" It is fitting that we inquire whether this unusual being is doomed to be a battleground for a conflict that cannot be resolved.

Much of the literature of mankind represents man as struggling with a division in his nature. Was he made to have one part fight against another part? In ancient Greek mythology there were pictures of creatures who were half men and half beasts. Mermaids were pictured with the upper part of a woman and the lower part a fish. These ancients did not seem certain about what man was. They were not sure whether he was all of one kind of stuff.

Paul of Tarsus wrote of his own inner struggles. He made what happened in him typical of what takes place in all persons. He saw himself struggling against two sets of influences and forces. Often the fighting was intense. It was not until he put all of himself in undivided loyalty to the One—that is, to Jesus Christ—that he found harmony. Then he could say, "This one thing I do" (Philippians 3:13). In the unified Christ he found the key to his own way to harmony.

Moderns Face This Question

Modern man faces these questions of tension. Contemporary biological and behavioral sciences use different terms but they are dealing with the same general question: Will man's equipment permit him to be unified? On one hand man finds the animal nature that pulls him to satisfy his animal appetites and desires. On the other hand man is a self-conscious person who seeks to transcend these biological impulses, who seeks to develop his higher powers. At first it looks as if the fight is for all time.

Man can work at achieving some kind of unity in three ways: (1) he can suppress the unifying and discriminating impulses within him and sink back to the animal level, with unity coming through the victory of the lower drives; (2) he can consider the physical body as evil, as hostile to his higher nature and seek to repress it with unity coming in conquest by the spiritual; (3) he can consider both the animal and the spiritual as essential parts of his nature, parts that can be harmonized, with the spiritual equipment developing and directing the biological equipment. All three of these can operate in a given society. To some degree they can exist simultaneously in one person.

The sound conception is that of the unitary person with the two phases blended into a working harmony. Here man is seen as a part of nature, but he is seen as transcending and as controlling this biological nature and as directing it to spiritual ends. It becomes the necessary framework for this spiritual expression. Here man is seen as having a physical and chemical nature, as electronic and cellular. But he is seen as something more. Man can live so that the material and the spiritual meet in mutual helpfulness. And everything in him can come under the unifying purpose that is God's purpose. Man can be a unity in a universe. As such he will be altogether healthy.

Questions for Discussion

1. What do you think prompted so many through the centuries to look upon "the material" as evil?

2. What do you think caused so many early and medieval Christians to consider man's physical body as evil?

3. What difference does it make in dealing with persons whether we consider "the material" as evil or as misused to evil purpose?

4. What do we mean when we say "evil is potential gone wrong"? How does this differ from saying "God created evil"? How was it necessary to create the possibility of "going wrong" if there was to be the possibility of the emergence of persons?

5. What kind of program of health would be worked out by those who truly believe in asceticism?

6. How is the "Word of Wisdom" a denial of the doctrine of asceticism?

7. How do the four fundamentals of Restoration theology set forth in this lesson support the idea of oneness between "the material" and "the spiritual"?

8. How does belief that there is spiritual reality in the universe affect the way we will go about developing inclusive spiritual health?

9. What is your reaction to the comment, "My spiritual health has nothing to do with the condition of my physical health—I rise above physical discomfort."

10. How does the Shema present a point of view that moves toward a unitary conception of the way God works? How may a conception of the unity of God help to effect unity in us as persons?

11. Distinguish between inherent evil in something and misuse of this something to evil consequences. Indicate how this something may be saved from misuse and be directed to healthful use. Fields for consideration: the physical body and eating; the physical body and sex expression; the physical body and rhythm.

12. What are implications for individual living, for family living, for congregational living, for Zionic community living of the principle, "Spirit and element, inseparably connected, receiveth a fullness of joy"?

CHAPTER 11

THE MINISTRY OF
THE HOLY SPIRIT

Rightly understood and soundly experienced, the Holy Spirit, the Spirit of God, is health fostering and health furthering. Wrongly interpreted and unsoundly practiced this Spirit, or rather what is purported to be the Spirit of God, can undermine health. These misconceptions can encourage superstition, fanaticism, and lopsidedness. They can make persons neurotic, nervous, volatile. Sometimes the Holy Spirit has been discounted or denounced because of the misemphasis and the misuse in the practices of those who testify that they "have the Spirit." Such things as handling poisonous snakes, speaking in meaningless gibberish, shouting out in scriptural exclamations, prancing about in dance steps, swooning to the floor, and the like are rejected by those who are looking for uplift and insight when God is at work in them. It is not enough to insist that persons ought to experience the Holy Spirit. It is imperative that the Holy Spirit be interpreted in terms of God being at work purposefully, consistently, lovingly. And this means health building.

A Dearth in Consideration of the Holy Spirit

During the past several centuries little was written about the Holy Spirit. Little was said in creeds. The Protestant Reformation did not appear to raise question or make statement. The Holy Spirit was not a part of the concern of these theologians. Dr. H. Wheeler Robinson once referred to "a relative neglect of the Holy Spirit." T. Rees in *The Holy Spirit in Thought and Experience* wrote in this vein:

> "It is a frequent and well-founded complaint that the doctrine of the Holy Spirit has been strangely neglected by theologians. Our theological textbooks, as a rule, pass over the subject with a few conventional pages."—Page vii.

And this dearth is apparent in the thinking of the common man. Dr. Henry Van Dusen in *Spirit, Son and Father* observes that if the modern Christian were confronted with the question that

Paul put to the Christians at Ephesus, "Have ye received the Holy Ghost since ye believed?" they would be bewildered and embarrassed. Dr. Van Dusen laments this "fuzziness and inconsistency," this "vagueness and confusion" concerning the Holy Spirit. His own interest is revealed in the title of his book: "Spirit" comes first.

Some Reasons for This Neglect

Through the centuries the Holy Spirit has been so little understood and so greatly misunderstood that many have chosen to leave this unknown out of their thinking. Some have identified it in such general terms and abstract conceptions that there was little to get hold of. Some have referred to this as the "catchall" of Christian theology. Many have surrendered it to fanatical groups who have gone to extremes on overt, exaggerated manifestations. One such was the religious sect that rose up in Hungary a generation ago. It advocated that salvation could be gained through laughter. This was a manifestation of the Spirit. Those who practiced this tenet laughed so boisterously that they were committed to the court as public nuisances. Unbridled hilarity without understanding brought discounting of such spirituality. Another factor has been the tendency of administrators to identify the operation of the Holy Spirit with ecclesiastical rites so that this presence was to come to the believer in *ex officio* administration of sacraments. It might be said that the Holy Spirit was suppressed by office and officialdom. These three factors in decline or denouncement operated: the overgeneralizing, the exaggerating and "fanaticizing," and the institutionalizing.

What Happened on the Day of Pentecost

Now and again we ought to pick up the book of Acts and read it as a connected story. Dr. Luke has made the early Christian community come to life. His former treatise closed with the departure of the Christ (Luke 24:49-52). He also tells how the disciples "returned to Jerusalem with great joy" (verse 51). The book of Acts opens with telling of the Ascension and of the condition of the unbelievers. They felt left alone after the departure of their Lord and Leader.

The disciples waited in Jerusalem. Jesus had told them to do so. They did one thing that looked to the future: they selected a successor to Judas Iscariot in the Twelve Apostles. The total picture indicates that they believed that Jesus Christ would be returning soon, so they could mark time until he should return. They were going to wait. But waiting for long without purposeful expression would be debilitating. Something had to happen in them, and before too long. The coming of the Holy Spirit was to meet this need. This Spirit was to come to these waiting and uncertain disciples to confirm, to comfort, to convince, to commission. Immersed in this energy-providing Spirit they were to learn that they would be able to receive this divine presence even if Jesus were not with them in person.

The Outcome of Pentecost

Those who like headline stories tend to emphasize the dramatic, observable, repeatable happenings of the Day of Pentecost: the "rushing mighty wind," the "cloven tongues like as of fire," the speaking in "other tongues." And the addition of "three thousand souls" comes to the fore. Those who seek understanding of the day endeavor to find out what happened in the lives of these disciples. These ask, What did the coming of the Holy Spirit bring to pass in these believers? These find that something happened in these believers that transformed them and sent them out to work with productive spirituality.

1. These disciples discovered that they could experience the ministry of the Holy Spirit when Jesus of Nazareth was not there in bodily presence. Without this discovery they would have been waiting for his return without expectation of spiritual empowerment. Now this Holy Spirit could be experienced anywhere.

2. They came to see how men of different languages and cultures could transcend linguistic barriers and find spiritual fellowship in common allegiance to Jesus Christ. To this date the revered language had been the Hebrew. The issue was yet to be met in the mission field when the question was to come up about admitting Gentiles into Christian fellowship and on what terms.

3. They experienced a commission to go into all the world with the good news of God's redeeming love, of the revelation of this love in the life and ministry of Jesus Christ, of the ministry of the Holy Spirit. Now the gospel was truly universal. They had seen its universality work on the Day of Pentecost.

4. They built up a community of spiritual fellowship made dynamic and harmonious by this Spirit. The picture given in Acts 2:42-47 sets forth what happened in the Spirit-endowed community. The members are studying together, supporting one

another in practical affairs, associating "with gladness and single-ness of heart," worshiping with "one accord." J. B. Phillips says in his translation that they met together with "common consent" (verse 46). The result was noteworthy: "Every day the Lord added to their number those who were finding salvation" (verse 47). Here was a witnessing community. The phrases in Luke's account are noteworthy: gladness, steadfast learning, common consent, fellowship, community in all things, respect by others, and reception of newcomers. Here were saints with a great commission, a good community, a glad convocation. Here was healthy spirituality.

Paul, the Spirit-Endowed Believer

What happened in Saul of Tarsus in his conversion constitutes a miracle of the highest order. Here was a man torn within himself, lashing out at the nearest target and believers in Jesus Christ. His inner turmoil is expressed in the comment made by him in the encounter on the road to Damascus. Phillips puts it this way: "Saul, Saul, why are you persecuting me? . . . It is not easy for you kick against your own conscience." This bewildered man was converted to a new allegiance. He found unity within. Later he could write to the Philippians, "This one thing I do!" (3:13). After Paul reached Damascus on that conversion day, Ananias went to visit him. He laid hands on Paul that he might recover his sight and "be filled with the Holy Spirit" (Acts 9:17). Henceforth Paul was a Spirit-endowed man and he grew in spiritual health. This Spirit gave a courageous, adventurous quality to his ministry. This Spirit prompted him to attest this ministry by the power of *edification* (I Corinthians 14). This Spirit impelled him to elevate to the fore the fruitage of love and wisdom. This Spirit supplied him with energy to do the otherwise impossible. This Spirit kept hope alive in him. In the closing days of his ministry this Spirit prompted him to write to Timothy, "God hath not given us the spirit of fear; but of power and of love, and of a sound mind" (II Timothy 1:7). Paul developed from disease to ease, from spiritual ill health to miraculous good health.

Out of God's Resources

Healthful living draws on the resources of the environment. The alert, wise person is aware of these resources and knows how to draw on them. The creative person goes to work at conditioning his environment. He does not remain a victim of whatever happens to be around him. He senses how foul atmosphere moves against healthy breathing. He sees how putrid food pulls down his nutritional condition. He is aware how rotten thinking bears in on his mental health. Stink and squalor, decay and deadness eat in on physical and mental health. He sees the opposite, too. He is sensitive to the beneficial results of clean air, deeply breathed, of nutritive food well digested, of natural beauty that evokes artistic response. Such a person is well aware that resources of the environment matter ever so much.

God's universe is charged with spiritual resources. It is up to man to discover how these are to be discovered, understood, tapped, and used for healthful living. We shall conclude that God provides the kind of universe with the kind of spiritual resources that will make man spiritually healthy. We come to see that these spiritual resources do not function automatically in the lives of persons. We have to qualify to draw on them. We come to appreciate that the Holy Spirit is the abundantly supplied resource available to man for healthy living.

The Holy Spirit for Health

In our study we shall think of the Holy Spirit or Spirit of God as the foremost health-producing factor in the universe. In Restoration theology the Holy Spirit is named as the power that "quickeneth all things" (Doctrine and Covenants 32:3 d). We may call this the *spiritual dynamic* of the universe. This Spirit expresses and reveals the nature and functioning of God. In May 1829 the pioneers of the Restoration movement were advised about the healthful functioning of the Holy Spirit. Here was good foresight: the counsel came before the founders talked about and prayed for this divine endowment. Paragraphs 6 and 7 of Section 10 forever lift the ministering of the Holy Spirit to a high level. Here would be healthfulness at its best. When these sentences and those that Jesus spoke in the Last Supper about the Comforter are brought together, we can use such descriptive phrases as these: *life-giving, light-affording, unity-producing, good-things-creating,* and *love-encouraging.* Jesus used such phrases as guiding into truth, as comforting, as prompting to love.

Considerations of the Holy Spirit in scriptural writings always speak in terms of living. Something dynamic is happening in a person who experiences the Holy Spirit. There is no suggestion

127

of inertness, of confusion, of aimless motion, of running down. Rather is there vitality, productivity, harmony, wholeness. In the early days of the Corinthian congregation Paul found it necessary to give members some basic instruction about the nature and the function of the Holy Spirit. Many seemed to prefer the more overt, spectacular manifestations such as speaking in tongues. In the fourteenth chapter of I Corinthians Paul spoke definitely about criteria for recognizing the Holy Spirit. The word he used is *edification.* He was saying that whenever the Holy Spirit ministers in a man's life he is *edified.* This means that he thinks and acts nobly, expandingly, constructively. This last word gives the clue. The words edify and edifice come from the same root. This root has to do with building. A man is edified when he is built up. When the total person is built up, he is edified; he is healthy.

Using Our Health Resources

Students of breathing say that on the whole we are careless, partial breathers. They say that many times we are sluggish and pepless because we do not get enough of the oxygen that God amply supplies for our good health. Some of this is because we do not exhale deeply enough to increase capacity for intake. God has given us a large lung capacity, probably more than we need most of the time. We can even get along on one lung. The more oxygen we breathe in, the more we have to give into our bloodstream, which in turn vitalizes our bodies. There is plenty of good air unless we humans cut ourselves short or contaminate it.

The total man is involved in good breathing. We assume the posture that nature intends us to have for good health. We do not hunch up, we do not stoop when we breathe well. We plan consciously until our better breathing becomes second nature. God expects us to use our body resources and our oxygen resources to achieve vitality and good spirit.

This necessity to draw on resources about us holds true in many phases of our living, to many operations of our bodies, to many developments in our spiritual living. Just as man needs to learn how to draw on and utilize the physical resources about him, so he must learn how to draw on and utilize the spiritual atmosphere about him. He has to learn how to use his own capacities as he reaches out to draw on these spiritual resources. These are part of his total environment.

The utilization of spiritual resources has to accord with God's way of doing. We do not squirt oxygen on the outside of our bodies by a spray; we have to take it into our lungs. We do not rub milk on the skin when we want nourishment; we have to swallow it and get it into the digestive tract. And the body needs to be in good condition. Nor can we go to reunion and purchase a bushel basket full of the Holy Spirit and absorb this with a few deep breaths. And this Spirit will not accord with personalities that are sensuous and sour and selfish. Man has to behave in God's way when he goes about assimilating the Holy Spirit into his personhood.

It is significant that so many times the words used to express "spirit" indicated "air." On terms of vital operation, those ancients were not so far off. They did not know much about the respiratory system but they found that air came and went and that man has to have it. We have been slower in discovering how very much man needs to breathe in "spiritual oxygen" in order to live completely, how man needs to do this well if he is going to be healthy.

When the Spirit Is Misread

After an unusually exacting series of meetings in a tensely "pentecostal" group, a woman remarked, "I'm not much good for a while after I have really been possessed." She meant "possessed by the Spirit." A man, once an exhorter-preacher in such a group that insisted on "the coming of the Spirit," told how he memorized passages of scripture and then put them together with fervor and emphasis without consideration of meaning and message. He said that the more he was "possessed" the faster, the more fervently he preached. Another "Spirit-led" man testified that when "the Spirit took hold" of him, he loved everybody, with all restraints and barriers gone. He confided how he felt especially close to the sisters. This kind of thing does not sound like healthy spirituality, or safe-and-sound spirituality. It is desirable to point out some of these misconceptions of the nature and function of the Holy Spirit. These misreadings undermine and jeopardize spiritual health.

In survey of many movements that stress the place of the Holy Spirit we are able to designate some manifestations, some interpretations that ought to be regarded as unsound and unhealthy. When the Spirit is observed as bringing about or contributing to any of the following conditions, something is not right. Good spiritual health will not come from these conditions.

1. When the experience discounts thinking, diverts us from

thinking, and weakens us in our thinking. Whenever a "thus saith the Spirit" becomes a substitute for thinking, danger is ahead. Whenever "the feel" of the Spirit pushes aside clear, exploratory, honest intellectual processes, whatever is considered to be this "spirit" needs to be examined.

2. When "spiritual experience" is separated from considerations of right and wrong, its foundations and effects need to be reviewed. Some so-called spirituality has nothing to do with ethics of daily living. Spirituality, so-called, that is divorced from matters of sex and shekels and social relationships is quite disassociated with the God who is righteous. One of the great tragedies is the separation of spirituality from the ethics of everyday living in the minds of too many religionists.

3. When what is ascribed as "spiritual" saps the energies of mind and body and does not build them up. Healthy spirituality is exacting, but it does not wear us down and leave us nervous wrecks. The man who testified that he could not relax when he was truly spiritual has a misconception of healthy spirituality.

4. When believers elevate overt expression, easily discernible, above inner transformation and insight. Many persons want the evidence of spirituality to be seen on the outside so that little discipline or development is required of the observer. This is especially true of manifestations of the physical body. Sometimes the degree of spirituality is thought of as being proportionate to the intensity and the motion of the performer. Thus if the person "possessed" is expected to jump, the one who jumps two feet is more "possessed" than the one who jumps only one foot. This applies to voice quality and the uttering of strange sounds. Observing these overt expressions does not require much of the observer. Nor does this require too much of the performer. Well do we inquire about the soul transformation and soul edification which take place on the inside of the person.

5. When "spiritual life" takes persons from social, domestic, and occupational responsibilities. Some "drawings of the Spirit" isolate devotees from their fellowmen. These draw apart and leave the running of social affairs to others. Sometimes they cannot be "bothered" with family living, with civic responsibilities, with improving the social order. These are too mundane for the "truly spiritual."

These are not all the misconceptions and misexpressions. They are enough to point up the problem. Whenever a man's "spirituality" excuses him from thinking honestly and clearly, prompts him to escape from unpleasant situations or exacting responsibilities, keeps him from developing his capacities for effective living, stimulates his feelings without judgment in expressing them, puts him under strain and pressure, such unhealthy effects ought not be attributed to the Holy Spirit.

Men of Insight Call Us to Make Sure

Time was when it was considered sacrilegious to examine the ministering of the Holy Spirit. Some felt that whatever is holy is not to be scrutinized. Once Socrates said, "The unexamined life is not worth living." We might say, "Unexamined spirituality can get pretty dangerous." Something with such great potentiality as the Holy Spirit can be misinterpreted and misdirected. We ever need vision and vigilance. And these can be developed and used with insight and understanding love. We are needing more examination, not less, but we are needing the constructive spirit that will not choke out all spiritual endowment. But we need ever so much to develop a sound, expanding, validated conception of what constitutes endowment.

Joseph Luff was a man of spiritual power in our church through many decades. He moved to Independence in the early years of the return of the Saints to the Center Place. He saw that if this region was to fulfill its rightful place the Saints would need a conception of wholesome spirituality. He said frankly that members needed to discriminate well when a "Thus saith the Lord" was expressed. He considered that everything should be evaluated and that some so-called "manifestations" were thinly inspired. He discounted some on the basis that the effect of them on the average mind was not to establish men and women in the truth that Jesus was the Christ. He considered some as coming as "merely a temporary gratification of the inordinate desire that clamored for them." He observed that "many of them communicated nothing, but were frequently a recital of oft-repeated phrases." He considered that some "manifestations" "had no beneficial effect upon the moral character of those most receptive to them." Yet what man saw the sound ministry of the Holy Spirit more indispensable to the spiritual life of a person and of the church as a whole than this grand man of our ministry?

In 1907 Joseph Luff expressed in song a message of prophecy to the Saints of Independence. It struck at the core of true spirituality. The fruitage of love was set forth as the highest of

131

ministries of the Holy Spirit, as the highest expression of the Zionic community.

If you would be rich, be holy!
Would you dwell on heights above?
Heed ye, then, this admonition:
Climb to atmospheres of love.

Love ye me and love all people,
Love as I have loved you;
This your calling—this my purpose—
Thus be my disciples true.

Then in this exalted station,
Your companion I will be;
Every promise of my Scriptures
Will be verified in thee.

Forth from thence your testimony
Shall to trembling nations go,
And the world confess that with you
God has residence below.

Here would be the kind of community with the kind of Saints described in the book of Acts after the Day of Pentecost. This hymn is saying that Saints who are truly led by the Spirit of God consider the life of understanding love the high revelation of spirituality. And the Saints are spiritually healthy.

Some Health-furthering Ministries

The Holy Spirit is at the heart of Restoration theology and life. This belief and practice, neglected for so many centuries, was "restored" in the Restoration movement. Early revelation to the church such as Section 10 gave sound counsel about the nature and the function of the Good Spirit. Here are some of the major contributions this Spirit can offer to our spiritual health:

1. The fruitage of saintly character as outlined in Galatians 5:22, 23. This fruitage is the primary evidence of spiritual living. Saints with these qualities are healthy.

2. The interpretation of the universe with inclusion of spiritual reality. Most world religions have some kind of idea of a divine spirit. The Holy Spirit can provide a point of contact with these other religions. The spiritual reality may be interpreted as the Spirit that quickeneth all things (D. and C. 32:3).

132

3. Motivation and impulsion for ethical conduct through the "Spirit which leadeth to do good" (D. and C. 10:6). We can be undergirded and strengthened in our righteous living.

4. Basis for the spiritual unity, the worldwide fraternity that transcends spiritual barriers as did that of Pentecost. Men can live happily and helpfully under the blending and bonding ministry of this Spirit.

5. Inner peace that emerges as one achieves personal harmony and oneness with God, the Source of harmony. The Spirit enables a person to bring scattered segments together in a unifying spiritual operation.

6. Enlightenment that involves meaning, expanding understanding, insight. The Holy Spirit quickens man's natural and cultivated powers and develops them. There is high estimate on what man has in native endowment and in what he can become as he studies with God in all departments of learning. This was set forth in the counsel to Oliver Cowdery in 1829 (See D. and C. 9).

7. Spiritual dynamic as the energy-producing spiritual reality of the universe comes into our bodies and minds and hearts. Such dynamic is available as we line up with God and live his way. If it were otherwise the universe would go to pieces. One man put it this way: "My run-down-by-myself life took on something new and vigorous as I began the walk-on-with-God life. The Spirit gave me new life."

The resources of God are available. Their functioning in us must be as up-to-date as the sun shining on the leaves in the garden today. The light and the warmth of God's Spirit can be that immediate. This dynamic expression of God is life-giving, light-affording, love-expressing, Through this Holy Spirit can come enlightenment, vitality, creativity, and harmony.

Questions for Discussion

1. Jesus talked about the Holy Spirit in his conversations with his Twelve during the closing weeks of his ministry (see John 14, 15). What did he indicate as the functions of the Holy Spirit? How do you see these as health-producing?

2. Jesus referred to the Holy Spirit as "the Comforter." How is it advisable to interpret this in the light of the second syllable "fort" as denoting strength? What is a common idea of what comforting means? How did Jesus' meaning connote affording strength?

3. What identifying characteristics of the Holy Spirit were set forth in the first instructions to the Restoration movement, given in 1829 in what is now Section 10 of Doctrine and Covenants?

4. Why do you suppose so many people have identified the "possession" of the Holy Spirit in terms of overt action? In this case how would you identify the most possessed person? How is this an unsound conception of the ministry of the Holy Spirit?

5. How may a person become a fanatic on the Holy Spirit under the definition of a fanatic as a person who dotes on one thing and divorces this from the rest of reality and experience?

6. How may the ministry of the Holy Spirit deliver us from the unhappiness that is described as "not knowing what we want and killing ourselves to get it"? How can the Holy Spirit develop our overview so that life can have meaning?

7. How would you interpret the Holy Spirit to one who agrees with the picture portrayed in John Steinbeck's *Grapes of Wrath* when the erstwhile preacher Jim Corey was conversing with Tom Joad? This was his report: "Jumpin' and yellin'. That's what folks like. Makes 'em feel swell. When Grandma got to talkin' in tongues, you couldn't tie her down. She could knock over a full-growed deacon with her fist." What does this sort of religion do to a person and to a group? What is unhealthy about it?

8. One student of inspiration says, "The Holy Spirit ever prompts me to explore, to discover, to put things together meaningfully." Do you see this as a valid criterion of the ministry of the Holy Spirit? How inclusive do you see this functioning? Does this include searching in the laboratory concerning molecules as well as searching in the worship room for callings to the ministry?

9. How is it good for us to get the inclusive picture of many manifestations of the Holy Spirit as set forth in the twelfth chapter of I Corinthians? How does this recognition help the person and how does it help the church?

10. What responsibility does this counsel place upon us: "The spirits of the prophets are subject to the prophets"? How does this call for good judgment? How does this contribute to our spiritual health?

11. Elbert A. Smith once wrote that "zeal without wisdom" leads to disaster and to spiritual disease. What does this mean? What safeguards are there against this?

12. Portray your picture of a spiritually healthy person when this good health is fostered and furthered by "the healthful Holy Spirit." Apply to a child of ten, to a youth of twenty, an adult of forty, to a senior adult of seventy. Make the person stand out clearly so you will suit the ministry to the person.
13. Consistent good health requires that we keep our bodies functioning all the time with life-building foods. Yet this does not mean monotony. How do you apply this to the maintaining of spiritual health through the ministry of the Holy Spirit?

CHAPTER 12

SOCIAL MUTUALITY IN
OUR COMMUNITY LIVING

"We're stuck together, so we might as well make the best of it," said one man to another marooned with him on an isolated island. Replied the other man, "It is fortunate that both of us got carried to the same island." These two viewpoints can be spotted around the world. One stresses the misfortune of having to live with and get along with other humans. It seems to suggest that life might be pretty enjoyable and decent if we did not have to have other persons around us. The other viewpoint looks upon man's living with others as an indispensable asset. This view expresses the desire to have others around even if some of these others get to be annoying and at times liabilities.

The gospel portrays the rightful living together of persons as an essential part of God's program. It indicates that man was intended to become a person and to live with his fellows. It affirms something more: men are designed to live together with God. It says further that when man learns how to do well, how to do this in God's way, he has untold resources for achieving spiritual health. This good way of living is one of social mutuality. There is an interrelationship, an intersupport.

Social Influence Can Go Two Ways

God does not provide us with a foolproof mutuality. He provides us with potentials that can be developed and used to our good or to our disability. We come to see that it is not enough for us to set up the goal of developing our potentialities. We have to see how and what for. Every person, every society can take potentialities to the left or to the right. Socrates once confessed that he had within him the potentiality to become a criminal, but that he had decided to turn away from this potentiality. He had decided to line up with the forces that moved away from criminality.

Our life together can be a source of good health or of ill health. One thing is sure: we are created and constructed to live together. It is up to us to determine whether our living together is going to be asset or liability. One family can subject a small child to pressures, to fears, to phobias, to insecurities, to filth that will bring about spiritual dyspepsia or spiritual ulcers or spiritual paralysis. Another family can create a climate of wholesome fellowship, of stimulation to creative goodness, of spiritual security. The question is not whether we are going to live in social relationships but in what kind we are going to live.

The Gospel of Social Mutuality

Jesus of Nazareth kept teaching that men are responsible to one another for the influence they exert upon each other. There was not the slightest hint that a disciple should think of living in a vacuum to himself. The Golden Rule (Matthew 7:21) enjoins every person to act with high consideration of every other person. Jesus interpreted ministering to others as ministering to him (Matthew 25:36-37). The giving of a cup of cold water could be worthy of commendation. The spirit of giving made a difference; giving was to be done in the spirit of Christ (Mark 9:38). He pointed definitely to adults' responsibility for their influence on children. He thundered out that malinfluence on a child was heinous sinfulness (Matthew 18:1-5). In his closing conversation with the Twelve he exalted the relationship he had been having with them and he called them friends (John 15:14). He designated the sacrificial giving of one's life for the good of others as the noblest virtue (John 15:13).

The gospel of Jesus Christ affirms that God designs men to live together in mutual helpfulness. It says that this is possible only as they live in a social order in which God is the center and source of helpfulness. It goes on to say that when men respond to God he will support them and unify them in living together in spiritual mutuality.

The Re-expression in the Restoration Movement

So often during the centuries after the early years of Christianity men came to think of living in solo arrangement with God. The man concerned about saving his own soul might go apart and live to himself. He would "withdraw from the world." The main thing was that he receive the sacraments of the church and this could be done alone with the priest.

From the earliest days of the Restoration movement the social mutuality which Jesus had preached so consistently was

137

taught anew. It was taught as a responsibility; it was set forth as a privilege. It was one of the tenets of primitive Christianity that was restored. This social responsibility, this spiritual mutuality was more than an option. It was a requisite for Christian living. Before the church was organized, there were given instructions about requirements for membership. Here was a sharply focused directive: "No one can assist in this work, except he shall be humble and full of love, having faith, hope, and charity" (Doctrine and Covenants 11:4). This kind of mutuality was basic.

The Basic Concern for Persons

When the youthful John Whitmer wanted to know what he should do as a participant in the new movement, he was probably thinking of some specific assignment. He was not told what he should do; he was told what he should *be*. The foremost thing was that he be concerned about others and about bringing them to God (Doctrine and Covenants 13:3). It would be good for him; it would be good for others. Oliver Cowdery and David Whitmer were told the same thing. They were told of the worth of every person in God's sight and of the genuine joy and deep satisfaction that would come as they would associate with those to whom they ministered (Doctrine and Covenants 16:3). Mere carrying out of dutiful warning to others would not be enough. Persons were to find happiness in lifting a brother Godward. Every man was to be concerned about his neighbor, warning him "in mildness and in meekness" (Doctrine and Covenants 38:9 d). The circle of this neighborliness was to extend to worldwide proportions.

It was not going to be enough to make one submit to living with persons. The competent and healthy member would want to live with others with wise helpfulness. He would learn how to do so. He would find satisfaction in seeing others join in the gospel of spiritual mutuality. He would thrill joyfully in association with those whom he would help Godward.

The Program of Building Zion

Early in the movement the pioneers were commissioned to build "the city" (Doctrine and Covenants 27:3 c). In time this community came to be designated as Zion. It was to be right here on this earth, on the Western continent. It was no celestial city that was to come down ready-made from heaven. Nor was it to be a city of the hereafter pictured after the manner of the much heralded city of Enoch. The qualities of this city of long ago were to be expressed here; the people were to be "of one heart and mind," they were to dwell "in righteousness," and there was to be "no poor among them" (Doctrine and Covenants 36:2). But these virtues were to be expressed in the relationship of Saints who would be living on farmland in Jackson County, Missouri.

The preaching of Zion brought ready response. The early Saints sang of the earlier city in which "as himself each loved his neighbor." It appears that they often caught the appeal of the new venture without catching the gospel of it. This gospel would stress the personal qualities, the interperson responsibilities, the help available in God for changing their lives so that they would be able to live in saintly mutuality. The program of building saints as brothers and sisters was an essential part of the program of building "the city."

The Idea of Zion Has Been Expanding

This preaching of Zion attracted converts. It impelled members to migrate to the place designated for the Center Place. This was in the summer of 1831 (Doctrine and Covenants 57). Now after a century and more we are able to see that the image of Zion and the motivation for moving to the place of gathering were not adequate. The motivation was often self-centered. The picture was often partial. Many took a hurry-up view about the way Zion was to come to be. They did not recognize the priority in gathering designated in Doctrine and Covenants 58:3 c. This first attempt at building Zion in Jackson County, Missouri, collapsed. So did the settlements at Kirtland, Ohio; at Far West, Missouri; and at Nauvoo, Illinois.

There were those who came to the conclusion that Zion was a fancied dream that would not work out. There were others who concluded that the idea of Zion was sound and that it is essential in the developing of disciples, but that the thinking of the Saints about it had to be worked through and made to accord with God's program and purpose for working it out.

More recently we have been realizing that a look-to-itself community, a flee-from-this-world city could not produce healthy Saints. More recently, too, we have been giving consideration to the kind of community that will promote spiritual health among those who build it and maintain it.

More than Aggregation

Merely bringing many church members together into one place will not further the spiritual health envisioned here. Mutuality involves more than getting persons together into one place. This could produce a horde or a mob or a mere aggregation. Mutuality involves more than doing things together. This could be done at the direction of some superior director without any sense of community among the participants. It takes sharing in something that has continuing, expanding, harmonizing possibilities.

Our modern times have much to say about getting along together, about making social adjustment. Our touch-and-go social practices can bring persons in proximity with one another, can get them to greet one another conventionally, without the inner soul of one ever touching, ever meeting the inner soul of the other. Only the veneers meet. The gospel of Jesus Christ calls persons to have an inner core that is genuine and enduring, a core that is worth meeting. It is this inner core that makes contact in spiritual mutuality.

Clifton Fadiman once wrote of this in *Holiday*. He suggested that in our modern living we are not meeting one another. "What we are substituting for friendship is friendliness, which is its enemy." He sees man alone and lonely in the great urban center which he calls Megalopolis. So man cultivates a conventional sociability which does not get beneath the surface. Fadiman comments, "We try to head off solitude by friendliness, universal-jointed amiability. We have no time to cultivate a smile within the heart; the smile on the lips will have to do." Yet he feels that this surface smile in megalopolitan life does not and cannot meet the inner needs of the person. It only alleviates conditions.

The gospel of Jesus Christ affords us a spiritual mutuality that is to further our good health, increase our spiritual competency, stimulate us in good works. This community is more than an aggregation of men. It is a fellowship of those committed to the work of God, united in the common endeavor of achieving his purpose in man, enlivened by the Good Spirit. The gospel affirms that this kind of mutuality is essential to first-class spiritual health.

Possible Services in Community Mutuality

The health-producing community examines continually what its effect is on the members who compose it. It keeps asking whether its objectives and methods accord with the divine intent for men as persons. It does not take things for granted. It does not assume that things will take care of themselves in an automatic way. It sets forth what it can do when it is functioning well. Here are major contributions that sound mutuality, well-balanced community can contribute to achieving spiritual health:

1. A sense of worth of every person in the sight of all other members of the community. This calls for the recognition of the right of every member to develop and express himself in accordance with his capacities. Each person is a recipient and a contributor in the total community life. It is of tremendous consequence for a planet or a satellite, a child, an oldster, a genius, a dullard to be viewed as having worth, as having the opportunity to live in his own right.

2. A recognition of the inviolability of every person. This might be called "personality protection." This protects any person from being absorbed by any other person or by any group. This guards against personal exploitation, against personal domination, against merging of personalities until a person may no longer have a distinct personality of his own. It is a tragic situation when a personality is so drained that there is nothing left to reveal, until even unphrased thoughts can be anticipated. In this wholesome community every person has an inner sanctuary that is not invaded by others. Here is the inner fastness of the soul.

3. A fund of growing language for person-with-person communication. This includes verbal symbols, gestures, emotional inflections, and more. Some groups have an impoverished language supply. For instance, Eskimos cannot converse about some things because they have no language symbols, they have no thought patterns in many fields of more mature thinking. The community that develops its members well keeps thinking on the frontier, keeps formulating new words for this expanding intellectual life, keeps refining and beautifying its resources for its methods of speaking. This includes adequate vocabulary for spiritual exploration, for spiritual interpretation, for spiritual stimulation. Some languages of the world are much richer than others in spiritual vocabulary.

4. A stimulation in creative goodness. A group can make things go, in this direction or another. The healthy community does things—does things with creative spirit, does things for the general good. It encourages members to develop and use their potentials in satisfying creative endeavors. Goodness is seen not as a listing of things members do not do but as a program of constructive activities that crowds out the less desirable.

141

5. A pacing of members on the road of community endeavor. This rises above cutthroat competition, above discounting of others. Here members are pacing one another on the road of Zion, with consequent stimulation. The motive is not to get ahead of everyone else but to encourage others to come up to the fullness of their potential. The steward is not satisfied unless he is functioning well. Nor is he content unless his brothers are achieving to their optimum.

6. A clean atmosphere for occupational, family, community living. The impact of the sordid, the sensuous, the shallow, the shameful presses upon us. Some of it is going to make inroads. Words, phrases, music, pictures, types of dress, advertisements, conversations creep in.

7. An elevation of values that are enduring, that emphasize the worth of spiritual health. Social standing rests on the basis Jesus advocated—service to others, motivated with understanding love. Keeping up with the Joneses becomes acceptable to the degree that the Joneses are keeping up with enduring spiritual values. The healthy community calls into question values that circulate under pressure from vested interests or from forces that do not see the total picture.

8. The art of achieving common consent that accords with God's mind and heart. This calls for the free, friendly sharing of funds of experience, of attitudes, of materials, sundry and important, that have bearing. The community uses the word "we" and this "we" includes God. The pooling includes things that range from what Gilbert Chesterton calls "tremendous trifles" to "trenchant truths."

Never in Isolation

This "good community" is a spiritual nucleus in the total social order. It has enough distinctiveness "from the world" to enable it to function, but also enough contact "with the world" to enable it to serve with Christian mission. There is no hard-and-fast boundary line between members and nonmembers. Those who are living in it maintain a two-way communication with those not affiliated with the church. They are ready both to give and to receive. "Sister Jones" is a good neighbor to Mrs. Jollis, who is a member of the Presbyterian Church, and with Mrs. McHone who is a member of the Roman Catholic Church. And they all work together for an upgrading community.

And this community of Zionic intent—we may call it Saintsville—senses its responsibility and relationship to the total social order. It has to have something to contribute to the general welfare. The concerns of its members run from the poor housing and lack of health-producing facilities of white folk and Negro folk a few blocks down the street to the no-housing and no-health situations and consequent suffering in Vietnam and in the Congo. This community is a voice of conscience and a hand of ministry.

Such a community pours out its energies, its prayers, its saintly heart for the good of the whole world, for the good of the local region, for the good of families next door. It is concerned with the spiritual health of all persons in all lands. And it has to maintain its own good spiritual health in order to do this. It realizes that inbred self-centeredness will lead to spiritual unhealthiness. It senses that only the community that is outreaching to bless others can be truly healthy.

When a Community Can Be a Liability

Moving several Latter Day Saint members together and calling it a church settlement does not make it a wholesome spiritual community. Calling it "Zion City" would not change its debilitating influences. For a time there could appear to be an inner peace, but this presumed peace could be deadening and could lay the foundation for future eruption. Here are some situations that would contribute to poor spiritual health.

1. Exploitation of persons by dominating persons or by domineering groups. A member may be tied by sentimental attachment or loyalty until he cannot assert his own personhood. It can be that "the one who cares less may exploit the one who cares most."

2. Lopsided community living that leaves out some essentials and overemphasizes some segments of social living. This lopsided emphasis may be on basketball, fish frys, or prayer meeting. The omission may be an appreciation of music of quality, sanitary toilet facilities, or periodicals of spiritual uplift.

3. Faultfinding, person-assassination patterns. Such negativism is contagious and crushing. Members of a church can indulge in a diet of roast preacher, hashed-over business meetings, and deviled general church.

4. Monopoly of participation and positions by a minority which discounts the abilities of others. The capable will and ought to come to the fore and to the top, but they come as under-

standing servers rather than as domineering managers who keep others from development.

5. Inbred viewpoints and patterns of living that shut off contact with the outside world in which the community exists. This may involve a holier-than-thou attitude or a sense of security in imagined walls that shut out extraneous influence. Confrontation with problems may be avoided by simply denying their existence.

6. Laissez-faire policy that assumes that all things will work out for the best in the long run. In this outlook there is no need for social planning, no need for screening influences that operate in the community, no need for setting up community goals. This may come from a belief that in the course of things everything comes through all right or from a faith that God will see that the outcome will be good for the faithful.

7. Watchful waiting that presumes that God in his own time will move in his way and that until then men are to "wait on the Lord." This attitude generally discounts human efforts to bring about the Zionic way of living and looks with disfavor on scientific research and social programs to enable the good community to come to be.

These Things the Community Can Do

The person in the Church of Jesus Christ should not expect that the spiritual mutuality afforded in this fellowship will undergird him in any kind of activity he may choose to pursue. The individual may not expect the community, local and general, to bend to his whims if these whims are contrary to the genius and work of the Church of Jesus Christ. What any person does has to fit in with the purpose and procedure of God that will be furthered through this life together of "co-workers with God." The individual will be supported to the degree that he and others have clear vision about where they are going and how they are going to get there. Here are basics that the community will be striving to develop:

1. Clarify the image of the kind of spirituality motivated, spirituality integrated, spiritually nourished persons we are needing in the community. These persons will not be identicals but will develop with diversity in skills and abilities in the framework of this general image.

2. Recognize and support spiritual values that are to be at the fore in the common life, values that are inherent in God's person-producing universe.

144

3. Develop spiritual fitness and sensitivity in persons for communicating with God for expanding revelation in the total field of person developing, church functioning, and community building.

4. Create and maintain agencies of diverse emphases and functions for servicing persons and families in their endeavors to live the "good life" together. Such agencies see clearly their roles in this way of living.

5. Provide the pastoral, counseling, and related ministries that enable persons and families to see themselves honestly, evaluate themselves soundly, and receive ministries helpfully.

6. Unify the community in common allegiance to God, in creative service with brotherly outreach, and in enlightening uplift and oneness through his Spirit.

7. Include all age groups, all interest groups, all fields of labor groups in a complementing, cooperating venture.

8. Celebrate the happenings that carry forward the hopes and the satisfactions and the assurances in working together with God in this kind of living.

"We're in This Together"

It is a great moment when two men strike hands together and say in word or in unuttered language, "We're in this together." It is a sacramental experience when these two men are saying also, "And God is in this with us." It is a lonely and a tragic moment when a man stands alone and feels that no one cares, no one understands what he is endeavoring to do. The fullness of aloneness comes when he feels that even God has left him and he says, "My God, why hast thou forsaken me?" It is fundamental that Jesus Christ experienced this bottom point of loneliness. It is significant that lonely men can realize that he appreciates how they feel when they stand alone. There is a great distance between spiritual isolation and spiritual fraternity.

The Church of Jesus Christ prompts us to live so understandingly, so daringly with one another, so fraternally with one another that we can say, "We're in this together." The Church of Jesus Christ also calls us to keep growing in conception of what this is in which we are together. The Church of Jesus Christ keeps calling us to develop in the arts of expressing this fraternity. The Church of Jesus Christ keeps calling us to express this cooperating fraternity in congregations and communities. And

145

the church affirms that in this spiritual mutuality are resources for spiritual health.

And It Works!

Don was a confused youth. He was disheartened. He belittled himself. He had been born out of wedlock. He had been raised by a grandmother who reminded him of how much she was doing for him. His mother was neurotic and alcoholic. He came to feel that he belonged nowhere and that no one really cared for him. He sought refuge in pentecostal religions, but the flush of feeling was always only temporary. He turned to liquor, only to increase his sense of defeat. In his own language he was "no good." He was invited to some meetings of the "Reorganized Latter Day Saint" church. He attended meetings; that was all. He continued in his discouragement and sense of futility.

Then he went to another congregation of the church. Here was a minister who took him at his face value, who listened to his story, who never lifted an eyebrow, who understood the forces that had been shaping his life, who saw that it would be a long, uphill climb to get this youth on his feet. Here was another minister who helped Don to get employment and who talked to him about the social responsibility of working well. Here was a family who invited him to come into their home, to sit at their table. Don had always been an onlooker. A youth leader consulted with the youth cabinet and they found something for Don to do in which he could express himself. He was not well-coordinated physically and was not at home on the playing field, so they guarded against showing him up to disadvantage. He had a good vocabulary and expressed himself quite well, so they helped him get ready for panels and discussions. The minister-friend made it easy for Don to come back to him and confide whenever he slipped back in his ways of living.

Don found himself. He found a way of praying above disheartened pleading about himself. He found friends in the fellowship of the Saints. He found means for going on in education. And the wise fellow-members arranged for Don to contribute in a two-way give-and-take.

Don found himself, his brothers, his God through the spiritual mutuality of those who saw, who cared, who reached out, who took him in.

146

Questions for Discussion

1. Contrast mutuality and one-sided helpfulness.
2. Illustrate the difference between the "let-me-do-it-for-you" approach and the "let's-do-this-together" approach.
3. How was the affirmation of the gospel of spiritual mutuality a "restored" tenet of the Restoration movement?
4. How may a community called Zion be a project of social totalitarianism rather than a community of spiritual mutuality?
5. Expand and interpret, "A person cannot share in spiritual mutuality unless he has a spiritual core in his personhood that can meet the spiritual core in another."
6. What did Clifton Fadiman mean when he said that friendliness might substitute for and crowd out friendship? Apply this to a congregation or to a community.
7. What qualities of a community or of a congregation might get in the way and block the realization of creative spiritual mutuality?
8. How may a type of social operation in a community block the development of initiative, sense of responsibility, and decision-making in members of the community?
9. How would a community or congregation of which you are a member go about adopting and assuring a person who comes from a culture that is different? A person whose language is different? A person whose skin color is different?
10. How would your congregation, your community proceed to further good spiritual health with parents who face the realization that their child is retarded?
11. How would your congregation, your family, your community go about improving the spiritual health of a youth or adult who is an alcoholic?
12. Designate qualities in the spiritual atmosphere of a family, of a congregation, of a community that constitute a wholesome climate for spiritual development. Avoid generalities like "faith"; make this faith functional and identifiable.
13. To what degree do you believe, "No one saves us but ourselves"? If this is so, what is the role of "the communion of saints"?
14. What bearing does the view defined by Emily Kimbrough as the outlook of her grandfather have on our living with spiritual mutuality: "I have never met anyone who couldn't tell me something I hadn't known before"?
15. What are some things you may receive through sound saintly association that you could not get in any other way?

CHAPTER 13

REPENTANCE AND FORGIVENESS
FOR RENEWAL

When an unpretending disciple said, "Repenting keeps me kept up," he was speaking of something basic in spiritual health. He was seeing the indispensability of repentance and forgiveness in healthy living. Today we are seeing this as more than an optional possibility; we are seeing it as a necessity. We are considering it as more than a regulation imposed; we are seeing it as available and incalculable resource for good health. We are finding out how repentance and forgiveness meet the demands of our own nature. And this is meeting the demands of God, for he designs us to be forgiving and forgiven, to repent and be restored.

Getting Right with God

Revival preachers have often thundered forth on the sermon topic, "Is Your Heart Right with God?" They would make it a direct-to-person question with the implication that sinners needed to do some thorough adjusting in their ways of living. There is basic soundness in the question. The man out of harmony with God and out of accord with God's universe is, as one confused man put it, "really fouled up." When we see God as forgiving, we cannot get along well if we are hateful and malicious, holding grudges and remembering slights. Nor does nature hold hatreds and practice get-even tactics. God has a universe that operates reliably and consistently in ways that we call "natural law." We have to accord with these. The man who goes against these takes the consequences of his actions. There is, however, no pouting God sitting on a judgment seat figuring out how to fling back his jealousy and dislike. God is concerned with man's getting right rather than with God's getting even.

Getting right with God means readjusting our living so that we accord with his nature, with his way of doing things. We do not ask God to cross his fingers while we do something that does not fit in with his way of doing things. We cannot expect to raise tomatoes in a temperature of twenty degrees Fahrenheit or run a gasoline engine by using ice water as fuel simply by petitioning God to do a special favor for us. If he were to do so, we would not have a universe that holds together; we would end up in a falling-apart confusion. And this holds true for matters of our own character. We cannot live hatefully in a universe in which God is forgiving. We cannot do well in a world in which orneriness persists when the Sustainer of this universe lives righteously and lovingly.

"Getting right with God" means getting in right relations with the Source of life-giving energies and equipments. This includes the full range of our contacts with everything in God's universe. Sometimes we talk and act as if God ought to consider us in full right relationship with him because we take care of some single field. This reminds us of the boy who thought he ought to be very healthy because he brushed his teeth night and morning in response to a contest in school. It did not occur to him that what he ate, how he slept, whether he exercised, and the like had bearing on the situation. A grown man looked upon paying his tithing in much the same way. Since he paid his tithing systematically, he thought he should be prosperous in all ways. Rightness with God is thoroughly inclusive.

God Is Gracious

Some of our pictures of God make him pretty severe and punitive. Because of such portraits of him many persons who have blundered and strayed, carelessly or intentionally, may carry for years a sense of guilt, of uncertainty, of non-forgiveness and apartness from God. They feel like the man who said, "My record in God's books is in the red." Or they feel as one youth expressed it, "After all the things that I have done, how could God ever forgive me?" Such self-condemnation and insecurity are destructive. They keep us from God.

Sometimes this inability to sense forgiveness applies to our notions about other persons. A husband had been rather free in his sex relationships prior to marriage. Then he came to know God and had come to sense genuine forgiveness. He became a loyal, understanding husband and father. But his wife never sensed how God had forgiven. Now and then reminding taunts were spoken in a self-righteous way. She seemed to be saying, "I did not sin as you did. How could God ever forgive you?" A breach developed between the husband and the wife. She had never learned the gracious and forgiving nature of God.

The gracious person is not resentful and vindictive. And God is altogether gracious. One youth put it this way, "God does not rub it in." An adult phrased it in this manner, "God does not rub salt in my wounds to hurt me; if he uses salt, it is to heal me." God is waiting graciously for every one of us. He waits for us to want to be forgiven. Quite early this portrait of God was set forth in the Restoration movement. In what is now Section 16 of the Doctrine and Covenants is this reminder, "How great is his joy in the soul that repents!" The gracious God reaches out to the returning, responding wanderer. He says, "My son, who was lost!" And the wanderer with confidence of forgiveness replies, "My Father!"

More Than a Word of Appeal

One day a man sat down beside me on a railway train. He had been drinking heavily and was quite relaxed in conversation. He told me the story of his life with lurid details. He had just visited a city for "sexual satisfaction" at a "reasonable price." He had been promiscuous in sex, indulgent in liquor, and drifting in employment. After a lengthy recital of the recent decade of his life, he turned to me with free frankness and said, "But everything is all right now, for I told Jesus about it last night, and he has forgiven me." Then he wanted to know if I did not think that way, too.

This man had little or no conception of what repentance and forgiveness mean. To him it was an easy retreat from consequences and an escape from God's displeasure. He was looking upon forgiveness as washing the slate so that he could start all over again in the same way of life. The plans he outlined indicated as much. True repentance would involve a change in his entire pattern of living, with the intent to live in a different way.

Ulcers of Hate and Guilt and Fear

Numerous studies disclose that a person cannot be happy and healthy as long as he carries a burden of dislikes, contentions, jealousies, self-denunciations, fears, and phobias. The body chemistry reveals how these states of mind, these attitudes lower efficiency and undermine health. One middle-aged woman was at the breaking point. Shortly after marriage she had turned to a man other than her husband and a baby had been born. Now twenty years later she was groveling in a sense of guilt and wondering how she could start anew. She was certain that God was going to make her pay the consequences by blighting her or her children. She was making life miserable for her husband and for the family. She was depriving them of the companionship of which she was capable. Her spiritual body was getting full of ulcers of anxiety and guilt and turmoil. Then a miracle happened. A wise pastoral counselor began by reinterpreting God to her. The get-even God she had been fearing was replaced by a start-anew Father who was wanting to help her sense forgiving and restoring power. She had not participated in the Lord's Supper for months. After pastoral consultation she renewed her covenant and started out once more with a sense of forgiveness and a new vision of God.

The book of Christian experience is crowded with stories of the lives of people who have found renewal. The book of Christian testimonies bulges with accounts of men and women and youth who got a new hold on life through coming to God repentantly and sensing his forgiving response. They tell how once they were sick with hatred and fright and how they rid themselves of these ulcers with God's help. The book of Christian theology tells of the repenting potential in man and of the forgiving quality in God.

A man told of his recovery from stomach ulcers. First, he honestly recognized that something was wrong and he sought help. He could not pretend; he could not cover up. He put aside diet that was causing distress and took a menu of softer and more "peaceful" foods. He relaxed under the discipline. He got hold of major factors that were causing him distress. Some of these were worries and tensions; some were apprehensions about competitors. He made a thorough reevaluation of his physical and his spiritual foods. And with all this he achieved a sound, realistic conception of God. The God of wrath and vengeance was replaced by a Father of understanding love. Not the indulgent God who would pamper him but a caring-for-him Parent who expected him to discipline his life and become thoroughly healthy. In time this man could say, "Now I am whole."

Basic Honesty

Healthiness always calls for honesty. There is no place for sham, for veneers. It involves the entire body, the entire mind, the entire self. It is as one youth said, "All of me with all of God." One of the most outstanding prayers I have ever heard was that of a rugged young man in the presence of four friends in a cabin on a lake. This is about what he said, "God, this morning there is no use trying to pretend anything. You know what kind of guy I am. Just now I feel that I am standing before you without any clothes on, just as naked as I can be. You see me just as I am. With your help I want to see myself as I can be." Here was the eloquence of humility and honesty.

A person always has to start from wherever he is. The prodigal son had to start from a pigpen. A man practiced in tangled business dealings had to begin by saying, "I'm crooked as a dog's hind leg." A woman wanting to start over said, "I am carrying ever so many jealousies and petty hatreds and I am just now recognizing them and admitting them." A good man starts from his own spiritual homeland.

God and his universe as he designs it are fundamentally honest. He requires a fair accounting of his debits and his credits, of his assets and his liabilities. It is not honest to list all our fears and disregard our confidences. It is not honest to enumerate all our weaknesses and omit the strengths any more than it is to glory in our achievements and deny our shortcomings.

There is no substitute for inclusive honesty in spiritual health. The honest person is going to see needs for rectification and renewal. He says to himself, to those worthy of trust, to God, "This is what I am, this is where I start."

Sinning Is Specific

In consideration of repentance we shall think of sin as alienation from God, apartness from God, dis-accord with God. In this sense we can think of ourselves as sinners. We all fall short of what we might be; we all have compartments of ourselves that are not responsive to God. Honesty requires us to see this. But this sinfulness is expressed in specific actions, in specific attitudes, in specific ways of thinking. The man who shortchanged another by five dollars, the woman who made a cutting remark about a neighbor, the youth who drove through a traffic light, the boy who "talked back" insolently to his mother, the oldster who sat nursing his complaints—all of these were sinning in specific ways. These situations could be rectified by applying general principles to specific shortcomings. Glossing over by general repentance will not take care of identifiable sins.

There is a not-infrequent idea that a kind of abstract forgiveness will cancel out abstract sinfulness. Then the person does not have to be bothered by concern with things done wrong, with things to be corrected. This is represented by the comment of the woman, "As long as God forgives me and assures me of glory, I do not have to be worried about patching things up with others." The honest man recognizes specific violations and wants to do what he can to rectify the situations. The truly repentant says forthrightly, "I did it."

Above Cataloguing

The truly repentant person looks to the condition of his own personhood. This transcends consulting catalogues of sins and of virtues. When this is done, the person thinks of going to a book to find out what is permitted and what is not permitted. He has little or no insight into what is taking place inside himself. The concern is with some list that God has designated or some list that a church body has drawn up. The legalistic catalogue indicates whether one may or may not do some specific thing. Such an approach misreads the nature and the concern of God. It also misreads what God is wanting to come to pass in the life of the person. God is looking to persons who choose with him rather than to legalists who dutifully honor his prescriptions.

To recognize specific sins does not mean that we are concerned with listing specifically forbidden and specifically permitted acts and thoughts. Rather do we express a universal quality in an identifiable situation. We endeavor to understand the motivations, the developments, the consequences in a person, in a group through what is done in a specific situation. When a man misrepresents material in making a sale to his financial advantage, something happens in him that has eternal effect upon his character. When a young man takes advantage of a young woman in sexual relations with or without her consenting, something happens in him that expresses a surrender, a self-centeredness that weakens the fiber of his personhood.

Not infrequently persons say something like this: "I would like to have a list of all the things that are wrong and all the things that are right so that I would know what I should do." These persons picture God as directing his people by setting down a collection of do's and don't's with suitable rewards for the do's and suitable penalties for the don't's. This does not get at the heart of spiritual development; it does not sense what God is wanting to take place in persons. It does not appreciate the true nature of repentance and forgiveness. These have to do with the "set of the soul" more than with "a set of stipulated orders."

Repentance Is Constructive

Repentance is constructive change within the person. Isaiah's classic call to repentance pointedly sets this forth. His opening chapter invites his countrymen to turn from externals which will do them no good to internal contrition. He makes a devastating indictment of what they have been doing. When he says, "Make yourselves clean," he is not thinking of ceremonial washings. He indicates the necessity of clearing away the wrong to make room for the right. This is his succinct wording, "Cease to do evil; learn to do well." The word "learn" is significant. There was to be nothing instantaneous, nothing automatic about this repenting. The way of the good life was to be learned. It was to be a life of effective self-management. It is no accident that the words disciple and discipline come from the same root. Isaiah was saying that repentance is more than quitting something. The good life is never a vacuum. The good replaces the not-so-good.

Repentance Has Social Implications

Repentance calls for understanding, according to Isaiah. He represents God as inviting, "Come now, and let us reason together." God is really saying, Let us understand one another, let us have common consent. He points up specific things for the contrite person to do. These have to do with relationship to others. Here is a quartet of directives: Seek justice, correct oppression, defend the fatherless, plead for the widow. Right relations with God involve right relations with all our fellowmen. Isaiah would be saying that a man cannot live in right relations with a God of love and righteousness if he treats his fellowmen with contempt, if he looks upon them with anger or revenge, if he deals with them in greed and dishonesty.

Forgiveness, a Relation between Persons

When we forgive we lay aside resentment and put aside dividing factors that keep us apart from others. There is restoration of lost brotherhood. Bitterness is gone. The two who formerly have been at odds now walk along understandingly together. This is expressed in the coming together of two elders of the church who had been at each other's throats. They had been uncomplimentary of each other in public. They had rationalized their actions by saying, "It is not a personal grievance, it is a matter of principle." When they became sufficiently honest to diagnose the

154

situation they recognized (1) that there was intense personal dislike and some jealousy, (2) that both were suffering from their hostile attitudes, (3) that their attitudes and conduct were hurting the life of their congregation, and (4) that their feelings, their comments, their actions were detrimental to their spiritual condition. Both began to see that they were unhealthy. One day they came together in a quiet place where they were alone. Their first comments were, "Something is wrong: let's see what it is." Neither covered up feelings and actions. Then two admissions followed, "I am sorry," and "Let's work together."

Not Remission of Consequences

Forgiveness is a restoration of relationship. It is not a remission of consequences. So often we tend to think that if we seek forgiveness and are forgiven, all undesirable consequences are blotted out. Not so. Restoration of good relationships should help us operate to alleviate undesirable consequences and to change the situation so that better things can replace the damaging ones. But there is no automatic blotting out of consequences. A young man who had been rather loose in his relationships with women married a young woman of unquestioned chastity. Through him she became plagued with disease. At first she was going to leave him as she resented what he had done. In time they came together with forgiveness and with resolution to try a fresh start. A new, well-foundationed love blended them together. With competent medical service health was restored and children came to their union. Her forgiveness did not blot out the physical consequences, but it opened the way to meet the situation together. Once when I was a lad, my mother left me to burn a smudge under a plum tree to kill infesting insects. I wanted a big blaze, so threw on inflammable material. The tree died. My mother was disappointed in me. She had trusted me. I said I was sorry. She forgave as an understanding mother would, but the tree did not come alive.

Early Emphasis on Repentance

The first preachments of the young Restoration movement focused on repentance. The first counsel, now in the Doctrine and Coventants (Section 2) was a direct message to the young prophet. He was told specifically that he would have to repent. This was in July 1828. He had been unwise in turning over 116 pages of manuscript for the Book of Mormon to Martin Harris.

The copy had been lost. The gift of translation had been lost. The sense of oneness with God had been lost. Joseph Smith was downcast and discouraged. The counsel was direct, "Repent of that which thou hast done" (2:4 b). The manuscript was never restored. God's forgiveness did not remove the consequences of Joseph's unwise procedure. In the restored relationship God could advise the young prophet how to proceed and meet the difficulty. The young prophet had to learn discipline through repentance before he was qualified to translate and to lay the foundations for organizing the Church of Jesus Christ.

This getting right with God was so important that the pioneers were told, "Say nothing but repentance unto this generation" (D. and C. 10:4 b). The counsel given here to Hyrum Smith is identical with what was said to Oliver Cowdery a month before (D. and C. 6:4 b). This relationship with God was basic for participation in the new movement.

Repentance in Specific Fields

In June 1831 at Kirtland some definite problems were recognized in life among a group of members. Some from Colesville, New York, had moved to Ohio and had endeavored to effect a settlement at Thompson. It was pointed out that certain of the elders could not go out and preach repentance to others until they righted some situations in the group life. One man was told that he would have to "repent of his pride, and of his selfishness" (D. and C. 56:3 a). Members of the entire group were directed to do some thorough repenting if they were going to continue in the movement.

"Behold, thus saith the Lord . . . You have many things to do, and to repent of; for, behold, your sins have come up unto me, and are not pardoned, because you seek to counsel in your own ways. And your hearts are not satisfied. And you obey not the truth, but have pleasure in unrighteousness."
—Doctrine and Covenants 56:4.

This unusual direction warned both the rich and the poor. The first group was told that their love for riches would canker their souls. The second group was denounced for their greediness and idleness. Apparently some preferred to take from others than to work on their own. It was not the possession of wealth or the lack of it that made the difference. It was the attitude toward wealth and toward others that spelled out the difference.

The sins denounced were recognizable. They needed correction and they called for forgiveness. These persons had been sinning concretely.

A Fellowship of the Forgiving and Forgiven

The church is a society of those who are trying together to get right and to keep right with God and therefore with one another. It is a laboratory in learning how to live "together with God." It invites others to join in this way of repenting and forgiving. Those who come in indicate their intention to stop sinning and to change radically their way of living. Such a society can be and is intended to be a resource for healthy living. It declares the health-giving gospel that men can forgive and be forgiven, that men can repent and be restored. In this sense we may think of the church as a clinic in which needing members confer and consult and cooperate in getting rid of health-defeating forces and in building up health-giving forces and fruits.

In a testimonial meeting a young man stood and related frankly the kind of life he had been leading. It sounded as if he had tried about everything that would take him away from straight-going, health-producing living. He asked for these basic things: (1) to be understood, (2) to be forgiven, (3) to be helped as a brother, and (4) to be remembered to God. Here he caught the functional benefits of repentance and forgiveness. Three things happened: (1) he felt relieved and honest, (2) he was assured by understanding brothers and sisters that they would stand by him, and (3) he was reminded through prophetic ministry that his Father was waiting for him, was wanting him, and would receive and help him. That meeting, with what followed, became a clinic in spiritual health.

New Strength Within

After a man had come out of the hospital where he had been treated for gastronomical ailments, he was asked how he felt. "Relieved," was his reply. He amplified this by saying that he had ceased his worrying, that he was relieved from pain, that he knew where to go for help, and that he felt he could be worth something now. He said pretty well what happens when a spiritually sick person turns from his unhealthy way of living, turns to a wholesome way with source of help, and starts anew. Confession, contrition, and consecration can give a fresh hold on life. There is no substitute for it. When assured of forgiveness and of God's help a wanderer testified, "I feel like a new man." This is what Paul said should happen when a person comes to know the forgiving, reconciling Christ. Phillips puts it this way, "If a man is in Christ he becomes a new person altogether—the past is finished and gone, everything has become fresh and new" (II Corinthians 5:17).

Questions for Discussion

1. Under what conditions are repentance and forgiveness a means for furthering spiritual health?
2. Under what conditions and what interpretations may repentance and forgiveness block the furthering of spiritual health?
3. What conception of repenting and forgiving should a congregation have if it is going to be a clinical laboratory in furthering spiritual health?
4. How would you counsel the woman described in Gross's *God and Freud* who had been involved in adultery with several men and who said that she was not worried that she had sinned against God, for he would forgive her, but she was concerned about how her friends would disapprove?
5. What kinds of unhealthy attitudes and thoughts and actions can undermine spiritual health and physical health? How do they undermine?
6. How may the sacrament of the Lord's Supper be a means of restoring a person through experience of repentance and forgiveness?
7. Apply to present-day living what Isaiah had in mind by "learning to do good." Illustrate how patterns of feeling and thinking and doing have to be built up.
8. How may we interpret God as indulgent in patterns of his forgiving so that we do not build strength in our spiritual health?
9. How would you interpret God's nature to persons or a group who think of him as getting miffed, as being jealous, as taking out his dislikes on persons?
10. How do you see as important the fact that repentance was stressed so much in the early days of the Restoration movement?
11. How may a Zionic community and a Zionic congregation function helpfully, healthfully in life situations that involve forgiveness and repentance?

12. What kind of God, what kind of gospel, and what kind of church would there be if there were no functioning of repenting and forgiving in them?
13. When soundly interpreted and practiced how are repenting and forgiving and being forgiven essential in a gospel of spiritual health?

CHAPTER 14

IMMERSION WITH
INVOLVEMENT

A radio program used the catching phrase, "All or nothing!" At this place in the script of questions the contestant had to risk everything on the forthcoming question. The Christian gospel is ever posing the same question. There is no place for the "hyphenated Christian." Jesus put it bluntly: "No man can serve two masters; . . . you cannot serve God and Mammon." The youth of sixteen put it this way at the time of his baptism, "When I get baptized, I am going in this all over." The voice of God is always reminding us, "All or nothing."

We express this getting in all over when we are immersed. The rite of immersion baptism is an eloquent expression of complete involvement. The total person in the total body gets in "all over." This was expressed by the ten-year-old boy who kept his coin purse in the pocket of his trousers when he was baptized. When his mother chided him for being so forgetful, he said he planned it that way. Said he, "I wanted my money to get in, too." In inclusive immersion there can be no segment of our personhoods, our possessions, our program of living left out. A man who caught this symbolism said, "Every bit of me gets in the water and every bit of me is to get in God's work."

The Power in Oneness

When John Bunyan pictured the character in *Pilgrim's Progress* moving toward the Celestial City, he had him meeting several persons who would never arrive there or who would arrive at a belated time. One of these was Mr. Facing Both Ways. Such a man would never be sure about which way he was going. He could never get clearly in mind that he was going in one direction. In today's parlance, we keep meeting another wobbling traveler, "Mr. Chronic Indecision." He cannot make up his mind. He keeps picking up old problems that he should have resolved and dismissed and going over them once more and then twice more. This is the kind of man that James had in mind when he wrote, "A double-minded man is unstable in all his ways" (1:8). He keeps trying to straddle the fence. Sometimes in religion this type of person is referred to as "spiritually schizophrenic."

The genuine Christian is not fighting civil wars within himself. He is not going over and over the same matters. He "hangs together." He has a unity that stems from his unifying allegiance to Jesus Christ. Every bit of him is focused in this unifying Person. All parts of him are dovetailed together in harmony. There is a oneness in him that evidences inner harmony, unifying purpose, and effective operation. He does not wear himself out or waste his energies on inner conflicts. A spiritually healthy person achieves oneness and he senses the power that comes with this oneness.

The New Power in Paul

When Paul of Tarsus first appeared in the book of Acts he was a confused man. We can see how his inner nature was calling for something bigger and nobler than his inherited Jewish religion. Yet his background was calling for loyalty to his inherited faith. In this confusion and inner turmoil he must lash out at something. Persons with inner insecurity and conflict tend to seek a target on which to vent their unhappy feelings. Paul found this target in the disciples of Jesus of Nazareth. To him they were dangerous and apostate. He lashed out against them with all his fiery vigor. He sought to discover them and bring them back to Jerusalem for trial. (His inner war reminds us to look for the source of a man's distress when he strikes out at targets; he may be seeking to relieve his own battlings.)

Then one day on the road to Damascus, Paul met the Christ. Paul's physical blindness typified the darkness in his own soul. He was led to Ananias, an elder in Damascus. His sight was restored. This was recorded of him, "He received sight . . . arose . . . and was baptized" (Acts 9:18). Then this happened, "He was strengthened . . . he preached Christ . . . increased . . . in strength" (Acts 9:19, 20, 22). The divided Paul became the unified Paul and the strong Paul. Later he wrote to the Philippian congregation concerning his own spiritual oneness, "This one thing I do" (3:13). He likened himself to a runner who was going straight ahead down the straightaway to the goal. There was no uncertainty about his destination and his getting into action.

Our Basic Need for Oneness

A man of the modern world appeared worried and ineffective. When asked what he thought his trouble was, he replied, "I feel all split up." He felt so divided inside himself that, as he said, he could not "get going." And this often applies to our social world as well as to ourselves. Sometimes it applies to a family. It can apply to a church. A society can be split into fragmentary and conflicting individuals and groups. A person can be this way, too. Sometimes we say that ours is a crazy world; sometimes we say this of ourselves. In the literal meaning of the word crazy, this is just what is happening. The word "crazy" comes from the French *écrasé* which means broken and shattered. When we as persons are pulled into fragments, when our society is broken into bits, we can say we are crazy. Then the disruptive forces assume the ascendency and prevent oneness, community.

Each person, each group has to have oneness if he or it is going to endure. Jesus phrased it this way, "If a house be divided against itself, that house cannot stand" (Mark 3:19). Lincoln borrowed this phrase in his famous "House Divided" speech in his debate with Stephen Douglas in 1856 and used it so definitely that many have thought of him as being the originator of this saying. Lincoln was saying that it would be impossible for the nation to endure half slave and half free. We have been seeing quite clearly during recent years that the psychic house totters and falls when it is split. We are seeing what Jesus was saying— that each of us needs a unified personality that makes for stability, for spiritual wholeness, for general good health.

The hymn popular a few decades ago, considered the favorite hymn of Chiang Kai-shek, begins with this testimonial, "O happy day that fixed my choice on thee, my Savior and my God." This points up how the divided self, with conflicting desires and unresolved strains, can be brought together with consequent happiness as every facet of a personhood becomes integrated in loyalty to the Christ.

Getting into Something

A youth at college was asked, "How are you getting along?" He diagnosed himself as outside the flow of life of the campus with this reply, "I'm not in anything; I'm outside of everything." This youth was lonely and apart. He felt that he should be living in the community but he did not know how to become a part of it. Every person needs a sense of belonging, the experience of community.

But merely "getting into something" is not enough. Often persons go about in feverish haste and motion when they feel

162

little or no sense of importance in anything that they are doing. When life has little meaning and when persons have a sense of futility in their living they often buzz around hither and yon with emphasis on being busy and on being in motion. Such persons are likely to mistake motion for meaning and speed for significance. One woman, enrolled in clubs and societies with membership on many committees and with appointment to many projects, confessed, "I have to keep going, for if I stop I get bored with myself and anxious about myself and my life." So the phrase should read, "Getting into something significant."

One man addled with living said, "I have no trouble keeping busy, but I have trouble in being busy in something that is worth my time and effort." The wise person wants something that has returns in living, something that is expandable, something that will make a better person of him, something that will enrich all who share in it and make it come true. A young man in the navy used his artistic skills to make a target. One practice and it was blown to bits. After a time or two of this experience, he concluded that he was not going to devote his skills to making something attractive as a target only to have it blown to pieces. We want to give ourselves to something enduring, something that will grow under our hands, something in which we shall grow.

Jesus Invited Men to Join Him

Jesus carried on a program of enlistment, involvement, immersion. Every person who would respond grew in this sharing with him. To those who would respond he gave "power to become the sons of God" (John 1:12). This power was realized as these men took hold with Jesus Christ and gave themselves completely to ministry with him. So many persons want a rich endowment to have on hand especially for emergencies. Some day it might be useful, might be needed. Jesus promised empowerment as his disciples moved out with him and went to work with him. They grew strong in the laboratory of ministering. There was no supply for the inactive to keep in storage.

Jesus' promises were always conditioned by how effectively and completely his disciples got involved in his work. He summoned Andrew and Peter and admonished them, "Come ye after me, and I will make you to become fishers of men" (Mark 1:15). Jesus always called his followers to become involved in his cause and immersed in his life-giving power. This is the way he works today.

Above Empty Living

Carl Gustav Jung, the late Swiss psychiatrist, said that the central neurosis of our time is emptiness. He is saying that many a modern, if he takes time to ask anything at all, is inclined to ask, "What's the good of it?" We see so many scurrying and scrambling along for material prosperity, for staying in motion, for putting up a front. Inside they find little of enduring purpose. So pessimism, confusion, uncertainty, cynicism flourish. The line is drawn between hollowness as one lives to himself and holiness as one lives with God. The "hollow men" realize a personal emptiness as they become separated from the Source of meaning and spiritual might.

We come to appreciate that God does not fill us with spiritual empowerment as we might fill a storehouse with grain in readiness for the day when we shall open the door and let bushels of grain flow out. We are not supply tanks or storage bins. We are persons, and persons can retain only through using and can get only through giving out. The gospel keeps reminding us that the person who looks to himself, who lives to himself, will eventually shrivel in himself and die in himself. Jesus kept teaching his disciples that those who drew on his supplies and gave out to others would never be empty in their living.

All-over Baptism

In the early days of the Christian movement baptism expressed the union of the believer with Christ. When Paul wrote to the Corinthian congregation he assumed that everyone in the church had been baptized and thus had become united in the body of Christ (I Corinthians 1:13). There was no question as to whether the believer should be baptized. The question had to do with meaning and function. It appears that immersion was considered the method employed. In *Encyclopaedia of Religion,* edited by Virgilius Ferm, in the article on "Baptism," Dr. Shirley Jackson Case observes, "At first immersion was the common practice but as the movement spread to territory where the needed water was not available it was deemed sufficient to pour water on the head or moisten it with the finger tips."

This getting in all over was compared to burial. Paul wrote to the Roman saints, "We are buried with him by baptism into death" (6:4). The "old man," the "sinful man" was to be buried and the candidate was to come forth as in resurrection to "walk in newness of life." In II Corinthians 5:17 Paul wrote that when a person affiliated with Jesus Christ and sensed his life-giving power, he became a "new creation" with all things becoming new. Such a person was "reconciled" to God; he would be at one with God. New power would come into his life. Every bit of his personhood would be involved in this new way of living.

A young man contemplating affiliation with the Church of Jesus Christ asked, "How would I be baptized?" He was not wanting some easy rite, some conventional procedure. He was wanting to know what would be the sound way for coming into the church. The answer was a simple one, "When you make your covenant to live with Jesus Christ, when you link yourself with fellow disciples in the church, every bit of you is to come in and be involved. The whole you comes in. Immersion is the form of baptism that expresses this. Every particle of your body is immersed in water and every fiber of your being is to be immersed in the work of God. When every spiritual cell and every spiritual process of your person is immersed in God's work, his life-giving power will come to you. Literally you will have new life. We expect you to get in all over. Jesus Christ invites you to get in all over. In this light how would you expect to be baptized?" His reply was immediate, "I want to get every bit of my body in the physical water and every bit of me in the spiritual water." And it was so. Persons who see baptism as complete involvement do not seek some easy, convenient rite. They want to get in all over.

There Can Be Narrow Involvement

It is not enough to say, "I lose myself in God." We can have such a narrow and confined picture of God that this picture does injustice to God and damage to us. Sometimes it is as if we were trying to get baptized in a tank or font that is too small. We cannot stretch in the cramped quarters. We have to curl up and stay folded up. A few years ago J. B. Phillips wrote a brief book with an arresting title, *Your God Is Too Small*. He reminded us that many persons were pushing out in their mental horizons, in their scientific explorations, in their social contacts while their ideas of God were remaining largely static. Often these sincere persons are defending an outgrown conception of God, a childhood conception not adequate for maturing adults. Dr. Phillips was not saying that God is too small but that the conceptions of God that many of us are using and often defending are too small and inadequate.

165

The person who is going to invest every bit of himself in the work of God is going to require that this work is big enough, enduring enough, challenging enough to warrant his commitment. The truly devoted believer cannot have lurking suspicions that Christ and his cause are too insignificant for him. He cannot fear lest some new discovery will show up the juvenility and partiality of his faith. He cannot hold back some part of his equipment because the God of his commitment is seen as too limited to include every bit of him. Rather must he see the call to keep on growing in his conception of God, in his appreciation of God, in his commitment to God. As J. B. Phillips suggested, we shall go beyond looking at God through a pinhole and getting a pinhole conception of him; we shall remove the shutters we have put up and let the Light shine in.

We are not to be baptized in the little conceptions that hinder our sensing the fullness of God. We are to be immersed in the work of God whom we vision only in part but whom we expect to appreciate more and more. This does not mean that we shall consider God so big that we shall have only a fuzzy picture and a faraway loyalty. We shall see the eternality and the universality of God in every manifestation of him. We shall sense his nearness while we are aware of his greatness. We can find this kind of revelation of God in the life and person of Jesus Christ.

Applied Involvement in the Restoration Movement

The Restoration movement reaffirmed this way of baptism and empowerment. The initial experience of Joseph Smith in the grove in 1820 was an enlistment. The youth had come to God with a simple question that he thought could be answered by *yes* or *no* or by a word that would tell him which church he ought to join. There would have been little edification in such answering. There came the impression of *light* which would symbolize insight and understanding and freedom. Out of this came the vision of God and the directive, "This is my beloved Son: hear him!" Here was the pointing toward the Son as the Source of continuing enlightenment. He was told that expanding understanding would come to him, that he should learn "the fullness of the gospel." He experienced a sense of commission: there was something for him to do. Years afterward, he wrote of this experience, "I was informed that I was chosen to be an instrument in the hands of God to bring about some of his purposes in this glorious dispensation." There was more for him to see. There was more for him to do. There was more for him to become.

As Joseph Smith began to carry out this assignment, he kept growing in his conception of what the job was, what his ministry was to be. In the summer of 1829 he was busily engaged in translating the Book of Mormon and in laying the foundation for the effecting of the organization of the church. Over and over this counsel came to him, "A great and marvelous work is about to come forth!" What he would be participating in was to be wonderful: it would call for the fullness of his own powers quickened by the Spirit of God. Here was no dwarf-sized enterprise, no tempest-in-a-teapot endeavor. God was going to be at work in a "big way." Such an undertaking would call for men to give themselves with big devotion. So would they be able to become big, entirely adequate for their assignment.

And there was not going to be any hurry-up, automatic coming to pass of this "marvelous work." Men were going to be working at it, with God. The pioneers were told to "seek to bring forth and establish the cause of Zion" (D. and C. 10:3). The Spirit would lead "to do good," would "enlighten" their minds, would fill their souls with joy (D. and C. 10:6, 7). Those who joined with God would be empowered to do their work as they gave themselves wholeheartedly to God.

When It Was Time for Baptism

Joseph Smith, Jr., experienced his initial vision of God and God's salutation to him in the spring of 1820. It was in May 1829 when he and Oliver Cowdery were baptized. Much had happened in the life of Joseph Smith during these nine years. In early April of 1829 Oliver Cowdery had come to Joseph Smith and offered his service as scribe for the translation of the Book of Mormon. The two men were studying and searching together. They were learning about the process of revelation (see Doctrine and Covenants, Section 9). They had come to wonder about baptism and had been searching for understanding about it. They were concerned about ministerial authority. Then one day in the woods near Harmony, Pennsylvania, where Joseph was then living, they were called to the Aaronic priesthood and this priesthood was conferred. Joseph Smith gave this terse account of what happened (*Church History*, Vol. 1, page 36).

"Accordingly we went and were baptized, I baptized him first, and afterwards he baptized me, after which I laid

167

my hands upon his head and ordained him to the Aaronic priesthood, and afterwards he laid his hands on me and ordained me to the same priesthood, for so we were commanded. . . .

"Immediately upon our coming up out of the water, after we had been baptized, we experienced great and glorious blessings from our heavenly Father. . . .

"Our minds being now enlightened, we began to have the Scriptures laid open to our understandings . . . in a manner which we never could attain to previously, nor ever before had thought of."

Joseph Smith continued his account by telling how his brother Samuel H. Smith came to visit him after a few days. The two men showed the newcomer what they had translated in the Book of Mormon to date; they told him of their larger understanding of the scriptures; they testified about what had happened in their own lives so recently. Joseph Smith wrote this significant comment, "He was not, however, very easily persuaded of these things, but after much inquiry and explanation, he retired to the woods, in order that by secret and fervent prayer he might obtain of a merciful God, wisdom to enable him to judge for himself." In time, he too was baptized by Oliver Cowdery. He went home a happy, thankful, and dedicated believer.

These three men took time to get their bearings, to build some foundation. They were not baptized until they had a working idea of what was involved in their choosing. They did not make a covenant with God until they had some understanding about what they were promising to do, about what God would be expecting of them, about what spiritual empowerment God would afford them. After the baptism these three men had a sense of commission, a feeling of divine support. They had endeavored to make ready for baptism and baptism was to help them make ready for their assignment in initiating the Church of Jesus Christ.

Into the Health-producing Process

The immersed person has all of him going in one direction with one purpose. He is going with God in God's work. There is a sense of wholeness in him. There is point to his living. He is steadfast and steady. He moves with God. One translator made the sixth beatitude read, "Blessed are they who are not double-minded, for they shall be admitted into the intimate presence of God." There is power in this single-minded, ongoing approach to life.

The immersed person exposes all of his personhood, all of his body to the life-producing forces of God. One youth said his religious life compared to the fellow who lay out in the sun to get "sunshine vitamins" but covered up everything but his feet and hands so he would not get sunburned. Sometimes this is about as much of ourselves as we expose to the light and warmth of God. A growing tree has all of its limbs and branches and leaves open to the sun. We can think of ourselves as intended to be totally exposed to the life-giving and light-affording rays of God's Spirit. Perhaps if we had a picture of ourselves in relation to God's empowering resources we might appear to have canvas covers over much of our selves, thereby shutting off much of our bodies, our spirits from what God intends us to have.

The immersed person looks to the fullness of God's available power. He means for *all* of him to be open to *all* of God. Sometimes we build up conceptions of God that shut off much of him; sometimes we set down formulas about the way God works with us that do not permit some of his processes to work in us. Often we are inclined to draw up finished ideas about how God makes his power available to us. Sometimes we dictate how God is to work within us. We vision a cellar with one small opening through which light can come. On the floor is a potato. A thin, struggling sprout is reaching toward the sun. Here could have been a healthy, growing potato if the walls shutting out the light had been torn away and the potato buried in life-producing soil. The truly immersed man who is baptized in all of God's edifying, enlivening power is totally connected with God without putting strings and stipulations on the way God is going to nurture him.

In the Name Of

The Great Commission (Matthew 28:18) directs the apostles to go teach all nations and to baptize them "in the name of." More recent versions make this read, "Go and make disciples of all nations and baptize them in the name of . . ." The great purpose was to develop discipleship in persons. Something good was to take place in persons. Sometimes this passage is stressed as if the main thing is to get persons baptized and to have this happen "in the name of . . ." Sometimes this is interpreted as if the repeating of the "name" would act as a magical charm to assure salvation. Such persons would consider the baptismal rite ineffective if the "name" were not mentioned specifically.

The word "name" expresses rich meaning. It expresses the idea of the personal nature and the personal response of those mentioned. It would help us to think of being immersed in the personal power and influence "of the Father and of the Son and of the Holy Spirit." The baptizing puts the candidate into personal relations that have life-transforming effect. He comes into direct relationship with God personally. As he is immersed his whole being thrills with the vibrant personal power of God. Henceforth he is involved in the mission of God to all men. He goes on to involve others and to see them immersed too.

Questions for Discussion

1. How is it not possible for a Christian to be "hyphenated"? Give illustrations of persons who are living in what might be called "hyphenation."

2. In what is a person immersed when he is spiritually immersed? What are identifying expressions of this spiritual immersion?

3. How does immersion achieve spiritual oneness? How does this spiritual oneness express spiritual health?

4. What ineffectiveness and unhealthiness occur in a person when he is divided within himself?

5. What was the nature of the spiritual oneness that developed within Paul? How was Jesus Christ the focus of his oneness?

6. How does oneness need to have an enduring, expanding quality? How may a person focus all his powers for a time on some inadequate center of loyalty only to find this running out and unsatisfying?

7. How are immersion and involvement inseparably associated? How is true immersion more than an act of a moment? How is it a continuing process?

8. How can immersion and involvement in the work of God enable a person to rise above spiritual emptiness? When may a person be said to be empty?

9. Interpret how baptism means the immersion of the total self in the totality of God. How may a person leave out some part of him when he is baptized? How may he shut out exposure to the fullness of God?

10. How was it necessary for Joseph Smith to go through growing and "readying" experiences before he was ready for the rite

of baptism? To what degree ought a person realize into what he is being baptized?

11. What happens in the spiritual health of a person if he is understandingly, fittingly, and completely baptized?

12. How may a person be immersed in the purpose and genius of another person? How does this happen when one is baptized in "the name of" Jesus Christ?

CHAPTER 15

DIVERSE MINISTRIES
IN THE CHURCH

The Church of Jesus Christ is a service agency. Basically an agency is an institution that chooses to carry on some function. Literally it uses its "agency" to decide what it is going to do, why it is going to do it, how it is going to do it, who is going to do it, and for whom this is to be done. It takes pretty good insight for a group to consider itself an agency. A very-much-alive agency keeps checking up on what it is doing. It is so easy, so tempting to start out with a purpose and plan and have this deteriorate after a while. The purpose and spirit may be lost as the so-called agency gets involved in maintaining itself, in keeping up its institutional requirements. This can happen in the church. After a time a church can become chiefly concerned in balancing its budget, maintaining good public relations, having complimentary publicity and the like until it loses sight of the purpose for which it came to be. The church must keep saying, "We are a service agency."

The major purpose of the church is to produce persons of eternal quality. The kind of person matters very much. The church is never a mass-production agency with the basic concern of enlisting names on its books. It is concerned with the quality of persons. Jesus always looked to having something good happen in the persons who came his way. He lived with them so that this could take place. If he had been merely concerned with numbers he could have had these by turning stones into bread and offering free lunch counter service or by providing miraculous healings that did not require any character change in the lives of those healed. He never stooped to this level. He lived with men that they might have "abundant life."

A Health-producing Agency

Jesus himself "increased in wisdom and stature" and he developed in relations "with God and man" (Luke 2:52). He took plenty of time: he did not begin his ministry until he was thirty. We shall presume that this is the way he wants all persons to develop in physical and spiritual healthiness. Many times he came across persons who were crippled in body or in mind. Circumstances had combined to make them invalids or incompetents. Sometimes he would bring to pass a fairly all-at-once healing. He would focus healing help upon the needy one. Then he intended this person to live healthfully with himself, with others, with God.

The church is intended to be a health-producing function in the life of persons. (1) It holds to the fore the image of the truly healthy person. (2) It interprets God as health-producing, as altogether healthy. (3) It makes possible association with healthy persons. (4) It enlists persons in health-producing activities. (5) It includes every phase of a person in its health program. (6) It provides ministers and ministries that service in achieving good health. (7) It enables the person to increase his qualification for utilizing the health resources that God provides.

The church is a producing enterprise. Its product: spiritually healthy persons. Its first emphasis is not on selling something, on displaying something. Nor is it a free charity dispensing institution. Its major concern is to help a person become a somebody, a somebody after God's design. Such a somebody is not going to run down at half-past time, is not going to go to pieces without any reason to keep on living, is not going to decline into ill health, is not going to collapse in social mire. Rather is this person going to achieve spiritual healthiness as he lives in the church as a participating member. Rightly functioning, the church is going to be servicing members and contributing to their continuing, expanding spiritual good health.

No All-perfect Agency

The church is never a finished product. It is an on-the-way process. It is made up of members who are growing up together. It is a laboratory school in developing saintly qualities. It is not an exhibition of persons who have already achieved celestial character. Some are further along in the growing stage than others. Some lag behind and some resist growing up. Some still live to themselves and want the world to revolve around them. They have not learned to focus on Jesus Christ and draw inspiration from him. Sometimes the company of devoted Saints does not know whether to put these careless and self-centered members out of the group or to retain them. Often they keep them in the hope that continuing association will encourage them to respond to God and live his way. Paul addressed the disciples at Rome as those "called to be saints" (1:7, K.J.). They were on the way in saintly living.

It is good for members and nonmembers to see the church as a society of those who are learning together and supporting one another in the business of producing persons of saintly character. This means that we shall measure and estimate a man in accordance with the gain that he has made rather than in terms of some stated and fixed standard. The humble man spoke well when he said, "I'm not yet so much in terms of where I am, but you ought to remember from where I have been coming." Jesus must have used this type of evaluation when he lived with Peter and Simon the Zealot and when he taught a woman such as Mary Magdalene.

Ministers Are to Minister

Jesus came to earth to live among humans that they might come to appreciate what God is like and how he cares for man. He came to draw men into right relationship with God through living with them and loving them. He could not be everywhere so he sent out other men to represent him, to witness for him. He chose them and commissioned them to go out to others. They were to minister in his spirit. First he sent out twelve men who were to be his special witnesses. Then he sent out seventy more men, and then still seventy more. When he sent the twelve out on their assignment he said, "Go to the lost sheep . . . heal the sick . . . freely give . . . fear not" (Matthew 10:5 ff.). These men were to minister to needing persons.

Ministering is always the reason for ordaining men to the ministry. There is no other reason. Sometimes we become confused and get away from this main purpose. It is so easy to think of the work of the ordained man as preaching, as baptizing, as conducting meetings, as making out reports, and the like. It is not unknown to look upon ordination with respect to its position, its honor, and to regard some ordinations as achievements. It is sound to think of ministers as shepherds who are to lead the sheep and feed them and shelter them.

A man had been a deacon for fifteen years. He had done what he had been assigned to do with more-than-usual effectiveness and reliability. Then something happened in him. He came to see that a minister was to be concerned with what was taking place in persons, that a minister is acting in the stead of the Christ as he serves his fellow-members, his congregation, his friends outside the church. He was honest enough to say, "I need to be ordained a second time. In many ways this would be my first ordination. Now I see what it is for. I have been receiving the offering; I have been ushering the attenders to their seats; I have been directing the parking of cars; I have been making out reports; I have been calling on families to get their pledges for financial support. But it has been busywork. I have not been a minister in the sense that I have cared for persons and have wanted to help them achieve spiritually. Now I see what it means to minister." This man at a belated time was discovering for the first time that ministers are to minister.

The Reaffirmation of Call to Minister

The Restoration stressed what had been emphasized about priesthood in the early Christian movement. These were basics: (1) The man who is going to minister for Jesus Christ needs to be designated by Jesus Christ, needs to know this Jesus Christ if he is going to be working with and for this ever living Christ. (2) The man who is going to minister for Jesus Christ is to be enlivened and enlightened by the Spirit of God, which Spirit will guide and strengthen in diverse manifestations. (3) The man who is going to minister for Jesus Christ is going to care for persons as persons, with understanding love. (4) The man who is going to minister for Jesus Christ is going to co-labor with fellow workers in the Church of Jesus Christ in ministering to others. (5) There are diversities of callings and ministries in the total company of ordained men, with ministers specializing according to their own natures and capacities, the needs of persons, and the needs of the church.

The Latter Day Saint movement affirmed the present-tense divine calling and the present-tense divine endowment in ministry. It also stressed the essential requirement for personal integrity in those who minister and the caring for those to whom they minister. There is no substitute for saintly character and brotherly caring. Nothing can take the place of conviction of being commissioned by Jesus Christ to live with his people as a ministering associate. Without this a man merely does chores, goes through routines, poses as a salesman, or fills a job position.

Specializations of Functions

One of the great resources in the Church of Jesus Christ for developing healthy persons is the variety in assignments and

175

functions. A man is not called to minister in a general kind of way. He is called to minister in specific callings. In 1887 the church was reminded again, "All are called according to the gifts of God unto them" (D. and C. 119:8). The possible diversity within a single office of ministry was expressed in the calling of two apostles to be evangelists in 1958. One would incline to one expression, one to another. This wide range affords to persons helps and ministries suited to specific needs and situations. It also enables a person to receive a wide expanse of ministries, thereby permitting and promoting development of his total personhood and affording expression in many fields of development and participation.

This specialization of function holds possibilities for many ministries to many persons in many fields. There is need for adequate portrayal of the structure and operation of the church with respect to its priesthood. What are these several callings? How do these several callings function in the nurture of persons, in the mission of the church? How does God work through these several ministries? A casual study reveals that here is a potential richness that is little understood by members. We find that moderns are wanting to know how these offices function and what their contributions are to be. Much of the time in the past we have stressed scriptural quotations that would "prove" that there should be certain officers in the church and that if we had them all we would be the "right" church. Today moderns are asking what they are for. One man put the matter this way, "If there are to be apostles, there must be a good reason for having them."

Right and Responsibility

In the church, administrators must be concerned with operational procedures. A body such as the church has to operate in an orderly, mutually sustaining manner. A body has to have a framework and its organs have to function together. But all this functioning in administrative and operational matters is secondary. They are the means for enabling the main mission of the church to be carried out. When the church's chief concern is with maintaining the framework rather than with realizing its major purpose it is in an unhealthy condition. Sometimes we act and talk as if our main concern is to see that the several offices and officers get along peacefully and effectively together. This is a sad day for the church.

In 1835 the young church was trying to see its way ahead

176

in administrative affairs. There was a scarcity in background. Strains and uncertainties had developed. Then came Section 104 of the Doctrine and Covenants. The phrase "right to officiate" appears. There is mention of "the power and authority" of the two priesthoods. There is emphasis on the number of men to be in certain quorums and the way these quorums were to operate. The stranger to the church might think that our main concern was with protocol and prerogatives, offices and official relations. It appears at first glance, as one man has said, to be a document on "quorums and quarrels." The closing paragraphs get at the real intent of ministry. All this administrative operation is to make possible the ministering of men in the fields of their specialization.

"Wherefore, now let every man learn his duty,
and to act in the office in which he is appointed, in all diligence."

Later on, in 1894 when strains had developed in matters ecclesiastical, this forthright counsel was given, "Ye are equal in worth of position and place in the work of the church; and if in honor ye shall prefer one another, ye will not strive for precedence or place in duty or privilege, and shall be blessed of me" (D. and C. 122:16). Definitely the church was told that the purpose of every office was to bring persons ministry suited to that calling. Never was it to be a means of gaining ecclesiastical preeminence or official ranking. The emphasis is not on "right to officiate" but on "responsibility to minister."

Each Ministry in the Light of the Whole

Considerations of ministry should start with exploration of what ministry is for. We get the total range of what God has in mind in pointing toward good spiritual health. Then we are ready to inquire what the specific functioning of some one office is to be. Any consideration of any one problem divorced from the total picture will be partial and probably detrimental. In March 1835 the Twelve Apostles had been studying their own field of ministry and had asked the prophet for guidance. The instruction entailed consideration of all the offices of ministry. To understand what a deacon is to do one must see this in the light of the total purpose of the priesthood and of the dovetailing of all ministerial functioning. The wise person will utilize the wide range of ministries in its entirety.

Specifics in Ministry

Let the ministries of the church be identified in the language of everyday living, everyday social relationships, and everyday needs of persons. When well visioned by administrators, members, and ministers these are seen as remarkable resources for building spiritual health. They may be considered as clinicians, counselors, confidants, companions, and so on. In this light here are available ministries:

The deacon, a specialist in socioeconomic matters in relating these to spiritual expression and development; a counselor and teacher in individual and family finance, an adviser in budgeting and contributing; a minister aware of the physical and other factors that condition spiritual well-being and worship.

The teacher, a specialist in human relationships, in associational life of persons, in reconciliation and repentance; a teacher in social ethics, in the arts of getting along together; a counselor in matters of attitudes toward and relations with others, a builder of spiritual atmosphere in congregational life.

The priest, a specialist in family living, in home conference and home worship, in parent-child relationships; a teacher in family study, in the development of children for affiliating with the church; a guide in matters of personal and family conduct; a minister in developing the congregation as a family of participants, notably in relation to the Lord's Supper.

The elder, a minister in a company of ordained men with a widening scope of ministries, with a wide range in possibilities for specialization; a specialist in the sacraments of the church involving laying on of hands and the ministration of the Holy Spirit in such rites as confirmation, the blessing of babies, the administration to the sick; the ordination of men to the priesthood with attention to spiritual development for and through these sacraments; the preacher; the teacher; the visitor; the counselor in matters that condition and further the insights, the attitudes, the participation of persons of all age groups for realization of spiritual health.

The seventy, a specialist in evangelistic ministry, alert and developing in seeing and expressing the motivation, the message, the methods, the materials of the evangelistic outreach to members and to nonmembers; the expresser of evangelistic love and concern for others; the teacher in enlisting persons in inclusive family and congregational evangelism; the witness of God at work in today's evangelistic ministry; the counselor in evangelistic expression.

The apostle, a specialist in affirming the worldwide mission of the church; an advocate of God's redeeming love and of spiritual transformation possible in persons and groups; an interpreter of personal living, family living, and congregational living in the context of the universal gospel, the universal church; a preacher and teacher of the universals of the gospel in terms of everyday life in the local area; a dare-big-things-with-God "special witness."

The bishop, a specialist in the socioeconomic affairs of daily living and church operation in the relation of these to spiritual development and health; a counselor in occupational matters, in location of persons and families; a guide in development of communities of Zionic qualities; a justice in personal conduct and relations with reference to church membership; a teacher in socioeconomic ethics; a minister in caring for the material needs and associated spiritual needs of members.

The patriarch-evangelist, a specialist in ministry to members with freedom from administrative responsibilities and with consequent possible objectivity and overview of the work of the church; an evangelist in sharing the good news of God to work in the lives of persons and in the life of the church; a revivalist through involving persons and groups in the challenging mission of the church and in exposing to the dynamic spiritual power available through the church, a counselor and confidant; a benedictory minister.

The prophet, a specialist in seeing with God the calling of persons and the mission of the church in the light of God's nature and purpose; a communicant with God in order to sense God's intent and outlook; a general calling the church forward in mobilization and devotion; a symbol of the church's belief in contemporary spiritual sustenance and revelation.

A Very Wide Range of Possible Ministries

When the early Christians at Corinth became somewhat lopsided about what they wanted in the expression of the Holy Spirit, Paul sought to lift them from their favorite and sought-for ministry. They were wanting the overt and more dramatic expression, chiefly the speaking in tongues. What he told them is as applicable today as then. These are basics in his instruction: (1) There is diversity in the manifestations of the Holy Spirit. (2) All manifestations are for the edifying of the recipients that they might "profit withal." (3) The basic ministrations of the Holy Spirit are expressed in spiritual development within the recipient, notably in charity, the love of God. (4) The fruitage of this ministration has lasting expression in the person. It is fitting that Paul said "and now abideth" when he listed the spiritual manifestation that had enduring nature. This treatise is in the twelfth, thirteenth, and fourteenth chapters of I Corinthians.

This diversity is perpetuated in the company of ministers of the church. One high priest, for instance, becomes a specialist in ministering to youth, another to senior adults. One bishop is at home on consumer economics for the family while another turns to community planning. One patriarch studies family relationships and counsels in this field, while another explores mental health and its spiritual implications. One seventy becomes a specialist in the culture in the Far East and in interpreting the gospel in terms of Oriental culture while another turns to the underprivileged areas in a metropolitan city. In the total church there ought to be available ministry in every field of human need.

And with the Nonordained

The services of the church include more than that which is often considered "ministerial." There are thousands of nonordained men and women who are proficient in saintly living, competent in selected fields of church participation, trained in professional fields, carrying on well in family living. There are ministers who are medical doctors, social workers, lawyers, psychiatrists, economists, educators, and more. In each of these fields are more specialized developments. There are the nonmember specialists and counselors to whom these ministers of the church can refer those needing special helps. We take a good look and consider ourselves in the initial stages of surveying our possible and our needed ministries and of mobilizing the resources we have.

Specialists in Generalization

It is said that when Frederick Madison Smith went to Clark University to investigate enrolling for graduate study, G. Stanley Hall asked him in what he wanted to specialize. F. M. Smith replied, "Generalization." He believed that for the work he would be doing he would need broad overview and sound integration. President Smith saw a need that has been increasing through recent decades. There are now so many departments in advanced study, each with a language of its own and with concentration on a smaller and smaller area of investigation, that we can have a world segmented into disciplines that do not speak the same language. We can examine a person from the standpoint of one narrow field and miss the picture of his total personhood. The times are calling for those who can see life in its overview, man in his total self in his total environment.

Today the Church of Jesus Christ can see and meet this need. Here is an agency that should have no vested interests, no specialized hobby to further. Here is a fellowship of ministers who ought to be endeavoring to see the total person in his total universe. The well-developed minister is looking to the whole man, whole in spiritual health. He may discover some single weakness, but he will see this weakness in relation to the total body, the inclusive self. We need spiritual diagnosticians, spiritual doctors who have a broad, deep God-view of every person.

Making Such a Church Come to Be

No honest member of the church would say that it has achieved the fullness of stature and the broad scope of effectiveness visioned in this consideration. It is basic, however, that we vision what the church can become. It is imperative that we be at work exploring how we can increase our effectiveness and move toward this competency in ministry. It is urgent that we see ministry in terms of ministering, that we look to what is going to happen in the lives of persons in the furthering of spiritual health. It is essential that we get hold of the marvelous potentiality God designs his church to have in meeting the needs of persons. All this is inherent as potential. We need to make it become real.

Just now we are looking at the church as having a wide scope of ministries that carry more possibilities than we have seen. Here are clinical, companionable, diagnostic, therapeutic, consultative, prescriptive, laboratory resources for developing persons and communities of excellent spiritual health. Such services are indispensable. They are of God's planning and provision.

Questions for Discussion

1. The church is identified as a service agency. How may a

181

"service station" publicize that it is for the service of the public while its major motivation is for itself? Could this happen in the church?

2. What difference does it make in the life of the church whether it considers itself a producing agency or a selling agency? What difference after a person joins?

3. What difference does it make in the life of the church whether we consider ourselves a health-producing and health-maintaining agency or a health-dispensing body?

4. If an elder is preaching, what should be his motivation in terms of the spiritual health of the people? How may he lose the spirit of ministering while he continues preaching?

5. What qualities of spiritual good health does a minister need to have if he is going to minister for the furthering of spiritual health in others?

6. How is the structure and administration of the Church of Jesus Christ unique in its inclusion of specialization of offices and functions in the ministry?

7. How is it possible for us to elevate some before-the-public ministries and discount some of the less apparent that contribute so much to the spiritual health of persons and congregations?

8. A conscientious youth once said that he seemed to have been ordained a deacon to pass out programs and take up the offering. In what essential ministries should he be schooled through several years in order to become a competent deacon who could minister to persons?

9. For what kind of ministry would a person consult an ordained teacher? What constructive ministry could this teacher bring to persons? How is the teacher often considered as a when-things-go-wrong officer? How can he function as a keep-things-going-right minister?

10. How do you see a seventy as a vibrant evangelist bringing good health to the members of the church?

11. What do you think Paul meant when he said the ministering of the Holy Spirit, and therefore the ministering of men endowed by the Holy Spirit, was to be edifying? What happens in a person when he is edified? How is this healthy?

12. How does good health require that we see the whole person in his total environment if we are going to further his spiritual health?

13. How shall we procure and evaluate the picture of ministerial

provisions and possibilities in the Church of Jesus Christ?
How shall we interpret these as provided by God to meet man's
needs?

Said a wise man to a youth, "Tell me what persons you've met and how you've met them and I will have a pretty good idea about how you are getting along." And then he continued, "I don't mean the ones you have said 'howdy' to but the ones you have meant 'howdy' with." The sage was wise in his observation. Underneath his comment were these fundamentals: (1) the important place of person-with-person association; (2) the necessity of living with persons if we are going to know them; and (3) the range of possibilities between kinds of persons and kinds of contacts. We are affected and we are measured by the quality of persons whom we choose to be with and by the nature of what we do together. The wise man might well have added, "Tell me what person you hold up as your ideal and I will tell you where you will be going."

An Immigrant Boy Had Friends

Once when Ellis Island was the main port of entrance for immigrants to the United States a boy in his early teens was applying for admission. When he was interviewed he was asked if he knew anyone in the United States. "Oh, yes, some wonderful persons." When asked who they were, he named these: Abraham Lincoln, Theodore Roosevelt, and Booker T. Washington. Conversation showed that he had more than a passing acquaintance with these three unusual men. One officer of immigration said that anyone who was acquainted with such Americans ought to be entitled to enter. It would be as if a youth going to England would have said he knew William E. Gladstone, Charles Kingsley, and David Livingstone. Whom we know, whom we select to know, how we come to know them measures each of us and indicates the health of our personhoods.

The Image of Our Ideal

"What person do you want to be like?" asks the leader of a group of boys of ten and eleven. The boys respond with names.

But this alone will not tell the story. We need to get hold of the boys' picture of the ideals they name. We need to see whether they are looking at the total picture of the man they choose or whether they are picking out some one segment of his character and achievements. A boy may select a baseball pitcher who can throw a curve with precision while his moral living can be as crooked as the curve he throws. Three boys named out of history Theodore Roosevelt. One was thinking of him as a "rough rider" on a dashing horse. One was seeing him as an afraid-of-nobody President of the nation. Another was looking at him as a crusader who was never afraid to stand up and be counted, as a square-shouldered man who wanted other men to be square. Each one of these boys was right, yet each one was incomplete in his picture. If the lads had had the same background and ability they could have turned out quite differently in life although in name they held before them the same man as their ideal.

We are seeing more and more that we need to consider a man in his wholeness. We may not select some segment or achievement in his life and hold this up as if this were the real character. When the maiden in "Song of Solomon" pictures her lover she says of him "he is altogether lovely." Another translation puts it, "he is altogether desirable." The general impression is that she thinks that she has seen every facet of his nature and that everything in him is pleasing. She may have been prejudiced by her affection for him but she was right in trying to get the total picture of the person she loved. We need to associate with a person in many activities, in many social situations, in many moods if we are going to have a sound appraisal.

There is one person who holds up under every examination, in every angle of his personhood, in every mood of his living, in every field of his expression. This is Jesus Christ. Paul wrote to the Ephesian saints that the goal was to move toward spiritual maturity, toward the measure of development expressed in "the fullness of Christ" (Ephesians 4:13). It is the complete Christ that is pictured as the ideal toward which we set ourselves. There is to be no reduced portrait of Christ, no one-sided conception of him, no one-track communion with him. Paul indicates that we are to "grow up into him in all things." He suggests that when the whole man comes into total relationship with the whole Christ, this man receives vital energy from Christ and he is united in himself and one with Christ. Here is the essence of spiritual health.

The Focus in Christianity

Who is the head of this movement? Who is the driving force in it? These are questions every person should ask when he considers becoming a member of any group. Emerson once said that every institution is the lengthened shadow of some man. Sometimes we talk as if we were lining up with some abstract principle or some impersonal cause. Such movements do not get off the ground. If they get started, they decline and perhaps collapse as the dynamic and magnetic power of the pioneers that impelled the start ebbs out of the picture. And we improve our chance for survival as we ask, How does this head of the movement express what the movement stands for? Sometimes there may be a group of persons who together take the lead and catch up the ideals and the purpose.

The dynamic core of the Christian faith is a Person. This Person expresses in his own life and person what the movement is for, how it operates, what it can do. Again it needs to be said that the heart of Christianity is a Person. Not a set of writings. Not a social organization. Not a set of beliefs. Not a liturgy or a complex of rituals. Not a theory about a person, but a person. This person is Jesus Christ. Yet he is expressed through rites, through literature, through a fellowship of believers, through a theology, through a faith, through a community, through a cause. His life, his personhood reveals what God is like, what God has in mind for man and his universe, what can take place in the life of man. Jesus Christ lives all this out in terms of human living, in terms that man can understand.

When This Person Focus Gets Lost

Many times Christians lose sight of this centrality of Jesus Christ as person. Many times believers in Jesus Christ lose personal contact with Jesus Christ. They come to look upon him as a historical figure who once lived in Judea and Galilee. Or they center on beliefs, on doctrines about him. Or they build up abstract ideas about him as truth and love and goodness. Or they use his name as a means of obtaining salvation. Or he becomes a myth to represent spiritual reality. Or he serves as a symbol of their values and hopes. Sometimes he becomes a symbol such as Uncle Sam in the United States or John Bull in England. He becomes a has-been, a never-was, or a hope-to-be. This is quite in contrast to the I Am who is present-tense, self-existent, and personal.

When this focus on Jesus Christ as person weakens or disappears believers concentrate on something else. This can be books, rites, beliefs, institutions, buildings, theologies, and the like. They look for priests or theories or ceremonies or rituals to do the saving for them. The intent of Jesus Christ is that each one of us come to know him so that the impact of his personality upon us will effect change in us as persons. It is a person-with-person experience.

The Power of a Compelling Person

Set before you two persons, with one having a strong, recognizable influence over the other. What is the effect on the one influencing? What is the effect upon the one influenced? Both are affected by the association. The range of possibilities is incalculable. The person in superordinate position can be dominating, arrogant, and draining. Or he can be stimulating, thought-provoking, and resource-developing. The person in superior position can make a slave, a weakling, a dwarf, or a criminal out of the one who looks up to him. Or he can help the other to stand on his feet, to live for what is wonderful, to line up with the good. What takes place in the life of the less dominant can be as varied. There is tremendous responsibility in exerting influence over another person. Every man needs to ask himself when he has the moral right to influence others.

Here is a question we always need to ask: What does this person do to those who look up to him? What does he do to me? And we also need to keep asking, What effect do I have on others? One youth said that his father was so complaining, so cynical, so undermining that after he had talked with his father he himself felt he was not worth anything. One man said that after he had been with one friend of his for an hour he felt as if the milk of his own soul had been curdled—so negative, so apprehensive, so cynical was his friend. On the other hand, one man said of a noble associate, "After I have been with John, I square my shoulders to make something worthful of what I have to work with." This kind of influence was well described by an Irish woman of poor means and almost peasant background when she said of Jane Addams of Hull House, "She allus pusha me up."

The Wholesome Impact of Jesus Christ

The Jews had many notions about what their Messiah was to be and do. Some of these were not fair to him, and they would not have a wholesome effect upon the people. Some thought of him as bringing them plenty of free food, deliverance from oppressors they did not like, leisure from labor, and material wealth. Some thought of him in terms of a monarch on a throne with splendor suited to his estate. Isaiah pictured him otherwise. He was to be a helper and teacher of the people, so that they as persons would be lifted up. In Chapter 9 he described him as counseling his people, as fatherly, as peace-loving, as orderly, as just, as zealous, as freedom-bringing, as light-radiating, as joy-producing. Such a person would further the realization of these qualities in others and in the social order. What is more, this majestic person was to care for persons as a good shepherd would care for his sheep, with gentleness and wisdom (Chapter 11).

This was no indulgent, give-them-candy kind of Christ. He would enable men to see themselves with true perspective. They would sense both their weaknesses and their strengths, their assets and their liabilities. They would learn how to see these in right relationships. A wise associate helps his friend to see himself and to evaluate himself aright. Jesus is the Christ of persons as they are; he is also the Christ of persons as they may become. He tells them they may become whole as they come to know him and live his way.

Jesus Christ Lifted Peter

Peter was a perceptive person, when he took time to see. He was this way with himself. When Peter first met Jesus of Nazareth he spoke out in his impulsive way, "Depart from me; for I am a sinful man" (Luke 5:8). At once Jesus sought to put Peter at ease when he said, "Fear not!" and told him of significant work that he would be doing. Jesus did not spare this rough fisherman. He intended to make an apostle of him and went about getting him to stand securely on his feet. So effective was the impact of Jesus upon Peter that he had only to look at him, meet Peter's eyes, to effect remorse in this man who had just denied that he ever knew him (Luke 22:61). It was this same Peter who stood on the Day of Pentecost and spoke out forthrightly and confidently to the multitude that had gathered (Acts 2). Later when danger loomed before him this Christ-inspired Peter spoke with "boldness" (Acts 4:13). This Simon Peter had been with this Jesus of Nazareth.

And Paul of Tarsus Was Changed

Paul, the Jew with Roman citizenship and Greek learning, became an integrated person when he met Jesus Christ, every whit of him. He was overbearing and dogmatic when Jesus Christ accosted him on the road to Damascus. Then and there he cringed at awareness of his faults and weaknesses. He "trembled" as he asked for instructions (Acts 9:6). He made a complete about-face. From this Christ there flowed meaning and purpose and strength. Right away he could speak "boldly in the name of the Lord Jesus" (Acts 9:29). Later in prison he could write confidently, "I can do all things through Christ who strengthens me" (Philippians 4:13). Here is the living testimony of what can happen in a man's life as he meets and understands this Jesus Christ. The soul-sick persecutor became the soul-searching apostle. New health came to him.

Not Always Healthful

Not infrequently we hear sweeping calls and promises such as "look to Jesus Christ and he will save you." We do well to be honest and admit that often when we look to Jesus Christ we see him through our own self-constructed spectacles. We do not see him as he is; rather we see him in the structure of our own wishes and backgrounds. We shall always see him through our own framework, but we need not limit him to this limited world of ours. We shall always need to see how his person and his purpose is richer than we can ever see. We should want to keep on growing in our experience with him and in our understanding and appreciation of him.

Some years ago Bruce Barton wrote the book, *The Man Nobody Knows*. As we look at it now we think that the author exaggerated the picture of Jesus as the business executive and the man-about-town. His introduction still stands as a portrayal of what a boy can think of this Jesus of Nazareth. The boy was not favorably impressed with the Jesus that he met in Sunday school. He appeared to this boy as a "killjoy," as "flabby," as "sissified," as a weak "lamb of God," who "went about for three years telling people not to do things." As a man Bruce Barton had to discover the magnetic personhood of this strong Man from the little town of Nazareth. Many a youth has admitted that he has drawn away from the Jesus pictured to him.

One young woman confided that Jesus always made her

nervous. Her grandfather had kept quoting from the twenty-fourth chapter of Matthew and had mixed the eighteenth chapter of the book of Revelation in the picture. Jesus became associated with warnings, disasters, plagues, and punishment. She said that the constant talking about the "second coming of Christ" made her feel "creepy." The phrase "abomination of desolation" (Matthew 24:33) had a depressing effect on her. Apparently this had been one of her grandfather's much-used phrases. To this young woman Jesus was a confirmed pessimist who said that things were in a bad condition and promised that things would get worse.

A middle-aged man developed the picture of Jesus as a neurotic wanderer who lived off what his apostles begged from others. He had kept the picture that an ascetic Sunday school teacher had built up about Jesus as denouncing material comforts and anything enjoyable. This otherworldly woman had quoted over and over the counsel, "Take no thought for the morrow." His own practical outlook rebelled at this. To him Jesus was looked upon as hostile to automobiles, athletics, cosmetics, food more than that required for existence, and the like. The Jesus he pictured did not belong to the modern world, to his world. He might be at home in a Zion of simplest tastes, of humble economy, with anemic saints. The slants given him in earlier years had covered up the courageous and creative spirit of the man of Nazareth.

This Jesus Christ who was altogether healthy needs to be seen in the fullness of his person, in the wide scope of his ministry. Then he becomes the greatest source of spiritual living in all the world.

The Christ of 1820-1830

A farm boy not yet fifteen years of age met this Christ in his father's farmstead in western New York in the spring of 1820. The story is told very simply by the youth himself. What happened in this young man through this meeting is of great consequence. What effect did it have upon him? What did it prompt him to do? Did it have any bearing on what the boy thought of himself? Did it narrow him or expand him? Did it stretch his heart or dwarf it? This experience gives the clue to the basic conception of Jesus Christ involved in the Restoration movement.

Joseph Smith told how he approached God to receive direction on a very simple question about joining a church. He wanted to know which one to join. If no more than a yes-or-no answer had been given, the youth would have remained in comfortable stagnation. He narrated that the key salutation of his experience came when the Father in his vision addressed him with the simple directive, "This is my beloved Son: hear him!" A few moments before he had been depressed and oppressed with a sense of spiritual darkness. This gave way to a sense of celestial light. He was amazed but not paralyzed. He was humbled by the light that shone on the woodland scene but he was not terrified. The youth kept his composure and remembered his question. His thinking powers were not blotted out. He came out of this experience with clarity and confidence. His faculties were alert. In the hours and days that followed he stood courageously for what he knew had taken place. He was quite aware that he knew very little and that there was ever so much for him to discover. The experience pointed him to significant ministry he would yet carry on. He was to find out that he would have to do considerable growing in order to get ready for this assignment. In months that followed this Son of God made the youth quite conscious of his "weaknesses and imperfections" (*Church History*, Volume 1, page 12), but he was prompted to seek forgiveness for his "sins and follies." He never felt smitten down or rejected as a contemptible sinner. He was hungry for further communion, for continued direction, but he never gave up with a sense of guilt. He had "full confidence that God would hear and manifest in due time."

Here was a health-giving meeting with Jesus Christ. It made Joseph Smith want to explore, willing to stand up for what he knew. It made him sensitive to God's call for clean living and prompted him to be anxious but not worried about the business to which God was calling him. Always there was awareness of light and invitation to goodness. Always there was insistence on personal righteousness and sound motivation if he was going to work with God. This does not mean that this meeting with Jesus Christ made him all at once a paragon of virtue. He had to keep working on his own personal conduct. Sometimes he slipped back. Sometimes he did not see things soundly. But he felt he had divine help in trying to develop. This much came out clearly through the years that followed: Joseph Smith was stimulated to make more of his own life, of his own self through his meeting with Jesus Christ.

The Restoration Movement Must Be Christocentric

Jesus Christ is the core of the Restoration movement. These things stand out as expressions and emphases of the ever living

Christ: (1) Joseph Smith was directed to turn to Christ as source of his understanding and strength. This applies to every believer, every participant. (2) The newly-brought-to-light scriptures, the Book of Mormon, focused on the universal Christ's visit to ancient America. He ever ministers to the "other sheep" of all the world that there may be "one fold and one shepherd." (3) The church organization was designated as "the Church of Jesus Christ." He is ever to be the center of allegiance and inspiration in the church. (4) The Holy Spirit was experienced as the vitalizing divine presence that cultivated the qualities of Jesus Christ and provided foundation for witness of him. This Spirit is ever the life-affording spiritual dynamic for enabling persons to be Christ-like. (5) Baptism and other rites were administered by those "commissioned of Jesus Christ" as expressions of covenanting with Jesus Christ. These are still Christ-with-persons sacraments. (6) Believers were to live together in a Christ-centered community as early disciples had done in Jerusalem after the Day of Pentecost. This community of those who live together in mutual helpfulness, in Christian spirit, was to be called Zion. (7) The Restoration movement is thoroughly Christocentric.

This Christocentrism is intended to be healthy. Rightly understood and with sound association, this Jesus Christ of the Restoration brings to pass saints of wholesome quality. In these ways is this Christocentrism wholesome: (1) It is present-tense in functioning. This gospel sings confidently, "Today the heavens are open to souls prepared to hear the wondrous revelation of Christ who's ever near." (2) It stimulates to creative expression with Jesus Christ. The highest expression of this creativity is in the creation of persons of eternal quality. (3) It harmonizes the person and the group into spiritual oneness. Here is a unifying focus for all of living. (4) It is a social gospel, concerned with quality of living in social relationships. This is a restoration of what Jesus taught and lived. (5) It appreciates the worth of every person as a potential child of God. As Jesus of Nazareth had chosen and lived with common fishermen, so now the Christ of the Restoration chose and lived with common farmers. (6) It affirms the way of joyful satisfaction through living with and working with this Jesus Christ. The directives "Fear not!" and "Be of good cheer!" are heard again. (7) It looks to one brotherhood as men are united in Jesus Christ. This is possible through common loyalty to the universal Christ.

The Christ of Immediate Experience

The Restoration gospel reaffirms what Paul said in his letter to the Colossians. He wrote boldly that a man can come into direct relationship with this Jesus Christ. He said there was no need for intermediaries, no call for interceding angels, no place for priests with privileged connections with God. Paul declared that Christ is all-sufficient. Each man can pray directly to God. Each man can receive inspiration directly from God. Ordained ministers are to help men come near to God, not to shut them away from God. Some persons have a more mature and a more effective communion with God. This is because they have been developing a more effective two-way communion, not because God is partial to some. The gospel expects men to increase their competency, to improve their communication, to develop their spiritual sensitivity as they keep on living with Jesus Christ. The gospel is not a way of secondary intermediatorship; it is the way of immediate experience of Jesus Christ.

Once William Hocking, philosopher, commented that great men and great causes have "kindling capacity." They can stir persons to creative and consequential expression. They stimulate men to dare, to drive on, to delve into the not-yet-explored. The Christ of the Restoration, the cause of the Restoration, has such kindling capacity. From the first it was set forth as "a marvelous work and a wonder."

The Restoration gospel affirms that this centrality in Christ is indispensable in man's achieving an inclusive, expanding, healthy selfhood. There is a central focus of selfhood in Jesus Christ. This person sees how God chose to actualize his own selfhood in the life and person of the Son who was known as Jesus the Christ. He sees how the selfhood of God was and is focused in Jesus Christ. This Jesus Christ becomes the norm of appraisal of his own self. He is more than a norm. He is source of achieving genuine selfhood. Such a self is no longer wandering and wavering, uncertain and insecure. He comes to sense his own worth as something of Christ lives in him. A unifying, a developing, a refining takes place within him. A new self comes into being. The believer does not reduce his worth and lower his condition as he lines up and accords with this Jesus Christ. He brings out his best and devotes it to the best. He stands before this ever living Christ and speaks in dedication.

> Thou strong young man of Galilee,
> The vigor of thy youth I see . . .

And that this teeming power of mine
Be set to noble works, like thine,
My strength I consecrate to thee,
Thou strong young man of Galilee.

As thou didst shed the truth of God
And lift man's vision from the clod,
I would equip my opening mind
To guide and lift confused mankind.

Thou holy man of Galilee,
Thy sinless life inspires in me
A valiant stand against all wrong,
And courage to be true and strong.

Such a Christ, such a conception of Christ, such a consecration to Christ develops men—men of thoroughly spiritual healthiness.

Questions for Discussion

1. What does this mean, "Each person needs a center for his identity"? What would be the condition of a person who did not have such a center?

2. Indicate in specific ways how a person's ideal of the person he would be like affects what he is going to become.

3. How and why is it necessary to have and use the inclusive picture of the person we may look upon as ideal? What can happen when we select some single phase of the person and concentrate on it.

4. How may misconceptions of Jesus Christ or partial conceptions of Jesus Christ get in the way of achieving wholesome influence of Jesus Christ upon our living?

5. How might Jesus Christ be placed as the center of our faith but not as a person? What other emphasis upon him might be made?

6. What made the impact of Jesus Christ upon Peter a wholesome influence? Upon Paul? Upon some other person of your choice?

7. What in the experience of Joseph Smith in 1820 made this a wholesome experience with the Son of God? What were the effects upon Joseph Smith?

8. How did the emphasis upon Jesus Christ as center of faith in the early Restoration movement differ from the picture of Christ in contemporary faiths of that day?

9. What is there in the life and person of Jesus Christ that points up the "kindling capacity" that William Hocking says great men and great causes have?

10. Lasting identity requires a man to see himself in relation to all creation, to the total universe. It is said that few men have this kind of identity, that for most of us our identity is diffuse, unclear, and unfocused. How can Jesus Christ help us to get hold of needed identity?

11. It is said that most of us who affirm allegiance to Jesus Christ have the focus of our concentration on him somewhat off center. What does this mean? Illustrate.

12. How is it necessary that we keep Jesus Christ at the center of our selves? What did the man mean when he said he focused on Christ differently in the prayer meeting than on the playing field?

13. How do you see this centralizing on Jesus Christ as a resource rather than a compulsion?

PART IV

PROBLEMS IN SPIRITUAL
LIVING IN MODERN LIFE

Growing persons will keep facing problems. Only the weak and incompetent will expect a condition in which there will be no questions, no strains, no unsolved situations. This section is recommending most urgently an honest, relaxed facing of our needs and our inadequacies in maturing spiritually. We shall give attention to identifying and stating the problems, to mobilizing resources that will throw light on solving them. We shall anticipate that we can mature through working through the situation "together with God." We shall not expect God to work out any problematical situation and give us the finished answer without effort on our part. Rather will God expect us to grow as he helps us to see the way through.

These problems concern the entire membership. It is to be the business of the congregation, of the family, of the community, of the entire church to provide an atmosphere and a social situation conducive to the solving of our problems. All of us need to understand problems, to appreciate what our brothers and sisters are experiencing even if we do not enter directly into the matter at hand. Zion ought to be considered a community with resources for solving problems, with skill in working at them, with disposition and ability to work with God in charting ways through. And Zion, too, ought to avoid the unfortunate, unhealthy conditions that contribute to spiritual ill health.

Not all problems in spiritual living are considered. Major ones, typical ones are discussed. All titles begin with a verb, indicating that we are to go into action. But going into action is not enough. Mere action can bungle a problem hopelessly and can draw the knots tighter. Each consideration refers us to that which constitutes good spiritual health. Each field contains possibility of promoting or of obstructing this spiritual health. No activity is good by mere name. The objective and operation matter ever so much. Thus fasting can undermine or contribute to our spiritual well-being. There is no merit in fasting without foresight. It is imperative that explorers see clearly what the problem is. We shall give attention to discovering factors that gave genesis to the problem and to forces that can enable us to get at the heart of its solution. We shall not point the finger and condemn persons. It is childish to say, "It is all his fault." Adults are little inclined to locate the "fault" as a solution. They would go on to discover how and why this "fault" occurred.

Those who explore these problems should put the questions out on the table without implicating themselves unduly. Honest persons will admit that there are some traces of these confusions and strains inside themselves. They will not stew and fret about it. They will see themselves as a whole in a whole situation. They will be able to smile at themselves and say with one man who discovered some of his idiosyncracies and shortcomings and creative spots for the first time, "I'm quite an interesting fellow!" It is healthy to enjoy one's self without overrating or underrating of either problems or achievements.

We could censure ourselves, excuse ourselves, adulate ourselves. We could do the same with others. We could blame the times— and there is plenty that muddles our thinking and our feeling in our modern complex. Rather let us tackle the problems as wise men do, saying, "Here is something to work on. Let's do it together. Let's permit God to join us in the exploration!" How healthy this can be!

CHAPTER 17

MANAGING FEAR
AND ANXIETY

The age in which we live has been called "the age of anxiety." Some have spoken of "anxiety, the disease of our age." Tenseness and uncertainty do mark our times. With this often goes a sense of futility and fatalism. Someone has characterized our Western civilization as "a shattered atom, a deflated dollar, and a worried look." This worrying attitude makes practical difference in daily living. Studies of industrial concerns have discovered that much of the inefficiency of workers is caused by worry. Medical clinics have found that many illnesses start with anxiety. Life insurance companies find that the majority of nervous breakdowns begin not in actual events in biological functioning but with worry. Hypertensions bring on heart failures and other diseases. Physicians find that anxiety affects the entire physical health. Dr. Charles Mayo once said, "Worry affects the circulation, the heart, the glands, the whole nervous system and profoundly affects the health. I have never known a man who died from overwork, but many who have died from doubt."[1]

Modern man needs to see what this fear and this anxiety are that are so perplexing and that can be so devastating. Modern religious leaders need to explore what religion can do in such a time. This requires that we (1) discover what brings on worry and anxiety, (2) understand what they are, (3) find out how to face conditions honestly, and (4) explore how sound religion can function in treating this "modern disease" and in bringing about good spiritual health. Today we shall do well to see what Jesus had to say about fear and anxiety and to note how he himself lived a life that rose above the "overanxious" conditions that plague us in modern civilization. We shall see how Jesus was a diagnostician and a physician and an example. Then we shall take a look at the reemphasis of this way of confidence in the Restoration movement of our own time. This Restoration gospel should minister in rising above worry and anxiety.

---

1. Quoted by K. Hildebrand, *Achieving Real Happiness*, Harpers, p. 166

Tension-producing Factors

Our times are an interesting mixture of reducing tensions and of increasing tensions. Several factors that used to distress men have been reduced. Science has abolished many fears and dreads that come out of widespread superstitions and traditions. Many linger on in the Western world and many continue in full force in backward parts of the world. On the whole, however, we are not afraid that some manipulator of black magic will work a spell upon us. We are not anticipating that some evil spirit will jump out of a tree as we pass by. The danger of want is being reduced so that in several countries there is no fear of starving. The dread of incurable disease is greatly diminishing. Diphtheria and smallpox, for instance, have been brought under fairly good control. Typhoid fever is no longer the menace it once was. Social services and medical science have brought relief to mankind. We have been developing a sounder conception of God so that we do not think of him as sending plagues on persons to suit his whims or ease his anger.

In spite of this reduction of these causes for anxiety, it appears that the total stock of anxiety has increased. So complex is the situation that it is not easy to free ourselves from fear and worry. Several factors make our age prone to tension and worry or to fatalistic acceptance of whatever comes. One man said simply this, "It's all too much for me, so I shall take whatever comes." He was giving up the idea that he could do anything about what would be taking place. Here are some of the factors that promote this worrying or this submissive outlook: (1) The tempo of our society is the fastest in history. Changes are coming so fast that we do not have time to clock them, let alone explain them. (2) Advance in communication brings the pronounced impact of news. Television and radio and press disseminate news so quickly and over so wide an area that we are exposed to a complicated picture of happenings. In one day we can get disquieting descriptions of disasters and horrors that may bring destruction. The man of two hundred years ago never had such an exposure to news. (3) Atomic developments and consequent possibilities of atomic warfare cause anxiety. On August 6, 1945, a bomb was dropped on Hiroshima—a blinding flash of light and a terrific explosion. More than 78,000 persons were killed. Moderns are thinking that all this could happen again on a larger scale. (4) Modern-day anxiety is on a global scale. Our concerns reach from Alaska to Zanzibar. There are no places exempt. There is no haven to which the fearing one may escape. (5) Competition is more insistent in today's world. The social order does not prescribe our roles and set up our limitations. When achievement is up to the individual, when the person's place in society is less set, each one is on his own and the competition can get intense.

How Persons and Groups React

There is no one way of reacting to this "age of anxiety." Here are some of the more widely practiced ways of responding: (1) There has been a great increase in the use of nerve tonics, sedatives, and drugs of all sorts. The use of "tranquilizers" is found in all age groups from children to senior adults. (2) Books and pamphlets dealing with "peace of mind," "soul uplift," and the like have been best sellers. Meetings that offer solutions and salvations in definite form and assured results have attracted large congregations. (3) Popular music has sung of "comfortable" help from God in such lyrics as those about "the Man Upstairs." (4) There has been increase in desire for medical assistance that would alleviate nervous and distraught conditions. (5) Consumption of liquor has mounted with apparent relation to nervous tension. (6) Keeping in motion, going somewhere has expressed the restlessness of the unsatisfied and the insecure. It is said that moderns keep hurrying to get somewhere so they may have more time in which to be bored after they arrive. (7) Demands for recreation, especially commercially provided recreation, have been on the increase as moderns seek release from strain, meaninglessness, and boredom.

Then there has been the honest searching by those who believe that in the gospel of Jesus Christ there are resources for enabling us to face our fears, to understand them, to utilize resources that God provides for spiritual health.

Fear and Anxiety

The words "fear" and "anxiety" carry separate meanings. This distinction is made here to help us diagnose the situation, not to be splitting hairs on terms. Fear means emotional agitation that rises out of a specific danger that we confront. Thus we can be afraid of a rattlesnake in the path ahead or of a flash of lightning that snaps about us. Anxiety denotes a deep-rooted concern, the object of which we may not be able to recognize. We may not be able to put our finger on what is causing the difficulty. Anxiety may be a reaction to an imagined danger. In morbid anxiety there is a general apprehensiveness. Seldom does the anxious one know specifically what he is afraid of. His explanations may be wide of the mark. Often this kind of worrier cannot apprehend what is bothering him without help from discriminating persons who can guide him in discovering the sources of his difficulty. Often the beginnings are in some childhood incident with the influence remaining while the specific happening is scarcely remembered.

Born in Fear?

Are we born full of fears and phobias? Hardly. Students of human nature have established pretty well by laboratory tests that at birth we have two major fears: fear of a loud noise and fear of falling. In former years we were inclined to assume that children were "naturally" afraid of the dark, of animals, of fuzzy things, and so on. Experiments have disclosed that babies between about four months and a year do not have these fears unless they have been caught from grownups. In other words, we are not born crammed full of fears.

While we start out with only two basic fears it is not long before we accumulate several. Fear of the dark, of death, and other common fears come from association with adults. In soundness to ourselves and in fairness to God we need to see how the baggage of fears and phobias we carry along come out of our social surroundings. Adults carry a responsibility of no small import in the matter of fears they impose on immature children.

The Constructive Use of Fear

Fear is not to be regarded as wholly evil. There can be a constructive and a protective utilization of fear. If we were without fear we could be careless and be destroyed. Fear can be a safeguarding factor in human society and in relations with natural forces. We do well to be on our guard against a speeding motorcar, a poisonous snake, an armed robber. Fear can protect us. It can bring into action what we sometimes call "emergency energy." It can bring out our reserve powers in times of danger and crisis. We do well to learn how to make fear work for us instead of against us. It is not enough that we learn to recognize whatever fears we have. It is not wise to surrender to them. Rather do we need to understand them, to harness them, to allow them to help us.

A fear with potential service in it can be exaggerated out of proportion and become destructive. It can be compartmentalized until it lives to itself and begins to dominate the rest of life. It is sound for us to take precautions against bacteria but the neurotic person can pull this fear out of proportion. Such was the case of the woman whose hands were cracked because many, many times a day she washed them compulsively in a strong disinfectant.

The understanding person does not say to another, "Don't be afraid—the thing you fear will never happen." Nor does he discount the fear. John S. Bonnell says he used to tell soldiers as they were leaving for the front, "Courage is not the absence of fear; it is the mastery of it. We are cowards only when we permit fear to dominate and control us."[2] Joanna Baillie puts it this way.

> The brave man is not he who feels no fear,
> For that were stupid and irrational;
> But he, whose noble soul its fear subdues,
> And bravely dares the danger nature shrinks from.

An officer in World War II carried out a dangerous mission, quite alone. He examined and disconnected a threatening explosive bomb. A friend inquired, "How can you do that kind of thing without being afraid?" Said the officer, "I don't. I am afraid, but I have to master my fears. If my hand were to tremble that would be the last of me." Silence. Then the soldier asked, "How do you master your fear?" Said the brave one, "I remember a verse my mother taught me when I was a boy, 'Yea, though I walk through the valley of the shadow of death, I will fear no evil: for thou art with me' [Psalm 23:4]. I need to feel I am worthy of God's help and then nothing else really matters."

Man's Capacity to Fear

Man has moral and spiritual capacity in his nature. The power we have to stand away from ourselves, look at ourselves, and evaluate ourselves makes us capable of concerns and apprehensions. We can be subject to discords and conflicts and concerns of which the nonhuman animals know nothing. Once a woman in great distress of mind spoke her feeling, "What would I not give if I had been born a cow!" She was thinking of some decision-making and problem-solving she would have been spared. The more we develop as persons in self-management the more we increase our

---

2. J. S. Bonnell, *No Escape from Life*, Harpers, p. 42

capacity to fear, to sense concern. The low-level moron has few fears, few anxieties, if any. It is also true that as we develop personally we increase our power for understanding our fears, facing them, and using them to advantage. The person incapable of fear is not in good condition. The person victimized by fear is most unhealthy.

Jesus' Counsel on Fear

The Christian Era opened with an affirmative salutation. It began with "Fear not!" (Luke 2:10). It did not end there. To tell a person not to be afraid is generally unsound and useless. This may succeed only in making this person feel guilty because he is afraid. This salutation at Bethlehem went on to give the basis for rising above fear: "I bring you good tidings of great joy, which shall be to all people." Then came the announcement of One who would transcend fear and enable men to rise above anxiety as they would live with this worry-dispelling Messiah.

Jesus said, "Do not be anxious about tomorrow" (Matthew 6:34 R.S.V.). The usual interpretation of the common version, "Take no thought for the morrow" does not do justice to what Jesus had in mind. Often this is taken to mean that we are to disregard the coming day to the point of improvidence. Not so. Jesus himself planned well the course of his ministry. The phrasing, "Do not be anxious" gets at what he had in mind. Paul continued this counsel when he wrote to the Philippians. "Be careful for nothing" (4:6) has to be seen in its original meaning or we shall get the idea that we are to be indifferent or careless. Another translation makes it read, "In nothing be anxious." When the total sentence is read we see Paul reminding us to be anxious in nothing, to be thankful in everything. He was saying that we can get rid of an anxiety by putting a thanksgiving in its place. Jesus was not discounting concern for daily material needs. He said that God was aware of these needs of ours. He was saying that undue preoccupation with these matters can get in the way of our living to utilize them well. Once a grocer deeply engaged in his business said he was so tied to a sack of sugar that he could not enjoy anything sweet. A workman said he lost his job because he got so concerned with keeping it that his work suffered. Jesus advised his disciples to be concerned with the major things and to face each day with courage and assurance.

Fear-producing Religion

Some expressions of religion increase fears and contribute to worry. We can picture God as so fussy, so exacting, so inflexible, so punitive that he becomes an ogre who makes persons shrink from him. Sometimes God is portrayed as delighting in man's suffering and punishments. A young man kept praying to God whom he wanted to please, to a God who exacted perfection. He was ordained to the ministry. This became a worry-producing experience. He kept wondering if what he was doing was pleasing God. He was concerned about suiting his administrative supervisors. His tensions increased until he "cracked up." Small children have gone home from sermons on hell and on the wrath of God afraid and trembling. A wrathful, jealous, vindictive God can strike terror and can deepen anxiety. A group of youth left a meeting in which the emphasis had been on impending disasters just before the end of everything and decided not to go to college that fall since destruction was so imminent. Some faiths can tighten the emotions and increase the fears.

The Undergirding Faith

Jesus placed foremost a fundamental faith in God. This means a faith that is endeavoring to know God as he is. This means a vital faith, which is something more than mere affirmations about the existence and character of God. It is a continuing communion with him and functioning cooperation with him. It is the faith of a Negro preacher who confided in his prayer, "There ain't nothin', God, that you and I can't handle together." This means a thoroughgoing faith that includes all facets of life, all phases of personhood. This faith calls us to sense God's purpose and plan so that we shall be able to line up with him in his total operation. This is not the faith that parades, "I can have anything I want, if I believe God will give it to me." Rather does it say, "I shall be secure and supplied as I am immersed in God's work and love." Fears and anxieties may be overcome as we develop goals and values that are of God, as we utilize resources that are of God. These are mightier than the evils that threaten us. Then we are able to say with the psalmist, "I sought the Lord, and he heard me, and delivered me from all my fears" (Psalm 34:4). And the hymn writer goes on to say, "Fear the Lord, you his saints, for those who fear him have no want" (R.S.V.). A saving fear was to replace a soul-sick fear.

Other Pointers of Jesus Christ

Some basic pointers about managing fear and anxiety emerge from Jesus' life and teaching. Because he lived in good hope, he could tell his disciples to be of good cheer. Here are major directives:

1. Jesus counsels us to live courageously with situations that cannot be altered. He asked, "Which of you by being anxious can add one cubit to his stature?" There is no point in worrying over being sixty years of age if that is what we are. There is no use pining away because we have narrow shoulders when we wanted broad ones. One woman told how she used to hate herself and even stick out her tongue at herself when she stood before the mirror. She made life miserable for herself and for those around her. Then she resolved to accept her body, her physical appearance as it was, do the best she could with it, and then go about beautifying her personhood. She achieved beauty in her inner life and she lived happily with herself. Reinhold Niebuhr is credited with this helpful prayer:

> God give me serenity
> To accept the things I cannot change;
> The courage to change the things I can;
> And the wisdom to know the difference.

2. Jesus advises us to look to our sense of values as a way of finding release from anxiety. We may fuss and fume over getting things that are not worth the effort. We may seek things that would get in our way. We may be wearing ourselves out "keeping up with the Joneses" when we ought to be lining up with Jesus. When we are converted to Jesus Christ we experience a transmutation of values. This brings a source of relief that many so-called believers seem to lack.

3. Jesus taught us to live richly in each day. He reminded us to put the qualities of eternity into every moment. In this way of living we shall not be reiterating the disappointments or the achievements of yesterday or borrowing troubles from tomorrow. He told his disciples, "Don't worry at all then about tomorrow. Tomorrow can take care of itself! One day's trouble is enough for one day" (Matthew 6:34, Phillips). One woman said she could wash the dishes for one meal quite happily but if she counted up and pictured all the dirty dishes she would be washing for the next ten years she would be completely undone.

4. Jesus reminds us to get rid of the impedimenta we are carrying. He referred to such a small thing as the particle in the eye. Such things as we must keep hold of, he will help us carry. Grudges, animosities, slights, and phobias are to be discarded. We shall do well to put into our program times for getting rid of the burdensome. Sir William Osler, the famous British physician, once wrote a little book, *The Student Life.* In it he urged all to "undress their souls" as they might undress their bodies each night on retiring. This undressing would include recognition and repentance with consequent forgiveness.

5. Jesus directed us to constructive action. There is no peace in attempting to escape from unpleasant situations by denying them or running away from them. We recognize the existence of fears and worries and then seek by productive action to replace them. An old couplet says, "He who fears and runs away will live to run another day." A straightforward directive is, "Do something about the cause of your worry." Get competent assistance. Associate with fellow builders. Plan for creative and satisfying work. Jesus practiced the way of productive endeavor: "My Father worketh hitherto, and I work." He identified the power that will help us as the "Spirit that leads to do good." There are no spiritual sedatives. The "workingsome" drives out the worrisome.

6. Jesus reminded us to make faith contagious. Fear is catching. Dr. Karl Menninger has commented that "fear communicates itself from person to person, from group to group, as certainly and much more rapidly than disease." So Jesus expected his disciples to live together in a faith-producing fellowship. In the same spirit the Restoration movement called Saints to build a health-producing community to be called Zion. Those who would share in the building of such a community would have "faith, hope, and charity." They would influence each other with courage and confidence. These should invite persons to come out of the infectious weather of gloom and doom and worry and scurry into a climate of fraternity and faith. Not infrequently worriers get together and feed on each other's neurotic concerns. Jesus told his disciples to expect to lift up their heads and rejoice.

A Message of Confidence

Jesus talked very frankly with his followers about perilous times. He said days would come when men's hearts would be "fainting with fear and with foreboding of what is coming on the world" (Luke 21:26, R.S.V.). He did not promise days without fear and danger and uncertainty. Rather he counseled them to make themselves equal to such situations. He told his people to keep their heads up, their outlook confident. God would still be in charge. They were not to be downcast or distraught. There would be no time for shallow optimism but for seasoned faith.

This message was reaffirmed in the Restoration movement. The powers mentioned in the foregoing pointers were reexpressed in this movement. The gospel was to be one of hope and confidence. There was to be no place for namby-pamby weaklings but for men who would draw on divine resources to make them equal to the demands of the times. Sometimes amateurs interpret the opening section of the Doctrine and Covenants as if it were a call to anxiety and discouragement. It was to be "a voice of warning" rather than "a voice of worry." The pioneers were told of the need of repentance so they would qualify for God's help. They were not directed toward distraction and despair. They would manage temptation to anxiety by getting immersed actively, creatively, hopefully in God's work.

Questions for Discussion

1. What conditions in our world order contribute to making our times "an age of anxiety"? Do you know of any age without problems that could bring on anxiety?

2. How is it unfruitful and unsound to tell a person, "Don't worry! Everything will be all right"?

3. Interpret, "The nature and content and use of a person's fears indicate his spiritual maturity."

4. When would you say a fear gets out of hand and becomes destructive? Apply to matters of physical and mental health.

5. How is it necessary to identify a fear and to discover its sources in order to evaluate it and to work on it?

6. What do you think of the suggestion that a person who wants to worry should select a time for doing his worrying so he will not weaken his working endeavors with worrying?

7. How can it become unhealthy for a person to worry about what God thinks of him and what he is doing?

8. Illustrate how we can handle some of the problem of worry by reviewing what matters most in life. What are some specific fears we could get rid of by reconstructing our scale of values?

9. Apply to daily life situations what Jesus meant when he said, "Do not be anxious about tomorrow."
10. How can the first section of Doctrine and Covenants be used as "voice of warning" or as "voice of worry"?
11. What grounds for constructive confidence may Latter Day Saints have in an age of concern about the end of the world and the collapse of civilization?
12. Formulate a few major pointers for developing an above-worry faith and way of life in today's world.
13. Interpret, "A healthy Saint faces facts and forecasts possibilities with God and with his brothers."

CHAPTER 18

RISING ABOVE
BOREDOM

The word "bore" is loaded with dislike. Most persons shrink from being a bore or being considered a bore. They do not want to be with bores. These are the dullards who without creative imagination or resourcefulness weary others by tedious iteration and reiteration, by concentrating on the uninteresting without sensitivity to the reactions of those about them. They keep going on in their own grooved world. When we say of a person, "He's a bore," we are implying that we would rather not have him around us. Sometimes we picture the bore as forcing himself on us. Whether we are working or conversing we seem to say, "Deliver me from bores." And a phrase expressing our own disinterest or our own disgust is, "I'm bored." Many moderns are either bores or bored or both. One man put it this way, "I'm fed up and there's nothing attractive to eat and I wouldn't want it anyway." Helpless within, this fellow would grab onto something outside himself, on some other person who for a moment would revitalize him and his surroundings. Boredom is not something new in the history of man, but it appears to be sharpened and more acute in modern times.

Hell as Boredom

Sometimes the word "boredom" is designated as the realm of bores. Here is a situation in which everybody bores everybody else. Here everyone is saying, "Nothing is going on here. Nothing to do." If this were stretched out interminably, this would be hell indeed. In fact, hell might be identified as a condition in which all who dwell there are unstimulated and unstimulating, bored and boring. In a drama that depicts Satan in his own realm, he is interviewed about his remembrance of the celestial regions. He is asked what he misses most. His answer, "The trumpets sounding in the morning!" In those remembered times there was something to give color and purpose to the day. There was something to call into purposeful action. On the other hand, we think of God, eternally creative, ever in action as Julia Ward Howe sang of him, "He is sounding forth the trumpet that shall never know defeat; O be swift, my soul, to answer him, be jubilant my feet: Our God is marching on!"

We can live hellish lives, steeped in boredom, right here and now. We can expect this to be increased as the years go by and eventually we can make this permanent in a hellish hereafter— the awful prospect of eternal boredom! Or we can rise above boredom and live meaningfully and thrillingly with God and with God's co-creators on earth. Then instead of waiting, and wanting the time to pass, we shall be wanting the time extended so we can do more and be more. Such is the outlook of those who sense the gospel of the good life, the gospel of Jesus Christ.

A Bored Hamlet

In Act I, Scene II of *Hamlet,* the prince of Denmark is in a room of state in the royal castle. He has just been conversing with the new king who is now his stepfather, his mother the queen, the prime minister, and others. All others have just left and Hamlet is alone. He looks back to the days of his father, recently deceased, and to the marriage of his mother to the present king. He feels overwhelmed and confused. He would like to take his own life but he fears God's "canon 'gainst self-slaughter." Then he speaks to himself of the futility of living, of his own boring existence. These lines of his stand as a great literary expression of the condition of those who find nothing stimulating in life and who become too perplexed or disabled to do anything.

> "How weary, stale, flat and unprofitable
> Seem to me all the uses of this world!
> Fie on't! Ah, fie!"

Hamlet distrusted the present king. He mistrusted his mother. He did not trust himself. He was resentful of things as they were but he lacked the fortitude to endeavor to right the situation. So he indulged in self-pity and resentment. He was bored without disposition to battle much of anything. So he lamented his helpless condition.

> "The time is out of joint: O cursed spite,
> That ever I was born to set it right!"

He let things drift as he lashed out here and there, without plan of action, without purpose for living. He was bored and inefficient.

211

What Persons Say about Being Bored

A roll call of persons who say they are bored brings out what they say makes them so. These may not be the causal factors, but these are what persons ascribe as reasons. Here are some of the major ones: (1) "There is no sense in what I am doing." Some have said they are just going in circles on a merry-go-round and have no way of getting off. They see themselves as facing a job of endless repetition, a round of chores. What's the use of it all, they ask. (2) "I'm not suited to what I am doing." Sometimes this is a complaint against the job and sometimes it is a complaint against the person himself. Here is a woman who sees herself writing a novel but she is washing dishes. Here is a stenographer in an office but she wants to be in a home where there is dishwashing. Here is a farmer who would like to be in a metropolitan region in market operations. Here is a salesman in a large city who would like to be out on a farm. (3) "I live with such uninteresting persons." This may be in the home, in employment, in the community, in the church. These persons consider those about them unstimulating with few interests. They can converse about the weather, items of health, and the cost of living. (4) "I'm always tired." Such a person may have debilitating health with biological factors causing fatigue or his own discouraged or defeated attitude may contribute to his lack of vigor. (5) "I'm not getting anywhere." Often conferences with these persons disclose that they do not have much idea about where they would like to be going. Some have goals that are too impractical for realization. Some have sound objectives but have been frustrated by combinations of circumstances. These persons feel they are on some sort of treadmill. (6) "I'm going it alone and nobody cares about me." Such a person usually wants to be on a team and to feel that teammates care. He is tired of solo playing in the game of life. (7) "Religion is mere routine." This person feels that he is merely going through a conventional round of activities, the same meetings, the same materials, and so on. And it may be that this is the case. (8) "I think that I am tired of everything." This sounds like the author of Ecclesiastes. This ancient man had tried wealth, children in his family, study, entertainment, social position, and more. The upshot of it all was meaninglessness. He concluded, "All is futility."

Here is a wide range of statements, but they all add up to the same thing. The person is saying, "I am bored with everything." He is also saying, "Life is unsatisfying. Life is monotonous." He comes to doubt that there is anything to give it zest and purpose. The French have a good word for this condition, *ennui* (an'we). This means dissatisfaction and weariness without promise of anything to give color to life.

The Universe a Continuous Creative Process

God does not provide us with a repetitious order of things. Change is always taking place. Koheleth in Ecclesiastes wrote, "There is no new thing under the sun." He lived his life from this viewpoint. He saw nature as a constant repetition. He said, "All the rivers run into the sea; yet the sea is not full." He thought of the wind blowing toward the south and then blowing the other way. No wonder this man was bored. Being God in the kind of world that he pictured would be an infinitely boring occupation. God would be sitting on a throne whose design never changes. He would be running a universe in which things happen over and over in monotonous repetition. Since perfection was thought of as a fixed condition God would never be causing anything different to happen. Being God would be the height, the depth of boredom.

But the universe we see today is not a monotonous round of what always has been. We are infantile in our conception of this cosmic order but we sense something of its unimaginable energy and creative power. Strange things keep happening. If there were a cosmic newspaper that had recorded things through a billion years, we would not find the story a wearying account of repetitions. It is not every day that Krakatoa erupts as it did in 1883 to send its volcanic dust from the East Indies around the earth. The dinosaurs and mastodons walk the earth no more; cows and sheep are with us now. We are living in a universe of change and diversity. It is exceedingly interesting, and man takes a hand in it to make it more so. He breeds and crosses plants and animals. He alters the contours of lands. He dams streams and controls floods. God did not supply us with a universe meant to be boring. We note a strange mixture of orderliness and predictability on one hand and of change and new situations on the other. We need both.

The Creation in the Restoration Message

Restoration theology pictures no has-been God, no forever-finished earth. Included in the Doctrine and Covenants is a digest of the revelation that God gave to Moses. Here God is portrayed as eternally creating. Here is a masterpiece sentence: "As one earth shall pass away, and the heavens thereof, even so shall another come . . . and there is no end to my works" (D. and C. 22:23). And what is more, God's creative expression in developing man as a person of eternal quality goes on eternally.

It is not unlikely that many who are bored with the business of living are thinking of God as one who might be described as the "Infinitely Bored." Certainly a God who exists in a finished creation, a fixed universe, a finalized calendar of events would never release man from the throes of boredom. Such a God is caught in a situation of sovereignty with little or no opportunity to live with zest and zeal in universal and eternal creative expression. Such a God can be a factor in producing or furthering this boredom.

Seeing Things Differently

The open-eyed person not only sees different things; he sees things differently. The prayer of Elisha for his young man-servant can be fulfilled in us, "Open his eyes, that he may see" ((II Kings 6:17). This youth was seeing the usual things in the usual way. Foremost in his picture were the Syrian hosts that had come to take Elisha. The prophet was seeing more. He said to the young man, "Fear not; for they that be with us are more than they that be with them" (verse 16). When his eyes were opened and he saw the helps that God was sending he became a different man. The affliction that came upon the invaders was blindness. The bewildered and the bored never see very much. What they see they do not see clearly and meaningfully.

The alert person sees things in wide perspective and broad possibility. He sees things differently. Any one of us tires if he keeps staring at the same things in the same way. A woman confined to her bed kept seeing the same design on the wallpaper until this made her irritable. She saw pink rosebuds until she was tired of pink rosebuds. One day a friend called, bringing a few roses, pink ones, from her own garden. The visitor talked of the enjoyment she was getting from her small rose garden. The invalid became interested. She fingered through catalogs that pictured roses. She learned names. She studied rose culture. Her friend kept coming to visit. She said that she made her dreary couch a bed of roses. Boredom gave way to "rosedom."

A woman went to the closet packed with her dresses and murmured, "Not a thing to wear." She was tired of everything she had. Her first impulse was to go out and buy a new ensemble. Uncertain and unsatisfied persons often want to buy new things, particularly clothes, to bolster themselves. The lift is temporary. Soon the thinness and monotony show up on the inside. The new clothes merely give a temporary covering to the drab interior of the person. A friend of resourceful spirit asked if she ever made a dress look different by wearing different flowers, different accessories, and by doing something different. She asked if she ever thought of dressing up differently on the inside. The woman bored with her wardrobe tried it. She discovered, "The dress is different because I am different."

The person who sees the same things in the same persons in the same places will probably be bored. Especially will this be so if he sees himself "in the same old way." A woman was quite perceptive who said to her husband, "Dave, would you try to do something different or wear something different? I am tired of things around here. To tell you the truth, I am even sort of tired of you." Both saw the situation and began presenting some other facet of themselves to each other and to their own selves. They lived more interestingly and they looked more interesting to one another. The bored atmosphere went from the breakfast nook, the book room, and the bedroom.

Healthy Christians keep their spiritual eyes in a good state of repair. Myopia leaves. Cross-eyed vision goes. Cataracts are removed. The healthy eyes see life more inclusively, more steadily, more meaningfully. Paul wrote to the Corinthians how we tend to "see through a glass, darkly" (I Corinthians 13:12). With expanding vision there is no place for boredom.

A Poet Who Was Not Bored

Robert Frost found life full of appealing things. He found something interesting in such a prosaic thing as a fence. As a freshman in college he used to take long walks in the woods alone. One day some upper classmen asked, "Frost, what do you do walking by yourself in the woods?" He said simply, "Gnaw bark." He was seeing things others did not see. He would take an idea or a situation and look at it from many angles, turn it inside out. He would find new meanings and new beauties even in common scenes and tired and timeworn phrases. This practice enables him to say, "The best thing we're put here for's to see."

215

Alertness to Learn from Others

Emily Kimbrough has given us a directive on living under the title, "How Not to Be Bored." She told of traveling with her grandfather on a train when she was a girl. He talked with the conductor and lingered to round out the conversation when the train stopped. As they were leaving, the grandfather remarked, "That was a very interesting thing he told me." The girl was irritated. She asked what a conductor could tell him that he did not already know. As if he had just come to the conclusion he commented, "I believe I have never met anyone who couldn't tell me something I hadn't known before."

Persons who can discover something interesting and worthful in others will never be bored. These others will not be specimens for study and observation but they will be persons in their own right. They will not be duplicates. They will be seen with humor, with understanding, with regret, with hope.

Jesus of Nazareth was a master in appreciating others. Every person appealed to Jesus in his own role and right. A Zacchaeus up a tree, a Peter in a fishing boat, a Martha in a kitchen, a thief on a cross—all these and more made up an album of persons to whom he turned with genuine interest and concern. He must have looked at the officious high priest, the doting mother, and the uncertain Pilate with a mixture of feelings. He listened to persons. He loved them. There was never a bored moment in his life among others.

The End of Boredom

Once Harrison R. Anderson preached a sermon on "the end of boredom." His text was John 10:10, "The thief cometh not, but for to steal, and to kill, and to destroy; I am come that they might have life, and that they might have it more abundantly." He pointed out that one way of life ends in deadness, the other in expansion. He affirmed that the new life that Jesus had in mind would "bring us to the end of boredom." The expectancy that life can be more than humdrum serves to make it more than emptiness and shallowness. Belief that life can be more than we have at the moment is a big factor in making this abundant life come to pass. Too often we underestimate the lifting power of Jesus Christ.

On the Misty Flats

Many persons start out with an artificial fling of excitement. They buy what they think will bring them whip-up and whoopee. This appeals for a while. Ultimately evil of this kind becomes humdrum, but not at first. The dosage of exciting potions has to be increased or this way of life grows stale. Many do not know either this first excitement of wickedness or the thrill of active goodness. They have not the courage to be good or bad. They lack the drive to be active in either goodness or badness. They live in the gray world of boredom. They do not ascend to the high road of right; they do not descend to the low road of wrong. They drift in between on the "misty flats," and we see that where they live is flat. John Oxenham put it this way.

> "To every man there openeth
> A Way, and Ways, and a Way.
> And the High Soul climbs the High Way,
> And the Low Soul gropes the Low.
> And in between, on the misty flats
> The rest drift to and fro."

A Lukewarm Congregation

Chapter 3 of the book of Revelation addresses the members of the congregation at Laodicea as in-betweens. These were the denunciatory words, "I know thy works, that thou art neither cold nor hot. . . . So then because thou art lukewarm and neither cold nor hot, I will spew thee out of my mouth." There can be no middle ground in allegiance to Jesus Christ. These people identified as "rich and increased with goods" were poor and blind and did not know it. For Laodiceans life eventually becomes stale. A Laodicean congregation seems at first comfortable, then conventional, then collapsed. It descends into the gray atmosphere of boredom on the misty flats.

For Living above Boredom

Again let it be said, the gospel is good news about abundant living. We need to see clearly what kind of person is visioned, what kind of persons we want to be. We shall look to see what resources are available for bringing about this kind of living. We shall identify the processes by which we shall go about achieving this good life. In this light we shall look at pointers for above-boredom living.

1. See things in their large relationship. This holds for persons, things, thoughts, everything. Anything in isolation is void of meaning. The whole universe exists in relationships. For a game to have appeal it has to be seen as a whole. To a novice a game, whether rugby or cricket, has to be seen in relationship. There has to be some goal to the game. A stroke in tennis is seen in the light of the total game, yet it has to be executed with accuracy and art as a unit in itself. Some see living only as a series of disconnected happenings. As such it is not understandable. It is boring. Jesus gave the eternal look to living.

2. Move into the not-yet-attempted. This does not mean hurried rushing into all kinds of novelties and taking all kinds of foolish dares. It does mean moving experimentally into fields not yet explored. When a person no longer meets new persons, no longer moves into new fields, and when he clings for security to what he has been doing, he is heading toward decline. Healthy faith is always calling men to pioneer. Those who insist on staying in their stable, settled ways of living will either become bored or boring, or both.

3. Select a focal point of interest in the program of the day, in the program of a longer unit of time. The nothing-to-look-forward-to outlook can stultify the soul. A crippled woman would always spice her day by picking out something to give color to the day—a letter to be written, a telephone conversation, a church periodical due in the mail, a radio program. A family would name highlights of the year—camping at reunion, the graduation of the son from high school, paying off the mortgage, a visit with relatives in the Rocky Mountain region. Life needs punctuation marks and exclamation points. Jesus had times that might be called mountaintop days, such as the Transfiguration experience with close friends and the Last Supper with his Twelve.

4. Associate with friends who have a zest for living. Some persons are catalogued as "wet blanket," "dry drooper," "sourpuss," and "dead timber." Such persons may complain and hold back until they sour the entire enterprise. Each one of us needs to minister to such persons and help them catch "the joy of the gospel." We also need to associate with those who will contribute to the upturn of our spirits. Sometimes persons who walk with downcast spirit will elect to be with a few with whom they can air and compare their ailments and their worries. Some testimony meetings take on this turn. Some groups cultivate the "ain't life bad" attitude. The Restoration movement visions associational

life in Zion that radiates cheer and confidence in its serious business.

5. Make acquaintances in today's world and in the world of yesterday who live zestfully and purposefully. The expanding circle of acquaintances and friends of a healthy person includes many out of the scriptures, out of history, out of church history, out of literature, out of science who "lived up." Among these are persons who faced frustration, misunderstanding, disappointment but who never gave up. We are encouraged as we get acquainted with Robert Louis Stevenson who was an invalid most of his life but who never surrendered to sickness of soul. At the center of our circle stands Jesus of Nazareth who radiated cleanness, confidence, good cheer whenever men would let him. We need to know him.

6. Practice praying in adventurous projects. The praying is a part of the project. The projects reach outside ourselves. It is healthy for us to think and talk with God about the needs and the welfare of others. One man revolutionized his life by getting concerned in an underprivileged family and talking with God about them. He brought them to know this God who meant so much to him. Then he could say, "After a while we get bored talking to God about ourselves, only ourselves, especially if we are not a very interesting subject to talk about."

7. Look for satisfaction in daily living. The healthy person identifies things that are satisfying. He does not disregard the unpleasant and unwanted but he does not concentrate all his attention on them. At one reunion a woman kept talking about how hard the benches were, how uncomfortable. And they were. Another woman said, "Yes, they are, but wasn't it a comforting meeting on uncomfortable benches." We can let one inconsiderate, garrulous camper get in the way of our enjoying a score of considerate, happy-hearted associates. God himself receives satisfaction and says, "It is good!" Life must be boring to the person who never expects to find anything rewarding and pleasing.

8. Interpret and experience the Spirit of God as enlivening and enlightening. When the Spirit of God is understood in his inclusive manifestations and ministries there is no place for boredom. One may feel restless and inadequate but not bored. It is good for us to keep hearing, "The Spirit quickeneth all things." Some persons put on dark glasses and keep their eyes glued to disaster and discomfort. They expect to hear in God's messages only doom and threat. The man ministered to by the stimulating, searching Spirit of God can never fall a victim to boredom.

The Restoration Gospel a Way of Vitality

The pioneers in 1820-1830 had no time, no situation that would lead them into boredom. The Restoration called for the adventurous, courageous spirit. Nothing like this movement existed anywhere. Over and over the word came, "A great and marvelous work is about to come forth!" Here was no finished product; everything was in process. Again and again they were told to move in a certain direction and they would receive counsel as they went on the way. Nothing dried and finalized in all this. Here was (1) a novel movement, (2) a large-scale adventure, (3) a present-tense operation, (4) an evolving organization, (5) a company of pioneers, (6) new scriptures, and (7) an on-the-job God.

Plan to Be Interested and Interesting

Let's be honest! Life can get boring. Often it does. The routine of occupation and of homelife can become so. The conventional operation of church services can lose sparkle. We can lose interest in our monotonous selves. We can listen only to humdrum conversation and pointless radio programs. We can gaze at faded wallpaper. We can keep eating the same kind of food. And God can seem to be going through a repetitious carrying on of his world work.

God does not expect us to surrender to an environment that is deadening. He expects us to be creative in arranging conditions of living that are conducive to looking-up and looking-out personal development. But he does not provide us with interest and zest as ready-made products. We have to use resources he provides for developing these. He intends that we use our own powers to bring this kind of situation, this kind of spirit into existence. This is the counsel of the Restoration prophet,

"The earth is full, and there is enough and to spare;
yea, I prepared all things, and have given unto the children of men to be agents unto themselves."
—Doctrine and Covenants 101:2 f.

The way of the gospel is the way of expanding insight, exhilarating spirit, exciting adventure. It prompts us to pray, "God, help me to discover thee in thy eternal freshness of spirit that I may release in my life springs of power that I may join thee in creative expression."

Questions for Discussion

1. How may God be pictured so that he will be, as one man said, "not very interesting or stimulating"?

2. What is your reaction to the comment that persons who are always bored are admitting their lack of initiative and resourcefulness in developing interesting activities?

3. Apply to daily living, "It is healthy to be bored with things as they are but it is not healthy to leave things so that we shall continue to be bored."

4. How is heaven sometimes pictured so as to appear boring to the dynamic person?

5. How may the universe be pictured as monotonous or as stimulating? Do you see it as resourceful, evolving, and appealing or as the expression of sameness?

6. How can you provoke interest and contributions to interesting living from those who appear at first "insensitive to others" and "grooved against change" in their outlook and pattern of living? Give instances of learning something of interest from persons who appear at first uninteresting.

7. How may we be incapable of appreciating persons of depth and insight so that they do not appeal to us? Does God ever affect us this way?

8. How may the Restoration movement be interpreted as an expression of free, adventurous spirit, of continuing exploration? How might it be interpreted otherwise?

9. Illustrate how a given activity may be appealing and interesting when seen as part of a purposeful whole but as drudgery when seen as a series of unrelated actions. Why, then, does God want us to get a mountaintop overview of his work?

10. How may praying become monotonous and, as some say, stifling? How does praying come alive as we get busy with God in interesting things?

11. How does the concept of the Spirit of God as "quickening all things" have bearing upon what will happen in us when we are inspired by the Spirit?

12. What do you see involved in "the stewardship of being interested and interesting"?

13. How may unsound interests lead us eventually into shallowness and then into deterioration and then into death of our spirit? What qualities identify a life-producing interest?

CHAPTER 19

LIVING BEYOND

LONELINESS

There is a general concern about loneliness. Eric P. Mosse in writing *The Conquest of Loneliness* said he designed it "for those who feel lonely—for everybody." He considers that "every man is alone" and that "every man can become lonely." Books on the aging speak of their sense of loneliness and of their feeling of being "pushed aside." Thomas Wolfe in *The Anatomy of Loneliness* looks upon it as "the central and inevitable fact of human existence" and as "the final cause" of "man's complaint." A woman puts the matter this way, "Who isn't lonesome? The difference between us is in how, and how much, and how often."

Dr. Mosse looks at loneliness as a disease. He speaks of it as something "to which everyone is exposed and to which anyone can fall a victim." In other words, loneliness is general, is serious, and needs to be understood, diagnosed, and met honestly. He considers it as a disease that can be treated and eventually cured. This sounds like strong language. Does this mean that the spiritually healthy person is never lonely? Does it mean that the person in good condition is always surrounded by understanding associates? Hardly. Rather is this saying that a person can be alone without being lonely, that a person can develop his own personhood so that he is able to share with others, and feel wanted. There is need to understand healthy aloneness in contrast to morbid and self-pitying loneliness. In this exploration we shall be inquiring about the contribution that healthy religion can make to this widespread problem.

Are We Born to Be Alone?

One observer with a psychiatric bent says that we are born into "an alien world." This sounds as if we had been dropped into a situation that was strange and unresponsive, that was neither friendly nor communicative. Many think so and live so. One song begins with this testimonial, "I am a stranger here, within a foreign land." This says that I do not belong here in this alien world and so I am born to be lonesome. Another hymn begins with this witness, "This is my Father's world!" This is not a placid belief that everything is all right and that life is going to be free from strain. The hymn goes on to say that "though the wrong seems oft so strong, God is the Ruler yet." There is battling to be done, there is a cause to be won, but we are not going to be crusading alone: God is in this great endeavor. It makes a difference whether we consider ourselves stranded in a hostile or indifferent country or residing in a universe with powers that will pull with us, with God.

Some see a universe quite without concern for man. W. H. Auden has phrased this view so well, "Looking up at the stars I know quite well, that for all they care, I can go to hell." Robert G. Ingersoll voiced this when he said that whenever man cries out for help, all that comes back to him is "the echo of his wailing cry." Those who see this kind of universe cannot call on anyone or anything for relief from loneliness in the midst of a world that seems too big, too complicated for them.

There is another view. This sees air and sunshine and soil and plant and animal life as contributive to man's living. There is oxygen to breathe, there is water to drink, there is fruit to eat, there are trees for shelter. These are not provided in packaged form. They are in the raw state, waiting to be discovered, tapped, and used in harmony with man's true needs and God's lasting purpose. The ready-to-use provision would make helpless parasites of us and we would never mature. The way of the universe is farsighted: it nudges us to become persons of resourceful nature and sound self-management. God's universe expects us to develop ability to stand on our feet rather than to go around propped up by an indulgent Santa Claus God. We are not born in a world that casts us off at birth to survive through calling upon our own resources without help from all that is about us.

More than Being with People

Companionship is more than being with a group of people. The solution for loneliness does not lie in providing the mere physical presence of others. Many times we feel most alone when in the midst of crowds. One can be moving with sidewalk traffic on a busy metropolitan street or be sitting in an amphitheater with thousands of other persons and feel no kinship with these multitudes. Sense of belonging calls for communication and joint participation. This means common language, common interests, common goals, common projects, common risks, common satisfactions. It is possible to be with thousands and not speak a common language.

A Roman Catholic attended one of our Latter Day Saint meetings and said, "I don't feel I belong here." The hymns were strange: he was not accustomed to group singing. The platform was drab and empty: he was used to an altar where he felt the "real presence" resided. The street attire of the elders expressed no color, no symbolism, and seemed ordinary in comparison with the priests with their ecclesiastical regalia. He enjoyed the friendliness but the meeting did not seem like "church" to him. It took a long time, considerable understanding on the part of member friends, and a willingness to learn before he felt at home in our meetings. And youth of our church did not feel at home in the mass of the Roman Catholic services. It seemed "a lot of getting up and down" and "Latin gibberish" to them. It takes a lot of speaking in the same language to feel at home, and this language includes that of heart and mind and hand. Sometimes mere intrapersonal greetings that follow conventional lines and expressions only add to the sense of loneliness.

Thronging together does not dispel loneliness. David Riesman has written *The Lonely Crowd* to characterize the middle-class urban society of our time in which persons flock together to escape their loneliness. In such a society men are concerned with obtaining social approval. They reflect like mirrors the expectations of others. The persistent concern is the threat of being left out or excluded. Moderns try to keep their social schedule filled for they do not want to fall into the vacuum of isolation.

The Way of Keeping Busy

It is easy in modern life to confuse keeping in motion with getting somewhere. The busy person may be devoting himself to something to which he is committed or his activity may be a cover-up for what is not on the inside. He may be hiding from others and even from himself the emptiness and the loneliness that is within. Some day an unexpected crisis may bring him into the realization of his true condition and he may come to see what has been driving him into social pursuits. On the face of things such a person appears to be "well adjusted." In time he may discover that he has kept busy with others because he lacked resources within to cope with the deeper needs of living.

Some Reactions to Loneliness

The lonely person is aware of apartness from those persons or those situations with which he thinks he would like to be connected. The person growing up keeps facing the necessity of making choices that regulate his own life and behavior. He can elect to line up with what others are wanting him to be and thus gain comfortable approval. Or he may choose to go a way that does not accord with prevailing patterns. Then he senses separation. Or there may be factors not of his own creating that separate him from the approved run of living. The price of complete independence with consequent separation is loneliness. The price of giving in to whatever prevails is surrender of true individuality. What do persons do? Note their possible reactions:

1. Hostility toward the persons, the groups, the society from whom they feel separated. Persons and groups can become targets of dislike and opposition. A youth not invited into a social or recreational club can crusade against the snobbery and the general undesirability of such cliques. A person can reject the ones who have rejected him. It is said that this is what the devil is doing after alienation from God.

2. Self-gratifying apartness. It is possible to rationalize that this apartness is best for the one withdrawing. The world may be too evil for him. There can be a certain satisfaction in self-denial, in a self-punishing relationship. One can say, "It is better to abide alone in a cabin than to dwell with many in the palaces of the ungodly."

3. Development of a dream world with self at the center. One can leave the unfriendly world and go to a castle of dreams where one amounts to something, where one achieves. The rags one wears may become silken garments. The club foot may give way in dreams to fleet-running feet.

4. Retirement to illness of body and mind. This can give excuse for inability to mingle with others and to achieve in the world of others. Sometimes physical symptoms may appear. Often this is visible in skin eruptions brought on by inner distress. In time illness or physical disability may be welcomed. This can excuse or it can elicit sympathy and attention.

5. Intense involvement in achieving success. The person may not feel personally accepted so he works ever so hard to attain the externals that are marks of success in the social world. These may be a house, an automobile, a record of salesmanship, clothes,

and the like. This achievement may take on a feverish quality. Yet such success may be covering a lonely heart.

6. Indulgence in drinking and other "reliefs" that give temporary covering-up of the inner hungers. Intoxicating liquors may become a cover-up for loneliness. Some have used smoking as a pipe-dream means of relaxing from aloneness and living in a fantasy of friendliness.

7. Flight to God. There can develop the outlook, If nobody in this world loves me, God understands and cares. This turning to God can take the form of seeking wisdom and strength for carrying through or the form of neurotic escape as a child might run to a parent rather than carry through on the playground. This can become unhealthy expression as it did when a young woman who never had young men invite her to date took to writing love letters to Jesus.

8. Association with non-present persons. This may be with persons in literature, in history, in scriptures, in contemporary life. These persons may be healthy or unhealthy, stimulating or depressing. The kind of person and the kind of association make a difference. It can be uplifting and wholesome to make acquaintance with men and women who have lived well, contributed well, and know God well.

9. Development of personal improvement program for increasing ability to associate with others. One man said, "My appeal to others is about nil. I can change some things, some things I cannot. I shall work on what I can improve." Such a program involves the inside of the person as well as consideration of externals.

10. Association with the not-well-accepted with whom the lonely person can hold priority of position. Some would rather be a big frog in a little pond than to be a little frog in a big lake. The socially uncertain often turn to those whom they can lead.

Compartments of Aloneness

The healthy person is unified. He has an allegiance to God that holds his life together. Yet there are many parts in his selfhood. The variety and the multiplicity of these several phases can give richness and provide interest to his life. A good man can have a place for baseball, for orchestral music, for woodland life and fishing, for mechanical engineering, for companionship with his wife and children, for the message of the Book of Mormon, for fraternity with fellow ministers, and so on. He has compartments for those several interests and emphases, yet he lines them together in one harmonious whole.

Such a person may have aloneness in one field and togetherness in several others. This can be very healthy. He may reflect while he is alone fishing on questions that he feels others would not understand. There may be things he does not share with his wife. If, however, such a man is alone in every field he will suffer from loneliness and will become quite ingrown. If he is always associating with others and never thinking independently he is likely to grow shallow and uncreative and subject to social pressures that demand that he adjust to prevailing patterns.

It is healthy to have compartments in which one is with others and compartments in which one is alone. God should be in both. Jesus of Nazareth dined with others and enjoyed their company. And on the night when he was choosing his twelve apostles, he went off alone in prayer: he and his Father were together. There were times when this aloneness and this togetherness were blended in a single occasion. For instance, at the Last Supper he wanted very much to be with his Twelve. There were times that same evening when he and they were far apart. He was alone when he talked to them about his impending death and about his departure. This is what he was thinking: Have I been with you so long and you have not caught what I have been trying to say? They were miles apart in spiritual distance.

Assurance through Living with God

A self-assured man said, "I'm completely on my own and I'll get there." He spoke a great illusion common to us humans, the self sufficiency of ourselves. So often we think, or act as if we think, that our potentialities are quite enough and that if we develop these and use them we shall do very well. It is true that God expects every one of us to develop our potentialities. This is our stewardship. He also expects us to do this in right relations with him, his universe, his people. It is an error for man to suppose that he can be independent of everything and everyone else. Without resources beyond his own, man cannot live at all. He has to draw on life-producing forces that are about him—on oxygen, food, liquid, warmth, and so on. Man cannot live on his own powers any more than a tree can live to itself in a vacuum, without the air, sunshine, soil, and moisture that the universe provides. Nothing is wholly self-sufficient.

And man needs the social-spiritual resources of the universe. He cannot become a person or remain a person without these. And he keeps drawing on the social heritage into which he is born. This will have weaknesses and drawbacks but it is better than a social vacuum. Our social heritage is not the creation of some one self-sufficient man but the centuries-long achievement of millions of persons working together and relying on each other. History reminds us that no man stands alone in self-acclaimed isolation.

The word usually ascribed to belief in one's own sufficiency is pride. A man thus afflicted is blind to his own inadequacies and his need to relate himself to others. Sooner or later he finds himself alone and unwanted. He becomes the fulfillment of the warning, "Pride goes before destruction" (Proverbs 16:18). His self-sufficiency leads in the long run to decline and defeat. One day he shall feel very much alone, unless his hunger for companionship becomes paralyzed.

The truly religious person senses his relationship with God as *creative dependence*.[1] He sees this functioning "not to stifle one's freedom but to exercise it through enlarging relationships." The maturing person does not "stay put" with God in some fixed image he carries but he keeps moving on with an enlarging image of God and keeps advancing "to the goal of mature responsibility through all his relationships." He senses expanding interdependence.

The healthy religious person combines both aloneness and relationship. He is apart from those who do not sense what is innermost in him. He is at one with God to the degree that he can communicate with God. He senses what Jesus meant when he said, "I am not alone, for the Father is with me" (John 16:32). Such a person is able to stand alone as far as humans are concerned against entrenched doers of evil, against smug and powerful leaders who twist things to their unsound plans, against stifling established institutions, against the dulled vision and sensuous tastes of masses. He senses that when he is with God his resources are stronger than the resources of those who oppose the good. He is assured that he is not going alone on a meaningless treadmill. He has something of the faith of the ancient Hebrew who said that as they were fighting for their freedom, "the stars

---

[1] Paul E. Johnson, *Personality and Religion*, 1957, p. 118

in their courses fought" against their enemy (Judges 5:20). He feels that one man with God is a majority.

Both Solitude and Communion

To be a person is to be alone with one's self. Man has dialogue with himself and comes to be aware that he has a self. He senses how it feels to be a person and to have individual distinctness, to be separate from the mass. As he grows to see himself as a person, he comes to sense how he is related to other persons—he sees himself through them. In all this he comes to feel incomplete and needing to be related to that which is beyond himself. He may search alone or with others. A person may be lonely either way. It takes both solitude and communion to effect good health as the searching goes on. William E. Hocking has called this "the law of alteration." This means the seeker goes back and forth from inner solitude to outgoing meeting with others.

The Life of Recoil

Some persons tend to shrink from those about them. Some are not at home with others. Some dislike association and involvement with others. We have come to refer to these as introverts. This simply means that these prefer to look in rather than to look out. This apartness becomes more pronounced if during childhood there is no one to understand and to help. In moderate degree this way in introversion can prove beneficial to those who have creative ability and resources for reflective thinking. The balanced person is both introvertive and extrovertive. If a child is thrust off to himself or if he finds no companionship in his creative bent, he may develop a permanent pattern of staying to himself. It was said of the poet Shelley that in his boyhood he "fled into the tower of his own soul and raised the drawbridge." Unable to make connections with others he turned to imagery, reflection, and day-dreaming.

This happened in the childhood life of Nathaniel Hawthorne and he was never able to come out of his shell. He was always shy and retiring. Critics say his writing needed more insight into life which might have come through association with others. In his *Septimus Felton* the chief character gives a picture of the author's mind, "I am dissevered from the human race. It is my doom to be only a spectator of life, to look on as only a part of it." When Hawthorne died, Emerson wrote in his journal of the "painful solitude" of the man and his death at the close of those lonely years.

Both nurture and nature figured in shaping these personalities. Shelley and Hawthorne would probably be regarded today as "problem children." They would not fit into the grooves of the well adjusted. In a way their superior intelligence and their several gifts tended to keep them apart from others. Much of the ordinary round of life would have little appeal and would express, as Hawthorne once said, "a good deal of nonsense." The well balanced person can blend the two sides as Kipling suggested,

"If you can talk with crowds and keep your virtue,
Or walk with kings—nor lose the common touch . . ."

Such a person can speak several languages, including the language of the inner soul and the language of the common folk. Those who recoil from persons will find themselves retrogressing into loneliness.

The Apartness of the Extrovertive

Today there is quite a tendency to put high premium on extrovertive habits. The person who can greet others easily, move confidently in social circles, and "go over in a big way" in social gatherings is considered the approved type. Such a person is supposed to have many friends. Often simple exploration discloses that such persons have many speaking acquaintances but few, if any, person-with-person friendships. One man who boasted of his wide circle of acquaintances eventually admitted that he did not have one person with whom he could converse soul-to-soul. We tend to forget that it is the *quality* of social contacts that counts most in building a healthy personality. Mere quantity may get in the way. Excessive social stimulation and surface contacts can weaken personhood. Indiscriminate sociability can be a hindrance. We do well to distinguish between the "child in the corner" who is brooding over slights and loneliness and the "child by himself" who is occupied in some absorbing interest outside himself.

Some so-called extroverts are always greeting somebody but meeting nobody. They address themselves to others but never get to know them. They may call others by their first names and shake hands with them and talk of "lots of little things" but never have community. An ordained man with ready flow of words confided that he did not speak to persons in particular but always to "audiences" in general. He did not sense connection with persons. Eventually he acknowledged his loneliness. The so-called extrovert can be very lonely. He may put on an act of sociability to cover up the social hunger that is on the inside.

Guidelines Away from Isolation

Wholesome association does not come by chance. It takes wholesome persons with healthy insight into their spiritual natures using effectively the art of spiritual communication to rise above loneliness. Such persons will know how to live with themselves and develop resources for appealing companionship with others. We do not simply say, "Now I am going to be likable; I am going to like others." This would probably end in defeat. The more we aim at popularity, the more we are likely to miss it. We have to learn how to live with God who never draws inside a heavenly shell. Here are some suggestions to help:

1. Develop interests in things outside yourself, in other persons.

The general rule is this: "Turn your attention away from yourself to things outside yourself, to things worth being interested in with others. Let the interest speak for itself." We care little for those who insist on talking about themselves all the time. A bore has been defined as a person who talks about himself when you want to talk about yourself. We like those who make us a part of their attention, their conversation, their plans. They make us feel that we count. We get along best when we and our associates are concerned in something outside ourselves in which we can share together. This has to be something worth sharing.

2. Look at yourself fairly and squarely—and not too seriously.

This takes honesty. This takes overview. This takes sense of humor. W. H. Barbellion in *The Journal of a Disappointed Man* comments, "There are people who have seen many things but they have never seen themselves walking across the stage of life." He goes on to say that most of us would not recognize ourselves. Some of us indulge in discounting ourselves, some in adulating ourselves. We need to see ourselves as we are in an inclusive picture. One young man did this and concluded, "I took a pretty good all-round look at myself. I found things that must annoy others; I found some things that can be put to pretty good use." One woman took an honest look at her raucous voice and concluded it was enough to irritate others. She said she oiled it and toned it down and put some warmth into it. She was wise enough to see that this had to come from genuineness on the inside. Taking inventory is not enough. We have to vision what it is going to take to put us in spiritual condition.

3. Commune with with God in outreaching expression.

Much of our praying can be considered self-centered. The pronouns *I* and *me* are pretty prominent. The lonely person can give praying a self-pitying and self-concerned quality. Truly healthy communion with God involves doing something creative and productive in God's program. Then we have something with which we can converse with God. Whenever we are concerned about the welfare of persons, identifiable persons, conversation with God does not grow stale. Then we are able to pray with those who share this interest.

4. Combine apartness and togetherness.

Make a place for being alone and for "being with." Here is a both-and relationship rather than an either-or program. Expect to have some time with your own self and to enjoy your own company. The person who has to be with others all the time is probably shallow or insecure. A resourceful person can carry on dialogue with himself when he is doing something interesting enough to talk about. But he also plans to converse with others as far as they and he can share. And God is always in this conversation. There is no absolute aloneness.

5. Cultivate the ministry of the Holy Spirit in creative manifestation.

Some views of nature and the function of the Holy Spirit support and validate the concept of living apart with God; but rightly understood, the Holy Spirit is the enlivening and enlightening divine personal energy that prevents our sinking into a little inbred, fixed order of things. The Holy Spirit draws us into relationship with all that is, prompts us into brotherly relationship with all persons that are. In wholesome thinking about the Holy Spirit no one can be a recluse or a reactionary.

6. Find what is stimulating in nature, in literature, in science, in history, in scriptures, in persons, in the church, in God.

This comment was made concerning a man of wide range of interests: "It is so interesting to travel with him. He sees things the rest of us never see and he makes them come alive." The common roadside is crowded with things to see. Trees have a character of their own. The clouds and the sunset are works of art. The local persons speak in their speech, their mannerisms, their dress the atmosphere of the region. To the spiritually healthy person God's universe is crowded with interesting things. Such a person is interested and interesting and he has an interested and an interesting God.

7. Associate with Jesus Christ as a Person who calls us into interesting adventure.

The three years Jesus of Nazareth spent in public ministry were crowded with stimulating happenings. He was always reaching out to others. Some pictures of this Jesus make him dull and lonely and withdrawn. Such a Jesus could and does encourage worshipers to become separated and secluded. The Jesus of the New Testament kept sending his disciples out to live among others and to minister to them. He advised them to go apart that they might be better qualified to go among others. The restoration of communion with the ever living Christ in our modern era reveals the dynamic, outreaching Son of God. No withdrawing here.

There is ample place for being alone in the gospel of Jesus Christ, as this gospel is portrayed in the Restoration movement. Joseph Smith went to the grove alone: he returned from the grove to minister to others. The first directive about the mission of the restored church was to all men. The Holy Spirit was to enable men to be spiritual brothers. The disciples were to bring into being a social order that was to be called Zion. The members were to bring in their oblation gifts for the assistance of those not so well supplied. The salutations "brother" and "sister" came to be used in the fraternity. Ministers were to go into homes to minister to all members; they were to seek out the lonely and needy. God was seen as the Father of all men everywhere. And the Saints sang of their fellowship.

Questions for Discussion

1. How may a set toward loneliness be developed in a child's early years? What kind of religious experience would lead a child into healthy contacts with others?
2. How may certain conceptions of what spirituality is prompt

a person toward loneliness? How may a sense of opposition to the world and the worldly prompt a person toward a way of spiritual isolation?

3. How may keeping busy be a cover-up for inner loneliness? How may this take place in a congregation or in the larger church?

4. How may one hide in a dream world of Zion or of heaven that can shut one off from association with other persons?

5. How is evangelism as the sharing of good news a way of moving out of loneliness? How would a sense of separation from other persons prevent evangelistic expression?

6. How did Jesus of Nazareth practice going apart from other persons? For what purpose? How can such going apart increase our fitness for ministry to others?

7. How may a person live in the point of view that it is more saintly to suffer loneliness than to enjoy friendliness?

8. How is it possible for a handshaking extrovert to be lonely? For what is he hungry? How may his extrovertive expression get in the way of genuine friendship?

9. How do you see the universe as friendly or as unfriendly? How may we expect God's universe to bend to our notions of what is friendly? How do you see the universe supporting us as persons?

10. Do you see our modern way of living producing more experience of loneliness? What kind of spiritual program and ministry can counteract trends toward impersonal relationships and services? How may this trend find its way into church life?

11. Under the axiom that the interested are interesting how can the church go about developing spiritual living that will be conducive to expandable interests that will make Saints interesting?

12. How may worship be an escape from loneliness? How can worship be an adventure into interesting living with God?

13. How do you portray the life in the church as "a great and marvelous work" that will deliver persons out of loneliness into creative fellowship?

CHAPTER 20

HANDLING SENSE
OF GUILT

Some words carry a harsh association. "Guilt" is one of these. There is a coldness and a finality in the pronouncement, "Guilty!" Generally a person is distressed who feels "guilt" in himself. This association goes back a long time. It is as old as man's sense of right and wrong. Man has always felt that somebody would check up on him and hold him responsible for his unapproved behavior. It might be the state that would check on him, or the gods, the tribe, the family, the club, or the business institution. This sense of guilt applies both to things he has done which he ought not to have done and to things he has left undone which he should have done. The term implies responsibility for wrongdoing.

Seen in the Larger Context

As we mature, we see things in larger relationships. Inches expand into light-years but we use both in measurement. At first we are inclined to think of a little world, often with ourselves as the central figure. Our world revolves around us. Some persons never grow beyond this. Others come to think of whatever we do as related to the great universe. In some the bigness gets so emphasized that they lose sense of small, immediate responsibilities. Our universe should keep getting bigger and bigger. Then things ought to be seen in the light of this increasing relationship. Yet small things are not left out. We think of life as becoming more complicated. We can see every action, every thought of ours involved in a great pattern of interrelationship.

In all this we can think of God as the center of everything or we can look upon ourselves as occupying the focal place. When we do the latter, we get out of relationship with the universe in which God is mover and unifier. The word we use for this self-centeredness is *sin*. While we admit that God is the center, we can picture him in such a limited way that we shut him out from ever so many aspects of the universe. This also makes us sinners.

We can shut him out from some parts of our selves and sin in this way. In healthy spirituality we see the totality of our selves in relationship to the totality of God in his total universe. As one man put it, "This is big business."

When we see life, when we look at ourselves in this larger perspective, we sense more shortcomings. We acknowledge that we fall short, that we are quite out of touch with God—or at least, partly so. This is not a matter of ignorance or ineptitude. It is the honest discernment of a perceptive soul. Some suppose that as we learn more and more and as the radius of our universe pushes out, we should lose the sense of sin. Not at all. The larger our universe and the clearer our conception of its operations, the more we sense the wideness and the complexity of the relationships in the life we are living. We should become more conscious of this bigness and these requirements of us. We see more definitely our need of right relations with God, with everything that is God's. We are aware that we sin and we honestly admit it. Strong and honest persons do not hesitate to do so. Weak persons who want to put up a front and excuse themselves cover up or deny their sinfulness.

There is a healthy and an unhealthy way of admitting that we are sinners. This sense of guilt can undermine us, weaken us, and consume our energies or it can stimulate us to rightness. The person who senses no guilt is in an unhealthy condition. The person who broods over it cannot cope with it and is also in an unhealthy state. The healthy person learns how to identify and handle his sense of guilt. This is so widespread that persons need to come to grips with the problem.

Cataloguing Sins and Salvations

So many persons say they want things down "in black and white." Once William Temple said his sins were all gray. We can only think that he meant they were not glaringly black or that his virtues were not angelically white. These intermediate shades bother many of us. Here the lines are not clear-cut. Many people want life categorized as either-or. They want listed all the things permitted and all the things not permitted, with specific penalties for specific misdeeds. Next they want specific identification of the method of deliverance for each misdeed. They want specification of sins, specification of penalties, and specification of means of removing consequences for misdoing. Usually they also want an authoritative pronouncement that the proper requisites have been met, that good relations have been restored and guilt removed.

Persons of immature spirituality want such listing for several reasons: (1) It provides them with an index by which they are able to know if they are "in bad" and how much. (2) It saves considerable effort at self-analysis and self-evaluation. (3) It provides definition and surety about penalty and remission of penalty. Especially is this so if there is some official or priest with recognized authority who can say "Released" or "Absolved." Then the wrongdoer is released from guiltiness and from punishment.

The Hebrews Began with Cataloguing

When the Hebrews stayed at Sinai on their way out from Egypt to their new home, they received a detailed code of the permitted and the non-permitted; they had a catalogued list of what pleased and what displeased God. Along with this went a listing of what they would have to do to get out from under God's wrath for whatever they had done or not done. Then the priest could assure them that the slate was washed clean. If some discomfort or ill fortune came to them, they jumped to the conclusion that they had done some specific thing that was displeasing to God. They would try to find out just what it was so they could make specific amends. They assumed that there would be some things for which they were guilty that they had overlooked, so each year there was a Day of Atonement when the scapegoat was offered and the slate of the nation was washed thoroughly clean.

In those days there was not much place for relativity. An act was wrong or it was not wrong. The people were not developed enough to make moral judgments and to choose the wise and right course between several alternatives. Usually they sensed their guilt in terms of ill fortune that they believed God sent them rather than in terms of what they themselves were. It was the overt act that counted.

Yet back in those Mosaic days there was some endeavor to get the people to sense a distinction between sins committed unwittingly and sins committed willfully. It was a long way from the time of Jesus of Nazareth when he taught that what was in a man's mind and heart mattered ever so much. It takes a more advanced moral development to make place for motivation and intention. Children are aware of this place of motive and intent when they say of another child, "And he did it on purpose, too." Higher levels of guilt include how we purpose and how we carry through what we have in mind. And this is harder to apprehend.

Lower Sense of Guilt

When sins and consequences are listed in specific terms, a person has a sense of guilt in proportion to the size of the sin he has committed according to the catalogue. Sometimes he measures his guilt in terms of the greatness of the person or the institution against which he has sinned. This latter view could put man in a helpless condition when he sinned against God, for God is infinite and man's sin against God would have infinite proportions. The guilt is identified not in terms of the condition of the sinner but in terms of external factors.

In this lower conception of guilt a person might feel no strain if he was sure he would not be caught. A man might say, "What God does not know does not hurt me." Guiltiness and getting caught are linked. It was of considerable importance when early people began thinking of God as being on a mountain or living in the sky. There God could see everything. Then it was not possible to go to the other side of the mountain and commit the forbidden without being seen. The view is still prevalent that one can do whatever he can get by with.

Guiltiness in the Person

On the whole, guilt is concerned with the state or condition of a person who falls short in carrying out his obligations. As one's own sense of rightness is heightened and one's sense of responsibility is deepened the person is able to evaluate more adequately and more readily. He does not wait for a policeman to arrest him or for a thunderbolt to come at him and strike him down. He says to himself, "I did it" or "I didn't do it" and "I am responsible." The genesis of guilt is from within.

On this higher level the person is concerned with what takes place within himself when he falls short. He is aware that he is not the man he might become. He is aware that he has deprived others of what he might have contributed. He is aware that he has not been cooperating with God. He points a finger at himself and says, "You're guilty." He is not concerned with fragmentary deeds that can be listed on an inventory sheet; he is concerned with his whole self, with his total spiritual health.

Asset or Liability?

Sense of guilt can tear us apart and depress us or it can stimulate us to become the person we are capable of becoming. Sometimes a sense of guilt pushes a person into such discouragement, into such discontent with himself that he becomes ineffective and neurotic. He can spend his time and energy brooding over how bad he is, how cast off he is, how hopeless he is. At the bottom of his troubles he is seeing God as vengeful and vindictive, looking at him as a creature born in sin, inclined to sin, and steeped in sin. Persons have gone into melancholia, have given up trying and even got rid of their "useless" lives as they have surrendered to an overpowering sense of guilt. Here religion is behaving very badly and the sense of guilt is a heavy liability.

On the other side are persons who have little or no sense of guilt with little capacity for it. They have little sensitivity to others and to God. They have little or no concern about what is happening to them or where they are going. They are living on a pigpen level of existence. They have no inclination to evaluate what they are doing. They have little basis for making evaluations of themselves. Their theme song can be, "It makes no difference what I do; and if I don't care, then why should you?" We can say that those who have an undue concern about guilt are on the priggish level and those without any concern are on the piggish level. Neither is healthy.

But the capacity for guilt can be cultivated and expressed as an asset. It can be the stimulation to sound evaluation of what we are and of what we are doing. It can be an impelling force in motivating improvements in our living. In healthy spirituality we admit that we are as we are, and we move toward realizing what we can become. We use our energies in moving on rather than in regretting where we have been. We see God concerned in helping us live with him in his way rather than in punishing us because we have been apart from him. The honest, hopeful person admits that he has fallen short in carrying out obligations but he also expects that with God's help he can rise above past shortcomings. He says, "I have sinned and come short," but he also says, "I can do all things through Christ who strengthens me." He believes that God understands what he has been doing and still cares for him even though He does not approve.

When Sense of Guilt Hinders

Thousands of persons suffer from a sense of guilt. Some become hardened and do not have the sensitivity to care. Some cultivate the sense of guilt until it gets out of bounds. There are many reasons for our experiencing this guiltiness. Sometimes it comes from a sense of having exercised bad influence on others. The evil effects of a person can permanently mar another life. Sometimes it comes from awareness of hatred and malice toward others. This remains as a canker sore inside. Sometimes it comes from consciousness of plain ornery behavior. The list might go on and on. It is enough to say that these feelings undermine health. Here are ways in which sense of guilt can hinder and harm:

1. When the sense of guilt is kept bottled within us, so that it festers in our personhoods; when there is no release through confiding in another, when the person feels too guilty to speak of his sense of guilt.

2. When the guilt is considered so deep, so despicable that it is looked upon as unforgivable; when offenders speak of having committed "the unpardonable sin."

3. When undue attention is given to weakness and short-comings so that energy is taken up with anxiety and remorse, which energy ought to be used in activity and remedy.

4. When targets are set up so that we spend time blaming others and excusing ourselves from blame. We feel guilty, but we keep saying, "It wasn't my fault." So we direct our hostile feelings toward parents or employers or associates or administrators or others. Or it may be the church. Or the state. The target is a relief-seeking device.

5. When God is pictured as vengeful and as taking delight in punishing sinners. Such a view shuts off possibilities of forgiveness and reconciliation and chances of receiving help.

6. When we make ourselves the center of everything so that everything revolves about us. Then we are inclined to say of some unfortunate experience, "Why did this have to happen to me?" We come to look upon ourselves as caught in a trap of circumstances. There may be a sense of guilt without honest admission of responsibility.

7. When we divorce ourselves from healthy social situations

that would help us to become revived and restored in wholesome living. Sometimes this grows out of the attitude that persons of good quality would not want to associate with such as I. Often persons with sense of guilt stay away from the Lord's Supper and divorce themselves from available help.

8. When we are belligerant toward those who persist in a good quality of saintly living. Sometimes we are inclined to read into their lives the qualities for which we are feeling guilty. Then it is easy to dub them hypocrites and pretenders. Then we can say, "If the truth were known, they would be not better than I am."

9. When we place the blame on the devil. This is represented by the comment of the small boy who invaded his mother's cooky jar. He told her, "It wasn't my fault. I was just standing there and the devil reached out and pushed my hand in." There can be a devil-blamed sense of guilt without admission of responsibility. Many things are laid to Satan that ought to be laid to self and society.

10. When we consider ourselves born in sin and inheriting guilt. Then we look upon ourselves as enmeshed in original sin and God-assigned guilt. One man put it this way, "I was caught before I got here. What right has God to blame me?" In this view we are born guilty.

The Strings of Guilt Get Tightened

Anna and John "had to get married." Their baby was born five months after their marriage. She was a member of the Church of Jesus Christ; he was not. She carried a sense of guilt about their premarital sex relations. When she talked to an elder after her baby was born, he reminded her of the enormity of her sin and told her that since God required a payment for everything, she might expect an unhealthy or a maimed child. This intensified her sense of guilt. She felt it unfair that her child should suffer because of her laxity. She lived several miles from a congregation and had been able to attend but once a month. Now she did not feel worthy to partake of the Lord's Supper; she considered herself unworthy to be with the Saints. Her sense of guilt deepened into despondency. It was then that she wrote a letter to me as a patriarch.

Theology—that is, the conception of God—was at the heart of her problem. The approach to her problem had to begin with consideration of her picture of God. It had to face frankly her misconceptions and those of the elder who had been advising her. This involved looking at God's loving concern for her baby, at his forgiving fatherly concern for her, and at his evangelistic concern for her husband. All this called for recognition of the consequences of parents' conduct upon their children. This would include the effect she was having on her child and her husband as well as herself through the despondent spirit she was carrying. As her understanding grew she resolved in humility and in honesty to go to the next service of the Lord's Supper and renew the covenant she had made in baptism. Again she would rise to walk in "newness of life." This she did. Both she and her family were "saved."

Her own sense of guilt had been adding to her guilt. She had been bringing a gloomy atmosphere to her home. In her sense of guilt for premarital relations she had come to look upon all sex relations as evil. Her anxiety about the baby had come to prevent a happy mother-baby relationship. Her husband was beginning to consider her religion, her church responsible for their unhappy homelife. Her later shortcomings were piling up to become more deleterious than the sin which had been worrying her. The strings of guilt had been tightening more and more and they were choking her spirituality. She had come to feel helpless and condemned.

Then came release and relief and renewal.

A Guilt Concern at Sunset

An eighty-year-old man in a home for senior adults wrote in scribbled hand, making a request that I come to see him. When we were alone, he poured out his anguished concern. He had never mentioned this anxiety to anyone. It was too close to his heart. He realized that before long he would be dying. An unusual fear and sense of guilt were plaguing him. Pitifully he told that he had been born out of wedlock. Would God hold this against him and reject him? With little else to occupy his thinking, this sense of illegitimacy kept gnawing at him. Would he be spiritually illegitimate, too? Yet he was sure there was nothing he could do. He felt helpless and rejected. Again the problem was theological.

We began by talking about God, about God's concern for every one of us. We went on to consider that God does not look at some single incident in our lives or at some small segment: he looks at the wholeness of us. The old man had read that unusual and usually misunderstood statement in James 1:15 and had concluded that this one misfortune in his life made him totally guilty. James appears to have been striking at the excusers who felt they could cross their fingers and get by on some matters. James saw this not as a single sin but as a sinful quality that could permeate the entire selfhood. Such behavior reaches into every fiber of our living. It is the total pattern of ourselves that matters, yet one phase of living can affect and reflect the whole.

This elderly man needed to see that God was not expecting him to march by and present a birth certificate. God would be concerned with what he had done with his own life in terms of what he had had to work with. Then it was time to say, "Let these sunset days be peaceful ones as you look forward to meeting a Father who understands and receives in loving-kindness." Sense of guilt left the old man. As he took my hand in parting, he was able to say, "I feel better and surer than I have felt for many years." His burden was lifted. He saw to some degree the God of new birth replacing the God whom he felt had been focusing on his illegitimate birth.

A Concern to Make Amends

A young man of twenty-seven was carrying very sensitively a feeling of guilt for the way he had treated his parents. He said he had disregarded their counsel. He had indulged in late hours and lost weekends. He had turned to drinking against their will. Now he was looking at all this with a sense of remorse and guilt. What should he do? Should he return to their farm and make things easier for them? In a survey of his total life program this did not appear to be the wisest course. It would take him from the larger work that he ought to be able to do. This came to be the decision: (1) He would give his life to the cause of Christ, the cause to which his father and mother were giving their lives. (2) He would write a message of appreciation to his parents and tell them of his deepening gratitude. (3) He would use his wayward experiences in understanding youth inclined to do the same in guiding them toward return. His guilt gave way to gratitude for God's patience and for the helpful ministry of friends.

The Gospel of Christ Can Lift Sense of Guilt

The gospel is essentially a message about getting right with God. Guilt involves a feeling of apartness, a break in good relations, and a sense of personal responsibility that this has happened. We need to learn how to go about getting right rather than fretting about our alienated condition. The Restoration gospel holds out these resources and guidelines:

1. Man is responsible to God for that over which he has control. He does not inherit guilt for what others have done who have lived before him—and this includes Adam. He does inherit consequences of their evil living but he does not inherit blame. The fruits of a father's life may be transmitted but not the guilt.

2. God is forgiving as man endeavors to qualify for forgiveness through forgiving others and through making amends for his wrongdoing. God does not hold grudges. He wants every person to know him and live with him. He plans a universe in which all of us reap the consequences of what we and others do, but he does not harbor vindictive judgments.

3. Ministers and members, reaching out in brotherly spirit, help those who have a sense of guilt to understand God and to find their way back to God. In the church there are counselors and confidants who will help the needing person to find release and renewal. The gospel teaches mutuality in carrying burdens.

4. Jesus Christ is the minister of reconciliation. He enables us to see that confused and contrary men can appreciate how forgiving God is. When men were doing their worst, this Christ was able to pray, "Father, forgive them, for they know not what they do." In the fifth chapter of II Corinthians Paul said that God was in Christ reconciling man to God. A man who knows Jesus Christ has neither grudge nor guilt.

5. The church provides for members to ask pardon of one another, to receive and to grant forgiveness. Members are to go to each other and seek to iron out tensions. The gospel teaches us how to say "I'm sorry," "I want to do right," and "I forgive you." Strong persons are not afraid to admit mistakes.

6. The sacrament of baptism expresses the immersion of man in God's lifting power and reconciling love. The man who "gets in all over" feels cleansed and restored to God. The person who is complete and genuine in his commitment to God is "raised up" to "walk in newness of life" (Romans 6:4).

7. The Holy Spirit affords sense of communion with God. The person drawn and directed and stimulated by the Holy Spirit is released from sense of guilt. There is something akin to the glow of brotherhood between two persons who have been

estranged. One day two men who had been at variance openly faced their differences, diagnosed them, and worked on them. They were members of the church. Both were elders. They discovered that they had a common allegiance to Jesus Christ and to his church and that this loyalty took precedence over their differences. They shook hands in renewing their covenant. Said one, "There's a glow in my heart." Said the other, "I feel like a new man." Both had felt guilty that they were holding feelings of dislike and distrust. Persons can experience this feeling as they are reconciled to God.

8. In the Lord's Supper we may renew our covenant with God and make a fresh start. We make confession and we endeavor to rechart our course. Every person needs to come to "the land of beginning again." Rightly received, this sacrament enables the covenanting person to make a fresh start, to sense forgiveness, to move forward again. There is no place for guilt in us if we go all the way.

Without Restraint or in Good Restraint

Some schools of modern thinking consider any sense of guilt quite undesirable. These would throw away any form of religion that makes a person feel guilty. If you have troublesome inhibitions in matters of sex or social relations, get rid of the inhibitions; then there is no sense of shame or guilt. On the whole this is an undiscriminating approach. We need to look over our conventions and our prohibitions and evaluate them carefully. Some of them do go contrary to human nature; they are ill-founded. Some do warp persons; some do tie them in knots. Something should be done about these unsound do-not's. This is something quite different, however, from saying that we should lift all bans and sound the slogan, "Let every man do as he pleases!" To do this is to reduce us to jungle living. One advocate of this approach put it this way, "I want to be free to do as I jolly well please and not feel sorry about it."

Three major courses are possible: (1) We can open the doors and remove all restraints. Then there could be no sense of guilt. (2) We can designate in detail what may and what may not be done, so that guiltiness is definite and penalities are specific. (3) We can construct a picture of saintly living so that we sense responsibility for the total self in a total situation. Here we sense satisfaction and dissatisfaction in terms of what we are in relation to what we can become. In a healthy way we sense our shortcomings and our shortsightedness. We admit that we have fallen short. We believe that God understands and wants to undergird us for abundant living. We are ashamed but we do not give up. We seek a nobler way of managing our powers with God as the Great Manager. This God does not submerge us in a pool of guiltiness and hold us under. He helps us wash ourselves clean and come out with "newness of life."

Questions for Discussion

1. How is the way a person feels guilt and the things for which he feels guilt a measurement of his spiritual maturity?

2. A very conscientious elderly sister in the church was distressed with a sense of guilt because she had eaten some fruit cake made with brandy. She was more remorseful because the cake had tasted so good to her. How would you go about helping her to find relief from her sense of guilt?

3. Under what conditions would you say that a person might be considered guilty by reason of ignorance? When might a person be held responsible for ignorance of conditions and consequences?

4. Sigmund Freud looked upon sense of guilt in religion as thoroughly unhealthy and undesirable. He interpreted it as childish reaction against a father against whom he was rebelling. He considered that a person should forge ahead in his own strength rather than relying on a God he feared. What do you have to say in reaction to this idea of guilt?

5. How may a person take punitive measures against himself to relieve a sense of guilt? How is this practiced in some strict sects or orders such as the flagellators? What is the purpose back of this? How may one use spiritual whips on himself instead of a physical instrument of flagellation?

6. Why do so many persons want a detailed listing of what God permits and does not permit? How does this program limit spiritual maturing?

7. What kinds of conception of God can develop an unhealthy sense of guilt? What makes this conception and practice of guilt unhealthy?

8. How is this an unsound conception of God: "All I have to do is to ask Jesus to forgive me and he does"? Do you see any spiritual requirements and responsibilities in receiving divine forgiveness?

9. How are the sacraments of baptism and the Lord's Supper means for enabling us to remove sense of guilt? What do you consider mature uses of these sacraments for achieving renewal and restoration?

10. Contrast inheritance of consequences and inheritance of guilt. Apply this to a child's biological and spiritual inheritance. Direct to a young man's comment, "God is not going to hold me responsible that my father was a drunkard before I was born, but he will hold me responsible for the way I influenced my father after I was old enough to understand the situation."

11. How would inability to sense remorse be an index of a rather low spiritual condition? What kind of person would never sense regret?

12. What provisions and services do you find in the gospel of Jesus Christ and in the Church of Jesus Christ for developing a healthy approach to remorse and sense of guilt?

13. How can this prayer of Reinhold Niebuhr give guidance in matters or responsibility? Apply it to some specific life-situations.

> "O God, give me serenity to accept what cannot be changed; courage to change what should be changed; and wisdom to distinguish one from the other."

CHAPTER 21

This study keeps saying that spiritual healthiness calls for *wholeness of personality.* Each person has to hang together with a fundamental unity. This unity has to come from within. Externals will not pull us together, yet we cannot experience this spiritual health without getting outside ourselves. We draw on health-producing forces and we live in health-affording relationships. If any one of us tries alone to put himself into one piece, he is likely to go to pieces.

This unity is achieved only through linking every particle in us with the oneness of things that we call the universe. No compartment is exempt. As soon as we start leaving out any part of body or mind, disorganization or inner strife sets in. Paul wrote of this to the Corinthian congregation and summarized his message in saying that "the body is one" and that "all members . . . are one body." So he says "there should be no schism in the body" (I Corinthians 12). J. B. Phillips had made a passage read this way, "God has harmonized the whole body by giving importance of function to the parts which lack apparent importance, that the body should work together as a whole with all the members in sympathetic relationship with one another" (verses 25, 26). He was using the individual body to symbolize the functioning of the church. It applies to our personhood as well.

Sometimes we disavow some part of our body or of our personality as if it might go off on a tangent by itself and function in its own world. So often this is the case with sex. In good health, sex is included in the total selfhood and it never goes off in an arena of its own.

Man's Long Perplexity about Sex

It appears that mankind has always been perplexed about what to do with sex, about how to include it in his total program of living. Too often it has been set apart as if it could run a program of its own. Studies in cultural anthropology disclose how important it has been in the mores of groups. Earlier man must have discovered that here was a strong biological drive that could not be ignored, nor suppressed. He must have seen quite early that this drive would wreck society if allowed to go undirected and unharnessed. So groups put regulations and prohibitions around it in one way or another. Man has struggled between two extremes. On one side he sought to place sex under specific controls as a part of his group life; on the other side he left it to go its own free way. Sometimes man thought of sex as a great concern of his God or his gods; sometimes he looked upon it as quite outside the sphere of what was holy. In some ancient cults the priests had sex relations with designated priestesses as a part of the rituals to insure fertility; in others anything having to do with sex was looked upon as too evil for association with a pure deity. Mankind has not been very consistent in this field. Sometimes he has been confused. This still holds true. Today persons and societies are not clear about the place and the position of sex, so moderns are also mixed up about the expression of sex. The church needs to be able to speak a clear, consistent voice.

The Hebrews Tried to Regulate

Regulations on sex cover many pages in the Old Testament. At first glance it appears to some that these ancients were too much concerned with sex. Not infrequently those who pick up these sections of the Bible conclude that these early Hebrews were more occupied with sex regulations than with anything else. Not so. They were trying to control in an orderly way a phase of life that got out of hand in many tribes and nations. They were trying to include sex in their total pattern of living. They had to do it on their own level, and God had to meet them on their plateau of moral insight and expression.

The regulations in the Hebrew code were pretty inclusive. They dealt with conduct in such matters as adultery, fornication, incest, marriage of near relatives, wearing of clothing of the opposite sex, care of body elimination, uncleanness after childbirth, and more. Penalties were severe and strictly enforced. Measures for ceremonial cleansings were provided. These are set forth more specifically in the books of Deuteronomy and Leviticus. And the Hebrews did achieve a higher level of sex behavior than did other peoples of the ancient world. Their family life held together when that of many others fell apart.

Modern Confusions in Sex Ways

In few areas of today's life are there more confusions and conflicts and uncertainties than in the field of sex. This applies to premarital, marital, and postmarital living. It applies to advertising, to recreation, to reading material, to music. It applies to education concerning man and his interpersonal relationships and to his life alone. Much of the time when we moderns do not see the situation well enough, we are inclined to let things drift with a whatever-happens policy. And most churches are not speaking a very sure voice. If there ever was a time when the Church of Jesus Christ needed to explore competently, to formulate consensus soundly, and to speak forth clearly that time is now. It is urgent that sex be placed in its rightful relationships in the whole business of living.

There are several reasons for this confusion. In general we are in what might be called a shift from sex-denunciation and sex-denial to sex-parade and sex-indulgence. Here are some specific factors that have brought on this change: (1) Use of sex symbols in advertising for commercial gain. It is said that these symbols are used to sell everything from silk stockings to hair shampoo, from movies to men's underwear. Moderns meet a barrage of sex-soaked stimuli. (2) Social mobility. Today in many places persons can become anonymous only fifteen minutes from home. It is easy to get away so that no one knows us. Then social controls are gone. (3) Spread of facts about the biology of sex. Moderns set themselves to learn about contraception and move into freer sex relations and feel quite "safe." (4) Clinical treatment of venereal diseases. There is a growing feeling that if a person gets "caught" he can get cured. (5) Breakdown of inherited sex mores. A few years ago these fears held persons back from promiscuous sex relations: fear of social ostracism, fear of pregnancy, fear of disease, and fear of hell. All these fears have declined and the old restraints are gone. (6) Popularity of the "experienced" person. The one who has not tried himself or herself in sex experimentation may be looked upon as outmoded and priggish. (7) Patterns of thinking about the worth of all persons, especially of women and children. There is reaction against unlimited fecundity that disregards the right of persons to worthful family living. (8) The feeling of the inadequacy or the irrelevance of current codes of sex morality. Many say that churches too often repeat legalistic statements with little application to the business of living. Churches are accused of being behind on facts and application of facts. There is call for application of what we know about sex to the total business of spiritual health.

A Confusion in Theology of Sex

Two strands of thinking come face-to-face. On one side we hear God saying to man in primeval days, "Be fruitful, and multiply, and replenish the earth" (Genesis 1:30). Here sex expression for reproduction is enjoined. On the other side the physical nature of man is looked upon as evil with sex as the most evil of all the biological equipment. Adherents of this view often consider that the original sin of Adam and Eve was their discovery of and experimentation in sexual intercourse. These make the seventh chapter of I Corinthians support the view that only the spiritually weak indulge in sexual relationships, that those of superior spiritual attainment refrain. These overlook the fact that Paul was concerned with maximum contribution to the work of the Christian movement. He felt that the man unencumbered by family involvements would be able to do more. Here he was not making a denunciation of sex. In this ascetic pattern of thinking marriage would be looked upon as a concession to inherent weakness in man. On the whole sex would be considered evil and sexual indulgence unclean.

This conflict and confusion has persisted through the centuries. The word "concupiscence" has been regarded as a naughty word to designate a terrible sin. It designates the use of sex for personal gratification. This concupiscence came into man with his fall in the Garden of Eden and this sinfulness was transmitted. Theologians taught this for many years, and some still do. The enjoyment of sex was sinful. Woman was blamed for leading man to fall into this expression of sin, so she was accorded special responsibility and a subordinate position. The superior status for both men and women was celibacy.

In the thinking of many churches this conflict remains. Man's inherited nature is still considered evil with sex at the core of this depravity. We need to distinguish between two motivations for celibacy: the escape from concupiscence and the greater opportunity afforded to serve God. The confusion is not yet resolved. Reaction against this inherited theology of the fallen condition of man and of the transmission of concupiscence has had much to do with the turn toward emancipation in a promiscuous freedom. The Church of Jesus Christ must face up to the need to speak clearly a sound theology of sex.

The Viewpoint of Permissiveness

We are hearing on every side that sexual standards have become permissive. This means that ideas of premarital continence and chastity are not realistic and are not relevant to modern situations. With moral standards broken down and society incapable or disinclined to work through and set forth principles for longsighted living, moderns are in a chaotic situation. We flounder in moral poverty and wallow in moral incompetence.

Thus sex is often placed outside the realm of morality. This is a rather common treatment of conduct situations. Many deal with smoking and drinking this way. One teen-age girl put it this way, "It's nobody's business but mine." Another youth said, "Sexual behavior is something you have to decide for yourself —nobody can tell you." A youth in his early twenties expressed this opinion, "It is up to me, if I want to, as long as nobody gets hurt." One man said frankly, "I don't think God is interested in what I do with my sex." A church-going young woman said that God was concerned with her soul, not with her sex.

Our era of permissiveness says, then, that sex is to be managed according to the way a person feels about it. This means that if it bothers a person to indulge, then he should not. If it bothers him to refrain, then he should not refrain. It holds that a person should not get tied in knots by adhering to repressive measures. Permissiveness says that if one feels healthier and happier in unrestrained sex expression, then he should disregard the old codes. On first thought it stands out that this kind of thinking applied to bodily harm of others would produce a jungle situation. We note, too, that ideas concerning what constitutes health and happiness need some searching examination. How inclusive, how integrated, how farsighted are the criteria for evaluating health and happiness?

Involvement of the Total Person

Animals practice sex on a biological basis. There are no person-with-person considerations. Yet animals have one advantage. Sex is stimulated and expressed in reaction to physical, biological stimulation. There are no advertisements, no pornographic pictures and printed materials, no sexually played up music or movies, no use of clothing to excite sexually. In this sense the bull and the cow in the pasture have some advantage over us humans in our modern social order. We can be victims of all kinds of excitations. And it is so easy for us to contribute to the excitation.

Animals are not geared to consider the effect
expression on another animal. Expression of sex
field. We humans are equipped otherwise. We
vision the inter-influence of all that we are and
do on other persons. Sex is one part of every pe__
be separated from his total personhood. Sex is one phase of ...
fluence on another person that has to be seen and expressed in
terms of the wholeness of the other person. Anything less than
this is on the animal level.

Moral considerations involve this wholeness. Whatever affects
another person is involved in moral conduct. If I overeat or under-
sleep and this affects my disposition, my relationship with others,
I have fallen in my moral management. Everything that affects
my contribution to or my detraction from the potential condition
of another person is within my sphere of moral living. Even my
thinking is included. Jesus once said that the man who looks at
a woman and lusts after her is committing adultery.

In sex matters the immature person wants pleasure without
responsibility for what happens to another. He does not take
time to think or he does not care. He does not foresee how the
emotional, the mental, the biological, the spiritual aspects of the
persons participating are involved. He divorces sex from its setting
in a for-a-few-minutes temporary satisfaction.

Affection and Affinity Too

Appetite in sex is God-provided equipment. Management of
this appetite is a God-intended stewardship. Integration of this
appetite with the total of our personhood is a God-purposed operation. Our physical bodies are not neutral as to sex. Our personalities are not neutral as to likes and dislikes. These two, our bodily
drives and our personal affections, are to be brought together.
There is such an indissoluble union between all parts of the human
personality that no one part is to be expressed without regard to
the other parts.

Let sex be considered as the physical expression of a merging
of two persons in healthy harmony. It is not the beginning that
leads the way. Rather is it the outcome of two persons living
together in well-founded, well-balanced affection. The physical
relationship in marriage comes in sequence out of community of
interests, of objectives, of loyalties, of loves. In such a relationship
there is concern for the happiness and welfare of the partner in
sex relationship. The sex relationship can lead to increasing

ity. Without this affection, without this affinity, sex falls to
ie level of animals in the pasture or the woods. This affection
goes beyond skin contact; it involves soul relationship.

More than Freudian Release

Any modern consideration of sex does not disregard the work
of Sigmund Freud. He did mankind a great service in stimulating
us to explore our biological and our psychological equipment and
in bringing to the surface our hidden, unconscious powers. He
guided us in seeing that we have forces deep within us that are
not to be ignored. He advised us that repressing or ignoring these
drives would not take care of the situation. Rather would such
measures complicate the situation and tie us to unhealthy strains
and complications. He presented sex as basic and foremost in this
natural stock of ours.

In Freud's analysis of what had been taking place through
the centuries he gave religion a place of low repute and censured
it for getting man into this tightened, repressed condition. He
saw religion as something that would go as man comes to understand what religion is and how it has damaged him. He saw
religion as "belief based on wish," as "illusion." He presented
this most pointedly in his book, *The Future of an Illusion*. With
religion out of the way man would be free to express sex without
the unsound controls of the past. This was primary in Freudian
thinking, for he gave predominance to the sexual urge. He said
it had to be brought out from its buried or denied condition. He
affirmed that it had to be released from the dominance of religion
that had been so busy in pushing it down and keeping it down.
With religion discarded, sex could be openly recognized.

Dr. Freud seemed quite unaware that there could be such a thing
as a healthy religion, one that is more than wishing and retreating
and repressing. He did not vision a religion that is honest and in-
tegrative. Dr. Elton Trueblood in his *Philosophy of Religion* says of
Dr. Freud, "All of his major illustrations are of three related kinds,
the pathological, the primitive and the infantile" (page 184). Apparently Dr. Trueblood visioned a wholesome functioning of a true-
to-man's-nature and a true-to-God's-universe religion.

We can say that Dr. Freud gave sex a new freedom. He gave
it a central place and then released it and left man without resources
or guidelines for handling what he let go. He gave it a prominence
that pulled it out of rightful relationship with man's total nature. We
might say that in Plato's manner of speaking he put sex in the chariot

seat when it should be seen as one of the essential horses drawing the chariot and needing a competent charioteer. Man needs something more farseeing than sex drives in the directing of his life. These drives need control and direction, but not denial. A healthy religion recognizes every drive that man has and puts God in the place of control.

Dr. Freud never recognized the fullness of man nor the fullness of the universe. He left out man's basic spiritual nature. He had no terms, no techniques for dealing with it. He left out the spiritual reality of the universe. He considered selected phases of man's nature and inheritance and emphasized these. He named *libido* as the great dynamic. By this he meant the drive or energy from primitive biological urges with sex at the core. He brought to the surface the unconscious forces in us. He did disservice in presuming that this essential part of us was all of us and that this sexual quantum in the unconscious is all. He ignored the possibility of buried spiritual resources.

Our world should be grateful to Dr. Freud for calling attention to the essential place of sex in our nature. We need not agree with his interpretation of what he found nor with what he would do to remedy the situation. Full and unrestrained release of something caged up does not necessarily provide a good solution. We have found that many who follow his theory are long on description and short on prescription. Dr. Menninger has reminded us that too often we presume that if we bore into personhood and then give a technical name to what we find there, we have effected a cure. Sometimes we seem to think that if we deal with one selected area we shall effect an inclusive cure. Especially is this true of sex, but we cannot treat sex as an isolated something. We cannot bring it into the open and let it go off by itself or take over the total personhood. We cannot ignore its relation to the total personhood or to the total universe in which spiritual reality cannot be forgotten.

Basics about Sex in the Gospel

Our scriptures do not give us a packaged presentation of fundamentals about sex. We cannot gather a few quotations and put together a final code of conduct. We must strive to understand how God creates man and what God has in mind for man. Certainly sex and marriage are in this picture. We acquire principles to guide us through a changing world rather than a collection of police regulations that give specific and closed directions. The Restoration movement rediscovers what Jesus was saying in this field and strives to relate this message to living in our day. Here are basics that we gather from the total gospel of Jesus Christ:

1. God's fundamental purpose is the developing of persons of eternal quality, which development includes the physical and the material aspects.
2. Sex is a normal, essential aspect of life, placed in man by the Creator, to be expressed in harmony with God's purpose for man.
3. Sex, like every other equipment of man, is to be managed by man as a stewardship. It is capable of good use or abuse.
4. There is a moral order in the universe that applies to all personal relationships. Sex is included in this field of morality.
5. Marriage and family life is inherent in God's program for man. It looks to procreation and to the personal development and personal fulfillment of man as person.
6. Sex and marriage are to be evaluated in terms of what they provide or do not provide for the well-being of persons.
7. Sexual relations in marriage are to be managed in respect to their contribution to the health and happiness of those participating.
8. An essential foundation for sex expression is love, with love interpreted in spiritual connotations rather than in terms of passing physical appeal.
9. Promiscuity is disruptive of personal stability, personal integration, capacity for enduring loyalty; it evidences indulgence on the basis of momentary satisfaction.
10. Children learn of sex in normal, healthy family relationships as equipment provided by God, to be treated in physically and spiritually hygienic ways and terms.
11. Sex problems are to be handled diagnostically and remedially for the rehabilitation of persons and the best interest of the social groups involved.
12. Children and youth are to be relieved of pressures from adults, from peers, from groups, and institutions into premature interest in sex and relationships between sexes.
13. Zion is a community with sound social standards and constructive attitudes in matters of sex, with adequate education, with wholesome social relationships.

14. Education in matters of sex is within the context of total personal development, as an integral part of total spiritual living.
15. The church provides ministry and fellowship for assisting persons to understand well and manage well their sex nature.
16. Wholesome sex life and wholesome family life can add to the total contributions that persons can make to the work of God.
17. Decisions of a person concerning marriage and non-marriage are made on the basis of the person's total health, temperament, life pattern and of the welfare of the other person involved. There is no fixed priority to marriage or non-marriage.
18. Considerations of sex are concerned with persons as "total integral human beings" (a phrase of Gordon Allport) in a total order of nature in which God is source and sustainer of life.

A Time for Sound Thinking on Sex

This is a great day for pessimists who look at sex. Society appears to be on the final downgrade as sensuousness moves on into promiscuity. But the church is not intended to be a surrendering institution. We can make this a time for advance in sex living, if we will. We can see that family life of former years was not as ordered and as heavenly as supposed. At least conditions are out in the open and we know what we have to face. Problems are enough to overwhelm us: pregnancy in the unmarried, homosexuality, "automobilism," contraception, promiscuous permissiveness, and more. There are varying attitudes from suspicion, denial, and "freedom" in sex. Sometimes it looks as if every standard in sex behavior has gone with the wind. And youth are seen inheriting their ways from adults whose sexual standards have become permissive. The times call for competence and effective articulation in discussing the situation.

The Church of Jesus Christ has to be on the alert. Youth are needing counsel and conference, not kicks for noncompliance. Adults are also needing a basis for morality in sex behavior. The gospel of Jesus Christ reminds us that our approach will be in terms of what happens in persons for their continuing health and happiness. This is what God wants in man. And sex will find its rightful place in the total spiritual selfhood of persons. God designs it so.

Questions for Discussion

1. What do you think prompted men of former centuries to look upon the material body and sex in particular as evil?
2. How may religionists be said to have added to man's confusion through looking upon sex as evil and at the same time at man's duty to procreate?
3. How do some youth, girls in particular, grow up with the idea that sex is "naughty" and "not nice" in their life views?
4. How may a person think of the stomach and gastronomical pursuits as separated from the rest of living? How may this happen in respect to sex organs and sex expression?
5. How is separation of sex from total personal expression a reversion to the animal level of living?
6. How would you go about developing a morality of sex with a person who says that sex is not connected with morals and that this is his own affair?
7. What bearing does the teaching, "The spirit and the body is the soul of man" (D. and C. 85:4 a) have upon the consideration of sex?
8. How may the gospel of Jesus Christ be said to emphasize the guidelines of love rather than rule books of regulations?
9. How does the gospel of Jesus Christ see sex as a potential for personal development rather than a plaything for playboys and playgirls?
10. What do you see as marks of maturing love which are foundational for sex expression? How does this differ from the spasmodic "crush" based on passing physical attraction? What are essentials for developing spiritual affection?
11. How may much of our modern approach to sexual problems and sexual therapy be one-sided? What do you see involved in an inclusive approach to a problem of chaos and confusion in a person's sexual life?
12. In terms of what is best for the person in the long run, how would you present a case in favor of premarital continence?
13. What do you set out as characteristics of the "saint" who has a sound, workable theology on sex and a healthy functioning program of living his sex life?
14. What agencies and services should the church develop and make available for ministering to children, to youth, to adults in matters of sex?

CHAPTER 22

EXPECTING
REAL HAPPINESS

Two women in their seventies were conversing about going to church when they were teen-agers. Said one, "I enjoyed going to church and looked forward to it." Replied the other, "Whoever expected to have a good time going to church? I never thought of going to church to be happy." Here are two widely differing ideas about the relationship between joyful living and spiritual living. Perhaps we need to inquire if there is any relationship. The contrast in views is pointed up in the reaction of two youths. In India a young native girl who did not know much about the Christian faith said to a missionary nurse from America, "Being a Christian must be very sad." When asked why she thought so, she told the nurse, "Your face never looks happy." A Japanese youth said to a fellow student in the United States when he spoke of his American friend's faith, "You are a Christian; you have a joyful hold on life."

These scenes out of life bring us face-to-face with some basic questions. They are pertinent to every life. They get at the nature of happiness and the nature of spirituality. Here are some of the major considerations:

1. What are qualities of real, continuing happiness?
2. Does a person set out to obtain happiness? Or is it a by-product of a way of living?
3. How may God be characterized as happy?
4. How does healthy spirituality involve happiness?
5. Is the "spiritual" person happier than the "non-spiritual" person? If so, how?
6. How may Zion be thought of as a happiness-producing community?
7. How is the ministry of the Holy Spirit conducive to experiencing happiness? Or is it?
8. What can the gospel of Jesus Christ contribute to the realization of happiness?

A Common Searching

In *Achieving Real Happiness,* Kenneth Hildebrand has written of the widespread yearning for happy living. "Our generation yearns for happiness. . . . All persons point to a thirst for happiness" (page 17). He points to swarming to the heart of a city in search of amusement. He mentions the millions and millions of dollars spent annually to purchase pleasure. This can be expanded with the billions spent on liquor and tobacco. We face daily the publicizing of places and products and persons who promise jovial and joyful days. We sense how millions are saying silently, "I want to be happy." It is likely that the larger percentage of those who are trying to come upon happiness or conjure it up in some way do not have any clear idea of what would constitute real happiness.

A Sense of Lack

An Englishman had spent twenty years away from his native island. After he had returned and had walked about the streets of London and other cities he was asked what was the major difference he noted between the city of twenty years before and the city to which he returned. The inquirer expected him to mention the electrically lighted signs or the window displays or the traffic or the modern clothes. Said the returned one, "The main difference I note is the emptiness, the drabness of the faces of the people on the street." He had been noting the unhappy and sometimes sullen facial expressions of those he had been meeting.

We can sense the spirit of unrest and dissatisfaction in the lives of those with whom we associate. Some personalities are likened to dry cisterns. Some are similar to volcanoes ready to go off. Some may be thought of as squeaking toys that speak no message. Some are compared to clabbered milk. One man said his neighbor was like a broken-down dog that never wagged his tail, and yelped only when he was uncomfortable. Voices are shrill or emotionless. Laughter, when it comes, is strident. Response to what might be enjoyable is forced or blasé. And some put on an act simulating happiness when inside there is only emptiness. These persons are like the man with a troublesome stomach who said that he felt hungry for something but didn't know what and that whatever he got did not taste good.

Is Religion Involved?

Suppose we should collect a hundred or more of these blank-faced, bleak-toned persons and ask them if they were participating members of churches, if they were praying men and women. How many of them would "be involved in religion"? How many of them would consider themselves "spiritual" in any sense, to any degree? Would we find any relationship between spirituality and happiness? And what would we mean by spirituality, by happiness?

Beyond Surface Symptoms

A fairly common notion of happiness is that the happy person is floating along on a fleecy cloud with never a care, never a discomfort. Love is a round of heart-tingling romance. Wants are always supplied. Associates are always saying kind and complimentary things. One's team wins all the games. No muscle pains or headaches mar the day. A harvest moon is always shining. God is the benevolent Santa Claus who provides fulfillment of wishes without delay. And moods are buoyant and hopes are high. The bands play and the dancers trip the light fantastic. The theme song is, "Ain't We Got Fun?"

Such a state of existence would be suited to fairyland children housed in a trip-along palace. They could suck lollypops, jump the rope, and ride kiddie cars. But they would never become persons who could face life decisively and courageously. They would never create a social order suited to achieving their purpose; they would be shaped by their environment. The counsel, "Stand up and act like men!" would be replaced by the slogan, "Skip along like little children."

Happiness and the Large Vision

These childish ideas of good times may be called this-very-minute notions. They carry the spirit of the small boy who said, "I want what I want when I want it and that's right now." The vision of satisfaction is a foot or a yard long. The lad who wants only an ice-cream cone does not see beyond this. The youth of larger vision sees the ice cream as a step in a longer sequence of happenings that fit together in a life program.

Happiness requires that we see our fortunes and our misfortunes, our comforts and our discomforts in broad perspective. The person who concentrates on a toothache and on nothing else is going to be quite unhappy. "We need," says Martin Ten Hoor, "to place ourselves in the universal scheme of things."[1] He advises that for composure and satisfaction we need to "break up the habits of exclusive preoccupation with their . . . temporary impact upon our own life," for this keeps us going round in a circle and focusing on our own little world. In other words, we need to see the significance of our experiences in the broad setting in which they occur. We need to develop this overview before the happy or unhappy experience occurs. If we wait until an overwhelming situation occurs we shall be too involved to "see life steadily and see it whole." The truly happy life sees things "in the long view and interprets the five-minute happening in terms of the centuries-long outlook." Said a wise grandmother philosopher to her neighbor who had a local affliction of distressing nature, "Stop looking at this boil of yours as if it would matter so much a billion years from now."

Beyond Self-centeredness

"Nobody's going to live in the kingdom of happiness if he looks toward setting up a throne on which he will be sitting as king." This is a good way of saying that the man who makes life a wheel with himself the hub and all spokes pointing to him is not going to find his wheel rolling along on the road of happiness. He is more likely to land in the rut of frustration and despondency. Jesus told us all that if we want to experience the good life, we have to turn outside ourselves. The person who starts the day by cataloguing his aches and pains or by listing the comforts he wants to achieve for himself is not likely to have a day that is rewarding. Jesus said, "Lose yourself in my work, that is, in some ministry for others in my spirit." An old Hindu proverb puts it this way, "Help thy brother's boat across, and lo, thine own has reached the shore."

This does not mean that a person is to disregard his own welfare and neglect his own development. Jesus meant us to regard ourselves as God's sons and daughters, each one with infinite worth. He was saying that no person could attain to full stature, that no person could experience happiness by focusing on himself, on his own little world.

A By-product in Life

We are seeing more and more that no man attains happiness by making it his objective in life. Generally those who strike out

[1]M. Ten Hoor, *Education for Privacy,* University of Alabama Press, 1960, p.54

to get happiness do not have a sound, inclusive idea of what they are going after. They often are thinking of some kind of good feeling that is attached to some specific thing or experience. If this is gained, it is not attached to anything big enough to promote continuing and expanding good feeling. We cannot identify any who have gone after happiness as an objective and obtained it. Comments Wilfred A. Peterson, "You can't pursue happiness and catch it. Happiness comes upon you unawares while you are helping others."[2]

The Beatitudes of Jesus

Once in the first days of his ministry Jesus conversed with his disciples about qualifications for and satisfactions in life in the kingdom of God. He talked about the kind of persons they should be and could be as citizens in this spiritual order. In Matthew 5:3-12 there is a collection of statements we have come to call "beatitudes." Each mentions a quality or virtue in a person and then designates the satisfaction that will come to such a person. Most translations have them start with "Blessed are . . ." Some translations have them starting "Happy is . . ." or "How happy is . . ." This is the basic meaning of blessedness. A collection of beatitudes is really a selection of qualities in persons that will enable them to be happy.

Jesus' beatitudes are usually looked upon as being calm and placid. Not so. They were revolutionary in their day. To appreciate them we should draw up a list of beatitudes that his hearers would have set forth and a list that the priestly leaders of his day would have proposed. They might have started with something like this, "Blessed are you who are born sons of Abraham, for . . ." but Jesus gave no priority to Jewish birth. They might have said, "Blessed are those who pay their tithing, for the windows of heaven will open upon them with good crops and abundant harvest." Jesus did not hold out bribes or rewards in material possessions. He pointed to spiritual qualities that would bring spiritual satisfactions. His beatitudes constituted a fresh approach to spirituality. It was revolutionary.

Jesus was saying that happiness does not depend upon a birth certificate or a bank account or public acclaim. He was saying, as wrote W. A. Peterson, "Happiness does not depend upon a full pocketbook, but upon a mind full of rich thoughts and a heart

---

[2]Wilfred A. Peterson, *The Art of Living,* Simon and Schuster (1961)

263

full of rich emotions." He was teaching, as Peterson has commented, "Happiness . . . depends upon . . . what happens inside of you. . . . It is measured by the spirit in which you meet the problems of life." Jesus of Nazareth taught how happiness comes to man as he achieves happiness-producing qualities within himself.

Look at one of Jesus' beatitudes, "How happy are the humble-minded . . ." Artificial humility is self-centered. It can be proud of its pride-shunning spirit as was Uriah Heep. The word humble comes from *humus,* the Latin word for earth or soil. The humble person has his feet solidly on the ground. If he is going to bear good fruit he will stretch upward to the sun while he maintains his footing on and his rooting in fruit-producing soil. He senses his reliance on God's resources. The beatitude says that the humble-minded shall sense the presence of God. And this is "real happiness."

God, the Eternally Happy One

Some portraits of God make him the acme of unhappiness. Often one of the first things that unhappy religious persons have to do is to consider God with "a new look." Not infrequently he is pictured as if his chief occupation is listing and lamenting about the sins of mankind. His countenance is seen as glum and morose. He is thought of as brooding over the slights and insults that men through the ages have given him. What he expects of man is struggle and strain. How could man ever be happy in the presence of such an unhappy God? The idea that God could ever be jovially happy would be quite outside the vision of some. Moderns need a theology of God that portrays his quality of enduring happiness. His is not a hep-up-happy or a slap-happy existence. His joy is deep and broad and longtime.

Alma's Counsel to His Son

Alma in ancient America had three sons. One of them, Corianton, had done considerable sampling in living. He had had lost weekends and lost weeks. He had associated with persons who drained him, who drew him down. In Alma's later years he wrote to his sons what might be called patriarchal blessings. He told Corianton that he would never be happy living as he had been living. These three things stand out: (1) Happiness emerges out of a good quality of living. He wrote pointedly, "Behold, I say unto you, Wickedness never was happiness" (Alma 19:74). (2) The person's picture of what constitutes happiness matters ever so much. Alma wrote of a man's being "raised to happiness, according to his desires of happiness" (Alma 19:68). (3) God's nature is happy and he purposes that men be happy in an eternal sense. He spoke of those who have gone "contrary to the nature of God" and are consequentially "now in a state contrary to happiness" (Alma 19:75). Alma was advising his son to discover the sources of happiness in the kind of living that God intended men to experience. He was saying what Lehi had said centuries before about God's intent, "Men are, that they might have joy" (II Nephi 1:115).

Alma's Own Testimony

Alma wrote down his own reflections about being happy. He had been going through inner turmoil because of the indifference and the hostility of his people. He sensed that he could not be effective dwelling only on what was wrong although he needed to be aware of their shortcomings. His comrade, Ammon, had just returned from arduous years among the Lamanites and had been reviewing his experiences. He had told of the turning to God of many Lamanites and of the transformation in their lives. With a thrill of happiness, Ammon had concluded, "This is my life and my light, my joy and my salvation" (Alma 14:125). Here was happiness of high order. Alma spoke out with the same message,

> "Yea, and this is my glory,
> that perhaps I may be an instrument in the hands of God,
> to bring some soul to repentance;
> and this is my joy."—Alma 15:61.

A People Can Be Happy

There is a contagious quality in an atmosphere of happiness. There is an interinfluence between those who are living together in a happiness-producing way. Zion is to be seen in this light. Such a community is to realize and radiate this spiritual quality. Those who want to be happy cannot move in and soak up happiness as a sponge would soak up water. They must come in and participate in the life of the Zionic community so that happiness comes as a by-product. There is no way to drop a coin in a slot, punch a button, and have a cup of happiness flow out. Nor can a person move into a Zionic community and have the Saints serve happiness on a silver platter in a ready-to-use package.

People have to plan to live together in ways that will bring happiness into realization. Nephi recorded how his people came to have a good atmosphere in their new colony. It had been necessary for him and his associates to withdraw from the segment led by his brothers Laman and Lemuel. This withdrawal was required for safety and comfort. The new colony reorganized its way of living and elevated values of spiritual quality. Then Nephi could record, "It came to pass that we lived after the manner of happiness" (II Nephi 4:43).

Later the Nephites came out of civil strife and military involvement with a stable government and with spiritual fullness. Their general, Moroni, was the chief figure in realizing this good condition. He encouraged the Nephites to be industrious: a marked prosperity came to them. He brought about a consideration of one for the other. He placed God at the center of all that was done. So the chronicler could write, "There never was a happier time among the people of Nephi, since the days of Nephi, than in the days of Moroni" (Alma 22:24). Such community happiness does not come by accident. It has to be lived for.

After the Ministry of Jesus Christ

The book of IV Nephi tells briefly, too briefly, what happened in the Nephite people after Jesus Christ had ministered to them. The story points out these things: (1) industry for the common good, (2) evangelistic outreach to others, (3) consideration of one another's good interests, (4) stable family living, (5) functioning faith in God. The historian mentions in particular that "there was no contention in the land, because of the love of God which did dwell in the hearts of the people" (IV Nephi 1:17). This was more than a selfish sentimentality; it was a functioning, servicing affection. Then could the chronicler conclude in one of the most appealing sentences in the record, "And surely there could not be a happier people among all the people who had been created by the hand of God" (IV Nephi 1:19).

The Joy-stimulating Holy Spirit

In the pioneering days of the Restoration movement some foundational instruction came before the church was organized. It was imperative that these forerunners have some idea of the nature of what should happen. They expected to receive the Holy Spirit. They needed to understand how and why. In the frontier revivals of those years there was considerable emphasis on the

Holy Spirit. The expression was looked upon as overt and dramatic. Shouting and singing and jerking were in the picture. This seemed to express an exuberant spiritual joy. These early Latter Day Saints were advised in 1829 about the nature and the ministry of the Holy Spirit. There was to be more than temporary excitement in a revivalistic congregation. There was to be continuing uplift that would lay the foundation for happiness. So they were told, "I will impart unto you of my Spirit . . . which shall fill your soul with joy" (D. and C. 10:7 a). Here is more than spasmodic outburst. Here is more than surface enthusiasm. Here is joy that rests on enlightenment, on creative goodness. This Spirit leads to real happiness.

Seriousness and Happiness

The happiness that endures is more than a flippant, carefree feeling. Shallow persons will have shallow happiness. Increasing the capacity for happiness in like measure increases capacity for sorrow. The low-grade person has neither capacity. There is no recipe or program for increasing capacity for happiness while deadening capacity for suffering. Jesus of Nazareth was extraordinary in his ability to suffer and to rejoice. And he felt both to the full.

Times of exalted joy come only to those who guide their way through situations that exact much of them and who come out with solutions and insights and mastery of the problematical situations. Archimedes could not know the happy thrill of finding the solution to a mathematical problem without searching and exploring. Only with insight could he cry out "Eureka!" (I have found it!) Only a youth who tried to find out about affiliating with a church, who asked God for guidance, and who sensed the darkness of confusion could know the deep happiness that comes in the directive, "This is my beloved Son: hear him!" Too many want bargain-counter, low-cost good feeling rather than well-foundationed happiness.

In the nineties the Reorganized Church had been going through some trying growing pains. Men of leading administrative quorums did not agree on procedures. In some ways the work of the church was blocked. A message to the church in the conference of 1894 advised members of the First Presidency, the Twelve Apostles, and the Presiding Bishopric to remain after the conference in council meetings to tackle their problems together. They were to seek divine direction as they counseled. They took up problem after problem. A common consent began to emerge. In the minutes of the Joint Council of 1894, now included in the Doctrine and Covenants, the secretary of the council could write, "The Spirit of the Master fell upon those present and the service and season was one of joyful solemnity and peace" (123:28 b).

Starting Where We Are

Many of us want to go to some other place so that there we can start out happily. If others will provide us with pleasant circumstances and congenial surroundings then our cares will leave us, and we will be happy. This fact remains: wherever we go, we have to take our own selves along. We cannot gain happiness through escaping what we do not like. Human need is a reality. Human misery and suffering are about us. Human weakness is apparent. We cannot close our eyes to these and run off to some imaginary ideal realm. First of all, there is no such land. Second, we could not be happy if we were to run off and hide away.

We work with what is available to increase this happiness, to improve our living conditions. We can learn to discover what is enjoyable where we are. One day a little boy was having a good time playing with one roller skate. Said a passerby, "Sonny, you ought to have two skates." The boy replied with a grin, "That's right. I know I ought to have two skates, but you can have a real good time on one skate if that's all you have." We experience this kind of happiness right where we are. We can have what may be called "the habit of happiness."

Jesus Christ, Eternally Happy

So often we describe Jesus Christ as "a man of sorrows and acquainted with grief." He was this, to be sure, but he was more. There was deep-seated happiness in him. He did not surrender to moods that would make him ineffective. In the Upper Room at the Last Supper he had cause to consider everything a failure. Even these men closest to him did not appreciate what was about to happen. He saw the betrayal in Gethsemane, Peter's denial in the courtroom, the jeering crowd, the long walk to Calvary carrying the cross, the crucifixion, and the spiritual aloneness. Yet he said to these men, "These things have I spoken unto you, that my joy might remain in you, and that your joy might be full. . . . In the world you shall have tribulation; but be of good cheer; I have overcome the world." He could speak this way because his happiness was rooted in something that was beyond what was going to happen to him through the next few hours. He wanted
268

these men to lead happy, purposeful lives. He expected that they would come to see the Source of his happiness. This is what he expects of all of us.

Questions for Discussion

1. How is wholeness of a person essential to deep and lasting happiness? How is it not possible for a segmented person to be happy?
2. What did Robert Louis Stevenson have in mind about happiness when he said that "good health is to be able to do without it"? (He had poor health most of his life.)
3. How is the longtime dimension essential in picturing real happiness?
4. How is the viewpoint in Luke 12:21 foreign to achievement of happiness? The comment is, "Take thine ease, eat, drink, and be merry." Why do many add, "for tomorrow we die"?
5. What pictures of God's nature and operation can make him foreign to happy living?
6. What constitutes a healthy expectancy of happiness? How does our conception of happiness condition what is going to happen in our achieving it?
7. What is your reaction to Abraham Lincoln's comment, "We are as happy as we make up our minds to be"?
8. Which beatitudes characterize ideas of happiness in the modern social order? Write five or six that say "Blessed [happy] is the man that .... for he shall ...."
9. What are beatitudes (conditions of happiness) that characterize your own family's beliefs and way of life?
10. React to the statement of John Masefield, "The days that make us happy make us wise."
11. Analyze what was happening in the Nephites when Mormon wrote of them, "Their sorrowing was not unto repentance, because of the goodness of God, but it was the sorrowing of the damned, because the Lord would not always suffer them to take happiness in sin."
12. What kind of "goodness" do you see correlated with what kind of happiness? Note Lehi's comment, "If there be no righteousness, there be no happiness" (II Nephi 1:90).
13. What is the quality, the foundation of happiness set forth in the counsel in Doctrine and Covenants 16:3 a about evangelistic ministry? In what does the joy consist?
14. How is the Restoration gospel a guide to living so as to produce the fruitage of "real happiness"?

269

CHAPTER 23

PRAYING WITH
ASSURING COMMUNION

We are equipped to converse. We need to converse. God makes us this way. At birth our potentials for becoming persons require interaction with other persons. Whenever men live together they work out symbols for communication. This includes a wide range of words, signs, gestures for conveying moods and meanings. The man who does not interact adequately with others goes undeveloped or declines after development. This conversing of humans carries a world of possibilities. At our best we are just beginners in the art of communication.

A Stewardship of Many Possibilities

It has been said, "Talking will either kill or cure." Another has put it this way, "Mere talking will not get us where we ought to be: it may get us off the track and it may get us going in reverse." So the question stands, How do we talk? Such comments point up that conversation is a stewardship to be managed. It is a field that requires development in us. It can expand our personhoods and increase our powers, or it can bury us in a bog of trivia. We can make our own selves the chief topic of conversation or we can reach out from ourselves into an expanding world. Each of us needs to build up a fund of worthful things to talk about. Each needs to develop the art of wholesome conversation. We are to cultivate friendships with those who will benefit us and will be benefitted by our common conversation. Conversation can be healthy or unhealthy. And this applies to praying.

We Can Learn to Pray More Effectively

Quite often we are inclined to think that spiritual experience such as praying comes to us intuitively and calls for no guidance. Some consider it sacrilegious to consider being taught to pray. Yet Jesus of Nazareth did this very thing. The opening sentences of the eleventh chapter of Luke tell how disciples came to Jesus after he had been praying and requested, "Lord, teach us to pray."

Apparently these disciples recognized the high quality of Jesus' praying and felt that he had something in his praying that they did not have. Throughout his ministry Jesus not only counseled his disciples to pray, he advised them that they should learn how to pray well. He meant that we should be students in (1) the motivation for praying, (2) the art of praying, (3) the content of praying, and (4) the relating of praying to the business of living.

When Paul wrote to the disciples in Rome, he was speaking to those who were newcomers to the Christian faith. He told them, in what is the eighth chapter, that they had been adopted by God and were now his sons. Accordingly they would be able to say, "Father." Yet he saw all of us as quite inadequate in expressing ourselves to God. To help us in this communicating is the available Holy Spirit. Paul put it this way, "The Spirit helps us in our weakness; for we do not know how to pray as we ought . . ." (Romans 8:26 R.S.V.). Paul suggests that our natures have to be transformed if we are going to be at home and capable in praying. He saw prayer as something more than undisciplined phrasings to God. We need to learn how to be effective.

Prayer, One Side of Conversation

Praying is one side of a two-way communion between man and God. In praying man reaches out communicatively to God. When God responds communicatively to man we call it revelation. In prayer man is opening his soul to God, manifesting his total self to God, as he is able. In revelation God is disclosing himself to man, as man is able to perceive. Both praying on the part of man and revealing on the part of God are required for the complete circuit of communication. Neither can be left out. In this communicating God is limited by our ability to express ourselves to him and by our ability to appreciate and understand what he is wanting to disclose to us. The gospel of the Restoration advocates the total circuit of communication which involves our praying and God's revealing.

Praying with Our Total Selves

Split personalities do not converse well. In healthy conversation a person talks with his total self. A young man discovered that a young woman he was dating had two sides of her personhood that were not harmonized, not integrated. She kept the two

271

parts well separated. She did not permit the values and interests of Saturday night to meet those of Sunday morning. Eventually the young man said, "I cannot talk with her; I never know which part of her I'm talking with."

This does not mean that the spiritually healthy person has a monotonously one-track type of life. Rather does it mean that he shall have many fields of interest and expression and will be pushing out in expansion of his circle of concerns and insights. But these will be harmonized into one well-integrated whole. At the center Jesus Christ will be the core of allegiance and the source for unity. The values and standards of the playing field, the business mart, the family living room, the municipal government, the library, and the prayer meeting will be the same. It is possible to participate enthusiastically in one field while the others are in the background. Yet there is no split in the personhood.

In effective conversation the total self is involved. Once one of our ministers was speaking in English to a congregation in Holland. The message was being translated by a brother who knew both English and Dutch. When it became apparent that the congregation kept watching the preacher intently as he talked in English, the translator mentioned this. Their reply: "He talks with every part of him. We want to keep our eyes on him, for he talks with his face, with his hands, with his body, with his voice. We do not want to miss anything." This applies not only to our bodies; it applies to our total experience. We converse with our total stock of experience, with our fund of faith, with our world of interests and appreciations. The person who converses with one segment of himself and with one limited field of experience will probably prove uninteresting and incompetent.

Good praying involves the wholeness of the person. When the body is relaxed, the mind clear, the heart clean and warm, the hand steady, the eye alert, we are in good condition to converse with God. While in a given praying experience we are focusing upon some given concern or problem or interest, we should be able to draw on the total unified resources of our personhoods and utilize them in this specific praying. Many of our resources are under the surface and may be spoken of as subconscious. This under-the-surface fund should include the spiritual resources we have been building up on the inside. We are not free to cross our fingers and pretend that some things are not there. We are not able to leave behind the intricacies and complexities of ourselves and take only one small segment when we converse with God. He knows the total picture. And we ought to recognize it and act accordingly. The best praying is done by the person whose life hangs together so that he is able to utilize everything in his conversation with God.

The Purpose of Praying

Conversation with a friend is an expression of fellowship. We like to be with a friend. We have things to share with this comrade. We feel relaxed with him and speak freely and frankly. We feel that we shall be understood. We do not weigh words or apprehensively work over phrases because of fear that he will misunderstand or take offense. Sometimes he and we will feel very close and sometimes farther apart. If things have gone wrong, we can admit what has happened, ferret out the causes, and rectify the situation. We have done things with this friend and we have much to talk about. Sometimes we say words; sometimes we are silent. Sometimes we commune without using words.

Foremost in our communion is our prizing our friend for what he is. There are no materialistic or self-centered motivations. We would not think of holding to him so that we can borrow money from him or receive substantial gifts. The very thought of this is foreign to true friendship. Yet we know quite well that if disaster should come our friend would be at our side and would give of himself and of his means. If this is a good friendship we are uplifted persons because we have been associating with this friend. We think up, we feel up, we live up. We see our true selves more clearly.

This kind of communion is what healthy praying is. We have a Friend. We prize him for what he is. We are uplifted as we commune with him. Yet we do not hold to him in order that we may get sizable gifts and easy benefits. It is good to be with this Friend, this Father, and to converse with him. And so we pray.

Answer to Prayer

So often we hear the phrase, "I know that God is, because he hears and answers prayer." When we listen a little more we are often able to put it this way, "I know that God hears and answers prayer because I got what I asked for." Scarcely could a person-with-person relationship survive on such self-centered motivation.

This is placing prayer on a rather low level. Prayer as communion with God is concerned with much more than asking for things and with waiting for them to come to us. Praying is fellowshiping with God. Certainly we have something more to talk about than making requests for things we would like to have. Certainly there must be something to say about what God has in mind and what he wants in us and in others. Certainly there must be great things to converse about outside our own small worlds.

How does a friend respond to us when we are conversing? Sometimes by a glance of the eye or an expression of the face. Sometimes through a phrase of acknowledgment or a word of appreciation. Sometimes through a handclasp. Sometimes through asking a question. Sometimes through reply to an inquiry. There are multiple ways in which God will "answer" us as we speak to him. Certainly the giving of some identifiable thing in response to our request is only one of these. It is rather immature to think of God's replying to us only through handing over to us something we have been asking of him. Sometimes we ought to expect that his response will be in assurance and communion that can hardly be described in words. More than one man of prayer has said something like this: "God answered me in silence through helping me to see that what I wanted would not be good for me." One man said, "God helped me to see that I would grow up to understand that one day I would be able to understand."

Some Unsound Conceptions of Praying

It is not sound to exhort persons to pray by giving the impression that any kind of praying will do. Some practices get in the way of health-producing communion with God. They block the achieving of sound spirituality. It is good for us to recognize some of these not-so-good practices, that we may turn from them to the healthier conceptions and the healthier procedures in praying. Here are some of the more frequently found undesirable and unsound practices:

1. Bargaining with God. This means saying to God, "If you will do so-and-so, then I will do so-and-so." One man prayed, "God, if you will increase my salary, I will increase my offerings." Friendship never thrives on bargaining. Terms for benefit to the one who is praying defeat or at least retard spiritual growth.

2. Begging with a "gimme" attitude. This is like writing a letter to Santa Claus. These prayers carry the tone, "This is what

I am wanting, so be sure to deliver the package quite soon." This makes our wants the criterion for "answer to prayer."

3. Changing God's mind. This assumes that if we are strong enough in our battering at God he will come through in our favor. Prayer is not to change the mind and heart of God. Rather does it look to changing us so that God will be able to bless us with what he has been wanting to bring to us, but which our condition has prevented.

4. Lining up the angels and the other forces in heaven on our side. This assumes that we may be able to mobilize interceding forces in our behalf. One man said frankly that he was needing some "heavenly political pull." Some think that the Son of God can do some imploring with God the Father in their behalf. This sounds like the youth who gets one parent lined up on his side to plead his case with the other parent.

5. Presenting a good case to God. This sounds like the attorney who works out a compelling brief to support his case. This seems to assume that God is a judge who is to be convinced. One youth prayed this way, "Now, God, I'd like to state my side so you will see how I look at this matter."

6. Adoring God. This can take the form of praising God so that he will be well inclined toward the supplicant. One youth said, "I feel like I ought to tell God what a good guy he is so he will be more inclined to listen to me." Adoration in this sense of expressing admiration and of narrating greatness is rather fruitless. God is wanting good laborers, not courtly adorers.

7. Dumping complaints and problems on God. This is something quite different from seeking for guidance and help in meeting annoying circumstances and facing problems. This attitude is expressed in the prayer of the woman, "God, you take over, for I do not want to be bothered with these things."

8. Begging for signs and wonders. Frequently those praying thus want shortcuts to solutions. These prefer an easy, sure, definite answer that places the responsibility on God and saves those who pray from the longer-time searching involved in working out a solution with God's help. Healthy praying develops the powers of the person; it does not afford easy answers that call for little or no insight on the part of the searcher.

9. Wanting special invasion of God in one's favor. Usually this kind of praying disregards the orderly sequence of happenings in God's universe. Each event is isolated, an occurrence in its own right. Often such persons think of every happening as

coming at the specific edict of God—and so God is expected to set aside the predictable course of his laws and manage things to the liking of his elect.

10. Getting "chummy" with God without demands upon the petitioner. This kind of praying is depicted in popular songs and programs in which God is addressed as "the Fellow Upstairs" or "my Heavenly Pal." Such communion makes no serious demands on those who beseech him as to what they are going to do with their lives. Erdman Harris speaks of this kind of conception of God in *God's Image and Man's Imagination.* He tells of a meeting held in New York City in 1957 in which a minister prayed before four thousand postal employees, "Bless the President of the United States. May he in wisdom be so directed by Thy will that he may accede to these requests for an increase in postal pay" (page 8). This shows how many look upon prayer as speaking to a not-too-critical God who is not highly expectant of those who are "chummy" with him.

Seeing with God

The spiritually maturing person looks toward discovering what God is purposing and how God is proceeding before he insists that God is so-and-so. He wants to discover whether what he is is wanting accords with what God is aiming to bring to pass. Before he insists on some identifiable blessing he tries to line up with God.

A conscientious elder was asked to administer to a woman seriously ill with a body malignancy. Some of the Saints were wanting a gathering of the members for a concentrated service of praying following considerable fasting. While the congregation was assembled the elders were to administer. Several felt that a display of God's power in healing would "strengthen the Saints" and attract nonmembers. The wise elder sought counsel of God as to what he should pray about. He came to sense that he should pray for the peace of the afflicted one and for a lifting of her burden. He told how in administering he made this simple, fervent prayer and had nothing more to say. The next day the woman who was ill said that a great change had come over her. She had held a terrifying fear of death. This was lifted and she was at peace. Her sufferings in body and mind ceased. In a few days she died calmly and contentedly. Later the elder said he had no intention of mobilizing the Saints to put pressure on God. He was not inclined to insist on a blessing of instantaneous healing unless he could see that this accorded with God's will.

Some Qualities in Wholesome Praying

Praying may be considered a "spiritual exercise." It is not enough that we spend hours praying. It may be that we can misdo the exercise. Once a girl started to take piano lessons. She took only a few. Then her teacher moved away. She kept on inventing her own techniques as she proceeded. When she took up her lessons again she was worse off than if she had never practiced. She had fallen into habits of fingering and reading notes that had to be unlearned. Warm intentions alone are not enough. Following the injunction, "Pray always!" is not sufficient. Here are some fundamental qualities in healthy praying:

1. Expanding and deepening conception of God's nature and purpose and process. How shall we be able to converse and commune with God as Person if we do not have some sound idea of what he is like, of what he is setting out to do, and of how he is going about his work? We cannot line up with God if we do not vision to some degree what he has in his heart and mind.

2. Working cooperatively and understandingly with God. Those who are doing things together have so much to talk about together. The prayer life of many persons runs down or runs out because they are not doing anything of consequence with God. Lazy, indifferent persons make ineffective "pray-ers." Praying is more than buzzing around on our own little projects which we want God to bless. It is sharing with God in his work and conversing about what God and we are doing together.

3. Being spiritually honest with God and with ourselves. The phrase of one man runs this way, "Now, God, this is the way things are." This is excellent to the degree that we set ourselves to see the total picture of things with thorough honesty. There is no place for pretense in praying. There is no place for partiality. One college student prayed this way before a few friends, "God, I am not going to pretend anything, for you know what kind of a guy I am." Well may we say, "Open my eyes, O Lord, that I may pray."

4. Maintaining a consistent pattern of praying. Friends are consistent with each other. One can rely on the consistency of the other. They keep up the friendly relationship and do not need to grab frantically for a friend when an emergency arises. They do not put friends aside until they feel pressure or danger. When John Glenn was asked if he prayed while on his astronautical flights around the earth he replied that he did not have a fire

engine type of prayer life. He meant that he did not put prayer aside until his house was on fire and he had to call out the fire department.

5. Expressing praying in meaningful and soulful language. Jesus spoke critically against "vain repetitions" and the like. The richer our resources of language in heart and mind the better we can speak to God. The frigid heart and the flitting mind can have little to say. We ought to be able to identify what we have in our outreach to God. Yet our praying ought always to go beyond our powers of expression. With Tennyson we shall keep on saying, "I would that my tongue could utter the thoughts that arise in me." Too often those who pray, especially in public, are inclined to "multiply words," to use "halo" words, and to fall back on traditional intonations of the voice.

6. Relaxing in the presence of God. We can become so tied up that we cannot reach out and speak to God. The phrase of the hymn is apropos, "and feel in the presence of Jesus at home." A considerate gentleman endeavors to get those who want to address him to be at ease and to be themselves. So shall they be able to reveal themselves to him. Jesus did not open his model prayer with something like "O Thou Awful One" or "Terrible Judge" or "Celestial Potentate." He said "Our Father."

7. Cultivating sensitivity to God and disposition to listen. We differ in sensitivity to other persons. Some of us pick up clues readily while others barge along oblivious to the feelings, the moods, the interests, the thinking of others. Some present their prayers of requests to God but do not stop to catch much of anything of his outreach to them. Basically a person cannot converse well with another person if he cannot pick up the clues and sense where the other person is. It is said that some persons never converse, never catch what other persons are thinking, for while the other person is talking they are getting their own speeches put together. Some are this way with God.

8. Planning to work ahead with God in matters talked over in praying. Praying is never escaping from responsibility, never retreating from reality. It can be looked upon as a "readying" session in which the person endeavors to equip himself for lining up with God, living with God, laboring with God, loving with God. Without this serious intent to carry on with God in his work, praying becomes an empty word-saying and mood-indulging. Great hymns of prayer express this desire and intention. Charles Wesley phrased it this way,

Forth in thy name, O Lord we go,
Our daily labor to pursue;
Thy mind, O Lord, we long to know,
And serve in all we speak and do.

9. Expecting the continuing ministry of the Holy Spirit as the prayed-about endeavors take expression. In this sense we may think of prayer as prelude to empowerment. The Spirit of God is promised to those who have reason to want this empowerment for effectiveness in their laboring with God. He who is experienced in prayer anticipates that the presence and power of God will continue as he keeps busy with God.

10. Experiencing the disclosure of God as God and man commune in two-way relationship. This rapport is the zenith of prayer. It is as when two friends can say, "We understand each other now."

Emerging Assurance through Praying

The assured person is confident and firm. Every one of us needs sense of assurance if we are to walk erectly and move forward in everyday living. We need the insight and the outlook expressed in the affirmation of the hymn, "This is my Father's world!" Such confidence requires that we see God's universe and him in his own way. A faith that is generated out of our own wishful thinking, out of our own fanciful imagination about the way things are and are to be will not hold up. It will collapse in the laboratory of living. Assurance comes as we see things as they are and vision how they can become, in the program of God.

Praying develops this needed assurance as we get to know God, as we line up with him. The more channels of communication we have the sounder this assurance can become. This is the kind of assurance that comes to a lad who is walking along with his family father. The two talk together. The father points out things for his son to see; he shares his thoughts with the boy. He will not provide him with a diet of candy and cake just because the boy asks for these. He wants the junior member to qualify to become a member of a father-son corporation. This is the way praying operates as God and man work together and talk together. God wants his sons to stretch and develop. He wants them to stand on their own feet, with him.

Through praying and through the work operations growing out of the praying we come to know God. Then we are able to say, God is available; God is reliable; God is understanding; God is consistent; God is continuing in his creative expression; God is concerned in us; God never runs down; God is self-disclosing. This is what we learn in healthy praying. This can be caught by small children. It is phrased in the boy's prayer, "God, you be sure to keep right on, for if you give up we're all sunk." This can grow in older persons. Equally well did the senior Saint pray, "Sometimes things get pretty confusing and many times I get confused, but, God, you always know where you are going." Such praying expresses assurance and serves to increase this assurance.

A Restoration Precedent

In the spring of 1820 a farm boy prayed in the grove of his homestead. This youth was thoroughly honest. He had something to talk about, for he was needing direction. In the Palmyra woodland there was two-way communion: the youth reached out and God responded. Basic assurance shaped up in the boy: (1) God is available and responsive; (2) God plans through the ages with ongoing purpose; (3) God is at work today in realizing this purpose; (4) God invites the person to work with him and promises sustaining power; (5) God is revealed through his ever living Son. This youth left the grove of prayer with present-tense assurance. This would need to deepen and expand. It would have to be kept up-to-date. The praying in that grove transformed a youth's life and it affected the course of history. He came out of the grove to live with assurance.

Questions for Discussion

1. What constitutes assurance that is sound and serviceable? When do you think assurance is well founded?
2. What do we need to understand about God in order to achieve this sound assurance? How can this assurance come through praying?
3. How is it essential to have something worthful about which to commune with God if we are going to have beneficial communion in prayer?
4. How would you go about making ready to converse with a gifted celebrity? Illustrate how you would make ready to talk with some specific person such as Albert Schweitzer, Winston

Churchill, John Glenn. How do you go about making ready to converse with God in praying?

5. What do you think constitutes "answer to prayer"? How do you see God "answering" you when you are not asking for some favor or specific thing?

6. When may prayer take on the quality of escaping or retreating or surrendering?

7. What is your reaction to the comment of a brother who said, "When I close my prayer I always say, 'I ask it in Jesus' name' and then I know I will get whatever I ask for"?

8. What essential conditions in a person's quality of living and program of living entitle him to ask God for specific things to come to him or to others? When does a person have the "spiritual right" to expect specific blessings from God?

9. A young woman of Protestant background commented, "In my church we spend lots of time in prayers of adoration but it seems we never link this with getting anything done." How can this be true of the praying of a person or of a congregation?

10. How was the praying of Jesus connected with meeting life situations? How was his praying fruitful in his ministry, his daily living?

11. What do you think Alma had in mind when he counseled his people to "pray continually"? How might this be so interpreted that praying would interfere with productive daily labor? What is set forth here as the fruitage of praying? (See Alma 10:27, 28.)

12. How do you see a balance between in-the-closet praying and on-the-job praying as highly desirable? How are both necessary to good spiritual health?

13. If you were to teach a course on "learning to pray" what would you set forth as basic characteristics of praying that produce good spiritual health?

CHAPTER 24

FASTING WITH
CLEAR PURPOSE

"Be ye clean!" is a continuing admonition of God to his people. It was spoken in the Hebrew religion and in the Christian faith. It is heard again in the Restoration movement. Conscientious disciples have kept asking, What constitutes cleanness? How do we go about becoming clean? How do we maintain this clean condition? How does God function in helping us to be clean? These are questions that we cannot afford to ignore. To preach, "Be clean!" is not enough. Our people are wanting to identify what constitutes healthy spiritual cleanness.

We Can Be Unclean over Cleanness

We are needing to see what constitutes a wholesome approach to cleanness. We can become victims of outlooks and practices that enslave us and stifle us and weaken our total healthfulness. A person can fill his day with washing the hands, with taking pills, with worrying over diet, with avoiding dirt, with spraying against bugs and germs, and with anxiety on these matters until he becomes antisocial as well as prosanitary. It is possible for a child to be so protected from dirt that he becomes unhealthily clean. A grownup can become neurotic over matters of diet, of ventilation, of sanitation. Such was the woman who would never shake hands with anyone until she had put on her gloves.

And this kind of thing can happen in our caring for our spiritual health. We can take joy out and put fear in as we scan rules and regulations and fret about invasion of spiritual microbes. We can consume time and energy putting up quarantine preventions until we become prisoners. Of one woman it was said, "She is unclean with worries about being clean." And it is so easy to seize a few special points or practices and presume that they cover the whole field of healthy living. This can vary from insistence on eating honey and whole wheat bread to closing our prayers in some one prescribed way. Such punctilious and partial programs can get in the way of spiritual healthiness. Fasting is one of the fields that can contribute to clean spiritual healthiness or to strained concern over spiritual sanitation.

The Widespread Practice of Fasting

The discipline of fasting has been widespread throughout the religions of the world. Usually it refers to abstinence from food. In the wider sense it may include much more. Often it involves any activity that provides bodily pleasure. This might include sex expression, bodily exercise, joyful entertainment, smoking, friendly conversation, and more. Fasting was prominent in ancient Hebrew religion; it was practiced by early Christians; it was in the life of Jesus of Nazareth. It came to have a large place in medieval Catholicism. It is emphasized in non-Christian religions such as Buddhism and Islam.

But there is no one picture, no one interpretation that runs through all these religions in the observance of fasting. Men have fasted for different reasons. They have included different items in their fasting. They have used different methods. They have kept their fasts with differing intensities. We may not look at two persons or at two groups and presume that they are doing the same thing when they are abstaining from food. One may have a fairly clear conception of what he is endeavoring to bring to pass; another may be only adhering strictly to prescriptions and to official directives. One may look to spiritual changes within while the other is thinking of observing rites with a view to gaining spiritual advantage. And this applies to two Latter Day Saints and to two congregations of Latter Day Saints.

Scarcity of Counsel Concerning Fasting

A cursory thumbing through materials on religious living discloses that there is little printed material about fasting. There is little to guide the person who is inclined to fast, little to help him see clearly why he should or should not fast, how he should or should not fast. A man of inquiring mind and professional training read the call to a time of fasting before an approaching World Conference. He was not hostile to the idea, but he said quite frankly that he wanted and needed to have some idea of what he was setting out to do when he was abstaining from eating two meals. He felt that many others had no clear conception of what they were trying to do and would be fasting simply because a call had been sent out. He said he did not know where to go to get the kind of counsel he was wanting. He felt that most members took fasting for granted and had no functioning insight into its purpose and process.

Cleansing through Catharsis

The word "catharsis" comes from the Greek, from an adjective meaning "pure" and a verb signifying "to cleanse." We use the word in medical practice to connote purging our body through getting rid of whatever obstructs healthful functioning of the body. Men of medicine remind us that when the body is doing well, it takes care of this elimination without need for purgative procedures. They counsel us to be wise in materials of food intake, in bodily exercise, in mental attitude and from these expect healthy bodily functioning that does not require continuing use of powerful cathartics. Sometimes, however, we may need to give attention to getting rid of what ought not be in our bodies. But this is to be done without doing damage to the body.

Catharsis applies to our personal living, too. We have come to see that we can bury unpleasant and unwanted experiences with their tightening feelings and thoughts. Sometimes these fears or hatreds or insecurities can get deep down within us and can fester there, causing dis-ease within us. In such a time the person needs to recognize what is buried, from where it came and what it is doing to him. Then he can recognize it, bring it to the fore, and in some way resolve it. In a program of good personal living we endeavor to avoid burying such unhealthy subconscious experiences. If we find such complexes buried we try to identify them and to remove them. Many a person has improved his spiritual health by getting rid of phobias, anxieties, and the like. One grown man, for instance, was living in strained relations with his wife. With the help of counseling he came to see that deep down he was holding resentment against a domineering mother who had always been cool-hearted in her relationships with her son. He had been making his wife the target for this longtime resentment. Catharsis brought better spiritual health.

This holds true in our relationship with God. Sometimes we need to see and admit what is on the inside of us and to plan to get rid of some things. One youth had been so thoroughly frightened with the fear of God his elders had generated in him that it remained to haunt him. He had thought of God as a stern old man peeping through spectacles to see what little boys were doing that was bad. Then this God would pounce down on the offender. It took a major purging program of several months to get rid of these ideas so that he could converse with God and work with God. One man, a priest, came to see that inside him was an unspoken dislike for a friend who had been ordained an elder. Inside was jealousy and a feeling of unfairness. A fasting experience equipped him to see, to acknowledge, to dispel his buried animosity. This cathartic treatment is indispensable to good health.

Some New Testament Advice

Purging was recommended by early Christian teachers. The writer of the epistle to the Hebrews spoke of the need to "purge your conscience from dead works to serve the living God." Some things had to go: they were incompatible with the creative work of God. The writer of II Timothy likened persons to vessels, "some for noble use, some for ignoble use." In 2:21 each disciple is urged to "purge himself from what is ignoble" that he may be fit for "the master's use." Paul advised the Corinthian saints to "purge out . . . the old leaven" (I Corinthians 5:7). Removal of sinful traits would make possible "fresh dough." In the second epistle of Peter believers were told to cultivate virtues in their lives, the fruitage of the Creative Spirit (II Peter 1:5-8). This would come with the cathartic process of purging out old sins (verse 9). The disciple does not get rid of what is undesirable and then remain as a vacuum. Rather is room made and a growing situation provided for the constructive nutritive experiences that further healthy saintliness.

Fasting Is for Cleansing

If fasting is abstaining from food or from something else, there must be sound reasons for practicing it. God does not ask us to do something such as fasting just to check us on our disposition to carry out orders. This would reduce us to the level of servile robots. God is interested in achieving something more than this in us. It will be well for us to take a look at what prompts men to fast and to examine how these motivations do or do not accord with what God has in mind for us. Here we set forth the thesis that fasting is a cathartic experience of freeing ourselves from what is unwholesome and of enabling us to take in strength-providing food that will further our spiritual health.

The Moslem Fast of Ramadan

Often it is good for us to look outside ourselves for some pattern for comparison and for evaluation. Foremost in the great fasts of the world is the Moslem thirty days' fast of Ramadan.

This falls in the ninth month of their lunar year. During this sacred month the faithful are to abstain from food, drink, and bodily pleasure from sunrise to sunset. As soon as it is possible to distinguish between a white thread and a black thread at dawn, no food or drink is to be taken. When at sundown the difference between the threads is no longer distinguishable he who fasts is released. When the fast season comes during the cooler months there is little hardship, but when it comes in the torrid season, it becomes a real burden. The observance is strict. Only the sick and soldiers are exempt.

Much of the observance of Moslem requirements is purely formal. The main thing is that the letter of the law is kept. Many feel that it is possible to fast all day and feast all night. The main thing is that Allah has commanded this fast and the devoted are to comply. Some of the more discriminating leaders see the desirability of looking to inner conversion and commitment, but the masses are concerned with carrying out the prescription as formally stated.

Some Not-recommended Purposes in Fasting

Some objectives for fasting are not to be encouraged. Some can lower spiritual health. Some can be practiced so that they actually undermine the physical and spiritual constitution. With the prophets of Israel we protest against the assumption that fasting is *opus operatum*. This means that the operation itself has value so that the person does not need to involve his inner self. Here are more common undesirable motivations:

1. To renounce the evil body. This view presumes that the material body is evil and must be suppressed if there is to be any spiritual advance. Fasting helps reduce any ascendancy of the body and puts it in its rightful place. The Restoration message calls for the full competency of the physical body as part of the soul of man.

2. To elicit the pity of God. It is thought that if we impose suffering on ourselves God will be moved to sympathy and compassion at our distress. The more we inflict denial on our bodies the more God will incline favorably toward us.

3. To please God through increasing our own discomfort. This is built on the idea that God enjoys seeing men suffer. This looks not so much to God's pity as to God's satisfaction in watching men inflict pain on themselves for his good pleasure.

4. To build up merit. This objective carries the belief that man's status is conditioned by the "merit" he builds up. Often this involves a kind of bookkeeping in which the assets are weighed against the debits. Some deeds are looked upon as building up merit; some are weighted more heavily. In this view fasting is often considered as carrying plenty of merit.

5. To make amends for sin. The contrite person with this view believes that he can eradicate God's dislike for his sins by carrying out prescribed acts such as fasting. The thoughtful person inquires if there is not some more productive expression that will bring good returns to himself and to others.

6. To increase the influence of our praying on God. This might be called "praying pressure." There is an old statement, "When praying will not get returns from God, fasting will." Sometimes there is a mathematical computation so that those who fast try to get as many as possible on the line of insistence.

7. To induce dreams and visions. In some religions the devotee goes a long, long time without food or water or comfort. In the weakened state the longed-for vision may come. Some American Indians used fasting as means of acquiring their personal "medicine," that is, their key word or password with the Great Spirit. This kind of motive is not infrequent in the Christian faith.

Some Possible, Commendable Benefits

Fasting does not carry automatic benefits. Its returns are conditioned (1) by the condition and needs of the person fasting, (2) by the purpose for which fasting is conducted, (3) by the nature of the person's relationship with God, (4) by the person's conception of the nature of the Spirit of God and his functioning in the process of inspiration, (5) by the total situation in which the fasting is carried on, and (6) by the utilization of the fasting experience for ongoing constructive returns. In this light here are some possible, commendable benefits:

1. Therapeutic effects of the physical body, effects of resting, reducing, and cleansing. This refers to more than recess for gastronomical organs. It refers to every organ of the body. It has been said that it would be good for all of us if we would plan soundly, suitably for rest from food consumption for suitable lengths of time.

2. Contribution to mental clarity and efficiency as the blood energy is freed for utilization in mental processes. It is well said that mental alertness does not come with stuffed stomachs and food-logged bodies.

3. Increase in spiritual sensitivity and clarity through concentration on spiritual exercise. When every fiber of our being is focused on some spiritual situation, there is possible a quickening of outreach and intake.

4. Symbolic putting aside of the less needed aspects of personhood; achievement of this abstinence of interest in what is less. Our expression of this abstinence in fasting helps to make this desire a fact.

5. Elevation of primary spiritual values. One youth observed that he put his emphasis on the cream of the gospel rather than on an ice-cream sundae. During the fasting we are saying that these things matter more than those things.

6. Unification of the total capacity of the person or of the group on one major concern. There is worth in a group's joining together at the same time to focus on needs, problems, shortcomings, goals. In effective fasting the total range of capacities can be mobilized on one single theme.

7. Economy in utilization of the person or group's resources. Said one youth, "I can do better feeling holy when I am not frying hamburgers." This was not denouncing hamburgers; it was saying that some things mixed do not achieve optimum returns.

What Isaiah Said about Fasting

The prophets kept making contrast between using a rite to express what was going on on the inside and using it as a thing in itself. They pointed up the inner discipline in contrast to mere external practices. The fifty-ninth chapter of Isaiah brings out this contrast boldly and definitely. Apparently the people were thinking that God ought to reward them well because they had been fasting. Definitely Isaiah said that the major concern ought to be with what went on in the inside. Particularly, he pointed to their social responsibilities and relationships. It was not enough that they go without bread: they should share their bread with the needy. It was not enough that they go about wearing sackcloth; they needed to wear this in their hearts.

"Why have we fasted, and thou seest it not? . . . Behold in the day of your fast you seek your own pleasure, and oppress all your workers. Behold, you fast only to quarrel and to fight. . . . Fasting like yours this day will not make your voice be heard on high. . . . Is not this the fast that I choose: to loose the bonds of wickedness, to undo the thongs of the yoke, to let the oppressed go free . . .? Is it not to share your bread with the hungry, and bring the homeless poor into your house . . .?—Isaiah 58:3-7, R.S.V.

What Jesus Taught and Did

Jesus lived a well-balanced life. He enjoyed eating with others. Sometimes his critics accused him of never fasting. But he did fast. At the opening of his ministry he fasted "forty days and forty nights" (Matthew 4:2). What he said and did has to be seen in the light of the Jewish background. The Pharisees made much of fasting and regarded it as a work of merit. It became the custom of the specially devout to fast on Mondays and Thursdays, although there is no evidence that this was binding on all. Jesus struck at display of fasting; he emphasized secrecy, privacy. For him it could never be done by rule or rote. Jesus advocated moderation and good judgment. He would have little place for the condition mentioned in Psalm 109:24. For him, fasting was to augment spiritual fitness.

Counsel to the Young Church of the Restoration

In the summer of 1831 the location of the land of Zion was designated. Soon after this the land was dedicated and the Saints were given basic instruction about their life in the community that was to be. The heart of this instruction was couched in the familiar directive: "Thou shalt love the Lord thy God with all thy heart, with all thy might, mind, and strength. . . . Thou shalt love thy neighbor as thyself." All other directives were to stem from this. They were given instructions about keeping the Lord's day and about the general quality of saintliness. Here was sound counsel about the nature of fasting:

"On this day . . . let thy food be prepared with singleness of heart, that thy fasting may be perfect . . . that thy joy may be full. Verily this is fasting and prayer; or, in other words, rejoicing and prayer. And inasmuch as ye do these things, with thanksgiving, with cheerful hearts, and countenances . . . the fullness of the earth is yours."—Doctrine and Covenants 59:3, 4.

This counsel indicates that partaking of food is compatible with fasting. Apparently it is a matter of *how* rather than of *whether*, in the matter of eating. Nor is fasting to be associated with mourning. Gladness and gratitude were inherent parts of the fasting. It was connected with achieving spiritual fitness in such matters as contrition and thanksgiving and praying and giving and making things right with the brothers. Here was expressed the concern of the prophets that the people of God be clean. There was to be no place for spiritual filth, for the intake or retention of anything contrary to God's nature.

Criteria of Good Fasting

Fasting is ever to further the good spiritual health of those who fast and of those affected by this fasting. Here are basic guidelines for healthy fasting:

1. It is an individual discipline suited to the spiritual well-being and efficiency of the person who is fasting. There are no identicals among persons as to needs, as to the constitution, the situation of the person fasting. There is no public exhibition.

2. It carries involvement of the total personhood of the one fasting. This includes body, mind, spirit, presumably in one harmonious whole. A person can hardly be said to be fasting if only the physical body is involved.

3. It carries as a part of it a wholesome tone of joy and thanksgiving. Healthy fasting carries a tone of confidence and hope.

4. It brings about a quality of cleanness in the person and in the congregation as the not-so-good is eliminated from the person or the social situation and the fruit-bearing Spirit of God enters with good spiritual nutrition.

5. It brings to pass increasing total spiritual competence. Emotions are refined; comprehension and discernment are quickened; love is deepened and broadened; values of superior worth are given superordinate standing; commitment is vitalized. The sense of the divine presence is immediate, compelling, and assuring.

6. It unifies in spiritual fellowship those who unite in soundly

appointed fasting. The salutation "Brother" takes on richer meaning.

7. It contributes to the well-balanced, well-tempered spiritual life of those participating and of those in proximity. There is no fanaticism. Such fasting follows the counsel of Paul, "Every man that striveth for the mastery is temperate in all things" (I Corinthians 9:25).

8. It sends the person into the business of living, into evangelistic stewardship with sense of commission and assurance. It does not breed recluses; it develops Saints who have been with God so that they are able to draw others to God.

Questions for Discussion

1. On what basis would you say, "Fasting is more saintly than feasting," or would you say this?

2. The Day of Atonement might be called an annual day of "spiritual housecleaning." Fasting was a part of the observance. On this day the people sought to catch up sins for which they had not made specific atonement. What might be the advantages and disadvantages of observing such a day?

3. If you were to work out a time of spiritual housecleaning for yourself or your family how would you include fasting as a part of the observance?

4. A rite is some specific action used to symbolize and express something that takes place on the inside of the person. Thus the rite of handshaking can be a ceremonial expression of fraternity. The partaking of bread and wine in the Lord's Supper expresses the renewing together of a covenant. What does fasting as a ritual express?

5. How do you respond to a person who comments, "I broke my fast when I forgot and took a drink of water"?

6. What are some items of catharsis that a congregation might consider in a fast in the preparatory period for a series of evangelistic meetings?

7. What items of spiritual cleanness do you see involved when counsel comes, "Be ye clean"? How might fasting contribute to realizing the cleanness counseled?

8. You have an important problem to face and a decision to be made. You plan a two-weeks' period of seeking light, in which fasting is to be included. How would you outline your

eating program for this period? What would you include in your fasting program besides food regulation?

9. How might the church go about preparing members to participate in a day of prayer and fasting before the opening of a World Conference of the church?

10. What could make the fast of Ramadan of Moslems a time of beneficial spiritual discipline?

11. Interpret and apply, "The wise person discovers what practices will achieve in him the maximum spiritual efficiency and good health." How does this apply to fasting?

12. What guidelines do you set up that will help in distinguishing between unwholesome worry about uncleanness and healthy practice of furthering spiritual cleanness?

13. How do you minister to a conscientious man who said, "I fasted until I was weak and tired but still the Lord did not take pity on me"?

14. What do you mean by catharsis? How can this contribute to achieving good spiritual health?

CHAPTER 25

STUDYING FOR
SPIRITUAL EXPANSION

Study is often looked upon as a cure for all ills, as a tonic for good health. This is not necessarily so. Study can build up or tear down. It can contribute to spiritual health or it can undermine health. It can narrow a man's living or expand it. Study is no unmixed good. Yet without it one cannot become a person. Without it the person cannot keep on developing personally. So the wise steward of study learns what it is and what it is for and how to use it to good returns. It is enough to say that the man who does not study dries up and declines; the man who mis-studies can misuse his powers and get on the wrong track; the man who understands broadly what study is and uses it to lifting purpose can expand in spiritual good health.

When Studying Goes Wrong

A young man was consigned to prison. He had been in a reformatory institution. His return to a penal institution came quite largely from "studying" with other young men "the tricks of the trade." He received quite an education in breaking and entering, in appropriating automobiles, and more. He might fitly have received a diploma on "Techniques in Burglary." A young woman went to live with an older woman. In two years the younger woman learned major negative attitudes toward living and the souring skills in complaining and fault-finding. She might have received a certificate in "the art of being against." A youth recently ordained a deacon was tutored by an older man. From the elder the younger man received a deeply entrenched schooling in "spirituality" that warped his life. His learning consisted in narration of sensational things, especially visions and dreams that had happened in this man's own life in which he was always elevated in his own sight as a man of great spiritual precocity while others were on a lower level and therefore discounted by him. The two men made collections of these "remarkable experiences" and perused them. And all these studyings went deep into the life of the learner.

One day the courageous Abinadi was denouncing King Noah and his priests. In a climactic moment he said to them, "I perceive that ye have studied and taught iniquity the most part of your lives" (Mosiah 7:112). They had become experts in misdirected study. One time Alma was distressed over the wickedness of the city, Ammonihah. He was inclining toward leaving the city to its own sinfulness. An angel addressed him and told him to return. With this directive went an interpretation of the factors working in the city. Here was one contributing cause: "Behold, they do study at this time that they may destroy the liberty of thy people" (Alma 6:22). The conniving people were studying government in reverse; they were wanting to find out how to turn everything to their own advantage. This can happen with politicians and priests and parents and producers.

A Senior Apostle's Counsel to a Younger Man

We think of Paul of Tarsus as a university-trained man. He had a trio of learning pursuits. He was schooled in Jewish learning of the Pharisaical type, in Greek thinking with its philosophical bent, in Roman life and government in which country he was a citizen. He used all this richness of education to good advantage in his ministry. One thing he had lacked and had needed: some central factor that could bring harmony into his education. This came with his conversion to Jesus Christ. Then he was able to sort over and sort out the ingredients of his learning and achieve an inner harmony in himself.

With such a struggle and with such a resolution of the problem in his own life Paul was able to give counsel to others. Timothy was very dear to Paul. The senior apostle regarded Timothy as his "own son in the faith." The advice given in II Timothy may be regarded as Paul's farewell counsel, as the mature outlook of his own life. He wanted his son in the gospel to keep studying, to keep increasing his competence in ministry. He knew quite well how Jewish scribes could argue over legalistic points, how Greek conversationalists in the agora could dicker back and forth for the joy of argument, how Romans could swing things around to political advantage. He wanted Timothy to rise above this kind of thing.

Paul warned Timothy against self-centered, unsound men who liked to hear themselves talk. These were the ones who made conversation a game of verbal ping-pong with phrases batted back and forth without serious intent to achieve understanding. These were of the nature of the man who said, "Let's have an argument; which side do you want to take?" One translation phrases Paul's comment about such persons in this wording, "who are always learning and yet never able to grasp the truth" (3:7). There are many in the field of religion who will quote "proof texts" in scriptures and pile up arguments without sensing the spirit and basic message of the gospel.

Paul saw learning as an integral part of his whole life, not as a section set off by itself. He denounced those whose so-called learning never proceeded beyond talking about matters (verse 9). For him worthful, wholesome learning had to be woven into the total life fabric. It was not ornamentation or surface expression. He told Timothy how this younger man had known Paul's thinking, his manner of living, his purpose, his personal qualities. He put it this way: "You, Timothy, have known intimately both what I have taught and how I have lived. My purpose and my faith are no secrets to you" (verse 10). Sound learning makes a difference in the life pattern of the learner. Paul advised Timothy to learn with purpose, to avoid fighting "wordy battles" (2:14), and to search in sincerity. He was to study with concern for God's approval rather than for acclamation by thin thinkers. In this setting Paul made this direct charge: "Study to show thyself approved unto God, a workman that needeth not to be ashamed, rightly dividing the word of truth" (II Timothy 2:15).

An Inclusive Program of Saintly Study

The entire curriculum of religious studying is inclusive. It is the total program of living. It is more than collecting a few facts and memorizing them. It is more than perusing printed pages. It is more than applying some formula. Rather it is a laboratory in learning. This involves appreciations, values, data for thinking, skills, experimentation. Study is much more than "book learning" and passing examinations. Its real testing is in the business of living, with thinking, feeling, acting included. Studying involves the total person in a total situation.

Paul wrote of this in his letters to the Thessalonians. He saw learning experience held together and given meaning in the unifying faith in Jesus Christ. He put it this way, "To sum up, my brothers, we beg you and pray you by the Lord Jesus, that you continue to learn more and more of the life that pleases God" (I Thessalonians 4:1, Phillips). He included instruction in brotherly love as part of the curriculum. This was more than theoretical study: it meant expressing love in everyday social relationships. He commended the Thessalonians for reaching out "to all the Macedonians." He went on to mention learning in their person-with-person relations. Quite frankly he wrote, "Aspire to live quietly, to mind your own affairs, and to work with your hands" (4:11, R.S.V.). He explained that thus they might "command the respect of outsiders."

Some Studying that Crimps

Some patterns of studying and some purposes for studying hem in those who hold to them. Some precedures are like blinders on the bridles of horses. They prevent seeing anything to either side. Here are some of the more commonly found forms of studying that limit:

1. Catechetical memorization. In true catechetical learning both the questions and the answers are given. The pupil receives both without examination. It is presumed that these are given by some authority that is not to be questioned. When a learner is permitted to formulate his own questions and when he insists on getting replies that pertain meaningfully to his own questions he has moved beyond catechetical learning.

2. Facts without relationships. A person can become a walking encyclopedia of data and statistics without having any conception of what they mean or of how or whether they hold together. Good learning always involves seeing relationships. Everything in the universe exists in relationships. It is possible to memorize scriptural quotations without sensing what they mean in terms of their setting and their application.

3. Closed mind approach. Generally these persons come to "prove a point" rather than to explore a field. This is the attitude of the Scotsman who said, "I am open to conviction, but I'd like to see anyone who could change my mind." Such mindedness tends to see only what supports an already believed opinion. Anything that does not agree is sifted out. In contrast is the prayer, "Open my eyes, O Lord!"

4. Segmentation of fields of study. This means that a field is fenced off to itself and treated alone. This is the way of fanatics and simplicists, those who have one simple solution for all things. Any area of research has to be separated to itself for treatment but not divorced from the rest of reality.

5. Popular fads. The history of education discloses many "latest fads" in education. Sometimes these dominate programs of study. The theme "Everybody's doing it" can be pretty powerful. The range can run from sects to sex, from counseling to committeeing.

6. Busywork. Here the main thing is to keep persons busy lest they have idle time that might get misused. The old adage, "An idle brain is the devil's workshop" warns to keep busy. Activity programs without purpose in terms of constructive living can be major detriments to sound education. This approach is often used with small children. Merely being active does not mean that anything significant is being accomplished. A crowded schedule does not mean that persons are being developed.

7. Final answers. So many persons want to get hold of the completed and closing-out word and solution. This seems to provide security and finality. Many want to feel that they have the total fullness of the gospel. They look for answers that only God is capable of having. These lose the thrill of exploring. They practically deny the ongoing experience of revelation that affords expanding understanding.

8. One-voice authoritarianism. One book, one person, one organization, one theory can become the sole reliable authority. The effect is narrowing and stifling. This is the *ipse dixit* attitude. This phrase was used to refer to a teacher looked upon as a final authority. When a statement was made that might call for amplification or support, his students would say *"ipse dixit,"* that is, "He himself said it." That was enough. Some use God this way, forgetting the many voices through which God speaks, the many fields in which he reveals himself. Some use the Bible this way, as if the Bible were the complete record of God's revelation and as if they had complete interpretation of what it says.

9. Prejudices against and phobias about some fields of learning. One man said he "saw red" whenever anyone mentioned the word "evolution." Another said he "tightened up" at the mention of Brigham Young. Another affirmed he would never read anything about communism or Marxism, for the thought of them made him nervous. There is the other side of prejudice in which a person is so blindly supportive of a proposition or doctrine that he gets a fighting spirit whenever anyone challenges what he believes in dearly. Recently a man said that this was the way he felt about the doctrine of the Virgin Birth. He was too emotionally involved to investigate it.

10. Halo words and phrases. In this study an aura of sanctity and sentimentality gathers around certain sayings. Their meaning cannot be examined. They carry an emotional association. The person feels good when he says them or hears them. They are taken for granted. Such words are "Zion," "God," "Atonement." Some "pentecostal" preaching puts these words and phrases and quotations together without intent to express a basic content. Some use John 3:16 this way.

11. Buildup of protection of "the word of God" against examination and interpretation. Adherents of this view say that if a message is from God it does not need to be reviewed and validated. These overlook that without understanding there is no revelation. They forget that untruths and half-truths can come forth as the word of God. Men who believe in revelation develop as they increase their capacity for revelation, as they reach out to God for revelation, as they study to get hold of the message and to examine its validity and apply it in daily living.

Testimonies of Spiritual Expansion

This expanding is more than a dream, more than a sermon. It is happening in the lives of disciples who rightly discipline their studying. If our lives were extended we might be able to effect balance and breadth that would include a wide world of fields of exploration. Most of us are able to take but one or two fields. These testimonies are out of the book of life of living Latter Day Saints. They are concentrated statements of original testimonies.

1. "I looked into a microscope in my biological studies and saw God at work. The field of cell structure and cell division became a present-tense miracle. I see ahead at least forty years of seeing God through the microscope."

2. "I have been examining Einstein's way of looking at the universe. I see a great mind and a reverent spirit formulating $e = mc^2$. I am finding as the British scientist has said that the universe is more like a great thought."

3. "I have been going over the history of human thinking. I do not know how man got started in thinking, but I know that he has come a long, long way. I marvel at the raw potentials for thinking that God has put in man. We have blundered and wasted our potentials many times, but we have climbed. I marvel at our native endowments."

4. "I have been getting into the field of geology with a touch of geophysics. My sight has been pushed out millions and millions of years. I see the grandeur in the long stretch of centuries and millenniums in which God has been shaping up this earth of ours. I see a God who keeps on the job."

5. "I have been stimulated by the counsel about 'light' that comes to us through the Doctrine and Covenants. I am beginning to see how a divine light pervades the universe, how this is revealed in the life, the person of Jesus Christ, how this can function in us. I am just beginning to sense this. How I expect to grow!"

6. "I have been studying the history of western Europe and of the opening of the Western Hemisphere. I look over seven or more centuries prior to 1820 and I am stirred to admiration as I see how God was at work in getting ready for this nineteenth century in America."

Counsels from Restoration Scriptures

The Restoration movement began as a study experience. The young pioneer expanded as he explored. He came to know God as a guide in exploration, as a source for understanding. Here are six essential steps in what happened: (1) A youth had problems to be solved. (2) He sought helps that would throw light upon these questions. (3) He disciplined himself for experiencing divine guidance. (4) He experienced foundational inspired insight. (5) He moved out on the basis of this insight and tested it. (6) He sought additional direction and understanding on the foundation of his earlier experience. (7) He communicated his findings to others and sought their experimentation concerning them. Through all this the questing inquirer expanded as he searched.

This earliest experience of Joseph Smith provides us with a sound, stimulating approach to study. He was at his best as prophet and teacher when he was following this way of exploring and learning. It prompted him to search with Oliver Cowdery to have increasing understanding about the way of God and the ministry of the Holy Spirit. It enabled him to write such revelations about study as the one which is now Section 85 of the Doctrine and Covenants, notably in paragraph 21. This was early in his prophetic ministry, in December 1832. It moved him to encourage the first Latter Day Saints who gathered to Independence in 1831 to provide schools. It guided him to arrange for the "school of the elders" in Kirtland. It was expressed in his own study of grammar and Hebrew and related subjects. It opened the way for him to speak to the young church about "light" and "truth" and "intelligence" in the noteworthy communication of May 1833, now numbered Section 90.

Through the years these counsels stand out, counsels about the way to proceed in study:

1. The way of inspiration is the engaging of man's capacities at their best. Man is alert and is applying the fullness of his powers. There is no place for a conception of a languid experience with the powers of mind becoming quiescent. The word to Oliver Cowdery is clear, "You must study it out in your mind" (D. and C. 9: 3 b).

2. The operations of exploratory study and adventurous faith are to be complementary, with both essential in the complete process of learning. There is to be no hostility between the trusting of the heart and the tutoring of the mind. The counsel, "Seek learning even by study, and also by faith," still stands. This is not to be an alternating experience but a two-phases-in-a-single-process procedure.

3. The curriculum is extensive, inclusive. The administrative leaders of the church were admonished to "study and learn, and become acquainted with all good books, and with languages, tongues, and people" (D. and C. 87: 5 b). The counsel in Doctrine and Covenants 85: 21 takes in disciplines of learning from astronomy to geophysics, from history to sociology. There is no limiting to a few books or to a few fields. The curriculum is universe-wide.

4. Specialization in fields of study are essential for ministries and stewardships. In 1906 Joseph Luff was called to be "physician to the church" and director of the anticipated sanitarium. He was referred to as having "been giving his attention to the study of medicine" and "preparing himself for usefulness in this direction" (D. and C. 127: 2 b). Here the ministry of priesthood and the ministry of medicine were linked together. The two were to be complementary.

5. Studying has social expression and social influence. The brotherhood of learners is recognized. The counsel, "Teach one another," was to carry through the school of the elders and through all the learning of the church (D. and C. 85: 36 a). The idea of the Zionic community was to run through the learning program.

6. Out of brotherly interaction enlightened by divine inspiration emerges common consent. The common mind is not superimposed; it comes to pass out of the sharing of brothers with brothers. In July 1830 Joseph Smith was directed to advise the young church, "All things shall be done by common consent in the church, by much prayer and faith" (D. and C. 25:1 b). Praying and group studying go together.

7. The program of studying shall be in the framework, in the faith, in the fellowship of the church. This is to be by virtue of the spiritual competency of those called to lead, with an outlook for spiritual growth. This is expressed in the direction to the church in 1940 (D. and C. 142:4).

Survey of the guidance expressed in the revelations to the church concerning study points up that members of the church are to keep on studying, and to do it *humbly, constructively, inclusively, exploringly, honestly, cooperatively, progressively, prophetically.* This last means that searchers endeavor to ascertain the mind and heart of God in all things and to speak forth this insight clearly, confidently, and reverently. This prophetic attitude applies to God in all his universe, in all his purpose, in all his processes, with all his people. It involves the divine mind in understanding cosmic rays, in estimating speed of light, in finding out about brain waves, in detecting interpersonal influences, and more. It applies to a four-year-old boy who is wanting to know about the stars, to a fourteen-year-old youth praying in a woodland about the course of his life, to a twenty-four-year-old college student wondering about depth psychology, to a thirty-four-year-old man just being called to the eldership, and on and on. The field of study is as wide as the universe, as far away as the galaxies, as near as our own inner hungers and drives. And God is to be enlightening us and stimulating us all in this business of learning.

The Outlook of the Healthy Saint

The gospel of Jesus Christ rightly understood prompts every person to healthy attitudes toward study. The healthy-minded person is not tied in knots because he has problems to solve. He is attracted by the immensity of what is yet to be explored. He stands up, as did Albert Einstein, with a sense of awe and wonder at the beauty, the complexity, and the order about him and in him. He feels the pull to discover. He is aware of the dynamic power of the Holy Spirit to quicken and enlighten his resources. He looks ahead to the years of this life when he shall keep on exploring and expanding. This is the first period in an eternity of seeing more and more.

This call to continuing expansion and exploration came to the church anew in the Conference of 1964. It is a modern-day call to the practice of revelation. It was encouragement and stimulation to those of searching spirit.

"Instruction which has been given in former years is applicable in principle to the needs of today and should be so regarded by those who are seeking ways to accomplish the will of their heavenly Father. But the demands of a growing church require that these principles shall be evaluated and subjected to further interpretation. This requisite has always been present. In meeting it under the guidance of my spirit, my servants have learned the intent of these principles more truly."—Doctrine and Covenants 147: 7.

Here is an admonition to spiritual study that expands.

A Prayer of Those Who Study for Expansion

A few Conferences ago the young people were considering a *studying* League. They concluded that Zionic harmony does not come by chance, that it requires the learning of the art of living together and of studying together. So the family and the League and the branch become schools in solving problems together, laboratories in human relationships. And God is the center in all this. These young people prayed this prayer together:

"O God of light, help us to cultivate the reverent and responsible spirit toward the stewardship of learning.

Deliver us from smugness, from indifference, from fear.

Enliven us in the disposition to share in the quest for truth.

Teach us how to expect the incoming of thy enlightening Spirit.

Open our eyes to see the wonders of thy universe and to find therein the disclosure of thy intent and thy way.

Grant us understanding of our callings to scholarship in mind, in heart, in hand.

Keep increasing within us the spirit of our Master Teacher. Amen."

Questions for Discussion

1. It is reported that a tribe in Africa some time ago wanted to build a statue of the devil and wished to put in his hand a suitable instrument as a symbol of his nature. They chose to put a microscope in his hand. This would represent man snooping into matters that were not to be investigated by man, for these were in God's domain. What is your reaction to this outlook? Are there other fields in which we might take a similar view? What would you put into the hand of the devil that would symbolize his intent to keep man in darkness?

2. A woman narrated how as a girl she had been put out of a Roman Catholic parochial school because she asked questions she said she was not supposed to ask. Could this happen in a Latter Day Saint school? What would constitute questions that a child is not supposed to ask? How would you guide a child of this nature?

3. A conscientious man said he would be shocked and helpless if a youth told him in his church school class that he did not believe in God. Another teacher of youth said he was so used to this kind of comment that it did not bother him. What would be your reaction? How would you go about exploring with a youth who said he did not believe in God? Would you explore or would you issue an edict?

4. What situations may place persons in the condition of ever learning but never able to get hold of truth?

5. How might we teach the mission of the church in the world in such a way that we would crimp the outlook of learners? How can we teach it so as to afford lifelong expansion of vision of the church?

6. What can happen in the life of a person who keeps pushing out in radius of learning, without any center or hub or nucleus to hold things together? What has to happen to our conception of God and to our communion with God as our world gets bigger and more complex? What happens if we try to hold to the God of our childhood in the universe of manhood?

7. What basic guidelines do you get from the Doctrine and Covenants about working out sound procedures in studying as persons, as congregations, as Zionic communities?

8. How are we tempted as we grow older to want to outline and systematize and complete our beliefs? How can we systematize

and coordinate what we believe without finalizing our statements? What is likely to happen to our thinking about revelation if we begin to fence in our world of believing?

9. Once F. M. McDowell surveyed some adult classes that had been "studying" the "doctrines" of the church over and over. He made this observation: "Each Sunday they come, chiefly to rearrange their prejudices." What did he mean? When and how might this happen among us?

10. How may study of the book of Genesis narrow or expand our conception of God at work in his universe?

11. This is a statement from a recent testimony: "I am so thankful to come into a church that not only affords me freedom to think but also encourages me to think freely." How can we see to it that this observation of a newly baptized person is always possible in our church life?

12. What qualities characterize healthy thinking? What qualities characterize unhealthy thinking? How shall we encourage "spiritual expansion through study"?

CHAPTER 26

TESTIFYING OUT
OF SOUND WITNESS

"I know it, but I can't tell it" is heard quite frequently. Sometimes this becomes an excuse for silence or for blundering conversation. Students of behavior and learning are telling us that much of this view is unsound. Those who say it are building up a wall of defense. Rather are we reminded that if something is clear to a person, he can in some way express this. He will try to communicate it in some way. If we were living next to a family of a different linguistic culture whose house caught on fire, we would make known to him what was happening in some way even if we did not speak his language. If we consider that what we see and believe is of great consequence, we shall go about trying to develop skills and means for expressing it.

This speaking out is essential for good spiritual health. Helen Keller, blind and deaf, says she did not start living until she began to develop the art of communicating. Once a woman inclined to hold everything to herself caught the picture of what has happened in Helen Keller and said, "If a girl deprived of seeing and hearing could learn to converse, certainly I ought to have something worth saying and some good way of saying it." The healthy spiritual person has something worth saying and some way of saying this well. This applies to his conversation with other persons and with God. This includes wisdom concerning when to speak and when to keep silent, concerning what to share with others and what to keep to himself, concerning how to speak and how to refrain from speaking. There is no substitute for the gifts of wisdom and discernment.

Testifying Is Essential

In terms of spiritual health, to testify is to speak out in witness to that which is worth sharing with others. It presumes that something is happening in the life of a person that is good enough to talk about. There are several reasons for wholesome testifying: (1) What a person is thinking and feeling on the inside needs overt expression in conversation and conduct. Any person who holds his beliefs inside in inner compartments is inclined to short-circuit what could come out in creative goodness. We are designed to act out and through what we converse about on the inside. (2) What is unexpressed can become inbred and self-centered. It can go unexamined if not expressed to others with expectancy of their reaction. We need to get our thinking out on the table where we can see it and where others can see it. We need more than our own scrutiny. (3) When a person holds in what means most to him, what has affected him most, he deprives others of the fruits of interaction. Once a man of our church worked alongside another man in a factory. Neither had any idea about the other's faith and convictions. One day quite incidentally the Latter Day Saint said something about his church affiliation and about the gospel of the Restoration. The other man said, "We have worked near each other for ten years. Why didn't you say something about this before? I have been needing what you have." (4) The person who does not talk about what is at the heart of his life may come to talk about things that do not matter very much. Then he gives the impression of shallowness or purposelessness. The image that the other person builds of the one who fails to testify affects what he comes to think of himself. (5) The person who refrains from talking about the biggest, most important values and experiences in his life shuts off possibilities of his own upward and onward development. He shuts off available inspiration from God that can come to him as he adventures in expressing himself. In brief, a program of spiritual health calls for testimonial expression.

Testifying Can Bring Clarity

"Don't tie yourself up. Tie your thinking together." So counseled a wise teacher. A capable Saint cannot be "in a scattered condition" in his thinking and doing. The capable person of conscientious nature and exploratory spirit cannot be satisfied with a jungle of beliefs. He cannot hold to an assembly of odds and ends. He needs a "gospel for living" that "hangs together." And his God has to be a source of harmony who can and will help him to bring things together meaningfully and functionally.

Testifying can do this very thing. It can help us get our experiences, our beliefs, our feelings, our convictions, our loyalties out on the table where they can be seen together. The witness beholding the totality of experience can arrange all of this systematically and meaningfully. A person cannot witness well who picks out a few dramatic things, pushes a few headliners to the front, and dwells on a few hunches. He has to see the whole story. In this way good testifying can bring spiritual clarity.

Writing Our Gospels

This seeing and narrating the whole story is what the four evangelists did who wrote the first four books of the New Testament. This is what Luke says he set out to do. The opening sentence in the book of Acts refers to his "former treatise" which dealt with "all that Jesus began both to do and teach." He intended to present an inclusive record. He was wise enough to realize that he could not tell and interpret any incident or saying out of the life of Jesus of Nazareth unless he saw the connected story of his entire life. This quality made Luke a first-class testifier. And John went even further. He interpreted this Jesus of Nazareth in his cosmic, eternal existence. He saw this Son as "in the beginning with God." These witnesses did not take some single happening such as a healing of someone ill or the catching of an unusual draught of fishes and build on this. They built on the total, connected life and ministry of the Man from Nazareth. They had lived with him. They had felt the impact of his life on theirs. Out of all this they could conclude, "Thou art the Christ, the Son of the living God" (Matthew 16:17). With this was the conviction that he could and would help them to "become the sons of God" (John 1:12). It is appropriate that these writings should be called "testaments."

It would be good for every one of us to write our gospel, our testimony. Each could look over his own life story with Jesus Christ and in the Church of Jesus Christ, and then tersely, clearly, coherently write down his way and his witness. Each one might give title to his writing after his own name, such as "The Gospel of Jesus Christ according to Paul Jones." Maybe no one else would read the account but the writing would do something for the one who wrote. It would prompt him to see and interpret every happening in the light of the larger overview of God at work in his life.

Testimony in Context

God always works in an ongoing, eternal process. He does not throw a few bits together without relationship. He is always calling his people to see this. When God wants a prophet to speak for him, he leads him to a mountain summit where the panoramic view is wide and clear. Here the prophet can see in many directions. He can get a sense of the way things piece together. In this way he is equipped to speak forth for God in the light of God's eternal plan and purpose. We are to try to do the same. When we tell of any happening, whether ordinary or extraordinary, we should see it testimonially in terms of its setting and its relationship in God's inclusive program. Only then are we able to witness for God soundly, fairly, adequately. Good testimony is always expressed *contextually*.

This difference between seeing a happening as an event to itself and interpreting it contextually is shown in the reactions of two men toward a prophetic message in a reunion. After the service one man spoke profusely to others about "the wonderful meeting," about "the word of God," about "the good feeling." When asked about the content he said it was that "the Saints should love one another" and that they "should work together in God's cause." For him the message of the morning was a thing in itself. He would go home and tell in a testimonial meeting how God had spoken to his people. And he did.

Another brother saw much more in the experience. In the district were several, including elders and some branch presidents, who were suspicious of and hostile to "the general church." Through previous years their attitude had taken a negative and caustic turn and it had spread. An atmosphere of fault-finding and of bypassing church administrators had developed. The Saints were being stunted in their spiritual development. Evangelism was at low ebb. Business meetings showed a cantankerous spirit. It is not unlikely that there had been lack of wisdom on the part of both local and general administrators. One thing was sure: this situation could not go on indefinitely. In such a time some conscientious members and ministers were seeking direction about what should be done. They felt that they must have divine guidance. So they prayed and tried to clear their own souls. Out of this situation an elder blessed with gifts of brotherly love, of prophetic insight, of wisdom stood and spoke at the reunion. He had lived with the message until it lived within him with strong and clear impulsion. He called the Saints to see the great mission of the church in terms of ministering to needing persons. He admonished them to seek to understand one another and to focus upon the things they held in common, that they might work together. The cause of God must go on. God wanted everyone to join in his work. If, however, there were those who would not make ready to join with their brothers and who would obstruct the work to be done, they would fall to the side, while the workers with God would move on. Then came the invitation to join together with God. They should put Christ foremost. Thus harmony and community could emerge and the Spirit of God come to guide and unify the congregations and the district. This second brother saw the setting that had called forth the counsel. He tried to see how members could carry out the counsel given. He became aware of repentance and renewal that would be required in members and ministers. He would be able to go home and testify of the leadings and the callings of the Holy Spirit. He could testify in context.

The Basic Testimony: It Works!

Producers of food, medicines, clothes, automobiles, and building supplies print testimonials of satisfied customers who are saying, "It works!" This is the kind of testimonial needed for the gospel of Jesus Christ. Such a statement would identify the product, indicate what it is good for, specify how to use it, and then climax with witness that it produces results. The gospel is good news about what takes place in the life of a person as the life-producing Spirit of God comes into his everyday living. It tells what the person has to do in order to be eligible for its benefits. It directs to the Gospel-Producer. It affirms that the erstwhile unhealthy person becomes healthy. It reports how disease-producing forces disappear. It narrates how spiritual exercise furthers vigor. It describes how the person seeking spiritual health associates with those who will help him in patterns of healthy living. It tells how the person, inadequate of himself, draws on the Source of spiritual health. The testimony of the man who had regained his physical eyesight is clear and to the point, "One thing I know, that, whereas I was blind, now I see" (John 9:25). This same thing can be said of a person who regains his spiritual vision as scales of hatred, ignorance, prejudice, suspicion, sensuality, and insecurity fall from his eyes and he is able to say, "Now I see." The great testimonies have to do with transformations that take place in persons. These say of the gospel, "It works."

A man of sturdy physique sat for his patriarchal blessing. He was a truck driver. He had been inclined to celebrate at both ends of the truck-driving line. He could hold his own in pugilistic combat. He could consume liquor quantitatively with the strongest drinkers. He could use profanity with emphasis and variety. He had dominated his wife and his children. Acquaintances had described his disposition as downright ornery and obstinate. Here he sat, with his Father speaking kindly, directly. His possible stewardships were indicated for reaching out understandingly to men of the type he had been. He would not lose his fighting strength but would refine it and use it fighting for the right. A miracle had taken place. This man who had indulged in what would satisfy his self-centered body at that moment was wanting to lift others. This man who had used God as a term in profanity was now turning to him as his Father. A glance at this man, now covenanted to walk with Jesus Christ, prompted one to say of the gospel, "It works!" He was a walking testimony. And this testimony had to include where he had been, where he was now going, and where God was calling him to go.

Not All Testimony Will Do

Not everything that passes under the title "testimony" is health-producing. Some testimonies get in the way. Some undermine health. Some cloud our spiritual vision. Testifying can go wrong. Testimony meetings can subvert the gospel. This ought not disturb us unduly, for anything that has great potential for good has also great possibility for going wrong. We do well to maintain a constructive, discriminating attitude toward testifying. We need to learn to keep it pointed toward clarity and constructive returns. It is good for us to identify some of the not-so-good types of testimonies. It will be desirable for us to use these descriptively rather than cynically. Titles are used to help them stand out.

1. "Jack Horner" testimonies, that point up self-righteousness and point out the evil ways of sinners who live other than we, the righteous, do. These carry the tone, "What a good boy am I!"

2. "Inside-information" testimonies that point up how the testifier has received some special information from God, some closed-to-the public data. This elevates the standing of the witness with God.

3. "Signs and wonders" testimonies that glory in the dramatic externals, signs that do not call for saintly fitness on the part of the observer.

4. "Can-you-top-this?" testimonies. Sometimes this happens in so-called experience meetings. There appears to be a strug-

gle for status with standing assured by the miraculous quality involved in what is narrated.

5. "Nobody knows" testimonies in which the theme borrowed from the Negro spiritual is followed, "Nobody knows the trouble I've seen," with a narration of problems and perplexities and sufferings.

6. "Private confession" testimonies in which scenes and happenings of rather private nature are reviewed. This is exemplified by the elderly woman who every Wednesday evening told of troubles with and prayers for "my wayward son and my adopted daughter."

7. Exhortative and homiletic testimonies, the first referring to exhorting the Saints, often the youthful Saints, the second to preaching. Neither of these is basically testimonial in nature.

Testimony from the Overflow

The good sister was saying something quite sound when she referred to her own testifying, "It comes from the inside of me. It just comes out naturally." She was speaking of what we may call "testimony from the overflow." This means that testimony is not something practiced up for the occasion. It is not staged for dramatic effect. It is not presented for impression on others. It is not for studied elevation of the testifier. Rather does it come out of the overflow of the soul, out of the fullness of spiritual resources. There is no preaching, no lecturing, no debating, no exhorting, no dramatizing, no parading. Rather is it the narrating as a witness of something that the person has experienced, that is worth sharing, that will help others. This overflow can be expressed by a congregation as they sing together, "I have found the glorious gospel."

Such a fund of resources does not come by chance. We build up this fund of experience. Those who testify have to live for something worth testifying about. A shriveled soul will have a shriveled testimony or none at all. A complaining, self-pitying person will testify with a poor-little-me outlook or with a why-did-this-have-to-happen-to-me attitude. The man who lives in the past will refer to "forty long years ago." Those who piece the gospel together meaningfully can have a meaningful testimony. Lives with present-tense interests in living with God will be able to share interesting testimonies.

The spontaneous witness of a fresh-spirited person is like the drink from a spring of clear, cool water. This is the way Jesus said it should be. He likened the experience of this spiritual revival as "a well of water springing up into eternal life" (John 4:16). There are never enough of this kind of testifiers, those who speak out of the overflow with reviving freshness.

The Need for Framework

An experience has meaning when narrated within its framework. Without this there cannot be clarity or understanding. Consider the testimonial use of an event that happened in the history of the church in Ontario, Canada. On the evening of December 29, 1875, a baptismal service was held at the river Thames outside London. A luminous shaft shone on the company of thirty Saints. John J. Cornish, the minister of the service, described it as "a very beautiful light from heaven." One narrator built this up with headlines, with emphasis of the spectacular and the dramatic. He added, "I would like to see such a light shine upon me." His wish sounded like the exclamation of a sign seeker. Another told the story simply, honestly. He saw how in those years foul and rough measures might be used against the Latter Day Saints. He caught the courage required to move out and be baptized. He sensed what would need to happen in himself to make possible such an experience. He caught what took place in the persons at the service. He caught their courage in adversity, the symbol of the light of the gospel amid darkness, the needed confirmation when opponents were persecuting. He remembered the assuring word, "These are my people." He stressed not the external light but the inner enlightenment. It was a dramatic story to the first narrator; it was a testimony of divine revelation to the second narrator who made a testimony of it.

An Essential in Healthy Testimony

Here is one measurement: The whole person tells the whole story in the whole situation with appreciation of the wholeness of God. At first glance this sounds as if a person would go on and on with a never ending narrative. Rather, it means that the testifier is aware of this wholeness and speaks accordingly. He may select a segment to be shared but he sees this segment in a larger setting. One young man told congregations how he had been very ill with an injury, how he had received administration, how he had felt a physical tug of knitting bones, how the doctor had reported a most unusual healing. By this he knew that God heard his prayers and he was thankful. That was all. He reported the material manifestations and the medical response. Another young man told close friends of a critical illness with typhoid fever. He mentioned how he was so worn out that he hardly had will to live. The doctors wondered that he survived. He told of his spiritual rebirth as strength returned. He told of his feeling that he was living on loaned time. He spoke of his intent to take care of body and spirit so he would be thoroughly healthy. He told of dedicating his life to helping those who are sick in soul. His life was transformed. He was seeing his stewardship in the light of what God wants to come to pass. Twenty years later he is living out this testimony. The greatest miracle in all this is the transformation of the man who came out of threat of dying to new insight for living.

What about God?

Every healthy testimonial expression involves a sound, expandable conception of God. The nature of God, the working of God, the purpose of God is at the heart of every good, sound testimony. It reflects how the testifier conceives that God carries on his work, makes contact with man, is concerned with the specific person. There is no substitute for a well-developed, well-validated, well-intended conception of God. There is no growth in spiritual clarity without this.

We can almost think of God cringing at times at things attributed to him. At other times we can think of him smiling at some things ascribed to him. We can single out events and lay them to him without seeing the full relationship. Some accuse him of killing a loved one who dies of appendicitis. Some thank him for bringing about conditions that suit their selfish little selves. Thus an old lady in one home for the aged in Lamoni several years ago expressed in a prayer meeting her heartfelt gratitude that God had opened the way for her to move from one home to the other. The way had been opened, as she saw it, by the death of an old woman in the home to which she wanted to go, thereby creating the needed vacancy. It is true that this woman wanted to move and that another woman had died, but it does not follow in the sequence of things that God got rid of the one by death to suit the wants of the other. So many times presumed "answers to prayer" are foreign to the very nature of God. In such times it is well for us to remember the honest prayer of a farseeing Saint, "Lord, help me to understand thee aright, so I will know for what to give thanks."

Testifying Is Enjoined

Jesus always directed his disciples to do what would be good for them. He was not occupied in getting them to do chores for busywork or to adore him to lift his own ego. He did not need this. In his farewell counsel to the apostles he told them to go out and witness (Luke 24:47, 48). He did this because they needed it for their own sakes as well as for the good of others. The two would go together. The disciple who would not testify would never identify clearly enough what he believed and what he was setting out to do. Something happened in Peter when he testified to the multitude on the Day of Pentecost. His sermon was essentially a testimony. He knew what had just been taking place in the congregation. He knew what had been happening in his own life. He spoke of what had been occurring and concluded, "whereof we all are witnesses" (Acts 2:32). Here was first-class testimony.

One day Jesus brought about the healing of a man who had been in the grip of an evil spirit. The man wanted to go along with Jesus. This was quite understandable. He begged to be taken. This would have been the easier way for the man. But Jesus told him, "Go home to your own people . . . and tell them what the Lord has done for you, and how kind he has been to you" (Mark 5:19, Phillips). So the man went home to testify. Thereby he grew. It is noteworthy that Jesus focused on what had taken place in the man as the core of his testimony, and appreciation of what God had done to go along with this. Jesus knew it would seem an anticlimax to a great experience to go back to the common and prosaic routine of ordinary life, yet he insisted that this man's testifying should be where he was living with others. This message is expressed in Kipling's poem, "Mulholland's Conversion." This man who worked on a cattle boat wanted to change jobs and preach the gospel where he could be "handsome and out of the wet." God is pictured as saying, "Back you go to the cattle boats an' preach my gospel there." The basic testimony in all this is that we have been with Jesus Christ and this has made a difference in us.

Not Whether but How

On the whole, religious movements carry a strong note of testimony in their earlier days. Meetings include testimonial expression. It was so in early Christianity. It was so in early Methodism with its class meetings. When numbers increase, when services become conventionalized, when professional ministers lead the services, this testimonial expression tends to decline. Some diagnosticians of modern church life label this disappearance of public testimony as regrettable, as indicative of a more anemic practice of congregational life. Yet there is little provision for testimony.

What are Latter Day Saints going to do? We, too, can succumb to conventionality and respectability and give up. This hardly seems the sound approach when we look at the potentialities in healthy testimony. There are problems, many of them, in connection with testimonial gatherings. It is easy to look at the fervent, dramatic, atomistic, individualistic testimonial life of the so-called Pentecostal bodies and condemn everything testimonial. It is true that there is dearth of leaders for conducting testimonial meetings of merit. It is also true that many participants do not know what constitutes adequate testimony. But inadequate observance by a group is hardly grounds for omitting testimony. On this basis many groups would have to leave out music.

Our approach is not *whether* but *how*. Testimonial expression is essential to vital, vigorous group life. It is indispensable for thought-out, reaching-out development of the person. The man who never states to others what he stands for, what God means to him, what happens in his life as he lives with God is likely to be other than clear in his conceptions or complete in his commitments. Moderns are needing the clarity and the consecration that testifying can bring to pass. We are needing to hear the counsel, "Tell a thing and get it clear."

A Directive to Testify

In the 1959 gathering of high priests at Kirtland, Ohio, this simple directive was spoken to these ministers. It is clear, concise, consequential.

"Return to other ministers and to your congregations and bear testimony. Tell them the Spirit that leads to do good is functioning, that this Spirit has been with you in this gathering. Encourage the spirit and practice of witnessing now among you, and arrange for adequate opportunity for my people to bear testimony."

Questions for Discussion

1. On what ground is it sometimes said that preachers do not make good testifiers?

2. What does an intellectually honest person watch when he speaks testimonially? What dangers does he guard against?

3. How does sound testimony require a good framework for soundness and meaning? Why should a happening not be told without relating it to a broad understanding that will give it meaning?

4. It has been said that the average modern Christian would be at a loss to know what to do if he were asked to bear his testimony to friends or to a congregation. Do you think this is so? If so, what has made it this way?

5. How can testifying help a person to clarify what he functionally believes? What kind of testifying will bring about this clarification?

6. What would be your criteria for determining whether a testimony meeting furthers the good health of those present? When would you say a testimony meeting has been wholesome and helpful? Some consider a meeting commendable if those attending leave "feeling good." To what extent is this a sound criterion?

7. How is it possible for a person to express himself testimonially with greater freedom when he is in a small circle of close friends and co-workers? What implication does this have for our planning for associational gatherings?

8. Some religious leaders are advocating the using of small groups of about six to twelve for conversational, devotional, testimonial association. This number is often designated as the ideal number for a "retreat" with the personnel selected with reference to spiritual companionship. What do you see in this suggestion? How would this permit a high level of testimonial expression? What kind of persons would you select for such a cell group for yourself? What would you plan to do?

9. How is it advisable for a person to survey his total world of religious experience and religious beliefs in order to interpret one specific happening clearly and soundly?

10. How would it be to the advantage of every person to write his own "gospel," his own account of his communion with God?

11. How might testifying enrich and vitalize and harmonize the spiritual condition of moderns? How do moderns need this in the world in which we are living?

12. How is testifying inherent in the Restoration movement? What lines of expression do you see calling for testifying? What insights do we need to do this well?

CHAPTER 27

PROPHESYING WITH
CLEAR VISION

It sounds almost daring to use "prophesy" this way, to put it in the present tense and to talk as if moderns were to experience it. Yet this is precisely what is being said. Here "prophesying" is set forth not merely as an option: it is considered an essential in the matter of good spiritual health. Those who are going to have first-class spiritual health are going to include prophecy in their program of living. In many cases this will call for some pretty clear rethinking about what prophecy is and how prophecy functions. Some conceptions of what prophecy is would make us anything but healthy. Sound insight about its nature and its functioning can bring in us something highly productive and health-providing. Spiritual vision is available and expandable through prophesying.

Present-Tense for Prophesying

Good health is always present-tense. Its functions are spelled with "-ing." And this applies to prophecy. There is a strong tendency to put this in the past tense. We are inclined to list the spiritual giants who were prophets in some former centuries. We might as well be content to read accounts of well-coordinated and well-disciplined athletes of ancient Greece and to study the aphorisms from them and about them. Their prowess and their vigor can guide and inspire us for living today, but moderns have to keep exercising right now if they are to have the body efficiency attributed to those Greeks.

This applies to spiritual exercising, to spiritual stretching. If prophesying is good for us, it has to be practiced in the living now. And it has to be practiced soundly, consistently, meaningfully. A young man wanted to pole vault. He got some equipment and started out on his own. He kept at it with a will. Later he reported to a coach who was a specialist in field events. The coach said, "Jim, you will have to undo what you have been doing. You will never get up and get over the way you are going at it." It is not unlikely that a good coach in spiritual exercise might need to tell many of us to change what we are thinking and doing if we want to "get up and get over."

Seeing What We Want to Happen

Two youths were running around the track in college. One was going through the drudgery of it. He was saying to himself, "How much more time? How many more laps do I have to do?" He had no heart for what he was doing. He had to get credit in physical education. He signed up for track and the instructor assigned him to run with a two-miler. So he was simply going around the track. There was no insight and no inspiration in what he was doing.

The other youth had the "feel" of the race. He wanted to get the stride, the stamina, the timing. He listened to the coach. He asked questions. He wanted suggestions for improvement. He was not saying, "How much do I have to do?" Rather was he asking, "How am I doing?" He was picturing what a two-miler was to be. He mobilized his resources of body and of mind.

This second youth kept close to his coach. The more he learned about running the more he wanted to learn. This represents what happens in the man who sets out well to run the race of life. He keeps close to the Great Coach. He wants to discover how the Coach looks at what he is doing. He believes that the Coach is not going to assign him to some field that he cannot handle. He believes that with the Coach's counsel and confidence he can see more than he is seeing, do more than he is doing. And we can think of prophecy as receiving increasing understanding, expanding vision from the Great Coach. Then the runner can move out and guide other runners as he learns from the Great Coach.

Prophecy Calls for Seeing with God

Literally, to prophesy means *to speak forth for God*. The great Hebrew prophets included phrases like this in their messages, "Thus saith the Lord." They felt that they were mouthpieces for God. They were so alive with their insights, so sure of their message, that they had to speak out. When Jeremiah saw the declining condition of Jerusalem and realized that the city and the nation were heading toward collapse before Babylon, he could not maintain silence. He knew that his countrymen would denounce him and accuse him of treason but he had to tell them of their precarious condition. With a view to the future of his people in God's program he had to try to save a nucleus for coming days. Once when he thought of saying no more, he realized he had to speak forth: "His word was in mine heart as a burning fire shut up in my bones, . . . and I could not stay" (20:9). The prophet speaks forth with a sense of commission: he has something that God wants him to say.

The man who is going to speak forth for God has to be with God enough to see with God. He has to live with God so he will be able to say what God is thinking and feeling, what God is planning and wanting. He has to be able to see and interpret events in the light of the whole picture of what has been happening, what is taking place, and what is going to be coming. It can be said that a prophet has to interpret a minute in the light of a millennium, a twinkle of light in the view of a galaxy, and a grain of sand in terms of a planet.

We want this closeness to us in anyone who is going to represent us and speak our mind. We want someone who has been with us long enough and closely enough to be able to detect and appreciate how we think and feel, what we think and do, why we proceed as we do. There is no shortcut. We cannot give a summary of our views and interests or hand a printed sheet to our friend. He has to live with us, work with us, laugh with us, sorrow with us, think with us, risk with us. Thus is he able to understand us as persons. Then we consider him qualified to speak out for us. In the same way the prophet becomes competent to say, "This is what God is thinking. This is what God is saying." He has been and is living understandingly with God.

The Well-rounded Prophet

When God has something for a prophet to say and something for a people to do, he wants them to perceive this in an overview that will give meaning to what is to be said and what is to be done. God is not in the habit of tossing out unrelated odds and ends to his spokesmen so they can reel off words without understanding. When God called Moses to lead the Hebrews to the land of Canaan and to start them out in their mission to the world, he wanted Moses to see this job in the light of God's total purpose through the ages. It is recorded that God took Moses to a very high mountain (see Doctrine and Covenants 22). There this prophet could look into the past and into the future and could survey all lands and peoples. Only then would Moses be able to interpret clearly what he was setting out to do. Sound prophecy always stretches the vision of the inspired prophet. He sees more and he sees more clearly.

The well-rounded, well-balanced prophet would need to be schooled in the curriculum indicated in Doctrine and Covenants 85:21. He would be at home in the worlds of learning from astronomy to zoology. He would see the workings in these fields with the mountaintop perspective and insight that God wanted Moses to have. He would be conversant with prophets from Amos to Zephaniah. He would know of lands from the Aleutian to the Zealand Islands. He would know peoples from the Aztecs to the Zuni and see how each had come to be. This list could be extended indefinitely, for all this is in the story of God's universe.

God cannot wait until he can develop a prophet with such well-rounded proportions and inclusive outlook. He has to begin where men are, with those who are available. They have to be men who will listen to him and respond to him. If a prophet has only the vision he can see from Mt. Moriah in Jerusalem, God will start there and speak through him. He will keep calling this prophet, whether he is Joel or Judah or Joseph Smith of Palmyra and Kirtland, to a higher mountain where a clearer and wider perspective is possible. This prophet will be both humble and confident as he "speaks forth" for God. He will realize his limitations and will want to see more. He will also be confident about what he has seen and has validated and will stand soundly on this. He will say with assurance, "These things I have seen." A prophet is always a man of extending vision and reliable verities.

One of the tragedies in prophetic religion is that often a man who has seen prophetically with God comes to consider his partial view as the fullness of possibility. He occupies his time in defending what he has seen and what he has written down and shuts himself off from the spiritual exploration that would expand his vision further. Another tragedy is evident when a prophet speaks from the standpoint of his segmented insight as if he were beholding the fullness of the universe. The wise prophet keeps the slogan before him, *Plus Ultra,* more beyond. He keeps praying, "Open my eyes, O Lord, that I may see!" Adventurously he continues, "New frontiers beckon me, known but to thee."

Dearth about Prophecy in Modern Writings

Tables of content and indexes in contemporary books on religion usually do not carry the word "prophecy." For instance, *A Handbook of Christian Theology* (1958) does not include it. It is not mentioned in such a book as *The Protestant Faith* by G. W.

Forell (1960). This is quite typical. Either modern religionists do not consider it safe or essential for contemporary religious living or they lack data or concern for discussing it. This lacuna says much about the place given prophet and prophecy in the thinking of modern scholars. Apparently its function is not very clear.

Encyclopedia materials on prophecy and prophets tend to refer to what took place in Old Testament times with limited place for what took place in New Testament times. Does this mean that prophecy is considered too outmoded for today? Does it mean that here is something too much outside the experience of these writers to enable them to discuss it? Or is it surrendered to extremists and fanatics? Has something else replaced prophecy? No. Concepts of prophesying as experiencing and extending spiritual vision indicate that prophesying is to be understood, encouraged, and utilized in healthy religion.

The Intent to Forth-tell

We cannot say too often that the purpose of prophecy is to forth-tell. This means simply that God has something to be said to persons and to peoples. It is right to presume that when God has something to say he has, as a wise old brother commented, "something to say." This good man was endeavoring to point out that God is not going to move persons to speak some non-essential gibberish, some make-them-feel-good compliments to his people. There is content in the message. This content will include both intellectual and emotional aspects. If there is no vision, no vitality, no verities to the message, it ought not be credited to God. Once when a "word of inspiration" was addressed to a congregation, an honest man, not wanting to be negative but intent on being honest, observed to a very good friend, "If that was God speaking, he must not have been very alert this morning. About all I could detect was that God said, 'Howdy.'" God must have had more than this to communicate to his people. Or did they want more than this?

Forth-telling is more than foretelling. God is looking ahead and is wanting his people to look ahead, too, with clear vision. He wants them to see and order their lives accordingly. Whenever God leads his people to peer into the future, it is always from the vantage point of the present place and time. Then they can start from where they are. Religion that prompts persons to escape into the future to some dream image and to try to return

322

from this imagined situation is not healthy. This prompts us to run away from things as they are into a fancied world of things as we would like to have them. This tempts us to fritter away our resources on dreaming. This may stimulate speculation about the future rather than building into the future. It may impel some persons to glory in acquiring top-secret information which they believe God has vouchsafed to them. Such persons may act as if they had inside information on top celestial secrets. This is devastating.

Prophecy is concerned with the future. Any conduct of merit always takes the future into consideration. If it does not, it becomes five-minute pigpen behavior with no consideration of what is going to happen tomorrow and next month and next year as a result of what we are doing right now. Jesus always called us to take an eternity-long perspective. But speculation about the future and foretelling what is going to happen is not high-grade prophecy. Sometimes prophecy may begin on this level but it must go beyond. Saul went out to find his father's asses and thought that the seer would tell him where they were. For the young men in Saul's family the seer was a sort of director of the lost-and-found department. God's directions were for very private matters, to avoid inconvenience. It look a long time for prophecy to rise above this level. It took a long time to lift the sights from the local barnyard to the great vision of God's work in which the barnyard would have meaning. It took a long time to rise above concern over straying donkeys to searching for insight.

With the Mind Quickened

Prophecy in healthy expression utilizes the powers of the total person. Intelligence is alerted and quickened. Thinking is not turned off. There is no superstitious aura about "spiritual gifts." Paul said he wanted the Corinthian saints to understand them. He wrote, "Now concerning spiritual things, brethren, I would not have you ignorant" (I Corinthans 12:1). Certainly they were not to be handled carelessly, through ignorance. They were to be expressed so that every person might "profit withal" (verse 7). He gave priority to the gift of wisdom. In the fourteenth chapter he gave instruction concerning the wise and orderly use of the spiritual gifts, and prophecy was in the list. He set forth edification as the basic criterion for evaluating the desirability of the expression of the gifts. He set forth these directives, "Let all things be done unto edifying" and "Let all things be done decently and in order."

Paul gave another very important word of counsel, "The spirits of the prophets are subject to the prophets" (14:32). He was saying that God does not treat men as robots who mechanically broadcast whatever God impels them to say with the fixed content that he prescribes. The prophet is to function with wisdom as to time and place and phrasing and context. Elbert A. Smith summarized the matter this way:

"Men were not to be parrots repeating the divine messages without understanding. Nor were they to be mechanisms moved like puppets under the prophetic spirit. Nor was the Lord to pour words through their mouths without their understanding. They were to perceive the will of God, clothe the message as best they might in their own language under the kindling influence of the Spirit, and all this under the eternal principle of man's free agency. They were to use wisdom as to when, how, and where they were to speak prophetically."—*Priesthood Journal,* April, 1940, p. 2.

Joseph Smith, prophet and president of the church, spoke to the General Conference of 1906 about inspiration and prophecy. This counsel is significant, for it removed any suspicion that the church looked upon prophecy as something too sacred for examination and interpretation. Rather does the prophet call members to procure sound understanding and to practice wisely the experience of inspiration.

"The influence of revelation upon me has always been to quicken, to make vivid and clear. And my understanding of revelation as we have it, is that every man stands before God upon his individual responsibility, and his individuality never will be taken from him unless he himself consents to it. And if he does, he opens the avenues of his soul for the incoming of a spirit that will ruin him."
—General Conference Minutes, 1906, p. 919.

Always with Wisdom

Vision is far-seeing. Prophecy is intended to enable us to see with God. Messages prefaced with a "Thus saith the Lord" constitute no revelation to persons or congregations if there is no increase in vision. It is possible that we focus on news items and overlook the basic message. There is hardly any revelation to a person who notes that a brother is called to be an apostle unless there is some insight as to the nature of apostolic ministry and the mission of the church in its apostolic aspects. Every conscientious Saint ought to ask himself when a message is spoken, What do I see and understand now that I did not see and understand? If he sees nothing that he did not see before, there has been no prophetic message to him.

Again Elbert A. Smith gave counsel about the essential place of wisdom in the manifestation of spiritual gifts, notably of prophecy.

"When dominated in their use by the gift of wisdom the various gifts bring healing to body and mind. They bring comfort and edification. The spirit of prophecy especially brings knowledge of the mind and will of God. Its province is not to foretell events; indeed that may be a minor function. By no means is it intended to make the one exercising it a fortuneteller or soothsayer.

"Given a lack of wisdom in the exercise of the gifts or a lack of wisdom in our attitude toward them and response to them, they become a source of positive danger leading to all sorts of follies and excesses and false and harmful reactions. . . .

"Spiritual gifts are intended in their proper uses both to comfort and edify the Saints. . . . They should edify the mind as well as warm the heart and fire the imagination."
—*Priesthood Journal*, April 1940, pp. 12-20.

Understanding for Evaluating

The Restoration movement provides that when the prophet brings a message to the church "purporting to be a revelation" it shall be examined and acted upon by the General Conference. It is expected that the message be understood. If it is not understood, the voting is only a perfunctory routine measure. As indicated, if there is no understanding there is no revelation, and the ministers and members are incompetent to implement whatever is outlined in the message. Today the Conference is asking that any such document be printed and made available to the members of the Conference so they may peruse and evaluate. This is sound procedure. Then the document is considered by the several quorums and these bodies report their findings to the total assembly, after which the official voting takes place. Sometimes the acceptance of a message has been delayed for a considerable time.

This consideration by members of the Conference is designed to protect the church against ecclesiastical dictatorship and unsound doctrine. It also carries another important function. It exacts something of members. They can grow in membership responsibilities, in conversance with the church, in insight into prophecy and revelation. And this applies to the total church. Every member is looked upon as carrying the responsibility of participating as an enlightened voter and steward. The member who only holds up his hand or speaks his aye on a supporting vote is not living up to his obligations. The commendable member studies the message and evaluates its merits in the light of all the resources he can mobilize. He is expected to grow in the process.

Official Versus Nonofficial Prophecy

No single person or no single officer has a premium on prophetic experience. The prophet who heads the church is spokesman in matters pertaining to the body ecclesiastical. This affords order and predictability. The "gift of prophecy," however, is not limited. Eligibility for prophetic insight depends on several factors. Here are some of the most important ones:

1. *Capacity for prophetic insight.* God can put into a person only that which he has the capacity to receive. One of our stewardships is the increasing of our capacity, and we vary with respect to this capacity. One person has a rich background in one field and another person in another field. We are not identicals. One person with extended training in astronomical sciences and geophysical studies would have more potentiality for revealment in matters pertaining to the relationship of planets and celestial movements than a person whose studies took him into the field of Bach and Beethoven; the latter would be more qualified for enlightenment in the realm of musical harmony and tonal relationships. The person with a rich background in biblical literature and Hebrew history and theology would be more capable in revelation of matters of pre-Christian faith than would the man schooled in agronomy.

2. *Rightness in personal character.* The righteous and loving and intelligent God can be discerned only by those who have these qualities in themselves. The person who is loving can appreciate the love of God, and this holds true for other characteristics of the Divine. The purity of God is not containable in a life of smut and spiritual disease. God is insistent that those

326

who represent him and speak for him must reveal him in the quality of their own living. A message about faith is futile if spoken by a person who is faithless.

3. *Spiritual sensitivity.* Some persons pick up clues and gestures from others. They can reach out of the fullness of their own personhood and be sensitively aware of the moods, intentions, the likes and the dislikes, the thinking, the conclusions of others. Others have a dulled spiritual epidermis. The personal feelings and thoughts of others float off them like the proverbial water off a duck's back. This personal quality applies in a cosmic way to our response to God. Said one man, "God has to knock me down before I catch on. Now my brother here can detect a wink of God's eye and know what it means."

4. *Resources and skills for expressing the revealed apprehension.* The person has to indicate the discernment to himself, if not to anyone else. The unindicated insight will not be clear to the person himself. Revelation involves both the insight and the interrelation of this insight, and it is truly clear and truly useful when it is spoken with meaning and beauty. Prophets draw on the riches of their literary and general resources. The poetic power of Isaiah is heightened and the philosophical conceptions of John are universalized as they speak under divine impulsion. It would be pretty hard, if not impossible, to express the great concepts of the gospel in the limited word forms of the Eskimo or the Tahitian language.

5. *Concern and interest in and commitment to the spiritual well-being of persons and social orders.* God is concerned with persons, his gospel has to do with the provisions for men whom he loves. No coldhearted, aloof-from-man recluse could see or voice the message of God about God's universe or his church. These are love-motivated and man-concerned.

6. *Overview of and insight into God's purpose and plan and process and personhood, in an eternal, universal program.* The prophet has to look from the mountain. The person who shuts himself within his own provincial two-by-four world is incapable of "seeing big" with God. The prophet has to stretch his heart and his mind. He has to get beyond his own spiritual myopia. Like Habakkuk he says, "I will stand upon my watch, and set me upon the tower, and will watch to see" (2:1).

7. *Blending of courage and wisdom in a prophetic stance and sight.* The prophet needs both. Courage alone can make him one-sided and fanatical. Wisdom alone can hold him to introspection

and hesitation. Both are needed for efficiency and soundness. With the two he is able to speak boldly and to speak soundly. He is able to say, "Thus saith the Lord."

A Community of Prophets

It takes more than one outstanding prophet to bring to pass a high expression of prophetic ministry. There is needed an advanced awareness in the people of problems and possibilities that are calling for understanding. A high level of spiritual insight in the people is required to discern a prophetic message that has depth and breadth. A ready willingness and ability to validate the message in the business of living and a more than ordinary awareness and association with God are also required. There is need, too, for uplifting and stimulating fellowship between people and prophet. This calls for a prophetic church and a prophetic community, Zion.

In such a prophecy-producing church community are forces that work together for prophecy of meritorious quality. (1) Members achieve a *basic unity* in their unifying allegiance to Jesus Christ who expresses true prophetic ministry. (2) Among the members are diversities in gifts and funds of experience that blend together to effect *balanced perception* of God and his gospel. This saves from lopsidedness and fanaticism. (3) Members pace each other and check each other in effecting a *wholeness* and *soundness* in their spirituality. (4) Members interact honestly and fraternally in achieving *common consent*—that is, a well-examined common mind. (5) Members practice, in group patterns of living, the disciplines that will further *spiritual health* and equip in learning and loving for prophetic experience of high quality. (6) Members see clearly the role of administrative ministers with reference to their prophetic functioning in our church with its *theocratic-democratic* nature. These are seen as specialized functions for the life of the body ecclesiastical. Such is to be the Church of Jesus Christ. Such is to be the congregations within this church. Such is to be a Zionic community originating and functioning in the genius of the church.

Questions for Discussion

1. How do you see prophetic inspiration as functioning in looking backward as well as looking ahead? How are both involved in sound management of our living?
2. What might happen in a conception of prophecy that encompasses the belief that an inspired person gives up his thinking

powers or suspends them while God moves in and takes over?

3. What was the situation in Corinth that prompted Paul to stress edification as the essential criterion for discerning the functioning of the prophetic gift?

4. Expand and apply the observation that prophecy is not an easy way to solutions and not a way to relieve us of responsibility. How is prophecy exacting of the person who lives through the total experience of prophecy?

5. What qualities of insight are expressed in the idea of standing on a high mountain and looking about? What can happen to our vision? Illustrate.

6. How does it require a prophetic insight to understand and appreciate the message of a prophet? How is this much more than expressing a vote on the message?

7. How can prejudices and phobias get in the way of experiencing prophetic insight? What kind of preparation is required if we are going to have clear spiritual vision?

8. How would you go about developing yourself through a ten-year program for experiencing prophetic insight about God's functioning in "outer space"? the origin of the American Indian? the spiritual potentials in a child of eight? Or would you prefer to have God give you everything in a sealed envelope in "one easy lesson"? How is healthy prophetic insight cumulative and expanding?

9. Under what circumstances would a dream or vision produce sound spiritual vision? What would happen to make it healthy and sound?

10. What are some fields in which you see prophetic understanding functioning in a Zionic community in the total business of living?

11. How can a congregation or a community of Saints practice healthy spirituality in which prophetic experience is an essential part? How may prophecy be a pervasive quality that runs through the total business of living and learning?

12. Why do you suppose that for many years prophecy has not been included in the manifestations of Christian living? Why is it so little known or expected today?

13. It has been said that prophecy could turn a man into a genius or a goose. What does this mean? Do you see both possibilities?

14. How are the hope and the health of the Restoration movement caught up in the way we "exercise prophecy"?

CHAPTER 28

EVANGELIZING
IN THE JOY
OF SHARING

"What qualities characterize a first-class Latter Day Saint?" This question was directed to a group of youth of the church. It was another way of asking what identifies a spiritually healthy Latter Day Saint. After the inquiry had been posed, explained, and related to the business of everyday living, a few minutes were designated for "thinking over." Then the replies were to be made and noted. Here was a first observation, "He's buoyant." It was expressed in a tone of voice that accorded with what the young man had in mind.

What did *spiritual buoyancy* mean? One early comment was, "He's always up." Another, "He's not down at the mouth." Another, "He has 'upping' power so he can pull others up, too." From the other angle, "He is not going to be mired down in despair." In the same vein, "He does not have a bad spiritual heart condition." Still another in youth language, "He's aloft in hope and help-up." This did not mean that the good Latter Day Saint is "floating around in the air," never touching reality. Of this it was observed, "When we are 'way up, we ought to see reality better." "Is a person to be like a pretty toy balloon, just floating around?" The return comment, "Anything that is really buoyant is always getting somewhere." There was a mixture of figures of speech as buoyancy in the air and buoyancy on the water were brought together. It was clear that the young people had the same quality in mind. In this applied interpretation, we can affirm that a basic quality of the healthy Latter Day Saint is *buoyancy.*

Buoyancy through Motion

Every airplane we see can remind us how young is the mastery of the air. The dream was an old one. Greek tradition tells of Icarius who made some wax wings that he might fly into the air. Modern air travel started as men believed that if they could get a vehicle into motion with wingspread they could move through the air. Birds were doing so all the while. Could not man invent mechanical devices that would enable him to do what his avian neighbors were doing? So Orville and Wilbur Wright made their flight at Kitty Hawk. A sputtering engine, a frail plane, a few yards of travel, but they got off the ground and moved forward. They demonstrated that it could be done. A new day had dawned.

These early experimental flights indicated some things that were very basic. (1) Man uses the atmospheric resources for keeping him up. (2) Man keeps in motion while he is keeping up. (3) Man moves forward with sense of direction. (4) Man employs propelling power. All the resources for getting up in the air had been around man, but he had never learned how to tap them and use them to lifting advantage. It took more than wishing and toying to get off the ground. It took experimentation and exploration that fitted in with the natural resources and operations of God's universe.

All this applies to spiritual buoyancy, and more. So often we dream of being blessed with the ability to "keep up" but we do not know how to proceed in getting there. The following apply to this spiritual buoyancy: (1) There are spiritual resources available for keeping man in a buoyant condition. Man has to learn how to tap these, how to line up with God so that these will be available. (2) These spiritual resources operate only as man is in motion with God. There is no promise of easy-chair buoyancy. But mere activity is not enough. We could become small-motor toy airplanes that fly around in a circle and then collapse. What we do has to be in process of keeping up, with God. (3) The upward and forward movement will have sense of direction and purpose. Mere acceleration is not enough. Man is to be orbiting and rising with God, in God's meaningful purpose. (4) The person looks to inner propulsion that utilizes the power-providing propulsion that God has available. There must be spiritual power, motor power. It is worth noting that the New Testament word for power has the same root as the word dynamite. This reminds us that dynamite can blow something to smithereens with lamentable destruction or it can contribute to constructive enterprises. Spiritual buoyancy does not come by chance, by wishing, by magic. It comes to those who learn to live for it. It calls for clear purpose, competent process, and saintly personhood.

The Need of Lifting Power in Process

How does a person experience this lifting power which enables him to have this buoyant spirit? Through the centuries the people of God have testified that there is such lifting power. They have relied upon it. In the Bible poets and prophets have thought of the hand of God holding them up. The psalmist wrote, "Hold thou me up, and I shall be safe" (119:117). The historian in Deuteronomy recorded this in Moses' benediction, "The eternal God is thy refuge, and underneath are the everlasting arms" (33:27). Now we are needing to take this general affirmation and discover *how* this lifting power can be functional. Something of understanding and application is required in us.

When we think of God working with us and sustaining us, we always fall short when we endeavor to describe what takes place. We go as far as we are able and come to the place where we have to use figurative language. Then we say that God is *like* so and so. We get along well as long as we accept these as figurative statements; we limit God when we begin to take these sayings literally and then legalistically. Sometimes God has been regarded as a shepherd who will hold us up with his rod. Sometimes he is thought of as a sustainer as we live in the ocean of life. In this figure of speech we see God holding us up so that we do not sink and drown. This confidence has prompted faithful Saints to say of this ocean, "The hand of the Lord will bear me up." More recently many are thinking of this buoying power in terms of phenomena in the air. Here the hand of God will keep us aloft.

This buoying power is not something that comes to sitting-down and waiting-for Saints. It is available to those who are working with God in God's way, in God's work. It is said quite frequently that we cannot steer a boat until it is in motion. Likewise we can say that we do not hold a plane in the air unless its engines are operating and the vehicle is in motion. In this same way we shall consider that a person has to be in motion if he is going to experience the lifting power of God.

This suggests that we shall need to be wise about praying, "Lord, lift me up!" To some this means that God will lift us up bodily and transport us from one place to another or provide a chariot or an escalator that will take us to the skies. We can believe that if the emergency should arise God could and would do these things, but this does not entitle us to sit expectantly and wait for him to do so. We are not free to pray, "Lord, set me in a well-cushioned, celestially directed chair, with sidetable for milk and honey." We should not pray, "God, keep me riding in the clouds!" Rather we shall discover God's lifting power which we can appropriate to bring to pass the buoyant spirit—and we shall be lifting with God. But we shall be doing more than pulling ourselves up by our own boot-straps. God is with us, pulling upward.

This spiritual buoyancy does not come by taking heaven-bound stimulants and keep-me-happy medicine. Moderns are inclined to want tonics and pills that will bring them a good feeling. The gospel of Jesus Christ looks to the reordering of our lives so that inner controls will provide an enduring quality. This gospel affirms that God provides power for spiritual lifting, and the church bears testimony that this power does come to persons. In a sound appreciation of this gospel we do not expect God to supply us with pep-up-with-power pills that will remove all strains and tendencies to fret in some automatic way. Rather do we want God to sustain us and direct us as we become busy with him in his work.

The Lifting Power in Working with God

The directive to buoyancy is clear: Become soundly and happily involved in God's work, and his lifting power will bear us up. The lifting power of God is available to those who qualify to receive. A man entered into a business operation that involved questionable dealings. He expected God to bless him in the venture, but God could not. This man went against the way of life that God has in mind for the world. He rationalized what he was setting out to do on the ground that he would have more funds from which to contribute to the church. But God would not be bribed by such thinking. This "dealer" could get no basic uplift from God, for he was not working in God's way. The man turned against the church and discounted God because he felt that God did not stand by him. One man twisted data of history and juggled scriptural texts in order to gain converts to the church. He wondered why God did not "come through" and "convince the prospects" of "the truth of the gospel." It did not occur to him that he was not bringing the gospel to his neighbor, that he was not representing the product in God's way. So this man grew discouraged about missionary pursuits.

Merely reviewing and observing the work of God will not bring this lifting power. One elder keeps praying for endowing power. He believes that when God empowers him he will do wonders. Meanwhile he waits. Now he is convinced that there is little lifting power in the church. Sitting on the sidelines and looking things over from the bleachers as noninvolved observers will not qualify us for good living. There is no place for disinterested observers in the work of God.

Nor is getting into motion enough. Buzzing around in a complicated schedule without insight into the basic thing that God is setting out to do may do little more than keep us going in circles. It is not enough to think that because we are very busy God ought to give us a lift; we may be busy getting in the way of what God has in mind. A woman was very busy ringing doorbells and handing out tracts and inviting people to services. She wondered why God was not blessing her and bringing converts to the church when she was working so assiduously with such a high sense of duty. What she was doing might have been used as material for a book, "How to Alienate People and Turn Them from the Church." She had never found the gospel of joy nor the joy in the gospel. If others had accepted what she was bringing they would not have known the buoyant spirit in saintly living.

The Joy in Evangelism

The thesis of this chapter is that persons can experience spiritual buoyancy through evangelizing. The -ing ending to this word indicates an active, contemporary expression: the person is doing something here and now. The spiritual buoyancy comes as a by-product of this evangelism.

Evangelism means *sharing the good news.* It comes from the Greek word in the New Testament, *euaggelion,* which becomes *evangelium* in the Latin and *evangel* in the English. We translate it as "glad tidings," as "good news," or as "gospel." The word carries a tone of gladness and "newsiness" and goodness. The general import is that God has some *good news* for man and that those who live out this good news will have joy and goodness in their lives. What is more, this good news is indispensable to man if he is to live the complete, continuing living that Jesus called "abundant." There is the further implication that this good news cannot be kept to one's self; it has to be shared. It will deteriorate if it is held in the confines of one's own life and person. The goodness will decline and the joy will die if the gospel is not shared. The first announcement of the Christian Era speaks as eloquently today as then, "Fear not, for, behold, I bring you good tidings of great joy, which shall be to all people" (Luke 2:10).

There is no such thing as a sad gospel, as a hopeless gospel. The person who feels that God is far away, that man is depraved and indifferent to God, that the world is totally steeped in sin, that history is moving toward the complete destruction of man, and that hell is waiting for the majority of men is incompetent to share the gospel. He has no good news to share. He has no Book of Acts to write, for he does not see God working effectually with men today. He has not heard Paul's counsel, "Be not moved away from the hope of the gospel" (Colossians 1:23). He has forgotten Jesus' closing admonition, "Be of good cheer" (John 16:33).

This does not mean that the person of buoyant evangelistic spirit sees no evil, faces no problems, senses no perplexities. If he has the wide-open eyes that a saint should have, he ought to be seeing things as they are—with inequalities among men; with misuse and exploitation of the powers of persons; with sensuous, self-centered motivations and schemings in men; with religions that hold men in bondage; with broken homes and confused children; with expenditure of billions of dollars for shallow indulgence; and more. Jesus saw all these things in his day, too. But he saw more. He saw that men could change their way of living as they turned toward God. He saw divine help available. What is more, he saw lives such as those of Peter and Zacchaeus and Mary Magdalene and Simon Zealotes turning into evangelistic expression. So Jesus could talk of a joy that would not go to pieces. When he was conversing with his twelve in their last evening together he told them that they would experience a joy that no man would ever take from them (John 16:22). He told them of the Spirit of God that would come to them to bear them up. He sent them out to tell others of the good news that he had been sharing with them.

The Restoration Reaffirms This Lifting Power

After the first few centuries of the Christian movement something of this early joyfulness went out of the church. The original good news became pretty much associated with life hereafter. It became priest-controlled. A man became most concerned with getting insurance for himself. This insurance was dispensed through the church and through its priesthood. Now and again there were outstanding missionary ventures for carrying the church to men of distant countries. One such was the dispatch by Pope Gregory of a group of missionaries to England in 596. But this was the work of a small group. The rank and file of the people did not participate. A century earlier Clovis, king of the Franks, had been baptized. All this had a remarkable political effect and ecclesiastical influence on the turn that western Europe was to take. But by and large all this was the work of a few dedicated priests.

The members as such did not share, they did not tell the message of Christianity. In fact, members were not encouraged to do this; it would have been an encroachment on the prerogatives of the priests, and the laity supposedly did not have the understanding and the authority to "spread the gospel."

The centuries saw a freshening and expanding of evangelistic expression. There was emphasis upon the performance of sacraments through the priests in Roman Catholicism and upon sermons in Protestantism. Of the opening of the nineteenth century F. Gerald Ensley observed, "The preacher of the age did not expect anyone to be 'saved' as a result of his homily, so, of course, no one was." He called it a time of "Arctic chill" and emotional flatness. Then came such a movement as Wesleyism with its emphasis on the availability of God's redeeming love for all humanity. The Methodist evangelists went out where the people were; they sang of "love divine." John Wesley preached good news and the common people hungered for it.

The Restoration movement renewed this evangelistic spirit and witness. It began with the declaration that the ever living Christ was speaking then and was interested lovingly in all men. Parley Pratt caught up the joyful quality of the message and the ministry of the first witnessing in the thirties.

"With joy we remember the dawn of that day,
    When, led by the Spirit the truth to obey,
The light dawned upon us and filled us with love,
    The Spirit's sure witness sent down from above."

In June 1829 the evangelistic tone was expressed in counsel to Oliver Cowdery and David Whitmer. These are some of the most stirring sentences in all Latter Day Saint literature: "Remember the worth of souls is great in the sight of God. . . . How great is his joy in the soul that repenteth. . . . If it so be that you should labor all your days . . . and bring save it be one soul unto me, how great shall be your joy with him in the kingdom of my Father" (D. and C. 16:3). Here the emphasis is on the joy in brotherly association with a friend with whom one has allegiance to and communion with Jesus Christ. Such a person will never be alone; he will be at home with the brother with whom he has shared and is sharing the *good news*.

Need for Big-time Vision

We are safer when we rely on several factors for health and happiness and hope. Believers in God are in a precarious condition who rest their faith on one experience, on one person, on one belief. A youth in the church tied his faith to one minister who was likable and creative. This man went to pieces in his daily living and the youth's spiritual life almost collapsed. An elder pinned his faith on certain interpretations of the Book of Daniel which he had been taught pointed to the time and nature of the Restoration. Study of history and of scriptures compelled him to give up his cherished arguments. He had rested almost completely on a narrow belief. For a time he was stranded in confusion. A wife centered everything in the ministry of her husband. He died unexpectedly and she was left empty-handed. He had been her chief interest and avenue to God.

Broad and continuing evangelism is not linked to any one doctrine, person, method, experience, city, or country. It is God-wide, world-wide, person-wide. Bishop Ensley said of John Wesley that he pushed the implication of his experience to the horizon in every direction. When a man does this there ought to be nothing small, nothing boring, nothing limiting in his evangelizing. The Latter Day Saint of big-time vision adds these broad dimensions to what he is doing: (1) His evangel includes *the whole of life*, the whole person. He is concerned with every phase of human living. (2) His evangel is for *the whole of humanity*. The evangelist will include paupers and plutocrats, sinners and saints, men of the soil and men of the skyscrapers, the unschooled and the scholars, those with fetish and those with free mind, the dark and the light and the shaded in skin color, the children and the childish, the socially insecure and the socially confident; the list might go on and on. The true evangelist may specialize on ministering to some one group but he will not hem himself in to any segment of humanity. Study of all these peoples in their settings and cultures would require centuries-long studies. (3) His evangel is for *the whole of time*. It is not something to be rounded out in five minutes or five years. Evangelizing will go on and on as long as humanity lives.

Evangelism, as *the sharing of good news*, applies to members as well as to nonmembers. There will always be need for persons to communicate about the good things that are to be shared. Without this, life will be stale and flat. True discipleship is never a thing of fits and starts. Saintly living continues as long as we live on the earth, and God intends it to continue after our life-span here. Our ideal is inclusive: *Evangelization of all of man and of all men for all time, through all time.* Such a view of evangelizing is wide enough and dynamic enough to stir, expand, and hold men's interest.

The French author Flaubert says, "The principal thing in this world is to keep one's soul aloft." Tissue paper balloons are not big enough or strong enough to do this. Ten-minute pastimes will not do it. Small-size church chores will not bring it about. The person of adventurous spirit needs the reminder, "Dare big things with God!" Pioneers respond to the call of the early days of the Restoration, "A great and marvelous work is about to come forth!" Every one of us needs this big-time vision that applies to our here-and-now.

Sources of Buoyancy in Evangelism

Evangelism is a person-with-person relationship. In the sharing there is two-way communication. The one who brings the glad tidings has something to give. Any person who receives also has something to contribute. For instance, the Latter Day Saint who tells his story to a Roman Catholic without getting something from the Roman Catholic friend is a poor listener, a less-than-ordinary evangelist. The Latter Day Saint who converses with a Buddhist or a Moslem without learning something about this other faith can never be an effective witness. And every time one witnesses sharingly he takes his conversational clues from the inquiries and the reactions and the convictions of his friend. In such an experience the person who is evangelizing is renewed by these sources of buoyancy:

1. The thrill of having some good news to share. Persons exude something as they say, "I have something wonderful to tell you" or "Here is something special—a special report, you might say." We are equipped to tell news with delight and enthusiasm. More than one person has said, "I want to tell you, in particular." The person with no good news to share is dying. And so is a congregation.

2. The sense of commission to share the good news. The Latter Day Saint who senses the mission of the church believes he is one of a company of believers whom God sends forth to tell others. With this commission is the promise of support as he goes about his witnessing. There is something lifting about feeling that one is a part of a great enterprise and the Head of the company gives this very person a personal commission. It is inspiring to feel that one is a working member of "God and Evangelistic Associates, Incorporated."

3. The varied world of persons and groups and cultures with whom to share the news. From big cities to small farms, from

rice eaters to potato consumers, from adobe houses to wooden structures, from fishermen to perfume makers, from stolid men to volatile talkers, and on and on. With such a variety in the more than two billion persons in the world, there ought to be no monotony. One enthusiast put it this way: "How could evangelism ever get monotonous with this indescribable picture of humanity near and far!"

4. The friendly association between the sharer and the "sharee" in communicating about the gospel. Evan Fry once pointed out that one cannot share the gospel with another until the two become friends. And friendship has two-way conversation. Life can never be completely dull as long as we are meeting others in this evangelistic sharing. This is not the impersonal contact of strangers on the street; it is the friendly meeting of man with man. Said one such sharer, "When I share the gospel I know how Jesus felt when he loved the rich young man with whom he was talking." Another said, "There will always be zest in my living as long as I like others and we share what is most worth sharing."

5. The continuing outreach in an expanding gospel world. One of the marks of decline and surrender to old age is the disposition to make no new acquaintances. Whenever the circle of our friends and neighbors closes up, we are in an unhealthy condition. Some lose the enlarging of this circle in their teens; others keep expanding their world in their eighties and nineties. The genuine evangelist can never close off his world. There are more people to meet, more to come to know, more with whom to share the gospel. The Church of Jesus Christ including the Orient, Africa, Europe, America, Oceania affords the richest of possibilities.

6. The creative expression that permits and calls for initiative and creative expression. In true evangelism there is no record played over and over. There is no servile following of some prescribed pattern of conversing. There is no fixed catechetical procedure. Each situation, each person calls for fresh insight and appropriate measures. And our insight into the message has to be expanding. John F. Garver observed to the clinic on evangelism in 1941, "Ours, too, has been a progressive testimony, and must continue so to be, as our vision and our understanding continue to expand." A system of proselyting that prescribes specifically what a person is to say and do will sooner or later kill the evangelistic spirit, the evangelistic opportunity, and the evangelist. There has to be creative expression and exploring spirit.

7. Refreshing communion with the Source of good news. When we catch the genuine genius of God, we see the freshness of his nature. He is not a weary old man sitting on a throne. He is a warmhearted evangelist. He is the source of the good news we are going to share. He has the spirit of one who is saying to us, "I want to share some wonderful news with you." Some never get this thrill out of working with God. For these, God has everything finished, everything created, every plan laid on the blueprint table. What an existence of eternal boredom this would be! The dynamic evangelist works with a God who is making news come to pass each day, and this God shares this zest with his co-workers.

8. The exhilaration of the ministry of the Spirit of God. In describing the Holy Spirit we employ such words as guiding, enlightening, enlivening, convincing. The evangelist who is lined up with God and experiencing this spiritual invigoration knows the thrill of this endowment. Missionaries tell of being directed toward specific persons and places and situations. They tell of insights that have come as they have shared their witness. They testify how persons have been drawn and moved by a Spirit they did not understand. Said one young missionary, "When a fellow is getting this vital help through the Holy Spirit, he sees nothing as impossible. He really comes alive."

Let these eight expressions and fruits of evangelistic sharing take place in a person's life and he will testify of spiritual bouyancy through evangelizing. And the possibilities never run out.

Questions for Discussion

1. Jesus Christ is the eternal expression of the bouyant spirit. He never gave up. He was never hopeless. How do you explain the upturn in his outlook when he was with his apostles that last evening, when he was facing crucifixion? (Read John's account.) How was evangelism involved in his outlook?

2. Why do "sunshine pills" and "pep capsules" fail to get at the source of a person's being depressed or up in the clouds? How may these be a temporary tonic for an emergency but not a source of continuing spiritual bouyancy?

3. When a man says, "I'm fed up with myself" how can sound evangelistic outreach help him?

4. Contrast "pulling myself up by my own bootstraps" with "dumping everything on God" and with "pulling up with God."

5. How does sound evangelizing enable the person to get in the pull of God's lifting power?

6. How may evangelism that is concentration on only one person, with one method, with tie-to-me motivation get in the way of experiencing healthy spiritual buoyancy?

7. How can continuing outreaching evangelistic expression prevent staleness in everyday living?

8. Contrast the immature viewpoint that in "sunshine living" one has no strains or problems with the more mature view that life's most exhilarating periods can be in meeting and working out problems. When may problem-solving depress and when enthuse? Apply to evangelistic contacts and communications.

9. Interpret in terms of spiritual buoyancy through evangelizing, "The lifting power of God is available only as we get into God's work where his spiritual dynamic operates." In this sense what are we to be doing if we are to expect God's lifting power?

10. How may the attitude, "Jesus, I My Cross Have Taken" get in the way of effective evangelizing? How may it prevent the person "evangelizing" from having a lifting experience? How may it prevent the recipient from discovering the gospel of joy?

11. Interpret, "Spiritual buoyancy does not mean that we have no pressures downward but that we have stronger pulls upward." Apply.

12. How does one participate in the evangelistic life of the local congregation with a big view of the world mission of the church? What difference does it make if the evangelizing person has this world view?

13. How does an evangelistic person keep "hopeful heart" when many persons he meets appear hostile or indifferent to the gospel?

14. What is the core of the gospel that you are sharing with others? What in it makes you want to share the good news?

CHAPTER 29

LOVING WITH
UNDERSTANDING OUTREACH

A man of good years observed, "There's healthy loving and there's unholy loving." Then he want on to say, "Much that passes under the name of love should not be under that name." Thinking persons are well aware of this. Gerald Kennedy considers "love" one of the great words that has been murdered during recent years. The word carries many moods and many meanings. Any person who is going to live healthfully needs to consider carefully what he has in mind when he "gets to loving." What passes under this term can wreck or recreate, enslave or ennoble. We cannot say whether the love of one person for another is good until we ascertain what the lover and the loved have in mind when they speak of their loving. Said one wise homespun philosopher, "If love is what I'm looking at when I see Sam Jones when he says he has the love of God in him, I don't want any of it. When I take a look at young Phil Baldwin loving up his girl, I would rather be without this. But if love is what Jed Hawkins and his wife have, when they're good neighbors to everybody, then I'd like to have ever so much of this."

In this modern day it is pretty important that we develop a sound idea about what love is, how it works, and what it does. We need to find out how we go about loving. Do we "fall in love" all of a sudden? Some talk as if it possesses us irresistibly in a moment. Do we "feel in love" with a torrid passion? Some describe it as taking hold so we cannot resist. Do we "fret in love" with "tugs that tear" at our feelings? Some consider that lovers must ever have "the blues." Do we "fashion in love" as movies and magazines of a sort would picture? Some act as if loving follows certain techniques and meets certain social approvals. Do we "fry in love" when it takes hold? Or is there such a thing as growing in loving and developing in being truly lovable? What constitutes love that may be called spiritual? Do we capture or cultivate this kind of love?

Love and Spiritual Health

This is pretty clear: the spiritually healthy person loves and his love is outreaching. Any kind of feeling tagged as "love" will not do. To be outreaching, love has to get outside the one who is loving. It may be that he is only loving himself. To be outreaching a person has to regard others as persons in their own right. He has to know how to regard them with understanding love. To be healthy in his loving the radius of his concern has to keep expanding throughout his life.

The person who does not do this tends to shrivel in his own little world. He swims about in the little pool of his limited circle and never finds the ocean of brotherly love. Jesus said quite plainly that all of us must lose ourselves in God's work and this means that we have to lose ourselves in loving ministry to others, for this is God's work. This is a natural law in God's universe. We can put it negatively first: The person who lives to himself and disregards others as his fellow brothers atrophies. We can put it positively: The person who reaches out for the welfare of others, understandingly, lovingly, expands in personhood, grows in spiritual health. This is as much a way of the universe as the rising of heated air and the diffusing through osmosis. This happens in human relationships and in God-with-man relationships.

There can be spiritual heart shrinkage as well as physical heart decline. And there can be spiritual heart repair. Love, God's kind of love, is indispensable for maintaining good health. Here is a case of life repair through expansion in loving concern for others. Alene Thompkins had financial means for comfortable living. Her husband had died three years before. She had no children. She had got crosswise with her church. She spent day after day in lonely self-pity. A wise counselor gave her this prescription, so stated that Mrs. Thompkins took it as such. It ran something like this: (1) Single out some specific group or person who needs a lift. (It was to be specific, for love does not function in generalities.) (2) Specify some identifiable thing of helpful nature that you can do for them. (General good feeling would not do.) (3) Approach the recipient-to-be with kindly greeting and gracious offering. (This was to be practiced, if necessary.) (4) Consider God as a partner in this business of giving. (Nothing was said about the church with which Mrs. Thompkins was at outs.) (5) Identify some quality or qualities in the person or persons that are commendable and appealing. (The experimenter was to expect that there would be some qualities that might annoy her.) (6) Look at the art of giving and the soul of giving as something that calls for development if one is to be competent, effective, and at home in reaching out to others. (7) Report to God on the project. (This would include awareness of one's own feelings. The woman was by practice a reporter and reviewer.)

So this finicky, worrying, self-centered middle-aged woman selected a young mother with three children, ages three, five, seven. They did not have enough clothing or food. The house looked as if an organizer and a cleaning woman were needed. Mrs. Thompkins took in a birthday cake with candles for the oldest. The expressions of joy were spontaneous. She even cut the cake and served it. She could report, "The day was delicious even if the house was dirty." Literally Mrs. Thompkins was saved. She came to love others for the first time in years. She began to reach out to other children. The next step was to the primary department in the congregation. She became spiritually healthy.

God Is Love

The scriptures keep saying "God is love." This is written quite definitely in I John (note 4:8). Sometimes love is so interpreted that persons do not want any of the kind of sticky sentimentality pictured as God's love. It can appear condescending. In this spirit the English workingman stiffened his back and said, "I don't want to be done good at." He did not want impersonal charity or hand-me-down kindnesses. He needed to realize how a man can be strong and love and be loved. God's love is strong, yet kind. He wants to strengthen the person he loves.

In some ways it would be better if we would say, "God is loving." This puts an active, functioning quality in it. Sometimes "Love," spelled with a capital letter, is thought of as abstract and apart, out there somewhere as if in storage. But love can never exist in a vacuum. It always exists in relationships. It is not vague and general. The love of God and the love he wants us to express is specific and applied. Gerald Kennedy in *I Believe* (page 84) says, "Too many of us talk about loving humanity, but do not love the man next door." God loves persons one by one. Yet he loves every person in our more-than-two-billion world population. So we, like Alene Thompkins, begin with specific persons and push out to include more and more persons in the circle of our loving concern. *God is loving.*

Qualities of God's Love

God has one type of love. He may express it differently in different situations with different persons, but it is ever the one love. So when we examine a given situation in which his love is

344

expressed we shall discover the qualities of his universal and eternal love. When God loves Jack Campbell, a teen-ager, or John Cowan in his seventies, he is expressing the same love. There is no two-sided sentimentality, no maneuvering duplicity in it. Here are qualities of this divine love:

1. It is person-centered, with undiminishing concern for man's welfare. Out in front stands the reminder, "This is my work and my glory, to bring to pass the . . . eternal life of man" (D. and C. 22:23). Man is never a means to something else in God's love; man is the foremost concern in God's loving.

2. It is dynamic, ever functioning. It is more than emotionless, general love. Paul's treatise on love in the thirteenth chapter of Corinthians tells what love does. It causes things to happen in the lives of persons.

3. It is inclusive and outreaching. Basically God is not concerned with sitting on a throne having persons adore him. He is not that self-centered. God is outgoing. Often we do God injustice when we picture him as wanting us to bow down to him. Rather does he want us to reach out and love with him and for him. This love of God reaches out "into all the world" to every person.

4. It is righteous. There is no place for sensuous self-indulgence such as characterized some of the Greek gods. They might invade the homes of other gods, plan trickery on other gods. God's love is consistently righteous, thoroughly reliable.

5. It is eternal in quality. There is no five-minute outlook to it, although the quality of eternity is expressed in the love at a given moment. This love of God looks to what will be good for a man in the long eternal range. God would not provide any person with something that would get in the way of his eternal welfare. He has no place for a momentary indulgence that would weaken the person and hurt others.

6. It is contagious. God's love is "catching." There is a chain reaction in its operation. Whenever a person senses this divine love, he too reaches out lovingly to others. If this outreaching spirit is not in it, it cannot be called the love of God.

Right well can we say, "This kind of love keeps God going." We do not picture God sitting in a celestial rocking chair pitying himself, wondering why some of his children are so unappreciative, contemplating quitting his creative endeavor with man. If he did, he would go to pieces in his own neurotic contemplations. God's continuing outreach keeps his love full and fresh. There are always newly developing persons to love. There are always new situations for expressing this love. God is the Great Exemplar of spiritual health through outreaching love.

The On-Earth Expression in Jesus Christ

Jesus Christ chose to come to earth to live among men of the earth. He came that men might realize what God's love is like, that they might be drawn by this love. It is worth noting that he chose to come. Some think that loving is somewhat automatic, something that chances to happen easily. Not so. Men plan to be loving; they learn to be loving, if they love at all. Jesus chose to love all men. Jesus, as the Son of God, revealed and reveals to men *how* God loves. He chose to do this.

Many forces shaped up against this revelation of how God loves. If Jesus had given in, they could have defeated his mission. He showed how his quality of loving rises above all forces that would hem him in and wreck what he was setting out to do. Many factors linked together to compel him to hate others. He did not surrender. His love reached high expression when he would not hate the priests that pushed for his death and the soldiers who carried out his crucifixion. He would not turn against the populace that railed at him and demanded that he be killed. He triumphed completely when he said, "Father, forgive them!" The lines of Edwin Markham's "Outwitted" had complete fulfillment in Jesus Christ.

> "He drew a circle that shut me out—
> Heretic, rebel, a thing to flout,
> But Love and I had the wit to win:
> We drew a circle that took him in."

There were no boundary lines in Jesus' world of love. When the Jew came to Jesus to inquire about eternal life, the well-to-do man who had "great possessions" but could not submit to using his wealth for others, Jesus, so says Mark's account, "looking upon him loved him" (10:21 R.S.V.).

Here are some of the qualities that Jesus lived out as he loved others. His life was essentially that of living in love. It was more than talking about it, more than giving directions about it.

1. Jesus Christ expected no adulation, no citation for his loving. He asked for no returns to him. The joy, the satisfaction was in the loving outreach.

346

2. He loved the ones who did not love him; he loved the ones who did not appear very lovable. He could minister for the good of others when the recipients did not say "thank you" for what he did for them.

3. He enlisted others and drew others into his way of loving. He sent men out to live with others and to love them. So would they achieve expanding self-realization. Whoever caught the tone of his personality would love others.

4. He showed men how to draw men through themselves to God. He practiced this, as he always pointed men to his Father, to his Father's love. A disciple who caught the quality of Jesus' love would not draw others *to* him but *through* him.

5. He harmonized love of God and love of man. There was no either-or about it. There was no questioning about which comes first. John pointed out definitely that a person cannot love God who does not love his brothers (see I John 4:20).

6. He indicated through association with his apostles and with other disciples how loving is expressed in *living with*. He called these men "that they might be with him." He went through the country with these men. John wrote in his account of the "last supper" that "he loved them unto the end" (13:1). He saw their strengths and their weaknesses, their limitations and their potentials. He met the requirements of the simple designation of love, "It happens when someone knows all about you and cares for you still."

7. He indicated how the breadth and quality of a person's love and loyalty condition what kind of life he is going to be living. Here we can well note both aphorisms, "Cheap loving makes cheap living" and "Deep living makes deep loving." Jesus showed how a man is conditioned by the quality of his love. Any kind of love will not do.

Some Not-so-healthy Expressions

Good health programs concentrate on wholesome ways of living. Most programs also include considerations of the not-so-healthy things that can happen. Love can get lopsided or off-center or dwarfed. Then it gets in the way of spiritual healthiness. Here are some of the possible undesirable expressions:

1. "Smother love," in which the one who is supposed to be loving another takes a dominating, possessing role so that the initiative and individuality of the person loved is held back or crushed, with consequent loss in self-management.

2. Clique concentration. This is in the spirit of the old prayer,
"God bless me and my wife, my son and his wife;
Give us good measure through all of our life."
Here one's own small group sets the boundaries for loving. In time
the outgroup is disdained or disregarded. The chosen circle holds us
in.

3. Skin-surface contacts. Persons who love this way either have
no depth or they cover up their depth so others cannot get to it.
The covering can be done with pretense or with partitions. Sometimes this results in merely shallow conversation.

4. Superfluity of things. Such persons are helpless without
lots of things. Insecure, uncertain persons tend to rely on "things"
to bolster them up and to attract others. In eating together the big
thing is chinaware, silverware, linenware with dishes of color, flavor,
and texture. The persons themselves never meet. Since the real
person never sees the other real person, they cannot love. In life such
persons dwell on things, not on thoughts. Persons with potentials for
deep affection use things as secondary means, never as major emphases.

5. Ego-satisfaction of the one who loves. Bluntly put, this
brand of love is saying, "I want you for what satisfaction I can get
out of you." This person is more interested in being loved than in
loving, in being wanted than in wanting, in reaching out for one's
own sake rather than for the sake of the other. The mother can
want a small child chiefly for the buildup in herself as she coddles
the child and is responded to by the child. A youth can want a
"steady" mainly for his own social security. A minister can enjoy
the glory of having persons look to him and rely on him.

6. Love at-the-moment. These are they who sing, "There's
no tomorrow; there's just tonight." The thrill of a moment's indulgence pushes out consideration of what the effects will be in
weeks to come. Divine love always has eternal perspective.

7. "Privatist" patterns. This view has been expressed quite
openly during recent years. It holds that matters of love in physical
and social aspects are in the realm of individuality, of private standards of conduct. In this view anything is permissible so long as no
one "gets hurt." This overlooks the fact that there is no such thing
as an all-to-himself person. Every one of us lives in a world of social
relationships and social responsibilities. No man lives to himself.
Dr. Stroup reminds us that the self is "contextually fulfilled." The
idea of "privatist" love patterns and standards is logically inconsistent
and out of harmony with the nature of God's universe. Everything
exists in relationships and these push out to universe-wide proportions.

Love in the God Context

Spiritual love is a person-with-person relationship in which God is at the core. The resources available in God can afford community, continuity, vitality, and vision. There is no place for the old saying, "Love is blind." Nor do we expect it to be deaf or handless. This love is wide awake. There are no opiates, no sedatives. Life and persons are seen as they are; they are imagined as they may become. Saint-Exupery once wrote, "Love does not consist in gazing at each other but in looking outward together in the same direction." In spiritual love two or more persons are looking together with God in his direction. Eyes are open. As the lovers look and love together the radius of their world pushes out. The scene ahead pushes forward. The two push together with God.

Such love involves the total person in the total situation in the total universe. There is a wholeness in it. Such love avoids building on some one skill or facet of a person. Thus someone's "divine dancing" or "heavenly hepping" or "angelic auto" cannot be relied on alone. The fullness of one person is associating with the fullness of another person in awareness of the fullness of God. There is nothing dillydallying about such love. It is active, dynamic in working adventurously with God and in reaching out with God. Like everything else in the world that is worth living for, it is exacting and costly. But the returns are worth all this. And it never runs out after five minutes. Those who live lovingly with God can say, "Love never faileth."

Contributions of the Restoration Movement

The Restoration gospel reaffirms with freshness and with contemporary application what Jesus said and lived out. Jesus used the setting and the patterns of his day. The Restoration message spoke in the language of the nineteenth century. It is endeavoring to speak in the thinking and social structure of the twentieth century. Our modern world is needing a sound identification of what love is. A few years ago Pitirim Sorokin, sociologist at Harvard University, said of our times, "All values are unsettled; all norms are broken." He said that mental and moral and social anarchy is reigning. In such a day the conception of love and the means of achieving this love need to be brought to the fore. Here are basics of the Restoration message:

1. Men can love one another and they can love God here and now. We do not wait for this to come to pass in some celestial city where "saved" Saints shall reside.

2. Enduring love calls for transformation of persons so they will be capable of loving and ready to be loved. This is the call to repentance.

3. Persons covenanted with Jesus Christ will build a city of fellowship called Zion. This will be a schooling community for developing persons who love with God and a witnessing community to testify of what can happen when men do love each other.

4. Persons in a collective fellowship called the church reach out to share the good news of God's redeeming love with all others. Thereby is the radius of the heart world of Saints pushed out more and more. This way of evangelism is the way of brotherhood in worldwide proportions.

5. In this sense of responsibility the Saints covenanted with God live the life of stewardship which expresses responsibility to God and to all men.

6. The family is a social group with common allegiance, with common consideration of members, with shared concern for sharing the witness of divine love with others. It is a laboratory in loving relationships.

7. The Book of Mormon as the record of what happened in ancient times on the Western continent tells of the loving concern and ministry of the universal Christ whose sheep are in all the world. It is a manual of inclusive love.

8. The Holy Spirit in ministering to men brings to pass the fruitage of love in the lives of the Saints. In the nature of things, Saints do love.

9. The practice of revelation keeps vital and contemporary the outreaching love of God as he discloses himself to his people.

10. The church as a fellowship includes persons of diverse cultures, racial stocks, lands, with central allegiance to the loving Christ and with continuing ministry of the Spirit that prompts to love.

This Kind of Love Expands

Lives take on expanding quality as they come to love with Jesus Christ. It happened in Peter. He went beyond his fishing nets in Galilee to fishing-for-men as his first calling. His world moved from the fishing village of Capernaum to Rome, capital city of the world. It happened in Paul. He grew beyond hunting out Christians to get rid of them to hunting out men who would become Christians to save them. His evangelistic field became the known world. He looked toward going to Spain. John Wesley grew beyond the town of Epworth in Lincolnshire until he could say that the world was his parish. And his brother Charles could sing of "love divine, all loves excelling," a love that encompasses every person. It happened in David Livingstone. The youth in a cotton factory near Glasgow caught the pull of the unbounded love of God. His love expanded until he set himself to rid the continent of Africa of the curse of slavery. He died on his knees among his native friends with a world-size love in his heart. It happened in Charles Wandell. He was baptized in New York state as a youth of eighteen. The ministry called him to distant places. His heart stretched to include the peoples of Oceania and Australia. He died, at home with God and with God's people, in a faraway country. It is happening in thousands of people today. Some travel to lands abroad. Others remain at home and there the life of the worldwide church with its universal mission flows through their homes and congregations. Recently a brother put his testimony this way: "God is stretching my heart every day. And I am just getting started. I never supposed my circle would include my brothers and sisters in the Orient, in Europe, in Latin America, in the Islands. *And I am just getting started!*" And as an afterthought he added, "Think of all the millions outside the church who are my possible friends!" He is on the way.

Questions for Discussion

1. How do you respond to the comment, "I don't have to do anything to love. God just put love in my heart, and there it is"?
2. In gospel teaching and preaching how is it not enough to simply declare, "Love others"? How is it necessary to identify what we mean by "love"?
3. How may members of the church practice a restricted group loving so that the church so understood can get in the way of the love that enlarges us?
4. How adequate do you consider this conception of love: "Love is to invest oneself in the life of another person, without thought of immediate return on the investment"?
5. How is it possible for a person to go to another land as an appointee without loving the native people as brothers and sisters?
6. How is outreaching love an essential to good spiritual health? What happens inside a person who does not reach out to others?
7. What happens in the life of an adult who, growing older, does not keep developing new and more friendships?

8. How many generations do you find in the circle of your loved-loving friends? How can life be enriched by speaking the language of several generations? How do you learn this language?

9. How do you see the Latter Day Saint movement, soundly interpreted, conducive to expansion in our world of fellowship? What do we do to insure this? How is it possible for the movement to restrict us with some interpretations?

10. How do you react to the comment, "A little church like yours must narrow your world"? How may a church of large numbers produce a small world of association? How can we make "a little church" function as "a big fellowship"?

11. How would you use the life of the church to save a member from an inbred, self-centered way of living?

12. How may a person rationalize that he is loving others in things he is doing when for the most part he is loving himself?

13. What qualities in Jesus' "loving in living" guide us in developing wholesome loving today?

PART V

UNITS FOR FURTHERING
HEALTHY LIVING

Now we come to a closing consideration: Who is going to be working in this program of spiritual fitness? To leave it all to generalized good intention is likely to be unfruitful. Every member is to be enlisted. Every minister is to be involved. Yet no new department (which might be called the Department of Spiritual Fitness and Saintly Health, the DSFSH) is to be set up in the church. What we are setting out to do must pervade the entire educational program of the church. This includes library, lecture, and laboratory expression. It must look to the entire range of life, from inception to death, and beyond death. The program will be the way of common consent, of common concern, of common consociation.

Five units of operation, five companies are indicated here. These can be interpreted so that they include all possible groups. They are to function in a complementary way.

1. *The general church* in worldwide operation shares and implements the health-affording gospel. The program is to be health-minded. The personnel are to be spiritually fit. The God of the gospel is to be altogether wholesome.

2. *The congregations* of the church are companies of Saints interested in the well-being of all members. The congregation builds a program of spiritual exercise that visions what will produce healthful living. The atmosphere and the activities of the congregational fellowship constitute a spiritual health laboratory, as a whole, in subgroups.

3. *The family* is a health center with provisions for continuing cooperation in conversation, in projects, in service, in study, in worship, in fellowship that blend together for the furtherance of family spiritual fitness.

4. *The member* sets himself to develop habits of living that "healthify." He works out a program of spiritual fitness that is suited to his nature and his needs. He has no shortcuts, no easy formula, no once-and-for-all cure. He plans to maintain spiritual health as long as he lives, and he is working at it now.

5. *The small voluntary groups* in which members of common vocabulary of mind and heart and hand come together for spiritual fellowship. These may be in the neighborhood, in the priesthood, in the age group, in the occupation. Such groups come together for a while, for a common interest, with a common sense of need. These stand above inbred pride or overemphasized fads. These are like the small companies with whom Jesus associated.

And through all these runs the evangelistic concern for sharing the good news of the gospel of spiritual health with all persons everywhere. Spiritual healthiness never thrives in fenced-in life.

All these groups are working here and now. They will enable the constructing of communities in which spiritual health is promoted. The core community is Zion.

The God of the gospel of spiritual fitness speaks today: Who will share my gospel of spiritual health? Who will live so healthfully that he will be able to share testimonially? Who will know me as the Father of Healthfulness? Persons, congregations, families, circles need answer now, Here am I: use me!

CHAPTER 30

OUR WORLD CHURCH
LEADING OUT ADVENTUROUSLY

Healthy churches live on the spiritual frontier. They may not settle down in conventional ease on Security Street. Any age calls for belief in adventurous faith. Once Elton Trueblood used the phrase, "the habit of adventure." This word "habit" identifies a continuing pattern of moving out beyond the usual, conventional ways of doing things. This is more than jumping up with a sudden, spasmodic spurt of daring. It means pioneering with purpose, frontiering with seasoned faith. Without adventure the church is in gradual retreat. Alfred North Whitehead has reminded us that "without adventure civilization is in full decay" and that religion without adventure is dead. A security-and-comfort-minded person, a convention-and-respectability-hearted church, and a we-have-arrived-and-shall-stay-here civilization are on the way out. Spiritual senescence has set in.

This need for adventure is ever with the church. It stands out more definitely in some periods. Such is the case today. The social order keeps changing with rapid tempo. It is almost dizzying to keep up with the change. The church is going to need wide-open eyes and keep-alert minds to read what is taking place. And it must see with God-inspired vision how the church is going to be relevant in such a mobile society. Otherwise, it will be burning kerosene lamps in a past-tense sanctuary while the world travels beneath arc lights on much trafficked boulevards. And the language must speak to the times, else the church will be quoting Chaucerian phrasing while society chatters in the lingo of the late twentieth century. Such a church will have diseases of atrophy and paralysis. The weary Christian will long for the good old days and will endeavor to hold on to usages and phrases and organizations of a "golden age" that is past. The disease might be called past-tense *praecox*.

An Organism Designed to Launch Out

The church is often likened to a human body; it is viewed as a social organism. At birth this body is more than "a hunk of clay" that waits for some potter to come along and give it shape. The infant organism wriggles and stretches and demands. It has a selective quality. It has a reaching-out quality. One wise friend with children put it this way, "These boys and girls were not designed by God to stay put." He rejected the notion that as a teacher his job was to mold the inert clay. He continued, "God made them to be curious, creative, cooperative; he expects them to launch forth and to lead out." And this is a pretty good picture of the way the church as an organism is intended to behave.

The Church of Jesus Christ is not some inanimate, insensitive dummy sitting in a rocking chair waiting for God to come along and give it a poke in the ribs to get it going. The living church is in motion and is seeking ways to express itself. It reaches out to God for direction and inspiration. It needs this to give meaning to what it does. Without this direction it could be merely hopping around and twitching like a person afflicted with St. Vitus's dance. To adventure is to do something more than get into meaningless and fruitless action. The prefix *ad* signifies that there is moving toward something. There is purpose in the moving. There is significance in the bodily expression.

The Church Needs Strenuous Exercise

In *Personality and Religion* (page 150) Paul E. Johnson says, "It is the privilege of a person to have religious adventures." We shall say this of the church. But this is not enough: we shall say that it is the *need* of the church to adventure religiously. Let this word "religiously" convey the requisite of associating with God and we bring forth the realization that God himself is adventurous in nature and that they who work with him will have to be adventurous, too. There is no place for stalemating and becalming in God's business. God intends the church to continue in strenuous exercise and pioneering courage.

Ideals and goals pointing toward a time of rest and ease are not quite true to God. There is nothing to indicate that one time God will retire from activity and loll in an easy chair. Nor would Saints who are to be like him be expected to go on a pension list with nothing to do. This would be the essence of senescence. The Church of Jesus Christ never punches a time clock and closes out for the day. It never gets superannuated. It can never get its exercise by proxy. It can never carry out its mission through reading a missionary manual with soothing poetry about the age when all men will have heard the gospel witness. The church has no choice if it is going to keep healthy: it will keep on exercising adventurously. The church will keep a young heart.

The Healthiness of Sound Restlessness

The Church of Jesus Christ is not called to sit down in placid peace and sing "All is well!" There needs to be awareness that some things are not as they ought to be and that the church is expected to do something about all this. The church has to learn how to be restless. There is no place for dithering worry; this is wasteful. There is place, however, for the dissatisfaction that prompts fruitful action. Well understood and well managed tension can be a constructive element in life. Athletes testify that butterflies in their stomachs push them to give to the full. Cicero, entering the Roman Senate to make one of his celebrated speeches, would show visible trembling. The church needs stimulation without staggering and work without worry. Our physical bodies are designed for tension and release. The church can learn how to use these factors.

In the year 1926 Dr. Henry Link wrote in *Return to Religion,* "All the material advantages of our civilization conspire to make our lives easier and our characters weaker" (page 178). He went on to say that it takes stern discipline to protect ourselves from the easy way of our environment. John Sutherland Bonnell in *No Escape from Life* observes, "With every year that passes the necessity for effort on our part is lessened. Multitudes are living today by the creed of comfort. We are producing a soft generation" (page 11). In some of his later lectures T. S. Eliot warned that even in our pleasures we are eliminating all necessity for endurance and fatigue. He saw us beginning to regard struggle, effort, and self-sacrifice as things to be avoided. This inclination away from the strenuous was described by Aldous Huxley in his *Brave New World.* In this new world pain, effort, struggle would be eliminated. In case there was such remaining there would be a new drug (soma) that would take all the rough edges off life. He wrote that if by chance something unpleasant should happen in this brave new world, there would always be "soma" to give us "a holiday from the facts." Near the close of the story a new character is introduced, a savage who has come from somewhere on the fringes of this anemic civilization. When he meets the head of this world order and this leader explains the new society, the visitor bursts forth, "It's too easy . . . I want God . . . I want real danger. I want freedom. I want goodness . . ."

The Church of Jesus Christ faces life with open eyes. The church says, "This is the way things are, but with the help of God, things will be different." God's counsel to the church admonishes us not to sit down and rest but to "renew our strength" and go on.

This applies to day-by-day living and to crises when it looks as if everything we have stood for with God is about to crack and go to pieces. The biographer of Edward Sheldon—the playwright E. W. Barnes in *The Man Who Lived Twice*—tells how this man, made completely immobile by a crippling form of arthritis which in later stages left him totally blind, "came to grips with destiny and from some hidden reservoir of the spirit drew strength to go on." He summarized, "In the moment of crisis he found a faith which would not only sustain him in the thirty remaining years of his life but would reach out in powerful and mysterious ways into the lives of other people." This has happened in persons such as Jeremiah and Paul. It has to happen in the corporate life of the Church of Jesus Christ.

The Malignancy of Bemoaning and Bespeaking Disasters

Honesty never covers up evils and maladjustments. But healthiness does not dwell on these as if they were the one thing that is happening. The church can become weak through concentrating on all the things that are wrong in the world and on the disasters that are going to come shortly. The church can develop spiritual melancholia. It is uplifting to catch the spirit of a person whose faith rises above his afflictions. In the latter years of Robert Louis Stevenson's lifelong battle with tuberculosis he wrote letters of such good cheer from Samoa to his friends in Europe that they could scarcely believe the reports of his actual suffering. In one of his letters he remarked, "I will not allow the medicine bottles on my mantlepiece to be the limits of my horizon." This has been a priceless testimony to millions. He saw his situation as it was, but he saw beyond all this. This is the way the church is to go in her world mission. We shall see fighting, starvation, disease, slavery, sexual indulgence, thievery, and more, but this is not our gospel. Like Stevenson we must see beyond the veils of suffering and sin.

During the recent months a preacher, bent on themes of disaster and doom, waxed eloquent about the many distresses and iniquities extant in the world. An air of hopelessness and judgment settled down over the congregation. The breaking forth of war was pictured as imminent. In a dramatic close he declared, "So the judgments of God are coming on the world!" A young man (we shall call him Carl), troubled by the outlook, approached the preacher and asked, "In the light of impending disasters coming on the world, what are we Latter Day Saints to be doing?" The answer was ready, "Flee, flee the judgments; flee to Zion!" The youth was more troubled and he continued, "Do you mean that God is giving up? Do you mean that I am to run away and leave the unwarned people to suffer God's judgments? I am not that kind of guy, and God is not that kind either. Go on with your fear and your gloom. God and I are going to a needing world with faith and with the gospel."

Today the adventuring church may not dwell on aches and pains in itself and on diseases and disasters in the world. In Madras, India, a missionary council of many Christian churches was held in 1938. War clouds were gathering and the outlook was not promising. Believers could not surrender to chaos. They could not go away with a message of hopelessness. They prepared "a message to all peoples." Its spirit can be spread abroad today:

> "Surely God is summoning us in these times to let go our self-sufficiency, to frequent his altars, to learn of him, and to make his ways known in all the relationships of life. . . . God grant to his church to take the story of his love to all mankind, till that love surround the earth, binding the nations, the races, and the classes into a community of sympathy for one another, undergirded by a deathless faith in Christ."

The healthy church is going to speak a positive message. There will be warning against sinful living, but there will be, even more, invitation to saintly living. The church will be living the way of hope in a way of world life that is hopeless. A few years ago with some prevision, this counsel came to a convocation of ministers. It speaks a commissioning message to all the church:

> "I send you forth to carry the message of repentance. This is a message of hope. Dwell not on terrors and disasters to come upon lands and peoples, but concern yourselves with tempests of men's souls. Tell how with repentance there is available redemptive power which can lift and heal. This is a message of hope."

It takes courageous hope and adventurous faith to go abroad in the world with such a message, with such a mission. Such a work is health-producing in the church itself and health-promising in the millions of men around the earth.

The Anemia of Silence

The healthy church knows when to speak and when to refrain from speaking. Jesus was a prophet in both respects. Before Pilate he said "not a word." In the temple courts those last days he lashed forth with definite assertions. He was clear and incisive. The church needs to know when to speak and what to say. There are times when silence is a deadly sin. Many times things go wrong and evil gets in control as much through the silence of otherwise good men as through the ingenious machinations of evil men. It is said that Socrates was condemned to death by the men who would have voted for his acquittal if they had voted. Sometimes a Saint is not permitted the easy luxury of speaking forth. A coward may refrain from saying something definite when he ought to be speaking forth. A fool is likely to speak out when he should familiarize himself with situations and issues before he gives his opinion. A radical will speak out with finality when he is seeing only a segment of the total situation. Koheleth counseled us, "Let us hear the conclusion of the whole matter."

Today the Church of Jesus Christ needs inspired and inspiring wisdom that we might speak forth on the side of God. The voice must be confident, with a clear message. It may not be partisan; it must see God as the Father of all humanity. It must not speak the voice of one nation, one culture. It must be the voice of the worldwide church. We can express ourselves in such generalities that we are quite safe. Some such opinions are above danger. There is the story that one Sunday Calvin Coolidge returned home from a morning church service. Asked what the sermon was about, he said, "Sin." Asked what the preacher had to say about it, he replied, "He was against it." He could have been more helpful had he made reply concerning some identifiable sin. This the healthy church must do, in the total light of the world situation and the intent of God. Sometimes silence indicates an anemic soul in the church.

Roads to Spiritual Health in the Church General

The health of any part, any branch, any member is conditioned by the state of general health. This is a two-way process of influence. The condition of spiritual health of any member anywhere in the church has bearing on the total church health. Here consideration is on the general healthiness of all through what is done in the church in its worldwide outlook and operation. What the church does in these fields makes significant difference to everyone.

1. The expanding concern, the outreach in operation, and the sense of mission on a world scale affects the spiritual condition of participating members and congregations. When the church takes root in India, Korea, Okinawa, Scotland, and Peru, something happens in members who follow the story and share in it. Hearts are stretched and sense of mission is pushed out. More and more we are seeing that the church has to push out to deliver the church in center areas from narrowness and provincialism. When Africa is under consideration some soul stretching takes place.

2. The coming of members from lands outside the Center Place and the visiting of congregations in other lands by members of the central and other areas makes for contacts which can lead to spiritual fraternity with world outlook. The salutation "Brother" and "Sister" is translated into every language in which the church is established. In this adventure lies one of the great possibilities before the church today. This adventure calls for enough brotherly interaction that members of lands of non-Caucasoid racial stock and non-American culture will feel at home in the fellowship of the church. And members in the home nation of the church will lose sense of condescension, paternalism, and colonialism in the fellowship with Orientals, Negroes, Polynesians, American Indians, Hindus, and others. There is a healthiness in saying together, "Our Father" with the brotherhood that this implies.

3. The review and the interpretation of the message and the doctrine of the church in terms of "universals" make these meaningful and applicable in all cultures of the world. The message of the church has been spoken in English in the phrasing and the thinking of a Bible that is Hebrew and Greek in its origin. The services of the church have been patterned after the ones held in the United States and British settings. Now Latter Day Saints must take a fresh look at all this—and what a healthy, growing experience it can be. Pressures for this looking from a world-size point of view are now appearing as we try to make the Restoration gospel and the Restoration church meaningful, appealing, and functional in lands such as Japan, India, and Oceania.

4. Explorations for developing and conducting programs of health in "missions abroad" can be stimulating and stretching. More and more alert members are seeing that the gospel must touch the life of the total person, the total community. Preaching sermons and distributing tracts and holding "cottage meetings"

may not be enough for other peoples—may not even fit. What is
the gospel of health that is to be shared? Certainly it must touch
the total man. This involves physical health, mental health, social
health, spiritual health. It will not be enough to dispense pills
and tonics, remove tonsils, and bring forth babies. Health emis-
saries will have to see health in terms of the total range of living.
We shall have to clarify what will constitute good spiritual health
for a diver in Tahiti, a fisherman in Norway, a dentist in Korea,
a day laborer in India. An exacting day is before us that can be
a health-producing day.

5. The facing of the problem of evolution in health lies before
us. We do not all start on the same level of healthiness, physical,
mental, or spiritual. A letter comes from a friend of the church in
Africa wanting prayers so the baby presently to be born will not be
victimized by evil spirits. We have to start where this family is. An
islander considers it safe to give a few grains of rice to a local deity
to insure good eyesight. We have to start where this simple believer
is. A European mother wants an elder to rid her of uncleanness after
the birth of her baby. We have to start with this mother's conception
of the application of Mosaic ideas today. A grandparent in the
United States recommends slitting a tree and inserting white horse
hairs to drive away asthma. We have to start where this grandparent is. And then there is the university student graduating in medicine and majoring in genetics. And we have to start where he is. A
tremendous program of appreciating the health views of other persons
and other cultures is before us. Some healthy soul-stretching is challenging us to better health.

Needed: Doctors in Spiritual Health

We are needing men and women of large vision who will look to
ministering to the total person. It is more than a pair of tonsils that
comes in for a tonsillectomy. It is more than a stomach that comes
in with an ulcer. The feelings, the fears, the faiths, the family connections come in, too. Farseeing men of medicine are enriching the
traditional program so that these other phases of the person are coming
in for consideration. We are needing doctors who are competent in
medical science and medical skill but who also are at home in the
field of spiritual health. Such men cannot have one kind of theology
for the prayer meeting and another theology for medical books and
research.

Albert Schweitzer was an unusual man in this respect. He was
a scholar in philosophy, notably of Goethe; of music, notably of Bach;

of theology; and then of medicine. He reached out to other cultures and worlds of thought, notably to India. And then he went to his missionary hospital at Lambarene in Africa. He saw all that he did in the light of his convictions about the meaning of life and of the universe. He saw every civilization, every culture founded on some conception of the total order of things. Basic in all this is "reverence for life." He saw that this has been declining and must be recovered. He affirmed the need of men who are "personalities sound enough and profound enough to let the ideas of ethical progress radiate from them as a force." All that he did in his simple if not rudely furnished hospital in Africa stems from this conception of reverence for life. He was more than a doctor of medicine for the body.

The Church of Jesus Christ has the potential for producing this kind of doctor. The physical and the spiritual are complementary. God is healthy and health-producing. Man is designed by God to be altogether healthy and integrated in this healthfulness. All mankind is considered as "of one blood" and intended for "one brotherhood." The ways of science are included in the comprehensive program of understanding man and the universe. The Holy Spirit is interpreted as functional in all approaches to understanding God and his purposes and plan. In this field of developing doctors of spiritual health the church can be adventurer indeed.

An Exacting Adventure in Loving

Our spiritual health meets with severe testing when we encounter those whom we have been traditioned to consider enemies. Once a Pole of aristocratic background came to the United States. When he discovered in New York that there were Jews in this country, he thought of returning home. He had thought that in this Western land he would be free from such horrible unpleasantness. The Hindu of high caste shrank from the shadow of an untouchable. Some of our church members have had allergies to Mormons and Roman Catholics. Our church has adventurous laboratory work in these areas. It may take a longtime clinical treatment to get rid of these phobias and animosities. This will not come by wishful thinking or by legislative enactments or administrative announcements. New attitudes have to grow in to replace those that are there. It was a tremendous experience after World War II when German Saints and Dutch Saints met. Here was a firsthand test of the power of faith in Jesus Christ. In some cases the miracle worked. In some cases it functioned in part.

One of the most moving and penetrating expressions of this soul surgery was made by Dr. T. Z. Koo of China before the Madras Conference in 1938. Japan and China were bitter enemies. He spoke with the honesty that permits healing to take place.

"My country today is being invaded by Japan. Before the war I could meet a Japanese Christian and feel we were one in Christ. But today with the Japanese army marching across my country, killing and destroying everything in its way, a sense of strain bears down heavily upon my Christianity when I face a Japanese. . . . Jesus challenges our complacency in this matter by telling us we should love not only our friends but also our enemies. As long as there is not a concrete enemy before us, or if the enemy is a thousand miles from us we can vaguely think about loving the enemy. . . . You can no longer take it for granted that we should love our enemy when he is actually standing before you waiting to be loved."—Quoted from R. P. Barnes, *A Christian Imperative,* pp. 107, 108.

Healing through Helping

The Christian gospel and the Christian Church calls for adventurous exercise. There can be, as John said on Patmos, no lukewarm condition. It has been said that a church can be neither sick nor well, but in that uncomfortable in-between stage in which the patient is well enough to keep going and carry on yet unable to do his work with zest, enthusiasm, and effectiveness. We may have some myopia on social and racial questions and there may be some creaking rheumatic joints in ecclesiastics, but this does not mean that we all have hardening of the arteries and spiritual dyspepsia. Sometimes our doctrine gets separated from the business of transforming lives and our worship gets divorced from work. Sometimes our message of spiritual health gets caught in terminologies and perimeter interests. But there is resilience and covered-up desire. There are resources to be mobilized and utilized. And this can be done.

The spiritual health of the Church of Jesus Christ requires that we get to the mission of sharing the good news of Jesus Christ with the conviction that this constitutes "a marvelous work and a wonder." Specific members and the World Church will become spiritually healthy through reaching out helpfully. This has to be done with worldwide vision, with consideration of individuals as potential sons of God—and it must be done adventurously.

Questions for Discussion

1. Illustrate how in the church the good health or the poor health of any one segment affects the church as a whole and how the health condition of the general church affects the life of the member and of the congregation.
2. How is the person, in physical body, in personhood equipped for and needing new, adventurous experience?
3. How does a person need the vision and the feel of a universal church to speak of and for this church in his own hometown?
4. What did the youth mean when he said he did not mind being a member of a small church but this small church had to have a big mission and a big world?
5. When is restlessness about our world mission healthy and when is it unhealthy? How may our concern get so big that it touches nowhere?
6. How might the church get lazy and self-satisfied in seeing and working at our world mission? What things might occupy our attention?
7. When the church opened the field in India on July 5, 1964, what did members need to know and understand and feel in order to be one in this missionary adventure?
8. What is the difference between "sending the gospel" to a distant country and "having fellowship" with members of another culture and country?
9. Would you react to a sermon on doom as did the young man Carl? When is proclamation of danger healthy and when is it unhealthy?
10. Specify a health-producing activity that would develop a member or a congregation in each of the five "roads to spiritual health" with these activities carried on in world-outlook perspective.
11. What qualifications are needed by a doctor of spiritual health? How would he go about his work?
12. What would happen in the spiritual condition of the church if we were to draw in all appointees from abroad and concentrate on a fifty-mile radius around Independence?
13. How is the present age a time calling for sound and spirited adventure in world missions and world fellowship?
14. What building up do you see as necessary for the church to have the health strength essential for adventuring as a world-wide church?

CHAPTER 31

OUR CONGREGATIONS
EXERCISING HEALTHFULLY

The word "congregation" has a functioning place in our Christian religion. If we were to drop it, we would have to get a new word to take its place. The early Christian writers had much to say about the coming together of believers. They never thought of a disciple existing in isolation. The first picture of the followers of Jesus Christ after the Day of Pentecost shows them living together in mutuality. They were a *congregation,* a *community.* They did things together. They sensed the need of being together. The account of this congregation, given in Acts 2:42-47, is one of the grandest in all the Bible. It describes a community in healthy operation. Every member, every branch ought to read it often. Here was a group in excellent spiritual health.

The Shaping of a New Vocabulary

Those writers of the records that in time were to become the New Testament had to draw on the Greek language for words that would best describe what went on in the new Christian movement. They used the word *ekklesia* which came to be translated "church." To the Greeks and Romans this word meant a convened assembly. It carried the connotation of being called by someone. In the Christian life it meant that the saints had been summoned by God. Another word that came to be used in the Christian writing was *koinonia* which carried the idea of generous sharing in contrast with selfish getting. It expressed Christian fellowship in which disciples shared in spiritual friendship. Those in this *koinonia* were partners and fellow workers.

The Way of Exercise

Paul was adept in describing how Christian living is exercising consistently, purposefully, and soundly. He must have been at home in athletic pursuits. Several times he compared life to a race that calls for discipline and tenacity. He applies this to himself, "I do not run aimlessly, I do not box as one beating the air" (I Corinthians 9:26 R.S.V.). Paul was considering the idea of teamwork in the athletic exercise. Well might he have used the slogan set forth by one of our church youth groups, "To pace one another on the road of Zion." He phrased this aptly when he was writing to the Corinthian members about achieving a congregation. They were to learn how to achieve the kind of congregational life described in Acts 2:42-47. He said pointedly, "We are laborers together with God" (I Corinthians 3:9). He might have put it this way: "We are all on the team together with our Head Coach, exercising and cooperating." A congregation is a company of Saints exercising in teamwork.

Good Exercise Is Indispensable

Congregational living is a gymnasium for exercising. It is a laboratory school, in the business of saintly development. The original connotation of gymnasium carried the notion of being naked during the exercising. This meant the athletes were to get rid of every encumbrance. Paul suggested this in his counsel to "lay aside every weight . . . and run with patience the race" (Hebrew 12:1). One of the essentials in the congregational gymnasium is that all on the team get rid of things that get in the way. This will include fears, phobias, hatreds, and insecurities. All will listen to the counsel, "Strip off whatever is excess baggage and hinders free movement."

"Learn to do by doing" is highly applicable here. There is no way to learn to swim other than by swimming. But this exercising has to be more than "going through the motions," more than "keeping very busy." Some exercising, some disciplining can undermine spiritual health. A child was learning to play the piano. Under his own fingering and that of a poor instructor he was bungling along. When a superior teacher came, this wise instructor gave the directive, "We have to start right." A second directive followed, "We have to keep practicing." These counsels hold in the developing and maintaining of our spiritual health. We have to start right. We have to keep exercising in sound ways. Going through motions without sound method and without sound theory can get in the way of achieving spiritual healthiness. There is no substitute for good exercising. We cannot go to the storehouse and purchase pills and tonics and ointments that will afford us first-class spiritual health. We need the sharing with healthy brothers and sisters, fellow athletes in the laboratory school, our congregation. We shall do significant things in a sound way. And the Head Coach is to be ever with us.

We Need Congregational Schooling

Each one of us needs to exercise in healthy congregational life. Here are some of the advantages that can come in such cooperative learning: (1) counsel in good growing from fellow workers; (2) encouragement and stimulation from fellow learners who pace us; (3) balanced cooperative exercise that enables us to do things that we cannot do alone; (4) group therapy and clinical help; (5) group witness to others of the healthy spirituality in the gospel and group reception of new learners in spiritual living; and (6) instruction and inspiration from the Great Teacher and Director in the congregational endeavors. Each one of us needs these services.

Jesus practiced this congregational schooling. He called twelve men to constitute a congregational laboratory school. They went with him in group experiments. Then he sent them out on their own, two by two. Worship for him was always related to the work he was doing. Then they returned and they reported on what they had been doing. They reviewed this together and he evaluated their ministries. Jesus was not concerned merely with keeping these men busy. Always he wanted them to "bring forth fruits," to become competent, consecrated ministers. Athletes often speak of having a "good workout." Jesus always saw that his spiritual athletes exercised and developed through sound, beneficial workouts.

Individually Too

Each one of us is an individual in our own right. God is not in the business of producing identicals in an everybody-the-same program. There are things in which all of us may share and should share. This provides community. There are also some things that belong to personal schedule. A great athlete has resources and qualities that are his alone. He has to train and develop to bring these out. The Olympic runner Jesse Owens had to do some things on his own. So it is with saints in process: they exercise together and they exercise alone.

Some Branch Quarantines

Quarantine signs used to designate that someone living in that house had smallpox or scarlet fever or some other contagious disease. They carried the warning "Danger" or the directive "Keep Out." These placards were put up to safeguard health.

It has been said that it would be well to have health inspections of our congregations. Some of these might have notices posted saying that their spiritual condition would impair the health of any who might come in. Here are some of the maladies which occur in congregational life that might be considered injurious to the health of persons living there and to those who might enter. These are diseases that "eat in" on spiritual health. They have contagious quality. Sometimes they produce malignancies. We wonder about effective inoculation, about improving the living conditions in the branch.

1. Pessimistic atmosphere that looks hopelessly at what is happening today and at what is expected to happen tomorrow. This pessimistic air is hard on our breathing. Children and youth catch this malady quite readily. It usually intensifies with the passing years.

2. Negative criticism that runs down persons and disheartens attempts to participate in congregational life. Opposite this is shallow optimism that presumes that everything is all right. Fault-finding negativism tends to cause spiritual ulcers.

3. Provincialism that hems in the attitudes, the beliefs, the practices, the contacts of members of the congregation. Outsiders are to conform. Insiders are to maintain things as they are. Narrowness and old age come prematurely. This provincialism presumes that "we" are right and that "we" have the fullness of the gospel.

4. Busyness that keeps persons in motion and on schedule without sound purpose and clear insight concerning what is being done. Motion and involvement become a virtue.

5. Tangency in emphases in practice and in thinking that stresses sidelines and secondary matters and shuts out the picture of the total gospel. Little things become items of major consequence. One branch's chief concern seemed to be taking care of their new hymnbooks.

6. Domination of the congregation by a few officials or a family or two, with consequence that those outside these groups may not share creatively in congregational life. This may take place with conviction in these who dominate that they are called to save the branch.

7. Immaturity in notions of spirituality which leads to unwholesome concern about "gifts," to unsound conceptions of what constitutes spirituality, to lopsided interest in signs and wonders which have little if any bearing upon development of saintly character. Some such branches pride themselves on their spirituality.

8. Repetitiousness in procedures that chokes out spiritual freshness and spiritual adventure. Ways become rutted and presumed

right. It has been said that some branches presume after a time that what they do customarily is set forth in the Doctrine and Covenants.

9. Otherworldliness, the undue concern about the hereafter as to comforts and rewards with exclusion of or discount of present-life undertakings and joys. This malady tends toward speculation and consideration of how much persons are going to get out of the glories.

10. Cynical superiority that discounts generally accepted operations and personnel. This malady prompts a congregation to set itself up to be the "judge in Israel." This is especially dangerous if members of the group so afflicted believe that they have special spiritual discernment in these matters.

11. Defeatism that concludes "we can't do anything here and now." This allows no place for the affirmation that it is up to us to make things come true. Sometimes this takes the form of waiting until God shall move mightily and assuming that until God does we are quite helpless.

12. "Adultism," the adults-only policy that excludes youth and children from significant participation in congregational endeavors. The present is looked upon as a time of "preparation" in which these immature members make ready; preparation in this concept does not include sharing in the laboratory life of the congregation.

13. "Proofing" that looks for final statements and closed-out proofs from printed statements and from inherited forms of argument, without quest for larger insight. "Proofing" may lead to hardening of the spiritual arteries and to atrophy of spiritual muscles.

14. Social apartness within the congregation that shuts out brotherly fellowship, restricts doing things together, and gets in the way of common inspiration. Mutual support and empathy are low.

15. Divorce from the life of the community with social distance from nonmembers. This may come from an exaggerated idea of sticking to the church, from guarding against incoming of worldly influences. Opportunities for evangelistic service are reduced.

16. The why-don't-they attitude which frees persons and groups from responsibility for getting things under way.

17. Defensiveness that presumes that all the "outsiders," all the nonmembers, all the social order are against Latter Day Saints, and against this congregation in particular. Such a view may consider smallness and social persecution desirable.

18. Isolation of worship from working with God, thereby leading to formalism and emotional indulgence. When the worship is over the service is over.

19. The be-at-ease-with-what-you-have mindedness, which can take satisfaction in shoddy, inadequate facilities or may glory in our

"unusually good" quarters and appointments. This says, "We are as we are, so . . ."

20. Apathy, which surrenders in fatigue, with loss of the pioneering tone and adventurous spirit of the Restoration movement.

Each Congregation Uses Its Potentials

Congregations differ. No two are identicals. So it is with persons. The wholesome person surveys to discover what he has to work with, how he can develop this, and how he can use it to good purpose. He is able to say, "This is what I am; this is what I am going to be!" His survey of what he is includes his listing of yet undeveloped potentials. His survey includes what he does not have and what he may never have. This exercise of "meet myself" has to be honest and hopeful. Thus Jimmy Durante used an unusually large nose to make him a "character" in the entertainment field and he became "Snozzola." Glen Cunningham used his resources against great odds and became a world-renowned runner.

Congregations need to do this same kind of inventorying. It is likely that everyone will find resources hidden, unknown. Then each will be able to say with the frank country preacher, "We ain't what we want to be; we ain't what we ought to be; we ain't what we're going to be; but thanks be, we ain't what we was." One small branch had a tired-looking building. Members hesitated to invite any friends and after they hesitated they did not. They had no building fund, no intention of building. Then a family with a conviction of the greatness of the church and with fertile imagination moved in. A resurrection took place in their hopes. The congregation came alive as they went to work to get a new church home. The healthy congregation behaves this way. It inventories. It formulates goals. It mobilizes resources. It develops manpower. It finds satisfaction in productive work. It makes members spiritually healthy.

Congregations Can Become More Healthy

A congregation that is going to be spiritually healthy does not contemplate a distant resurrection and wait for it. Its members believe that the Restoration movement says that restoring power is available here and now. They believe that this refreshing power is available to them. They believe that they have to do some sound exercising where they are. And this does happen. One congregation had no one to play the piano. First they waited and hoped. Then they prayed. No one moved in. They looked around and encouraged a young woman to take lessons. It was a branch project. They went through her struggles in trying to play the piano for hymn singing. She would never make a concert artist but she could make an accompanist for hymns which were not too difficult. Something happened to the entire congregation. And they learned something about hymns and hymn singing.

One congregation had only two ordained men. One was halting in speech, the other limited in background. Neither was very inspiring for preaching or presiding, for members or for nonmembers. Some felt that the branch was crippled and unpromising. Others would not give up. In branch council sessions, not too well directed, there was worked out a panel personnel for considering topics pertinent to congregational life. The older brother could respond in good spirit, with good counsel, when someone laid the setting in fields in which he was at home. The other brother opened up more freely when he felt he did not have to "preach all alone." Ministers, meetings, and members took on new spirit in such a cooperative endeavor. Good teamwork brought good team results, and other workers were developed.

Let a Congregation Be Itself

Healthy persons dare to be themselves. They have some conviction about themselves and go about living what they are able to be. They do not parade their weaknesses or their strengths. They accept themselves not in self-love but in self-knowledge. Then they do not need to indulge in excuses, in masks, in pomposities. They do not dislike themselves; they do not distrust themselves; they do not discount themselves. It is the same with congregations.

A congregation does not ape some other congregation. It does not envy any other congregation. It does not spend its time and energies trying to keep up with the Joneses. It says, "If we can't be an oak on the top of the hill, we'll be a wonderful shrub in the valley." Such a congregation will observe what others are doing and will utilize what they discover, but they will not grow grumpy under comparisons. They will see that congregations in rural Maple Grove, in metropolitan Toronto, in tropical Honolulu, in farther-north Anchorage, in Center Stake Stone Church are not going to do all things the same. They will learn how to be themselves in their own right while they live in the ongoing stream of the advancing general church. Yet each congregation will visit in spirit with others. The Master of all congregations speaks to each one: Discover yourself; develop yourself; devote yourself.

A Good-Life Congregation

Read Acts 2:41-47. Here is pictured a congregation of vigorous spiritual health. The believers, recently baptized and covenanted to Jesus Christ, were constituting a new community. Dr. Luke gives us a concise picture and a brotherly appreciation. The opening sentence of this second chapter makes a good prelude: "They were all with one accord in one place." They had come out of this tremendous experience of the Day of Pentecost with (1) a sense of immediate divine presence, (2) a sense of spiritual fellowship in spite of diversity in languages and cultures, (3) a sense of mission to the world. Now they were to live out the gospel they had come to know. Here is what they did that made them a healthy congregation:

1. They were ever learning and exploring together. The record puts it this way: "They continued steadfastly in the apostles' teaching and fellowship." They constituted a school of fellow explorers.

2. They shared their possessions for the good of all. Much has been made of the statement that they had "all things common." The statement has been used to "prove" many socialistic theories. They must have had a common treasury. The main thing of the story is this: they distributed "as every man had need." The big thing was their sense of mutual responsibility and their ministry in the material things needed for living. They must have been a working people.

3. They met in the temple "with one accord." J. B. Phillips' translation has it read that they met "with common consent." Here is a picture of harmony rather than of identity. It is noteworthy that they did not break with the Jerusalem city.

4. They associated in fellowship meals in their several houses, eating "with gladness and singleness of heart." Church dinners for fellowship are not a modern creation. Selling tickets may be. They did something more than attend a Sunday morning meeting together. Here was spiritual fellowship of the first order. The members were happy and healthy.

Team Qualities in the Healthy Congregation

Well might we have a brochure entitled, "A Manual for Players on the All-Branch Team." The roster would include every member who wants to be on the team, who works at being on the team, who wins "on the inside" as he functions on the team. Such a manual would picture a team that brings out the best and uses the best in the members who compose the team. It takes a team of good quality to develop sturdy, healthy players. It takes a team that focuses on the spiritual objectives of the game. Such a company says with the poet,

"There is far too much glorification
     Of money and pleasure and fame;
     Let's find, whatsoe'er be our station,
     Our joy in the love of the game."

These are qualities of the kind of congregation that will develop and utilize good players and impel them to give of their best:

1. Regard for the worth of every person as a son of God with recognition of differences between persons, with respect for his individuality in his native capacities and his cultural background. The branch is not a factory to manufacture identical members.

2. Vision of a total program in which the congregation is participating understandingly. To be interested a participant has to see what it is all about. Without this the round of things is drudgery. A player has to see the game as a whole. A health-producing congregation has objectives to be realized—objectives in bringing good things to pass in the lives of persons.

3. Association for the developing of common understanding that includes "common consent" and the building of morale, a common group spirit. This association is the quality that enables a congregation to say, "We are in this together." In certain sports such get-together is called the "huddle."

4. Acquaintance with great team members of former and present times. Specialists in a field study the skills and the theories and the lives of those who have made good in their profession. This holds for tennis players, musicians, statesmen, and others. Through this acquaintance the congregation builds an image of a good member of the congregation and seeks to bring this into realization in congregational living.

5. Training in techniques and group teamwork. It is imperative that every member discover and train for effective participation in some field. It is demoralizing for one to come into the congregation and do nothing more than attend meetings. Members must have something to do that will call forth creative expression and contribute to the congregation's mission. An athlete on a track team trains for the mile, for the quarter mile, or for the javelin throw; he does more than "go out for track."

6. Balance of concentration and relaxation. The runner calls on every bit of reserve that he has as he runs the half-mile. Then he relaxes and recuperates. The team as a whole uses all its potential in a meet and then enjoys a sociable, nourishing meal together. The healthy congregation works this way, too. There are cycles in the group enthusiasm and concentration.

374

7. Review and evaluation of what is being done. A football coach calls his men together and goes over the recent game. Such a review brings out strengths and weaknesses, cooperation and lack of it, commendation and discount. Such review and evaluation is of worth to the degree that it is sound. The branch does well to learn when and how to say, "Well done, good and faithful servant."

8. Counsel and clinical service for those needing guidance and instruction and encouragement. The healthy congregation is a school affording this clinical service. All persons of all age groups, of whatever equipment and level of achievement, are eligible and cared for.

9. Sense of belonging to and participating in the larger league of the game, with interplay with other playing groups. In this sense the congregation is a branch of a worldwide church. This sense of belonging to the larger league gives color and largess of spirit and greatness of mission. The congregation that lives to itself will shrivel into unhealthiness.

10. Rapport with the Head Coach, the Director of the church. The team feels at home with the Source of inspiration, instruction, integration. Once a great university had an athletic song that read, "With the Grand Old Man to lead you, without a peer you'll stand!" This is the spirit of congregational members who are following Jesus Christ and growing as they follow.

The Congregation Enjoys the Exercise

"I want to get out on the field and stretch my muscles," said an athlete. He continued, "I want to flex my arms and legs and work up a good sweat." No sense of martyrdom here. He enjoyed stiff exercise. Genuine Saints like to stretch their spiritual muscles. Another youth said, "I want to get out on the playing field with God and work up a good spiritual sweat." He said that if he ever got that involved and gave himself completely, he might become a hero there as he had become a much-cited football player.

The health-producing branch likes the feel of stretching spiritual muscles in things worth working and risking for. A tired congregation without the thrill of adventure is on the way out. The we-have-arrived branch is declining. A congregation's members working hard in a well-planned building program said they were combining fun, faith, finance, and fellowship.

Questions for Discussion

1. When would digging a ditch be drudgery and when would it be a play project? Apply this to some activity in the life of a congregation.

2. When might an activity in a congregation be aimless running or beating the air? (See I Corinthians 9:26.)
3. What did the youth mean by "working up a spiritual sweat for God"? What would be an example of such an experience? When would sweating be meritorius?
4. What qualities in a congregation might make it produce such unhealthy influence on members that it might well be quarantined to keep persons out of it?
5. How would you go about developing a healthy condition in such a branch?
6. Under what conditions might a man say, "I feel less healthy when I leave our prayer meeting than when I arrived"?
7. How and why ought congregations, like persons, dare to be themselves in the light of their own resources and conditions? What distinctive activities might a congregation engage in that would bring out healthy individuality? That would make it queer and self-centered?
8. How was the congregation in Jerusalem after the Day of Pentecost a healthy home for the disciples? (See Acts 2.)
9. How might it be unhealthy to maintain breakneck speed and white-hot enthusiasm in a congregation's program? How is it possible to mistake feverish activity for productive effort?
10. How does healthiness require seeing a person in the light of his abilities and using him accordingly? Interpret the comment of a coach, "It is disastrous to try to make a short-distance runner out of a man built to hurl the shot." Yet how is it possible for a person to miscast himself by not seeing hidden potentials? What happens in a person who is miscast and required to do something for which he is not fitted?
11. What qualities mark a first-class coach in any activity? How are these expressed in the "coaching" of Jesus Christ in the congregation team?
12. Translate this into wholesome branch life:
    "It ain't the individual or the army as a whole,
    But the everlasting teamwork of every bloomin' soul."
13. How do we generate team participation in children of the congregation? How do we keep it alive in older members?
14. Apply to the work of your congregation and to the exercising of members this quotation from Kipling:
    "Gardens are not made by singing:
    'Oh, how beautiful!' and sitting in the shade."
    What would constitute sitting in the shade? How might one get overheated?

CHAPTER 32

OUR FAMILIES FUNCTIONING
AS HEALTH CENTERS

Each one of us, as a general rule, starts life in a family group. Here in the first years each gets "the set of the soul." Here each puts together habits and attitudes in sleeping, eating, speaking, keeping clean, and much more. Each is born with bodily equipment which functions in patterns and routines suggested and directed by family habits and values. These patterns are conditioned by the equipment which each has at birth. This also applies to mental life. Each starts with his own mental inheritance. Then comes the stimulating and exercising of this mental equipment in the family circle. What the family does can retard or advance the thinking life. One family can encourage and equip to explore and expand; another can restrict and fence in. What happens during these first five to seven years of childhood is ever so consequential. What takes place in early childhood continues on in the person's world of outlook, of attitude, of self-conception, of relationship with others, of capacity for living and for thinking. Rightly did the young parents of a newly arrived infant say, "We must do this right, for there really will never be any undoing."

Spiritual Health Too

This applies to spiritual health. The family with good healthiness in spirituality will stimulate and develop the child in good ways. There is a contagious quality in the spiritual condition of family living. Fears, phobias, confidences, conceptions will carry over from parents, from other children, to a given child. The reaction will be two-way. If parents, one or both, have a God for occasional contact in time of urgency, a God of black-and-white rules, a God of finicky spirit, a God of jealous nature, this will be the God the child comes to know. And the reverse conceptions apply also. If God is left out of family life, the child will have an empty place in his growing experience. A girl of twelve confided that her mother was always wondering if every specific word, every specific act was pleasing God. This girl came to look upon God as the "Great Snoop." Another girl had a mother who thought of God's role as providing whatever she asked for, without consideration of personal rightness or of God's purpose, so she conceived God as listening on a kind of cosmic telephone system to hear requests from "here below." "Sometimes," she confided, "I have to call two or three times." Said a twelve-year-old boy, "I got the idea from my dad that tithing was a kind of insurance. He paid up so things would turn out well. That meant here and now as well as hereafter." In contrast, another boy said, "Our family paid tithing just as regularly as we paid the electric bills. No question about it. I got the idea that it was the right thing to do and that we were sharing in God's business."

Grandparents Are in the Picture

Grandparents affect the tone and the theme of family spirituality. In the terms of youth a grandfather can be a "sourpuss," a "saintly patriarch," a "self-centered prude," a "first-class storyteller," or more. Many a youth has testified, "I got most of my religious training and belief from my grandmother [or grandfather]." There is a difference in grandparents. One youth observed that from one grandfather he saw the church as the biggest enterprise in living, a great undertaking with God. He got the feeling that it was something worth getting into. Then he said his other grandfather always wore dark-tinted glasses—"The church was a pain in the neck; the members needed working over; and even God could stand a little advising, particularly from Grandad."

What Kind of Love?

Healthy spirituality involves healthy loving, in both giving and receiving. "God is love!" say the scriptures. We need to realize that not everything that passes under the name "love" is the kind of love that inheres in God. Some love ascribed to God is neither fair to him nor wholesome to the person. Said a youth in his late teens, "The God that I pictured from my childhood teaching was pretty much centered in God himself. He wanted everyone to tell him what a great guy he was. He would smack down anybody that did not approach him just right. I got the idea that I could get things if I approached him on the right side and gave him gifts he liked. Then he would love me." He said he got this in his family life and from his Sunday school teaching. He had to have a revolution in the way he thought of "divine love."

To exhort to love is not enough. Loving has to be lived out in accordance with God's way of loving. And God's way has to be seen soundly, healthfully. This love always asks what is best for the person loved, for the person loving, for persons round about. God's love is expressed at the moment but it is expressed in the perspective of eternity. It looks at what is going to be best for the person in the long view, in the wide range. It looks to the total self of the loving and the loved. This delivers from indulgence and affectional incest.

Such a conception of love provides foundation for love expression—family living that is conducive to good spiritual health.

1. Give love; do not barter affection. This applies to person-with-person and to person-with-God relationship. The two are to operate together. God loves us whether or not we love him. No baiting is involved. Our response to him does, however, condition his response to us. Healthy love is outgoing without consideration of getting something back, even love. Yet love can have depth and breadth when there is reciprocity. But reciprocity does not mean baiting or bartering.

2. Extend the radius of the circle of those loved. At first the family circle is small. In a sense the child is the center. The world of interest and experience should continually increase. The circle of affection should push out and out. The family is a laboratory in brotherly outreach. By printed page, by radio and TV, by flesh-and-blood persons, the world life can be brought into the home. Parents and children join in appreciating and caring for others. Said a lad of a church family, "When I was five we sent a Christmas gift box to a family in Holland. We signed a card and sent it. We located where they lived. We had a family worship as we sent off the box. It stretched my heart. I loved the Dutch boy I had never seen."

3. Understand the whole person in his setting. "Wholeness" was prominent in Jesus' vocabulary. He saw every phase of a person. He wanted the person to hang together in spiritual unity. Aunt Nancy is more than the sugar cookies she bakes or the scar on her left cheek. Seven-year-old John is more than muddy shoes or a dimpled smile. To love or to hate on the basis of some one phase or some one ability is not sound.

4. Focus on the worthful and the lovable in persons. This

does not overlook the not-so-good. God is aware of our short-comings and our blunderings. He helps us to build up the noble and the worthful in us. This tends to crowd out the less desirable. We shall accentuate the worthful in others and express appreciation for it, helping them to feel useful and wanted.

5. Practice looking together and working together in projects in which goodness is creative and forward-looking. Love is more than looking at one another; it is looking together at something worth looking at. Sound family love means looking together with God. Whenever we look with God, we labor with God. The family does family-size projects with God. So do they grow in loving with God.

Honesty with Wholeness

Healthy spirituality has no pretenses, no veneers. It looks to "the God of things as they are" (Kipling). It also sees potential for bringing to pass "things as they shall be." It sees things as they have been. In short, spiritual honesty sees the whole picture. It does not cover up with excuses, false fronts, and the like. It sees how every person has to start from where he is when he moves toward where he ought to be. The prodigal son starts from the pigpen. The prince starts from his palace. Each person works with what he has and makes the most of it. So the Wells family admitted to themselves that they were incompetent in their English expression. They wanted to increase their competency in church and in community life. So they circled the table and studied together. They prayed. Said the mother, "We have the ain't-got-none type of talking and we don't want to stay that way." Pretending would have worked to their detriment.

The family is to be a training school in honesty. This means getting the total picture. It is not strictly honest to get hold of some one liked or disliked quality of a person or a situation and separate it from the total context. God does not do this, nor should we. If a person makes a mistake, it is not fair to distort this beyond its relationship to all else, nor is it honest to disregard it. True honesty carries the picture of wholeness. This applies to Dad's eccentricities, to Mother's peculiarities, to Junior's unpredictables.

If family life is to further and deepen spiritually it must cultivate spiritual honesty. It will see both strengths and weaknesses in each person, in the family, in the congregation, in the general church. It will see each as it is; it will also vision what each can become. The honest family will have price tags on things and experiences as evaluated in the total scheme of living. It will try to see God's values in God's perspective.

More than Clinics

A "center" is a functioning association. It lives out what it sets out to do. The family, as a health center, practices healthy spiritual living. Evaluation and exercise go together. Diagnosis is related to doing. Occasionally a family takes on the nature of a clinic. Then the emphasis may be on designating symptoms and diagnosing cases. One such family almost substituted for the greeting, "Good morning!" the inquiry, "What distresses do you have today?" Once in such a family the greeting of a visitor, "How are you today?" elicited the reply, "I'm spiritually not so well, nor physically either. I couldn't sleep last night." Conversation disclosed that the "afflicted one" had spent much of the night listing her physical and her spiritual aches and pains. In the home of a couple just over seventy years of age, breakfast conversation consisted chiefly of review of distresses and diseases and disaster. The major early morning ritual was going through the pills and tonics taken, with a listing of maladies and an inventory of prices of medicines. All of this is caricatured in the line "You look all right this morning; how am I?"

Sometimes mental hygiene is preoccupied with abnormalities and diseases. These need to be explored, but there also needs to be consideration of factors involved in healthy-mindedness. So with spiritual hygiene. There are sin and self-centeredness in our world, true, but accounting and lamenting this will not produce healthy spirituality. We need to identify the truly spiritual person and to determine what makes him so. We want to find out how he and God live together so as to produce this spiritual healthiness.

Too often in our modern world we give emphasis to a clinical approach—that is, to what is wrong inside a person and in his relations with others. A name is given to the malady. Often the person is counseled to break with factors that helped bring on the malady but he is not pointed toward persons and practices and resources that will build improved mental health. Here is where sound religion ought to enter into the picture. Long ago we were advised to "cease to do evil, learn to do well." The family is to be more than a clinic to diagnose: it is to be a center to develop spiritual healthiness.

Family conversation will reveal whether the group is making the "diagnosing" or the "doing" approach. A recording of family conversation would bring out whether emphasis is upon what's-wrong conditions or on what's-good desires and interests. When a person is not in good spiritual health, it is well to see this honestly, but reviewing it and rehashing symptoms and discomforts will not restore good health. Neither fateful pessimism nor foolish optimism will bring to pass good health. It will take some thinking up, reaching out, and moving on to get into the life-giving powers of God. One youth made this observation: "The kind of conversation we have at our meals is enough to give us all poor digestion and spiritual stomachache." A girl once confided, "I got fed up on religion on my mother's steady diet of finding fault with others and feeling sorry for herself." Conversation in the family can carry disease or provide spiritual buildup.

In Centers Persons Do Things

Today community centers are operating in metropolitan centers and in smaller cities and villages to further the well-being of persons and the welfare of the community. There are gymnasiums and swimming pools. There are halls for dramatic expression. There are classrooms for learning cooking, sewing, interior decorating. There are sites for camping. With this goes instruction in theory and practice in the field concerned. There is "talking-about" but there is emphasis on participation. One director puts it this way, "We offer facilities and counsel but we cannot do the things for them."

Let the family be considered a center for achieving spiritual health. This means the family will do things together in a healthy way. Then spiritual health will be a by-product. There is no substitute for doing health-producing projects in a health-producing way. And we do these with God, the Source of spiritual health. A family of four was asked to conduct a twenty-minute devotional service as the first session of the church school. They were advised of this six weeks in advance. The theme was "Testifying of God's Love." They might have planned it so Don, the son, would have announced and stated the theme; Dorothy, the daughter, might have read the scripture. Mother might have told a story and Father offered a prayer. This would have been unrelated participation. This family, the Baldwins, talked about the love of God. They decided that before they could speak of it to others they would need to do something so they could experience outreach to others. Don invited to an evening meal two boys of his school who might be said to live on the other side of the tracks. The family talked about a suitable menu, a program for arriving, for getting seated, for conversing. They planned the evening this way: There would be a game of ping-pong. After the meal there would be a short ride and the boys would be deposited at their homes. As usual, there would be a prayer of thanks at the opening of the meal. Mr. Baldwin would do this so the boys would see a man pray. The Baldwins prayed as they worked on their project. They wanted to "testify" in a helpful way. After their entertaining of these two not-so-privileged boys they had the heart to lead a worship service. The spiritual health of the entire family picked up.

Yes, a family center does things "together with God" in a health-producing way. The family explores and exercises.

Discipline and Desire

Being spiritually healthy should be the common desire of all members of the family. No member can be happy by doing things he "has to." There is no place for the attitude of the father of artistic taste who said to his ten-year-old son concerning a symphony orchestra concert, "You're going to like this if I have to thrash you to make you like it." One mother heard in a class on religious life in the home that there should be scripture reading in the family. So she came home and brought forth the Bible, the Book of Mormon, and the Doctrine and Covenants. She was going to see that her family heard them through. She started in without preparation, understanding, or expression. The family responded with indifference and then with rebellion. The experiment brought only damage. Her attitude had been, "You'll listen, whether or no." Strict discipline without like or desire will not create a healthy atmosphere.

God designs us to be self-managing persons who chart our courses in accord with his life-producing plans. He wants us to *want* to. Every directive he gives us is for our good health, never to satisfy some whim of his for giving orders. This quality is to pervade family living. Parents should not give orders to satisfy their desire to be boss. The parent looks to the welfare of the immature child as he insists on obedience before the child can manage himself. Gradually the child learns to make decisions. One day he stands on his own feet. Good health looks to the emergence and to the expansion of self-management. When this management looks to and lines up with God, it is designated as spiritual.

Healthiness calls for understanding. Religion often makes much of "obedience" and "commandments." Jesus kept breathing new meaning into both words. He kept developing his disciples above servility and pointed to a relationship of discernment and desire. He did not vision puppets pulled by a string. George H. Preston in *The Substance of Mental Health* (page 43) says this concerning healthy self-management:

> "Absolute obedience is no virtue. Obedience is a means to an end, never an end in itself. A competely obedient child might be an extra arm for its father or an extra pair of legs for its mother, but it would always be a part of someone else, never an independent adult. As soon as orders and directions ceased, the child would fall in a helpless heap like a puppet with loose strings."

The family as a spiritual health center will look to the development in each person progressively through the years the desire to be spiritually healthy and the intent to live in health-producing ways. God will be consultant, counselor, provider, in the business of being spiritually healthy. And parents will function as co-workers with God. The family will assemble resources for doing the job well. The word "we" will be very prominent in the health operations. There will be "common consent," "common concern," "common conference," and "common communion."

The Family as Health Center

Imagine a sign like the following placed on the bulletin board of your home. It gives a professional flavor to the project. Perhaps you would include the persons on the staff.

THE DAVID F. BROWN SPIRITUAL HEALTH CENTER
A Station in God's Health Program
Operating Twenty-four Hours Each Day
Motto: SPIRITUAL HEALTH IN EVERY MEMBER OF OUR FAMILY

Such a center will have effective outreach. Those who come and tarry will sense the healthy atmosphere. They will see how the family members work together in mutual support, in contagious faith and stimulating hope. They will see how the family faces up to problems without excuses or escapes. They will observe how the family does health-producing activities together. Then the Browns, because they aim at wholesome living, will be able and qualified to speak to those who come their way about the fullness of the gospel. Spiritually healthy persons and families are free to witness of a health-producing gospel.

Habits of a Health Center Family

1. The habit of *enjoying* spiritual health. Some religionists have extolled the frail body as if it would be wrong to have good health. There is no virtue in being run down in spirit and sad in outlook. Saints are to *enjoy* spiritual well-being in God's sense of being joyful.

2. The habit of complementing *spiritual* health and physical health. The two go together. Neither is to be discounted. It is unsound to develop a husky physique for no reason other than to exhibit it. The gospel of Jesus Christ elevates and blends the two.

3. The habit of programming for healthy living without fussing about it. One doctor told a young mother her child would probably have better health if she threw her thermometer away. While he believed parents should be informed about body temperatures and have equipment for ascertaining this condition, he saw that the children could not spend their time sucking a thermometer and mothers occupy themselves in reading one. It is not unlikely that some persons need to get rid of their spiritual thermometers. Fussiness and faith do not go together.

4. The habit of facing spiritual health situations honestly and squarely. A family need not disintegrate or go into a panic when someone has a stomachache or a headache. They endeavor to see why and treat the situation accordingly. Nor should a family go into a state of worry when someone exhibits a spiritual pain or perplexity. This applies to many strains. Once a young teen-ager told his mother he was having adolescent doubt. Wisely she set up a situation as if this were a problem to be diagnosed and the two enjoyed the probing and the prescribing.

5. The habit of bringing in competent counseling service. Counselors may come into the home or family members may go to the counselors. Such advisers will see the questions clearly before they work on solutions. Matters in spiritual health may range

from omission to commission, from theology to sociology, from sacraments to sex, from baptism to agnosticism, and so on. The wise family knows how and when and with whom to consult.

6. The habit of praying so that God's health-producing resources can enter into daily living. Such praying seeks to cooperate with God. It says, Guide me that I may be healthy. Help me to be whole! It does not ask God to do the exercises for us that would enable us to be healthy; rather it encourages us to buckle down to consistent living that will strengthen our health.

7. The habit of sharing in building community living that visions and fosters spiritual health. Family members see they can be healthy to the degree that others whose lives touch theirs are healthy, too. This is Zion building.

8. The habit of identifying and releasing tensions. Saints do not hold grudges, cover up festering sores, pretend love when there is dislike or hatred. Covering up cankerous situations gets in the way. The gospel of spiritual health releases from fears and strains. This gospel does not direct us to agree with everybody and condone everything. The healthy man stands up against evil but he does not get tied in knots while he does so. The healthy family can have harmony with diversity. They know how to talk things through rather than "scrapping things out" or "forcing festers in."

9. The habit of interpreting the health of members according to the needs and natures of persons. We differ in metabolism, in gland operation, in digestive tracts, in nerve sensitivity. We are not identicals in capacities and sensitivities for spiritual health. Wise is the family that senses this. David and John were brothers. One was at home in things of machinery, one with thoughts in engineering. One was ready to go to work enthusiastically as soon as he got up in the morning; the other needed time to "get going." One wanted someone to give final, finished answers about God; the other wanted to explore and expected relative statements about God. One heard "Thus saith the Lord" and that provided sufficient evidence; the other asked what the content of the message meant and how much God was in it. The family got along well because the parents sensed the differences in the spiritual needs and hungers of their two sons.

10. The habit of keeping in touch with persons, programs, printed materials that contribute to healthy spirituality. Just as physical medicine keeps expanding, so should spiritual medicine.

Just as competent men of medicine want to keep up, so ought men of ministry. A church that believes in and practices continuing revelation is expected to keep growing in matters of spiritual health. Health cultivates and is always contemporary.

11. The habit of identifying healthy spirituality in terms of wholeness of persons and fruitage in wholesome living. The family is able to perceive men and women who are truly spiritual in spirituality that gets beyond surface expression and conventional forms and functions deeply in personhood. Then shallow spirituality will not satisfy truly healthy Saints.

12. The habit of involving our health-affording God in all aspects of well-balanced family living. Such a God lives on the playing field and in the prayer meeting, at the kitchen sink and at the altar, in the keeping of financial records and in the making of friendly visits. Such a family has one God. So shall the family be one fold with one Shepherd.

Questions for Discussion

1. How is the family environment so important during the first five years of a child's life in conditioning his spiritual life?

2. How may the parent's conception of God and of communion with God affect a child's spiritual health?

3. How may too great, too constrained concern about spiritual health get in the way of achieving good spiritual health in the family?

4. How is doing things together by members of the family essential for laboratory expression in achieving spiritual health? What kind of projects promote this?

5. What kind of family praying can undermine spiritual health? What kind can promote it? What praying might be unhealthy in family living?

6. How may "church workers" become so involved in "church activities" that their own family drops behind in spiritual health?

7. How would you go about developing a sound conception of spirituality, of "spiritual persons" in your family? How would you lay a foundation before you planned likes and dislikes? How would you make spirituality in persons appeal to youth?

8. How can the gospel appeal to your friends, as they come into your home, through the spiritual health of your family life?

9. What are some functions the family can perform more effectively than any other social group to further spiritual health?

10. Picture a spiritually healthy family in terms of what the family does and thinks and feels. Have you been in such a family?

11. How does the realization of our church mission require spiritually healthy families?

12. If your family is thought of as a health center, what are some of the things you would put on the agendum for discussion in one of your meetings?

CHAPTER 33

OUR MEMBERS DEVELOPING
HABITS THAT "HEALTHIFY"

There is no such word as "healthify" but there ought to be. For this consideration we are coining it with the meaning "to make us healthy." The thesis of this consideration is simple: what our habits are in "spiritual exercise" conditions what our spiritual health will be. It is of utmost importance that we give sound and continuing attention to what these habit patterns are going to be and how we are going to manage them. They can make or break our spiritual health.

We Live by Habit

Right after birth the random expression of our organism tends to fall into patterns of response. We call this habit formation. The physical equipment prefers and the social environment insists. A habit may be thought of as a disposition, an inclination, a preference left by previous experience. It is quite an elaborate process to weave the many habits of a person together into an integrated whole. A person's habit system can become a server or a master.

Habits are insistent. They are not trappings to be donned or removed at a wish. The set of the organism has something to say. The environment, physical and social, exerts pressure. A youth who has learned fingering on the piano in his own awkward way is not free to drop it and pick up another system by saying, "I will change." Conversion does not come at an instant. Habit patterns involve moods and attitudes. Thus if we form a thorough dislike for a person, however much we wish to be well disposed toward him we do not alter our attitude by saying, "He is all right!" This applies to desirable and to undesirable habits.

It is urgent, then, that every person learn something about habit management. He needs to develop a clear notion of the kind of person he wants to be, and what he considers of most worth. Then he must develop and manage a program of habits that will enable him to realize all this. Our habit systems must be progressive. They must be evaluated continually. A habit can enslave us or free us. It can pull us backward or point us forward.

Habits are needed for efficiency. If we had no grooves, no patterns, and we had to think through our responses for each situation, how tiresome all this would be and how ineffective would be our responses. Habit expression frees us to give attention to more complicated features of situations. This applies to conveying bread to our mouth in a meal and to reaching for the bread in the sacrament of the Lord's Supper. In both of these there is a great variety in expression. Thus in one congregation the receivers of the bread in the Communion service chew the morsel; in others convention requires that the bread be dissolved in the mouth. Habits of simple social usage do not have uniformity and we have to choose how we are going to develop them.

The Counsel of William James

Several years ago William James presented in his *Psychology* what still remains the classic treatise on habit. He was really preaching a sermon about habit programming. He wrote that we are making for ourselves a heaven or a hell, here and now, "by habitually fashioning our characters." He points out the fallacy of the comment of the drunken Rip Van Winkle in Jefferson's play as he excuses each fresh dereliction by saying, "I won't count this time!" But the body, the personality, the society count it. William James says that his action is stored up to be used against him when the next temptation comes. It is fortunate that the advantages of good habits are stored up, too.

The wise person gives attention to the kinds of habits he wants to build and incorporate into the self. Dr. James reminds us to make our nervous systems our allies instead of our enemies; our habits are servants to achieve the good life rather than slave drivers to hold us in worn-out or worthless ways.

Ranking foremost in habit consideration is the habit of forming and using intelligent habits. Here are a few of these essential habits: The habit of openmindedness with the tendency to discount prejudice; the habit of inquiry with the habit of seeking and stating problems and their explanations; the habit of self-reliance with the tendency to work on one's own and use one's own resources. This list might go one and on. These are enough to indicate that the person who wishes to develop and maintain good spiritual health must look to achieving a pattern of health-producing habits. They will function as effectively as habits of breathing fresh clean air, eating nourishing food, and brushing the teeth in caring for the physical body.

Fifty-three Habits that Further Spiritual Health

This is not a year's calendar of habits, one for each week. Rather does it stand forth as a program of habits which are to be incorporated into a coordinated, balanced way of living for good spiritual health. These recommendations recognize that when a person acts spiritually, he acts with his whole self. There is no divorce from his "physical" living, from his "mental" living, from his "social" living. Whatever furthers healthy living in any of these fields makes for good spiritual health.

Our General Outlook toward Living

1. The habit of seeing things and thoughts and persons in relationships, with broad overview. This calls for seeing from the mountaintop. It avoids narrowness and provincialism and five-minute wishes.

2. The habit of discarding whatever gets in the way of spiritual healthiness. This includes grouches, phobias, superstitions, hatreds, and the like. These clog up the spiritual system.

3. The habit of thinking honestly, seeing fairly, and facing facts and situations as they are. One cannot answer a problem by denying its existence. Good health calls for spiritual integrity.

4. The habit of exploring with zest and sound purpose to discover what has not been seen to date. This is requisite for seeking revelation.

5. The habit of finding satisfaction in well-executed creative endeavor. There is joy in productive effort, in the use of initiative, in doing a good day's work.

6. The habit of expecting that in the long run, in the large view, the right and noble will prevail, with divine support. Here the conception of the right and the noble is seen in God's perspective rather than in conventional notions. There is no surrendering to the idea that evil will win out.

7. The habit of distinguishing between what is beyond one's power to change and what is within one's powers to change partially or comprehensively. This includes gracious acceptance of what one cannot alter.

8. The habit of singing in one's heart, in one's family, in one's congregation songs of many moods and messages for life's full repertoire. The healthy person has more than one dirge or one lyric.

9. The habit of expecting that each age of life can be a "golden age," rich in its own pursuits and possibilities. This includes the habit of looking toward each coming age of life with anticipation.

10. The habit of praying as communing with God that one may discover his way and accord therewith. This connotes rising above asking God to change his planning in order to satisfy one's whims and wants.

11. The habit of observing and enjoying the useful and the beautiful in God's universe; of lining up with God in bringing to pass the beautiful and the useful, thus revealing God and helping man.

12. The habit of working with God to achieve good life rather than of expecting God to "do it all." This calls for the habit of joyful, adventurous cooperation with God.

13. The habit of expecting God to be thoroughly contemporary in manifold expressions of his creativity; of permitting God in one's thinking, in one's living, to be truly contemporary as well as historic.

14. The habit of relaxing in one's communing with God in the confidence that he understands our natures and our needs and will assist accordingly. There is no place for abject fear or servility in this relationship.

15. The habit of maintaining consistent, continuing relations with God and with God's people without bargaining with God or endeavoring to bring God to one's own terms for some specific situation.

16. The habit of disciplining one's life for the ministry of the Holy Spirit to develop spiritual "fruits" in one's personhood, which discipline is healthy management of life without unhealthy tensions, denials, and discount of any phase of the total body or total personhood.

17. The habit of relying on God's basic fairness and his love for every person, on his fatherly provisions for life here and hereafter, without bent toward speculation or concern about rewards and securities in the hereafter.

18. The habit of seeing one's sins as shortcomings, as alienations from God's person and plan, with identifiable recognition of the nature of one's sinfulness and sins.

19. The habit of immersing one's self more understandingly, more effectively in God's life-producing spiritual power and ongoing endeavor. This calls for developing insight into God's nature and program.

20. The habit of responding to the invitation to meet the living Christ, to listen to him, to draw inspiration from him, to work with him. This looks to a continuing revelation of Jesus Christ.

21. The habit of sensing the majesty and eternal greatness of God, and also the love of God that reaches out to blundering and needing persons, such as I.

Our Getting Along with Ourselves

22. The habit of discovering one's own resources for becoming a "son of God," of developing these potentials and devoting them to God and to God's people as a stewardship.

23. The habit of blending food and fellowship at meals with relaxation and enjoyable response. There is realization that the atmosphere one creates has bearing upon good digestion of body and of mind.

24. The habit of laying problems and anxieties on the table at the close of the day before retiring for sleep. Excess baggage is not taken to bed.

25. The habit of maintaining resiliency and power to adjust to changing situations while maintaining a core of principles and values that are valid in new conditions. This differs from the chameleon that surrenders to and changes with every new situation.

26. The habit of accepting consequences for what one does without alibis, without blaming others, without whining for easy ways out. The honest person says, "I did it and this is the outcome."

27. The habit of maintaining cleanliness in body, in mind, in feelings, with inclusive concept of cleanliness and without fanaticism on a few points or patterns; without strain in carrying on a program of spiritual sanitation.

28. The habit of modulating one's voice and managing emphases and phrasings that express one's spiritual poise and values.

29. The habit of managing one's financial resources in terms of balance of income and outgo, in terms of major needs and an inclusive program of living. This involves participation of partners where they are involved. It calls for freedom from control by prevailing patterns of wants.

30. The habit of maintaining a sense of humor that is clean, without barbs, that sees the incongruities and oddities of one's own self and one's own way of living, as well as those of others. Such humor provides relaxation and expresses one's appreciation of the truly worthful.

31. The habit of sensing one's own worth in God's sight without concentrating on one's own status and security. The gospel does not lead to self-pity, to self-adulation, to self-crucifixion, to self-parade, to self-indulgence.

32. The habit of conversing constructively, creatively on topics that are expandable, and contributive to personal and social welfare.

33. The habit of inventorying one's self, one's family, one's social groups, one's church in the light of enduring worth and contribution to God's purpose, rather than a keeping-up-with-others rating.

34. The habit of anticipating something interesting in persons, places, situations, that contribute to one's fund for living.

35. The habit of meeting persons in life, history, literature, the scriptures who will contribute to the understanding of what life is all about and how persons go about living.

36. The habit of searching for the source of unpleasant and undesirable factors rather than identifying whose "fault" it is.

37. The habit of expressing gratitude to others and to God for the truly meritorious things that come to pass, with sincerity and joyful artfulness.

38. That habit of finding satisfaction in service expressed for the well-being of others, without concern for recognition or reward for what one does.

39. The habit of appreciating and enjoying persons in their own culture patterns, judging each person on his merits.

40. The habit of arranging for occasions to be with others and for occasions to be alone with God, with awareness of the essentiality of both occasions. The aloneness is required for creative insight, for spiritual vision and renewal.

41. The habit of sharing the gospel of Jesus Christ in person-with-person-relationships for the spiritual uplift of these persons, with joy and competency in the sharing.

Our Participation in the Church's Life and Mission

42. The habit of interpreting and validating the gospel in terms of the transformation of persons toward and into Christ-likeness; the habit of finding satisfaction in this transformation.

43. The habit of using scriptures for getting hold of principles and procedures that will guide in the business of living.

44. The habit of seeing the roles of all age groups in God's program for the church, with insights into the contributions available in each group and the services needed by each group. No group has a monopoly; no group is to be merely tolerated. The habit of speaking the languages of many groups.

45. The habit of associating work and worship in the work of

the church, as in one's own life, of seeing the partiality of work without worship and the emptiness of worship disassociated with working with God.

46. The habit of observing the Lord's day in fellowshiping with the congregation and the family in worthful endeavors, for recuperation, and for freshening in spiritual healthfulness.

47. The habit of contributing intelligently and cooperatively in achieving functional common consent in church life, with ability to contribute in materials and methods and spiritual sensitivity.

48. The habit of considering salvation as a continuing experience in which the person, the family, the church, and society come into oneness with God, with consequent healthful living. The habit of seeing the services and sacraments of the church functioning in this continuing salvation.

49. The habit of participating in the Lord's Supper as a means of starting anew, for sensing forgiveness, for recommitment, for fellowship with followers of Jesus Christ.

50. The habit of sensing diversities and relativities in the spiritual achievements of members and ministers of the church, with appreciation of God's ministering to each person, to each group in accordance with their levels of spiritual living; the habit of wanting the higher levels of spirituality.

51. The habit of recognizing one's mistakes and omissions in relation to other members of the fellowship, with honest willingness to improve one's relationships, with God's help.

52. The habit of observing the festivals, the anniversary times of the church, with freshness and intent to celebrate the spiritual meaning and further service to others.

53. The habit of reaching out to others at home and abroad with a sense of the divinely intended oneness of all persons in all the world, with a growing sense of fellowship with persons of all continents, cultures, colors.

Maxims of Spiritual Health from Jesus Christ

Jesus of Nazareth lived healthfully and he spread health wherever he went. He was concerned with every phase of healthful living. He gave attention and healing to leprosy of the body and leprosy of the spirit. Here are some of his outstanding directives to his disciples about living so as to merit good spiritual health. Taken together, they assure spiritual healthiness.

1. "Seek ye first to build up the kingdom of God, and to establish his righteousness."—Matthew 6:38.

Spiritual living calls for active searching. There is no place for anemic sitting down and waiting. The disciple is called to constructive work with God as expressed in "build up" and "establish." Here is designated priority in what one does.

2. "Be of good cheer; . . . let not your heart be troubled."—John 16:33, 14:1.

This magnificent counsel was given when it looked as if his cause was collapsing. His enemies were doing their worst. Jesus looked through and beyond and saw with longtime perspective. There is no place for surrender, for fruitless anxiety. Keep moving ahead with hope, was his counsel.

3. "Let your light so shine! . . . I give unto you to be the light of the world!"—Matthew 5:18, 16.

Throughout his ministry he spoke of himself as "the Light of the world." He kept speaking of spiritual living as enlightened, as radiating this light. There is no place for darkness, ignorance, blindness. This call to be the light assigns man a high and significant responsibility. Man is to be somebody in God's program.

4. "Follow me, and I will make you fishers of men!"—Matthew 4:18.

The Master himself goes before as guide. He invites disciples to evangelistic ministry that will make something worthful and productive of them. There is to be no mere sitting in the congregation, no occupying observers' seats. They are to be in the laboratory of ministering. So shall they develop.

5. "Love thy neighbor . . . love your enemies."—Matthew 5:45, 46.

Spiritual health has no place for barriers that separate the loved from the not-loved. Jesus pictured hating as destroying the one who hates. The one who hates is sick. Jesus himself loved a man when he disagreed with his way of life. Jesus' circle of living is all-inclusive.

A Life of Unhealthy Habits

This portrait is of a member of the church, an ordained man. Often we are inclined to think of persons of unhealthy spiritual habits as being outside the church. Not so. There can be and are twisted, worrying, anxious, self-centered persons inside our fellowship. We shall call this man Floyd Oliver. He tries to keep busy in congregational matters. He takes the *Saints' Herald*. The Bible, the Book of Mormon, and the Doctrine and Covenants are on his table. He pays his tithing. But he is not spiritually healthy. Here are some of the habits that undermine Floyd's health. He has the habit of reviewing the sins of the world and being thankful that he is not addicted to these sins. . . . He ponders on disasters to come on mankind with belief that he will be spared. . . . He has little or no sense of humor, for he is commanded to ponder on "the solemnities of eternity." . . . He is irritated by children and youth, for they get in the way of his performing his ministry. . . . He testifies of his afflictions and wonders why these had to happen to him, while he vows to submit to "the will of God." . . . He considers himself "the head of the house" and finds no place for the way of common consent in family living. . . . He preaches much on the afterlife and wants assurance that he will receive celestial glory. . . . He wants to "magnify his office and calling" and considers that he is not being used to the full extent of his preaching potential.

A Life of Healthy Habits

This man is also a member of the church, an elder. He is forty years of age, a mechanic. He and his wife have three children, two sons 16 and 13 and a daughter 10. We shall identify him as David Calkins. When their youngest child, physically and mentally retarded, died three years ago David opened his heart to understand parents who faced similar problems. . . . He says of his sons, "Teen-agers are unpredictable—that is what makes them interesting." . . . He conducted family sessions on purchasing a new car and replaced himself on two of the committees, finance and engine efficiency. . . . He pledged himself to support the recently elected president of the branch—he himself had been nominated but not elected. . . . He smiled when told that a friend had made a caustic comment about him, with the observation, "Well, he has an interesting topic for conversation." . . . He reviewed a prophetic message given at the recent reunion and asked himself, "What are the implications of this for what I shall be doing?" . . . He visits elderly Sister Cochran and reports to her the up-and-coming news of the church. . . . He enjoys his work as custodian of the branch's church building and thanks members for their cooperative support. . . . He has this inscription above his desk, from R. W. Emerson, "See how the mass of men worry themselves into nameless graves, while here and there a great unselfish soul forgets himself into immortality."

A Call to Spiritual Healthiness

This is a great day for the Church of Jesus Christ to affirm the gospel of spiritual healthiness. Statistics and observation reveal that millions of persons are needing this gospel. On all sides can be seen persons troubled with low-grade spiritual health. Some collapse. Some are torn by worry and anxiety. Some find life meaningless with little or nothing to live for. Some feel lonesome and unwanted. Some are victimized by fears and phobias. Some are centered in themselves and are concerned lest others do not sense their importance. Some carry along guilt and cast-off apprehensions. Some are dominated by hot tempers. Some are held captive by sins and passions. Some say simply, "I'm no good." Others exalt themselves as if too good for association with those about them. Some hate life but are afraid to die. Some want to get rid of themselves. Some put on artificial fronts to cover up the emptiness on the inside. And the list can go on.

The gospel of good spiritual health can be shared with such persons and such groups only by those who are themselves in good spiritual health. The Man of Nazareth lived out the spiritual health he spoke. His great purpose, his enduring confidence, his inclusive love, his adventurous faith, his integration of everything in him in one effective harmony, his interest in all persons from children to the old and from the poor to the rich, his fruitful praying—these and more stood out everywhere. He was the living witness of spiritual health. Our world needs learners in Christ's school of good spiritual health who will go among moderns and live out the message of spiritual healthiness.

The company of health-speaking ambassadors will say to the world, "Our gospel comes to you not in word or in print only but in spiritual hope and health revealed in and made possible by the Exponent and Exemplar of spiritual health." Such persons are spiritually fit. Living in this condition is so wonderful that they want to keep on living here and hereafter.

Questions for Discussion

1. How may habits serve us well in providing economy, stability, ease in what we do? How may habits get in the way and prevent our moving on to better ways of living?

2. How may habitual ways and patterns assist and hinder in conducting meetings?

3. When are habit patterns helpful and when retarding in our practices of praying?

4. How may habit patterns stultify or stimulate speaking?

5. To what degree and in what manner may we say that habitual forms are desirable in thinking and talking about the gospel?

6. How would you go about rebuilding the habit program of Floyd Oliver? In what ways is he spiritually unhealthy?

7. What are some additional habits that you would recommend for the spiritual health of David Calkins?

8. Of the fifty-three habits listed as conducive to good spiritual health, which ones do you consider call for cultivation in your own life, in the life of your family, in the life of your congregation?

9. Interpret, "You have to live with a person quite awhile to ascertain whether he is spiritually healthy."

10. What qualities would you include in a listing to designate *spiritual healthiness* that you would want in a witness of the gospel of spiritual health? What qualities would qualify a person; what qualities would disqualify a person?

11. Expand the statement, "Saints are spiritually healthy persons."

12. Interpret, "When a person fusses and fidgets about his spirituality, he is not very healthy."

13. How may Philippians 4:8 be considered an epitome of the gospel of health when thinking is seen in relation to doing? How does this necessarily include God and his Spirit?

14. List seven to ten basics about "healthifying" persons that you see as fundamentals in the gospel of good spiritual health needed in our modern world.

CHAPTER 34

OUR SMALL COMPANIES
FRONTIERING IN
SPIRITUAL FELLOWSHIP

There are possibilities to be explored in small fellowships of spiritually healthy persons. There is need for such fellowships in terms of what they can do in modern life. These can be circles of voluntary nature in which adults or youth come together for mutual support and inspiration in saintly living. As a rule these do not come together through the suggestion or the direction of some central organizing agency. Persons who come together in such groups feel that they have "something in common," that they can grow in spiritual healthiness through associating wisely and informally together. They have a sense of genuine fellowship that does not require a name, that does not call for a constitution. The word *we* is important and descriptive. The words *brother* and *sister* are meaningful salutations.

Where Two or Three Are Gathered

This idea of the power and desirability of the small fellowship is long-standing and mature. The Talmud of the Jews has the saying that if two sit together and there are words of the Torah between them, the *Shekinah,* that is, the presence of God, rests between them. This passage is saying that the glory of God's presence is found where two agree in meditation on the sacred law. Jesus may have been stimulated by this when he was conversing with his disciples during the latter days of his ministry when he said, "Where two or three are gathered together in my name, there am I in the midst of them" (Matthew 18:20). This counsel of Jesus set forth (1) the association with one accord, (2) the spirit of the gathering "in my name," that is, in the nature and the spirit of Jesus Christ, and (3) the promise of the presence of God. The fulfillment of this promise was to carry the disciples through many a dark and dangerous time in the years that followed Jesus' making of this statement.

During those first centuries of the Christian movement there were no public meetinghouses, no "churches." Often congregations must have been small as they met in private houses. When Paul wrote to Philemon he saluted "the church in thy house." How large the circle was we do not know. It is likely that the group was fairly small. Here would be "cottage prayer meetings" and "cottage classes." It has been said quite often that the strength of the early Christians lay in these meetings in homes. The small circle groups enabled the disciples to have the believer-with-believer association that these tried and courageous Christians were needing.

Unlegislated Fellowship

Fellowship is essential in Christian health. There is no substitute for it. Medically speaking, we can say it can be prescribed for a person, but it cannot be purchased. It can be pointed out as necessary, but it cannot be provided in the sense that it can be served "ready-made." Nor can any group legislate it. The church can provide conditions out of which fellowship may emerge. It can provide instruction and contacts out of which fellowship can develop. Only when persons are working together toward a common, worthful objective, with common allegiance and language for conversing about it, can there be fellowship that will endure and expand. The Christian faith lived in common provides such fellowship.

This deeper fellowship calls for more than sitting in a meeting together; it requires more than attending the same reunion. Two members of the church may sit side by side and be worshiping with quite different conceptions of God, of what constitutes the gospel, of the ministries of the Holy Spirit, of what Zion is to be and why. Spiritual togetherness requires more than enrollment in the same church, more than proximity in congregational gatherings. It is said that for this fellowship persons in common cause have to share and care and dare together. There is a spontaneity about this, a spiritual freshness in it.

The Circle of Sharing

It is likely that the word "share" came out of Anglo-Saxon practices of sharing or harvesting together. When the dividing took place each worker was to receive his fair portion. It was presumed that a man would participate in the labor and then would participate in the returns. The original idea carried the notion of joining in common endeavor.

If there is to be this two-way sharing, there must be limits to the size of the group. As congregations get larger and larger the talk flows one way—from the platform to the members below. There is legitimate place for the sermon, for the lecture, but there is also a needed place for the smaller circle in which every member is a participant, a speaker and a listener, a giver and a receiver. This kind of sharing is possible only under conditions that permit and encourage sharing. If a group is too small, it can fall short of richness through diversity. If it is too large some begin to feel like audience or the group falls into small subgroups for conversation and interaction. Sharing implies that all participate, that all contribute and are sustained. In such a group there is something more than the addition of the several persons; something more comes through the total interaction, a plus element. In such a group, says Elton Trueblood, this general rule applies, "Make all, within your society, members of the crew and permit no passengers." And we may well add, "Let Jesus Christ be the Conductor on the journey of exploration."

Beyond One-sided Emphasis

Some small groups do anything but further spiritual health. They get off the main road and get diverted in emphases on tangents and hobbies. One such group composed of members of four or five families decided to achieve first-class physical health by dietary regulations; by following the commandments of God in these matters they would find, as consequence, a more-than-ordinary spiritual fitness. This fitness would come from the fact of obedience rather than the fruits of obedience. There would be no meat-eating, no use of white sugar, no purchase of canned vegetables and fruits. They would use honey, fresh vegetables (carrots in particular), whole wheat flour, and plenty of milk. They referred to their project as the Full-o'-Health Fellowship. One of the first weaknesses of the group lay in their growing holier-than-thou attitude. They developed the we-are-not-as-other-men outlook. This led to an inbred spirit that is defeating. What is more, they elevated and extolled a few things and pulled these out of their rightful relationship with all the factors involved in healthful living. Their narrowness and apartness brought on other conditions that were not healthy, but they kept glorying in the conviction that they were blessed of God for their adherence to discipline.

Another small group moved apart in reaction to the worldliness about them. They would have to save themselves through banding together in a company for redemption and rehabilitation. They focused on withdrawal for prayer, for reading the scripture, for denial of some wants. In all this there grew up the outlook that it was meritorious to do these things inasmuch as God had commanded them. It was the carrying out of these rather than the experiencing the fruits of doing them that was rewarding. In time quantity and intensity came to be the criteria for merit. These persons reveled in their closeness and their holiness. Their true spiritual health declined.

Another small group used to get together to examine and apply "prophecies." They would bring together passages of scripture that carried an apocalyptic spirit, the passages that they believed referred to the "last days" and the "signs" that pertained to their coming. Some of their signs were woven together until dates for the end of things were settled upon. One of the unhealthy qualities that grew up was their presumption of superior spiritual insight. Inasmuch as God was inspiring them, those who thought otherwise were not sensitive to divine inspiration. This tendency is quite common in such self-centered groups. Their ideas become the criteria for adjudging the ideas of others. The group would not admit to their meetings those who would not be "sensitive to the spirit of prophecy." The longer they continued and the more they deliberated on their chosen passages the further they got from the ongoing life of the church, the less fruitful became their deliberations, the less healthy became their purpose and their problem.

A small group of youth began meeting together for "spiritual uplift." They believed that they should strengthen one another. They hit upon a specialized technique: it was the way of confession and soul clearance. They would not bury their evil thoughts or their evil desires. Nothing should fester within. They would speak with utter frankness about their inner life. The purpose of confessing in order to set things right was lost, if they ever had it. Instead, there came to be a satisfaction in the dramatic rehearsal of dreams and thoughts, especially if these were "sinful," particularly in areas of sex and hostility. There might have been an inducing of unholy thoughts in order to have more to confess. The persons with the more dramatic "testimony" came to have higher standing. In the heyday of the meetings a member said, "We feel so close together."

It is quite evident that assembling of small face-to-face group-ings may be to the furtherance or to the undermining of spiritual health. Some may turn to one-point interest on things ranging from yoga to fasting, from numbers in prophecies to numbers of prayers, and make the world of health hinge on this one thing. The concentration deepens with the interaction with others of this bent. Others may associate to explore and enrich the whole range of spiritual habits and hungers and happenings. Here again, what is capable of going so right is also capable of going so wrong. This calls for wise cultivation of this field of tremendous spiritual possibilities and powers.

Jesus' Use of the Small Group Ministry

For the development of a nucleus who would carry on his ministry, Jesus of Nazareth did not try to see how many he could get in the company of believers. He did not try to make headlines in the newspapers, so to speak, by heralding happenings of colossal scale and dramatic quality. He selected twelve men "that they might be with him." They ate together, they walked together, they tackled problems together, they studied together, and they planned together. At the heart of all this was Jesus the Christ. It has been observed that a good range in number for small fellow-ship groups is from six to twelve. Jesus lived with twelve men in associational teaching. On the closing evening of their life to-gether he addressed them as friends.

There were times when Jesus wanted a smaller, more select circle. These were times that called for concentration and com-mon understanding. When he was going to the mountain for worship that would culminate in his transfiguration he asked Peter and James and John to be with him. There was the case, too, when he invited them to go with him for a healing of unusually exacting requirements. Jesus' way of conducting this gives us insight into his motives and methods. Whenever he called these three men apart, he always sent them back into the busy life of everyday living. He intended that the experience in this smaller circle would qualify them to return. He invited the more spiritual-ly qualified that they might be so inspired and instructed that they would be able to contribute a better ministry. Jesus by his selection of these closer, more responsive friends for more exacting activities has enabled us to perceive why and how we shall proceed.

Healthiness in Comradeship

Many times a year ministers and members will say in confidence, "If I only had someone to talk with, someone who would understand, someone with whom I could speak right from the heart and feel that I was being understood." Men and women who have carried problems and inner confusions have said when once they could speak out, "I have needed for so long some person or some small company of genuine friends to whom and with whom I could let myself speak out." When these people were asked what was lacking in the friends and ministers they did have in the church, these were major answers: (1) "They would not understand what I'm trying to say." (2) "They are not able to keep a confidence." (3) "They would start out giving me 'right answers' and advice before I could tell my concerns." (4) "They would raise their eyebrows at what I would be disclosing." (5) "They would give me a scriptural quotation." (6) "They would tell me to pray." (7) "They would wonder if I have some secret sin." Turn these around and it is easy to discover what they would want in a small circle of understanding friends.

Such comradeship is more than getting together on a park bench and airing opinions about the weather, the national economy, the standing of teams in baseball. All this may be good for casual conversation but it does not meet the needs of those who need health service in spiritual matters. Said one youth in the midst of confusion and insecurity, "I want to be with a few friends who can help me get at the heart of things and at the heart of myself. I do not need somebody to tell me to pray. I want some friends who have the genuine art of praying in a way that is sound. I need some friends who are on the way themselves, some friends who will understand how I want to get on the way." Said another man, "I want some friends, maybe only one, who will listen when I tell how I feel and will make me feel I am understood, without telling me what a mixed-up guy I am."

A minister who had had an emotional illness that had necessitated his taking extended time for recuperation put his feelings this way: "If I could have let off steam and aired my feelings without feeling I would be a sinner if I were to do so, I would not have got into this mix-up. I did not feel free to go to my administrative ministers and I did not have regard for local ministers as counselors. Those with whom I might have talked were not around. So things buried deeper and deeper and then the top blew off." This man had no inner circle of comrades. He attended priesthood institutes and went to prayer meetings, but by and large these were not comradeship groups. Said another, "I felt that I was not getting along well in my ministry and that I was not pleasing my supervisors. But I could not talk about this, so I just kept on worrying. I felt that my way of interpreting God would not agree with theirs."

Every one of us needs comradeship in which we share with inner-circle friends some of the things that are in the inner sanctuary of our lives. These friends need to be so healthy in their spirituality that we come from them with a feeling that we have had the windows of our souls cleared, the air freshened, and a bouquet of flowers placed on the table.

Codes for Circles of Fellowship

It is wise to think through the nature of our involvement in a group and the kind of group it is before we take out unsigned membership. A few church families in an area planned to hold get-togethers for sociability and service. A newcomer family joined in, but soon found that they did not have time for what was going on. The presumed "circle of saints" turned out to be a bridge club, unnamed. This couple was not prudish about playing bridge but decided that there was going to be little if any spiritual comradeship. They and three other couples of their age began meeting, as convenient, to talk about what was going on before the Conference of 1964. They examined the *Saints' Herald* to keep in touch with what was being printed. They read the resolutions that were to come before the Conference. When a minister of the general church came their way, they invited him to meet with them in a conversational circle in a living room. They invited two other couples. That evening they asked questions and exchanged viewpoints. At the close the minister rounded out the evening with his call to them to join in developing an intelligent and concerned church mind. They sat in silence for a few moments and then the minister offered a prayer that grew out of the fellowship of that evening. Said one man, "I saw tonight how to approach the problems of the church." Said another, "It was good to get so many things out on the table." Said a third, "Now I believe we shall be able to pull together and with God."

Out of such an experience the following codes may be set up for such groups. These are the groups that are looking to the health of the church and to their own health. These are the mem-

406

bers who would pray, "Lord, deliver us from being cranks or crackpots!" They will come together not out of snobbery but out of common spiritual concerns. They will leave someone out for much the same reason that six or seven violinists would not invite a tone-deaf person who preferred bowling to bowing.

1. Keep in mind the picture of total healthiness.
2. Practice the stimulating fellowship of the healthy.
3. Recognize individual differences in health needs and health capacities.
4. Look to the wholesome influence upon those outside the group that can come from a well-operated group association.
5. Explore what is being done in this field of spiritual health.
6. Build up a library of materials pertinent to the activities of the group.
7. Associate worship and work in the life of the group.
8. Expect to enjoy the pursuit and the practice of good health.
9. Incorporate the life-providing ministry of the Holy Spirit integrally.
10. Keep in touch with the *Director* of the Spiritual Good Health Service.

Qualifications for Circle Groups

Jesus demonstrated that there are some memberships that come only through spiritual fitness. When a doting mother asked him about giving priority in positions in the kingdom to her own two sons, Jesus inquired about their ability and fitness for such responsibility. There would be no favoritism. When the apostles began to argue about high status in the kingdom, he was very specific in saying that such standing would come only through service to others. Highest standing would be through greatest service. He left the idea that there would be relative levels of status. Only those would get in the upper brackets whose lives of ministry entitled them to be there. Suppose Judas Iscariot had heard that Jesus of Nazareth was going to take three men with him to the Mount of Transfiguration and had asked Jesus for an invitation. Would Jesus have asked him to go? Hardly. This was not a matter of favoritism but of fitness.

One day before the Conference of a few years ago, a small company of men got together to help lay a foundation for the Conference. They did not assemble by virtue of holding high office in the priesthood of the church. They did not get together through "knowing the right persons." They did not plan to have dinner together as a social gathering; this was to be a fellowship with conversation, meditation, and prayer. One man was not asked because he would have "griped all evening." Another was not asked since he "would want to hold a preaching service." These men wanted a circle for sharing concerns, convictions, companionship, and commitment. And God was in their midst.

Five men went apart in a wooded area by a lake. They were together for almost three days. They had to build a common foundation as they started. After their group-prepared breakfast they sat around the table in conference for two hours or so. They left time for the men to be alone or to take walks by two's. In the evening they sat by the lake, sometimes in silence, sometimes in consideration of a problem, sometimes in testimony. At the close of this evening circle, with the moon shining on the lake, prayer was natural. A brotherly handclasp was the climactic ritual as they turned toward the cabin. The fitting testimonial of one man spoke the heart of all, "Fellows, I have a new hold on life." Together these five had been in a spiritual clinic. Only those would join in such as this who, seeing what it was to be, would wholeheartedly want to go.

One time five other men went to a lakeside for two days. They took one ride on the lake together. They did not go fishing. They conversed. They went off alone at times. The fitting close was a service of the Lord's Supper. Each man prayed without compulsion in the midst of his friends. These men understood the backgrounds and the life objectives and the problems of the others. There was no need to guard words. One prayer was eloquent in its simplicity and sincerity. Here was part of it: "God, you know what kind of guy I am, so there is no use for me to pretend. These friends of mine know me pretty well so I cannot put on any pretense with them. I feel as if I were kneeling before you without any clothes on, with you looking right through me. Yet I feel you understand me and that you care for me. And my friends do, too." Here was praying of the first order. Here was comradeship of intimate sharing. Then there was testimony from each, sealed with the covenant of the bread and the wine. Without announcement, these five men formed a circle with hands joined for the benedictory prayer. They stood for a moment in eloquent silence. The senior member said, "It has been good to be here."

The sense of fitness for participation comes from within. Those not qualified would say to themselves, "I don't belong here," and they might continue, "But I am going to become qualified." This latter observation can indicate a major mark of fitness.

Evangelistic Motivation for Including

One of the most fruitful expressions in evangelism is the bringing into a group of wholesome evangelistic spirit persons who will be benefited by the good health of the group. Those adopted may be members or nonmembers. They catch the pulse and the promise of the gospel through being in a group that radiates good news and good spirit. A man, baptized after two years' exposure to such a group, said he "caught" the gospel through the conversation and the communion with Latter Day Saints. These members talked of the church in a meaningful way. The nonmember sensed how much the mission and the message of the church meant to these friends of his. Praying was no trimming; it was an integral part of their life together. Jesus Christ was as present-tense as the current calendar. So in time he lived out the story of Joseph Smith in the Palmyra grove in 1820. This newcomer said he was not preached at; he was reached to. The healthy group was the agency.

This reaching out to others, this inclusion of others—as many as the group is able to include in fellowship—insures against inbreeding, against self-admiration, against having-arrived-at attitudes. This reaching out applies to the family next door and to the family across the ocean; it applies to those of our racial stock and to those of other color. Today, and even more tomorrow, our evangelism will proceed through adopting into spiritually healthy groups friends who are needing the lift and the light that can be caught in small circles of spiritual vision and verve.

Some Agendums for Small Groups

A group has to be doing and thinking something significant if it is to be spiritually healthy—and there are many fields for group exploration. Here are some major ones that are pressing upon the Church of Jesus Christ for sound insight and expression: The nature of man, as God intends him to be; the ministry of the Holy Spirit as God designs this Spirit to function; the church in organization and administration as God expects the church to operate in a world mission; the society of all mankind as God creates men to be, to live together; the gospel of Jesus Christ as God anticipates this good message to function in transforming men's lives in today's world; the family as God sees this primary group carrying on in our complex society; the Restoration movement as God plans this to be functioning for the spiritual restoration of persons and societies in the living now; the Book of Mormon as God expects this to witness of the ancient Christ in ancient America for today. Each great field can be broken down so that it can be handled. Thus groups may study and diagnose the church of this very year as we need to survey program and personnel and power in the light of the mission to be accomplished. The field is unlimited. The need is urgent. Small groups who see this will leave behind the trivia of our conventional society and go exploring with God. They will rise above complaining and concentrating on "small talk" and assassination of character.

The Church within the Church

Arnold Toynbee has reminded us that civilizations need the small, consecrated, creative minorities who see the way ahead and pour their very life out for the good of the whole. Such effective minorities have a sense of mission and a sense of fellowship. Such is the nature of the Church of Jesus Christ. Members catch the soul of the Christ who pours out his life and love for the good of all. He asks his disciples to catch this call to outpouring ministry, in love. That they may do this, Jesus Christ advises his followers to band themselves together in the church as a minority in the world. He intimated that in the church itself there should be a selected nucleus, an inner circle, of those who would see more clearly and give more consecratedly.

This inner circle practices the health-producing discipline of living together with God. They have what one South American has called "an unlimited liability for each other." They have, too, an unlimited concern for all others. Within the inner circle are those small, prophetic, creative groups who are exploring to see with God, to work with God. And the promise of Jesus holds, "Where two or three are gathered in my name, there am I in the midst of them." Where Jesus Christ is, there is health.

Questions for Discussion

1. What are some things the small group can do that the large group cannot do in developing spiritual healthiness in persons? What are some things the larger group can do?

2. How is joining together in groups of fellowship a development rather than a legislated or an administered operation? Can fellowship be legislated?

3. What are things that a small group can do that will be conducive to spiritual development of those participating? How does this constitute good healthiness?

4. How may small groups get off the track and in the way of furthering good health? In this sense, define a crackpot group; a "like-ourselves" group.

5. What do you suppose were Jesus' considerations when he selected the three men to be with him on some special things he did? What saved these projects from being self-centered?

6. What qualifications would be required to join in a group of six to nine persons for considering the problems and the agendum of the next World Conference? Who would not be qualified?

7. In what way is the observer right who says that if we had some healthy small groups in which those who carry the load might share, there would be a reduction in breakdowns in health, in disaffection from membership and ministry, and souring of persons?

8. When may an administrative presidency or quorum function as a small-group fellowship in good health? When may they be only an administrative group?

9. When a youth says, "I want to be sure that I am understood when I blow off steam," what does he have in mind? When and how is "blowing off steam" a healthy expression?

10. How may small, healthy groups be foremost in our evangelistic expression in modern life for evangelizing both members and nonmembers?

11. If you were going to share in a small group what topics and problems would you like to explore? What qualities in persons would be needed to do this healthfully?

12. How may the small circle be the nucleus for radiating the gospel of Jesus Christ in countries to which the church as such has not gone?

13. Interpret, "Jesus Christ can live only in a group of good spiritual health, yet he comes to those who are needing to become spiritually healthy."

GOD OF HEALTH AND HOPE

Tune: Regent Square

God, the Source of life eternal,
    Self-sustained, with boundless wealth,
Infinite in strength supernal,
    Free from magic charm or stealth,
        O renew us! O restore us!
        Grant us power through righteous health.

Christ, the Son of God, revealing
    How we may this health achieve,
Bring to us thy hope and healing;
    From our weakness give reprieve.
        O receive us! O redeem us!
        Teach us how we shall believe.

Spirit, cleansing and creative,
    Stir our souls with lifting power,
That our lives be offerings votive!
    Let thy witness be our dower!
        O revive us! O refresh us!
        Help us live well in this hour!

Church of Christ, with restoration
    Of thy gifts of days of yore,
Bring to us the revelation
    Of the Christ, thy Open Door.
        O renew us! O restore us!
        Grant us health forevermore!